OECD Studies on SMEs and Entrepreneurship

SME and Entrepreneurship Policy in Israel 2016

OECD
BETTER POLICIES FOR BETTER LIVES

This work is published on the responsibility of the Secretary-General of the OECD. The opinions expressed and arguments employed herein do not necessarily reflect the official views of the Organisation or of the governments of its member countries.

This document and any map included herein are without prejudice to the status of or sovereignty over any territory, to the delimitation of international frontiers and boundaries and to the name of any territory, city or area.

Please cite this publication as:
OECD (2016), *SME and Entrepreneurship Policy in Israel 2016*, OECD Publishing, Paris.
http://dx.doi.org/10.1787/9789264262324-en

ISBN 978-92-64-26230-0 (print)
ISBN 978-92-64-26232-4 (PDF)
ISBN 978-92-64-26379-6 (e-pub)

Series: OECD Studies on SMEs and Entrepreneurship
ISSN 2078-0982 (print)
ISSN 2078-0990 (online)

The statistical data for Israel are supplied by and under the responsibility of the relevant Israeli authorities. The use of such data by the OECD is without prejudice to the status of the Golan Heights, East Jerusalem and Israeli settlements in the West Bank under the terms of international law.

Photo credits: © PhotoAlto/Getty Images, © David Wasserman/Brand X Pictures/Getty Images, © Tim Pannell/Corbis, © Andersen Ross/Photodisc/Getty Images.

Corrigenda to OECD publications may be found on line at: *www.oecd.org/publishing/corrigenda*.

Foreword

This publication presents the OECD country review of small and medium-sized enterprise (SME) and entrepreneurship policy in Israel. It forms part of the programme of work of the OECD's Working Party on SMEs and Entrepreneurship, served by the Secretariat of the Centre for Entrepreneurship, SMEs and Local Development. The report is part of a series of country reviews of SME and entrepreneurship policies undertaken by the OECD in countries that express an interest in co-operating on an external assessment of their policy challenges. Recently reviewed countries include Canada, Italy, Mexico, Poland, the Russian Federation and Thailand. The present review was requested by the Israeli Small and Medium Business Authority on behalf of the Israeli government.

The country reviews aim to provide a comprehensive assessment of the structure and performance of SME and entrepreneurship activity, the business environment and framework conditions for SMEs and entrepreneurship, the strategic framework and delivery arrangements for policy, national SME and entrepreneurship programmes and the local dimension of the policy. The studies also provide international comparisons of data and policy approaches. They offer specific recommendations for the countries concerned, often illustrated with inspiring practices from other countries. They aim to provide valuable insights to the stakeholders involved in making policy improvements in the reviewed countries and to offer inspiration for policy development in other countries.

The country reviews may include chapters of special relevance to the country concerned, as agreed between the OECD and the participating country. This report includes special chapters on entrepreneurship and SME development in the Arab Israeli minority population and on the development of medium-sized enterprises in Israel. Special chapters in other review reports have focused on issues such as cluster development, women entrepreneurship and policy evaluation.

The methodology for the review studies includes completion of a fact-finding questionnaire by national government authorities on SME and entrepreneurship conditions, policies and programmes, a study mission to the participating country by the OECD Secretariat and international experts, comments on the report by a steering group of OECD Working Party members and stakeholders in the reviewed country, and a peer review of the draft report by government delegates in a regular meeting of the Working Party on SMEs and Entrepreneurship.

Table of contents

Tables

Figures

Acknowledgements

This report was prepared under the management of Dr Jonathan Potter, Senior Economist, Centre for Entrepreneurship, SMEs and Local Development of the OECD. Dr Jonathan Potter steered the review process, edited the publication and authored material. Mr Marco Marchese, Economist at the Centre for Entrepreneurship, SMEs and Local Development, authored chapters, provided editorial assistance and supported the management of the review process. Mr Stuart Thompson, Economist at the OECD Centre for Entrepreneurship, SMEs and Local Development, authored a chapter and provided editorial assistance. Ms. Nathalie Gosselin provided technical support.

The review was prepared at the request of the Small and Medium Business Agency (SMBA), Israel, in the Ministry of Economy and Industry. Important support for the organisation of the study and inputs to the work were provided by Mr Ran Kiviti, Director SMBA, and Dr Nir Ben Aharon, Head of Research and Policy SMBA. Support for the chapter on the Arab Israeli minority population was provided by Mr Saif Aiman of the Authority for Minority Economic Development.

Members of the Steering Group of the Working Party on SMEs and Entrepreneurship for this study were: Mr Zenta Senoo, Ministry of Foreign Affairs, Japan; Mr Henrik Noes, Danish Business Authority, Denmark; Ms Piret Triberg, Ministry of Economy, Estonia; and Ms Sofiene Lourimi, Ministry of Finance, France.

The following experts provided substantial written inputs to the report: Prof. Francis Greene, University of Birmingham, United Kingdom; Ms Susan Joekes, London School of Economics, United Kingdom; Prof. Helen Lawton Smith, Birkbeck, University of London, United Kingdom; and Ms Lois Stevenson, Canada.

Many individuals and representatives of relevant organisations in Israel provided vital information, assistance and comments for the report through the fact-finding questionnaire, the study mission, supplying background reports and data and making comments on the report. Their support is gratefully acknowledged.

The project was carried out under the direction of Ms Miriam Koreen, Acting Director of the OECD Centre for Entrepreneurship, SMEs and Local Development.

Abbreviations

AUD	Australian Dollar
BERD	Business Expenditure on R&D
CAD	Canadian Dollar
CBS	Central Bureau of Statistics
OCS	Office of the Chief Scientist
EITC	Earned Income Tax Credit
EU	European Union
EUR	Euro
FDI	Foreign Direct Investment
FTA	Foreign Trade Administration
GBP	British Pound (Sterling)
GDP	Gross Domestic Product
GEM	Global Entrepreneurship Monitor
HEI	Higher Education Institution
IIA	Israel Innovation Authority (formerly the Office of the Chief Scientist)
ICT	Information and Communications Technologies
IEI	Israel Export Institute
ISED Canada	Innovation, Science and Economic Development Canada (the federal industry ministry)
KIA	Kibbutz Industries Association
KIEDF	Koret Israel Economic Development Fund
MAI	Manufacturers Association of Israel
MEDA	Authority for Economic Development of the Minority Sectors, or Minorities Economic Development Authority
MSE	Medium-Sized Enterprise
NBFI	Non-Bank Financial Institution
NGO	Non-Governmental Organisation
OECD	Organisation for Economic Co-operation and Development
PISA	Programme of International Student Assessment
R&D	Research and Development
RIA	Regulatory Impact Assessment
SMBA	Small and Medium Business Agency
SMBF	Small and Medium Business Fund
SME	Small and Medium-sized Enterprise
TEA	Total Entrepreneurial Activity
USA	United States of America
VAT	Value Added Tax
VET	Vocational Education and Training

BASIC STATISTICS OF ISRAEL

2014, unless otherwise noted; numbers in parentheses refer to OECD average*

LAND, PEOPLE AND ELECTORAL CYCLE					
Population (million)	8.2		Population density per km²	370.9	(34.9)
Under 15 (%)	28.1	(18.1)	Life expectancy (years, 2013)	82.1	(80.5)
Over 65 (%)	10.9	(16.0)	Men	80.3	(77.8)
Foreign-born (%, 2013)	22.6		Women	83.9	(83.1)
Population groups			Population of largest cities		
Jewish (%)	75.0		Jerusalem	849 800	
Arab (%)	20.7		Tel-Aviv Yafo	426 100	
Other (%)	4.3		Haifa	277 100	
Latest 5-year average growth (%)	1.8	(0.6)	Latest general election	March 2015	

ECONOMY					
Gross domestic product (GDP)			Value added shares (%)		
In current prices (billion USD)	306.2		Primary sector	1.3	(2.6)
In current prices (billion NIS)	1 093.7		Industry including construction	22.1	(26.6)
Latest 5-year average real growth (%)	3.8	(1.9)	Services	76.6	(70.8)
Per capita (000 USD PPP)	33.3	(39.0)			

GENERAL GOVERNMENT Per cent of GDP					
Expenditure[a]	41.2	(41.9)	Gross financial debt[a]	67.1	(115.2)
Revenue	37.7	(38.8)	Net financial debt (2013)	62.5	(73.6)

EXTERNAL ACCOUNTS					
Exchange rate (NIS per USD)	3.571		Main exports (% of total merchandise exports)		
PPP exchange rate (United States of America (USA) = 1)	4.006		Manufactured goods	34.9	
In per cent of GDP			Chemicals and related products, n.e.s.	26.2	
Exports of goods and services	32.3	(53.8)	Machinery and transport equipment	24	
Imports of goods and services	30.6	(49.8)	Main imports (% of total merchandise imports)		
Current account balance	3.7	(0.02)	Machinery and transport equipment	29.2	
Net international investment position	21.3		Manufactured goods	22.8	
			Mineral fuels, lubricants and related materials	17.6	

LABOUR MARKET, SKILLS AND INNOVATION					
Employment rate for 15-64 year-olds (%)	67.9	(65.7)	Unemployment rate, Labour Force Survey (age 15 and over) (%)	5.9	(7.3)
Men	71.5	(73.6)	Youth (age 15-24, %)	10.5	(15.1)
Women	64.2	(57.9)	Long-term unemployed (1 year and over, %)	0.5	(2.5)
Participation rate for 15-64 year-olds (%)	72.2	(71.2)	Tertiary educational attainment 25-64 year-olds (%, 2013)	48.5	(33.5)
Average hours worked per year	1 853	(1770)	Gross domestic expenditure on Research and Development (R&D) (% of GDP, 2012)	4.2	(2.4)

Note: The statistical data for Israel are supplied by and under the responsibility of the relevant Israeli authorities. The use of such data by the OECD is without prejudice to the status of the Golan Heights, East Jerusalem and Israeli settlements in the West Bank under the terms of international law.

* OECD average of latest available data is calculated where data exist for at least 29 member countries.

a) 2013 for the OECD aggregate.

b) 2012 for the OECD aggregate.

c) 2011 for the OECD aggregate.

Source: OECD (2015), "Country statistical profile: Israel", Country statistical profiles: Key tables from OECD, *http://dx.doi.org/10.1787/csp-isr-table-2015-2-en* and Central Bureau of Statistics of Israel (2015), Israel in Figures 2015.

OECD Studies on SMEs and Entrepreneurship
SME and Entrepreneurship Policy in Israel 2016

Executive summary

Israel is one of the most successful economies in the world for technology-based enterprises, which account for approximately 10% of business sector employment. Israel has great foundations in fields such as Information and Communications Technologies (ICT) and biotechnologies, in which productivity, business start-up rates and high-growth entrepreneurship rates are all very high, reflecting some exceptionally strong framework conditions for high-technology industries. Israel has the largest share of early-stage and seed venture capital funding in GDP of OECD countries, a rate of adult participation in tertiary education that is fully 16 percentage points above the OECD average, the second highest ratio of R&D expenditure to GDP in the OECD and a large base of R&D-based inward foreign direct investments.

Alongside this high-technology success story there is a second economy consisting of SMEs and entrepreneurs operating in traditional sectors. These businesses and entrepreneurs are largely detached from the high-technology economy and in general do not enjoy the same high profile successes. While being extremely important in terms of numbers of jobs and contribution to value added, the productivity levels of typical Israeli SMEs are low compared with SMEs in other OECD countries, and most traditional SMEs do not engage in any innovation. There is also a productivity gap between medium-sized and large enterprises in manufacturing, which is larger than in most other OECD countries. The scale of informal entrepreneurship is high and Israeli women and Arab Israelis lag behind in high-value added entrepreneurship.

This report examines how government policies and programmes in Israel can start to address this dual economy challenge and harness the potential of SMEs and entrepreneurship for broader economic and social development.

Key findings

One of the remarkable strengths of SME and entrepreneurship activity in Israel over the medium-term has been its high rate of nascent entrepreneurship and new business ownership. In recent years, Israel's stock of businesses has grown considerably, as business births have exceeded business deaths at a rate of approximately 3% per year. On the other hand, the growth has been weighted to lower value-added sectors such as construction and transport, and more needs to be done to raise rates of start-up success and SME productivity and innovation.

Among the strengths of the business environment for SMEs and entrepreneurship in Israel are the country's strong recent economic growth, a flexible labour market, relatively low taxation and low administrative burdens for business start-up. On the other hand, a complex system of business licenses and permits, product market regulation constraints, and a lack of systematic entrepreneurship education hold back SME growth. Furthermore, innovation policy is mainly oriented to R&D support rather than broad innovation, tertiary education is favoured over vocational education, and whereas risk capital for technology projects is relatively abundant, debt finance for traditional SMEs is constrained.

The Small and Medium Business Agency (SMBA) is the government's core agency for SME and entrepreneurship development. It plays an important role in strengthening business development services, access to finance, and guiding government regulation decisions for SMEs. However, the SMBA lacks some common supports that could help it co-ordinate and prioritise policy across government. It has no national SME and entrepreneurship policy strategy to refer to, no inter-ministerial SME and entrepreneurship policy co-ordination body, and few multi-annual budgets.

National government operates many successful programmes for SME financing, innovation, and exporting although there a few specific additional niche interventions that would be merited in these areas. Large strides have also been made in access to loan finance through the merger of three previous government-guaranteed loan funds into the Small and Medium Business Fund. Significant progress has also been made in business management advice through a new network of MAOF business centres. On the other hand, there are gaps in provision for SME workforce skills development, targeted public procurement, and support for social target groups. Furthermore, the resources for business management advice for non-high technology SMEs are well below those earmarked for technology support.

Although national government is the main player in SME and entrepreneurship policy in Israel, local authorities also have a role to play by ensuring an effective permit and licensing system and the availability of land and premises. They are often constrained in these tasks by small budgets and professional staffing capacities as well as by limited inter-municipality co-operations. More could also be done for the promotion of locally-specific supply chains and clusters by national enterprise and regional policies.

The Minorities Economic Development Authority (MEDA) is leading an impressive range of projects and programmes for the Arab Israeli minority population, which will be boosted by the implementation of the government-wide economic development plan for the Arab sector for 2016-20. These interventions should focus on improving finance, skills and premises in order to support Arab SME growth and diversification.

A further policy priority should be to address the productivity lag of traditional Israeli medium-sized manufacturing enterprises. A multi-pronged approach is needed for this group of firms that combines actions for workforce skills development, improving management skills and practices, access to finance, supply chain development, targeted public procurement and innovation.

Key recommendations

The report makes many detailed recommendations on how the Israeli government can pursue this agenda. Key recommended actions include the following:

- Increase programme support such as innovation and consultancy for productivity growth in SMEs operating in traditional non-technology sectors.
- Prepare a national SME and entrepreneurship strategic policy document.
- Create new structures for SME and entrepreneurship policy development and co-ordination across government.

- Create a national entrepreneurship education strategy and expand support for workforce development in SMEs.
- Provide capacity-building support to local authorities on regulations, procurement policy, and site and premises development and encourage the creation of distinct local clusters and supply chains.
- Boost financing, property and management capability support for Arab-owned businesses.
- Develop a dedicated package of workforce skills, management development, investment facilitation, innovation and supplier development programmes for medium-sized enterprises.

Chapter 1

Assessment and Recommendations

This chapter summarises the main findings of the OECD's review of SME and entrepreneurship policies in Israel. It identifies high start-up rates and a successful high technology sector but low productivity and innovation in traditional SMEs and uneven participation in entrepreneurship across social groups. Policy challenges and recommendations are presented on improving the business environment, the strategic framework for policy, national SME and entrepreneurship programmes, the local SME and entrepreneurship policies, SMEs and entrepreneurship in the Arab Israeli population, and strengthening medium-sized enterprises.

The statistical data for Israel are supplied by and under the responsibility of the relevant Israeli authorities. The use of such data by the OECD is without prejudice to the status of the Golan Heights, East Jerusalem and Israeli settlements in the West Bank under the terms of international law.
This document and any map included herein are without prejudice to the status of or sovereignty over any territory, to the delimitation of international frontiers and boundaries and to the name of any territory, city or area.

1. SME and entrepreneurship structure and performance

SMEs play an important role in the economy

SMEs are of great importance to the Israeli economy (OECD, 2015a). SMEs account for 99.8% of all employer businesses in Israel, 68.7% of the business sector workforce (Figure 1.1) and 62.3% of business economy value added. Both medium-sized (50-249 employees) and small businesses (10-49) contribute larger shares of business numbers, employment and value added to the business economy than the OECD average. On the other hand, micro businesses numbers and employment are slightly lower than the OECD average, although micro firms in Israel still contribute more than the OECD average to business sector value added.

Figure 1.1. **Employment by enterprise class size, total business economy, 2012 or latest available year**

Percentage of total employment

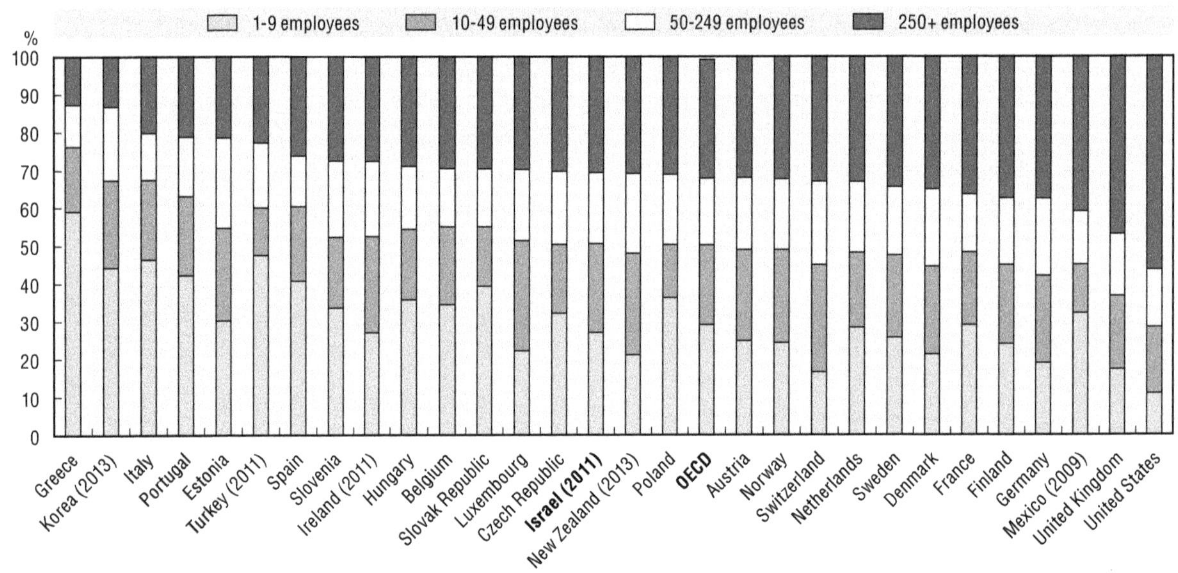

Note: Countries are presented in descending order, from the country where the SME sector as a whole (up to 249 employees) accounts for the largest share of national employment to the country where it explains the smallest share. All countries present information using the enterprise as the statistical unit except Korea and Mexico which use establishment. For Canada and the United States, data do not include non-employer enterprises. Data for Korea include financial services. Different size classes apply to Australia (1-19; 20-199; 200+), Korea (1-9; 10-49; 50-299; 300+), Mexico (1-10; 11-50; 51-250; 251+), Turkey (1-19; 20-49; 50-249; 250+).

Source: OECD based on OECD (2015a), *Entrepreneurship at a Glance 2015*, OECD Publishing, Paris.

StatLink http://dx.doi.org/10.1787/888933421241

Israel boasts strong entrepreneurship intentions and start up rates, but gaps in capabilities

One in ten Israeli working age adults report being actively engaged in early-stage entrepreneurial activity, which compares favourably on an international basis (Figure 1.2).

Figure 1.2. **Total early stage entrepreneurial activity rate across OECD countries, 2013**

Percentage of adult population (18-64 years old)

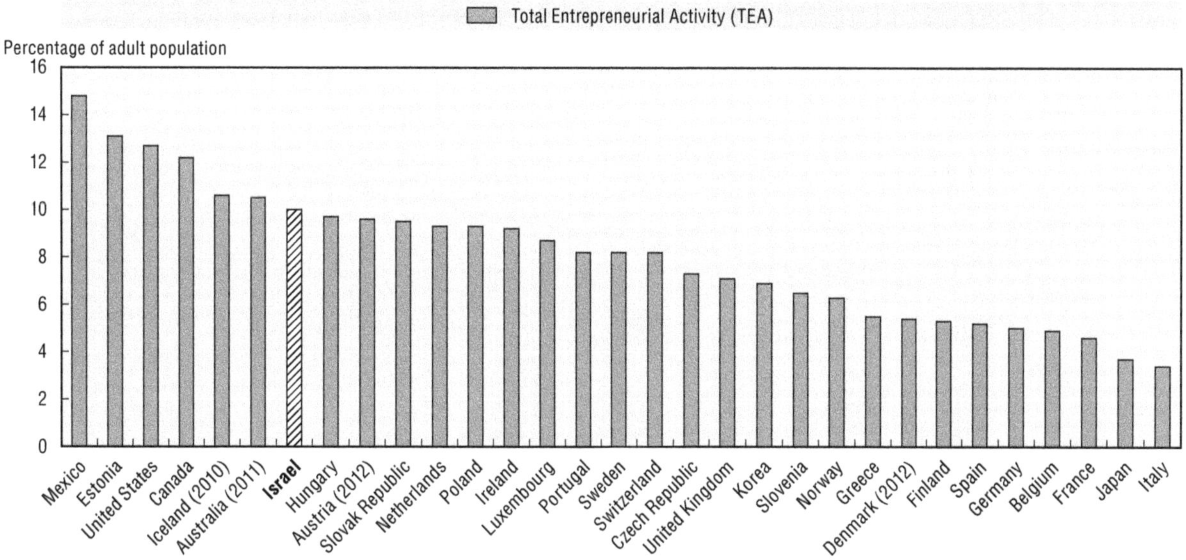

Note: TEA rate: Percentage of 18-64 population who are either a nascent entrepreneur (i.e. actively involved in setting up a business he/she will own or co-own; this business has not paid salaries, wages, or any other payments to the owners for more than three months) or owner-manager of a new business (i.e. owning and managing a running business that has paid salaries, wages, or any other payments to the owners for more than three months, but not more than 42 months).

Source: OECD based on the Global Entrepreneurship Monitor (GEM) database, *www.gemconsortium.org/key-indicators.*

StatLink http://dx.doi.org/10.1787/888933421253

Furthermore, nearly one-quarter of Israelis express the intention to set up a business within the next three years. This is the third-highest value among the OECD countries for which data are available, and double that of other entrepreneurial economies such as Ireland and the United States.

However, only 36% of working age Israeli adults consider that they have the right skills and knowledge to succeed in business, and more than one-half of those who can identify existing opportunities for business creation report that "fear of failure" could prevent them from taking concrete steps towards establishing an enterprise.

Israel has a growing stock of businesses but weak business dynamics

During 2004-11, the number of businesses grew by an annual average of 3%, resulting in growth of one-quarter in the stock of businesses (Figure 1.3). This reflects a high rate of business creation in the Israeli economy at the same time as business deaths have been low. Furthermore, Israel ranks among the best performers in the OECD area in generating high-impact SMEs in services sectors (OECD, 2015a). Approximately 4.5% of service sector firms were high-growth SMEs in 2012 and 2% were gazelles. On the other hand, Israel generates fewer high-impact SMEs in manufacturing than many benchmark OECD countries.

Although Israel has a high business birth rate, its rate of entrepreneurial churn (i.e. the sum of business births and deaths) is more modest (Figure 1.4). This reflects low business death rates and a significant excess of business births over business deaths. It is leading to healthy growth in the enterprise stock. In the long-term, however, attention will need to be paid to whether low business deaths becomes a burden to the entry of new firms, the growth of young firms and the increase of SME productivity. This could occur if policy

Figure 1.3. **Number of enterprises in Israel, 2004-11**

Absolute numbers and annual percentage growth rate

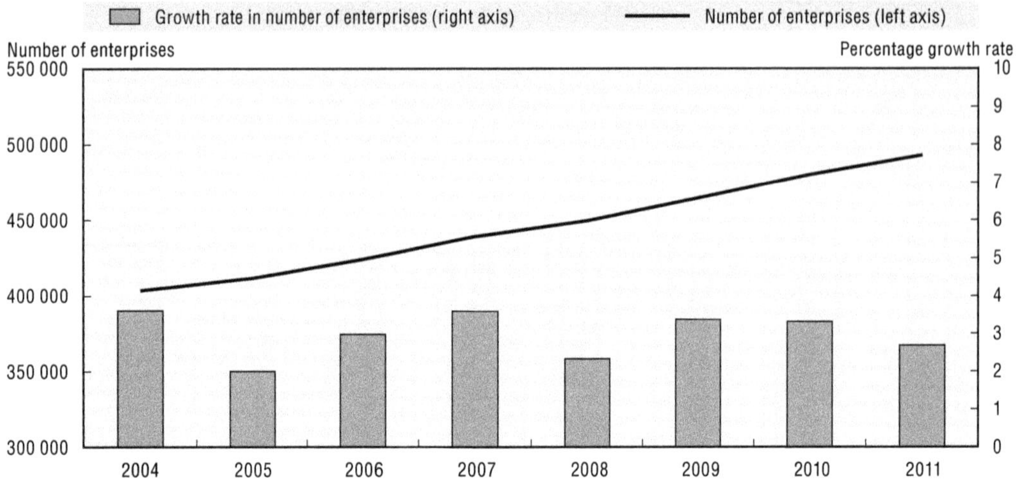

Note: Data also include non-employer firms.

Source: OECD based on CBS (2013), Business Demography: A Collection of Statistical Data from the Business Register: 2003-2011, Publication No. 1541, Jerusalem.

StatLink http://dx.doi.org/10.1787/888933421269

Figure 1.4. **Annual employer enterprise birth rates, death rates and churn rates across selected countries and Israel, 2012 or latest available year**

Percentage of employer enterprises

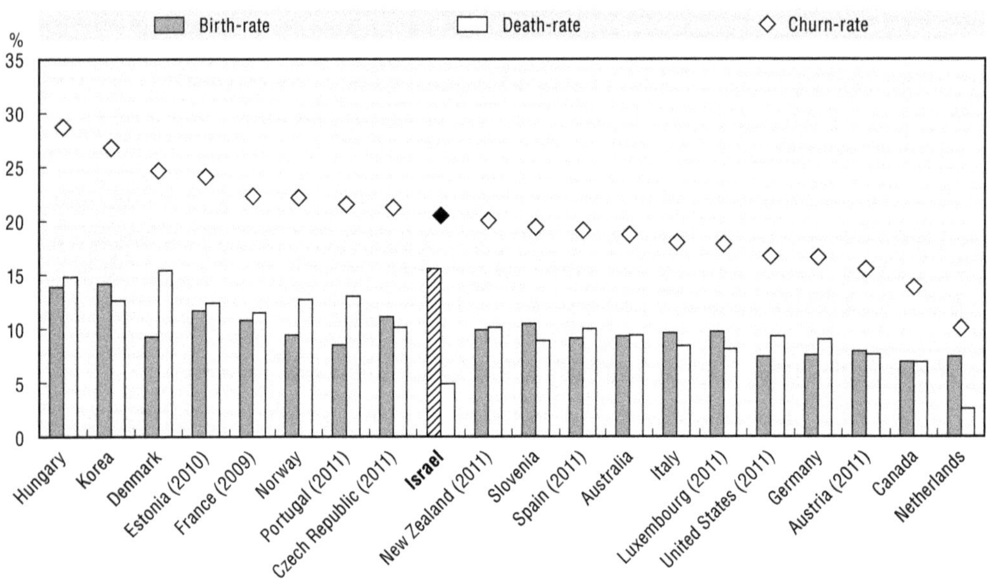

Note: The business churn rate is the sum of the business birth rate and the business death rate.

Source: OECD based on OECD (2015a), *Entrepreneurship at a Glance 2015*, OECD Publishing, Paris.

StatLink http://dx.doi.org/10.1787/888933421273

provides excessive protection of incumbent firms. Attention also needs to be paid to the quality of start-ups, since recent growth in business numbers has been weighted to lower value added sectors such as construction and transport. Furthermore, Israel has a large informal enterprise sector, which is estimated at 22% of national GDP (Schneider, undated; Schneider, Buehn and Montenegro, 2010).

There is scope to strengthen SME innovation and productivity

Israeli SMEs account for 42% of the value of national exports, which is a significant share compared with other OECD countries (OECD, 2014a). Nonetheless, only 15% of SMEs are currently involved in exporting, which suggests that there is a large latent pool of new exporters in the SME sector. Furthermore, Israeli SME innovation rates are not high by international comparison, despite the great success of Israeli high-technology industry. The share of national business expenditure on R&D undertaken by SMEs (27%) is below the OECD average. Moreover, less than one-half of Israeli SMEs engage in any form of innovation, whether technological or non-technological, and a relatively small proportion of Israeli SMEs combine both technological and non-technological innovation (Figure 1.5). This suggests the need for work to build up the innovation capability of existing non-high technology SMEs in Israel.

Figure 1.5. **Innovation in SMEs by type of innovation and compared to large firms (total), 2010-12**

Percentage of all SMEs and large firms covered by national innovation surveys

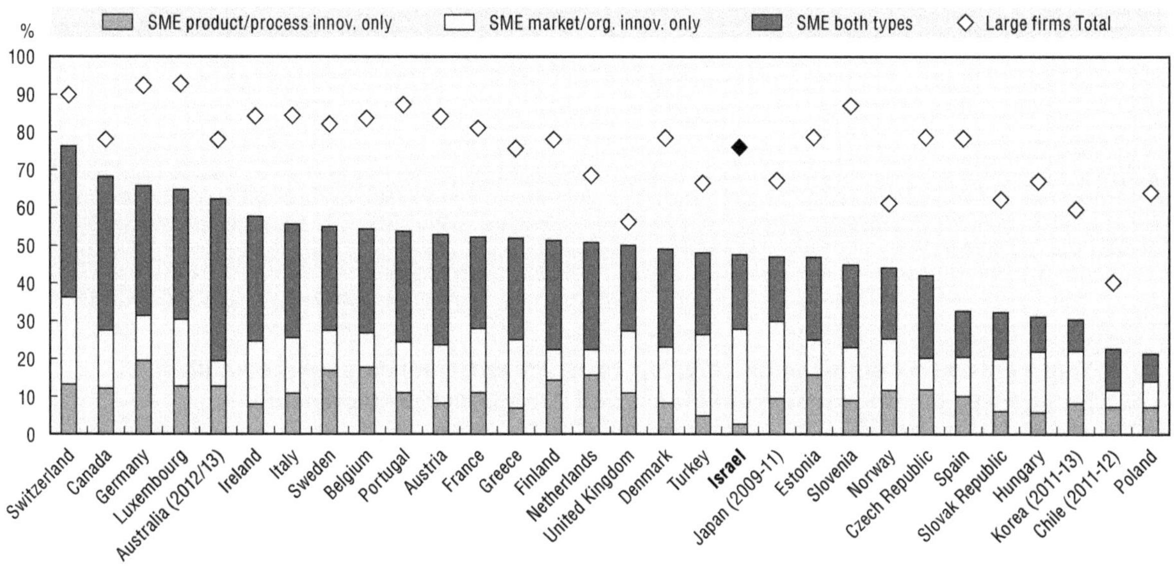

Note: International comparability may be limited due to differences in innovation survey methodologies and country-specific response patterns.

Source: OECD based on OECD (2015b), *OECD Science, Technology and Industry Scoreboard 2015*, OECD Publishing, Paris.

StatLink http://dx.doi.org/10.1787/888933421283

There is a major gap in productivity levels between SMEs and large firms in manufacturing, which is greater than many other OECD countries (Figure 1.6). The productivity gap is particularly large compared with other countries for firms of 20-49 employees. There is not a similar gap in productivity between SMEs and large firms in services industries. The productivity gap is likely to reflect both low capital investment and a large gap to the technological frontier in manufacturing SMEs. This requires interventions in a range of areas, including improving access to long-term investment finance, improving workforce training, strengthening management skills and supporting innovation and market expansion.

Figure 1.6. **Labour productivity in manufacturing by business size class and sector, 2012 or latest available year**

Percentage of labour productivity in large firms (250+ = 100)

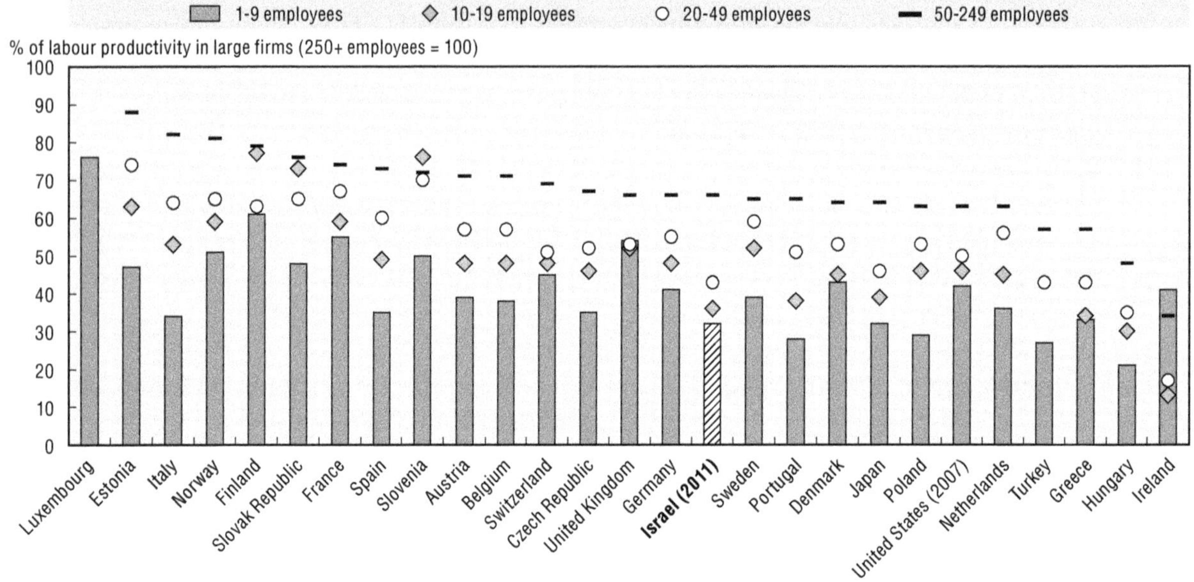

Note: Labour productivity is measured as the current price, gross value added per person employed. For comparison purposes, data are presented for each country as percentage of labour productivity in large firms (i.e. index 250+ = 100). Financial services activities are not included in the services sector. Data are presented in descending order from the country where the gap between mid-sized (50-249) and large firms (250+) is the smallest.

Source: OECD, based on OECD (2015a), *Entrepreneurship at a Glance 2015*, OECD Publishing, Paris.

StatLink http://dx.doi.org/10.1787/888933421292

Youth entrepreneurship is healthy, but there are entrepreneurship inequalities for women, seniors, recent immigrants and Arab Israeli entrepreneurs

The total early-stage entrepreneurship activity rate of young people of 25-34 years old was above that of the adult population in 2010 (20% for young men and 12% for young women), indicating positive conditions for youth entrepreneurship. However, across all working ages, Israeli women were less than half as likely as Israeli men to set up or run a new business in 2013 (OECD, 2015a). This is the second-largest gender gap among OECD members. Women were also less likely than men to set up businesses that grow. One of the issues is a gap in perceived capabilities for entrepreneurship; only 29% of Israeli women report having the necessary skills and competences compared with 49% of Israeli men (Menipaz et al., 2011).

There are also important variations by ethnic community (Table 1.1). The total early-stage entrepreneurial activity rate is highest among Israeli Arabs (6.9%), followed by Israeli Jews (5.7%) and Russian immigrant Jews (3.5%). However, only 8% of Arab Israelis involved in starting or running a new business expect to employ at least five workers within five years, compared to 15% of Israeli Jews and 25% of Russian Jewish immigrants. Furthermore, the rate of self-employment in Israel's senior population is far below the corresponding levels in most other OECD member countries OECD (2013a).

Table 1.1. **Total early-stage entrepreneurial activity by ethnic background, 2009-10**
Percentage values of adult population (18-64) in each group

	2009	2010	2009-10 (unweighted average)
Israeli Jews	6.3	5	*5.7*
Male	8.2	7.9	8.1
Female	4.6	2.6	3.6
Arab Israelis	7.3	6.5	*6.9*
Male	9.4	6.5	8.0
Female	4.9	6.5	5.7
Russian Jewish immigrants	4.2	2.8	*3.5*
Male	5.8	3.3	4.6
Female	1.8	2.4	2.1
Israel (total mean)	6.1	5	*5.6*

Source: OECD based on Menipaz, E. et al. (2011), GEM 2010 Israel National Entrepreneurship Report, Ben Gurion University of the Nagev, Beer Sheva, *www.gemconsortium.org/docs/2290/gem-israel-2010-report.*

StatLink http://dx.doi.org/10.1787/888933421358

Key recommendations on SME and entrepreneurship performance

- Adopt measures aimed at increasing the sustainability and growth of small businesses and young businesses.
- Take measures to increase the innovation activities of the bulk of SMEs in services and traditional non-R&D based manufacturing.
- Increase policy attention to productivity upgrading in medium-sized manufacturing enterprises.
- Reduce the scale of the informal economy through a review of tax and regulatory measures that may discourage formality.
- Expand entrepreneurship training for new and potential entrepreneurs, particularly among under-represented groups in growth-oriented entrepreneurship, including women, seniors, recent immigrants and Arab Israelis.

2. Business environment and framework conditions

Domestic macroeconomic conditions are favourable

Business creation and the growth of the SME stock have been supported by favourable macroeconomic conditions in Israel over the last ten years, including rapid economic growth, macroeconomic stability and labour market flexibility. However, the labour market participation of Ultraorthodox Jewish men and Arab Israeli women is low, and Israeli labour productivity levels and growth have lagged behind those of the EU countries and the United States.

Aspects of the regulatory environment remain restrictive for business creation and SME development

The administration required to start a business is relatively simple in Israel. However, other aspects of business regulation remain difficult despite recent legislative reforms. For example, the system of business licensing and permits administered by municipalities is complex, as is the administration of the tax system. SMBA is playing an important role in regulatory simplification by advising the government on the impact of new legislation on SMEs and new businesses. This has so far been carried out through informal consultation with private sector business associations and chambers of commerce. Nonetheless, the use of more rigorous methodologies such as the Standard Cost Model could enable a better estimate of the impact of legislation. Product market regulation is also very restrictive in Israel relative to most other OECD countries (Figure 1.7). State control in the economy is relatively high, and large firms have significant opportunities to exercise market power. This creates a barrier to the entry and growth of SMEs.

Figure 1.7. **Product market regulations across OECD countries, 2003 and 2013**

From 0 (least restrictive) to 6 (most restrictive)

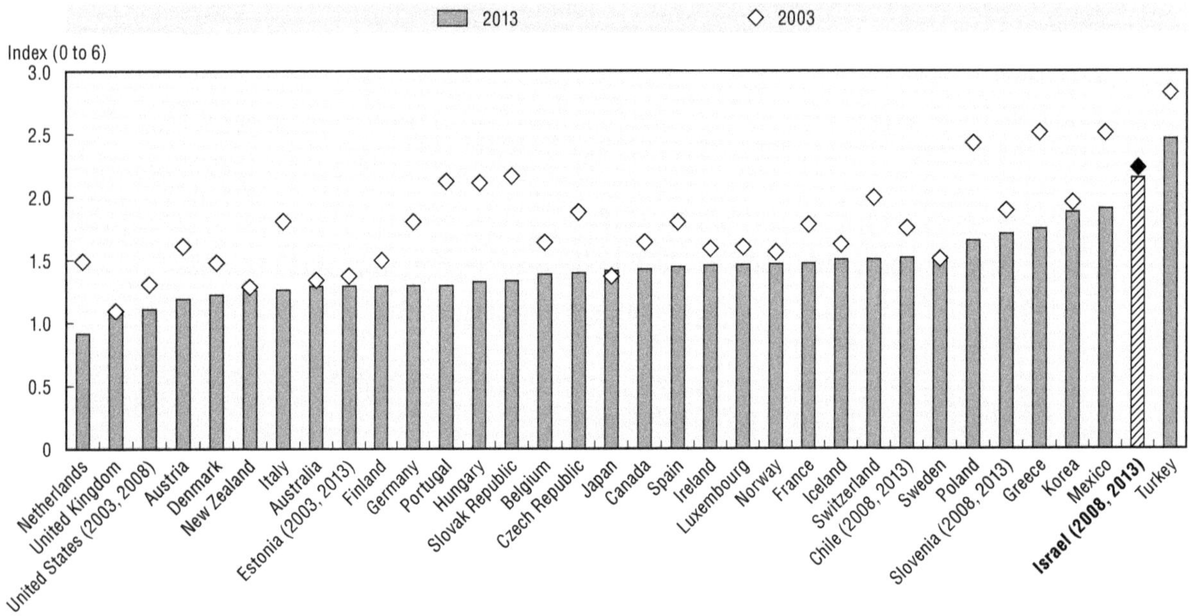

Note: For Israel, data refer to 2013 and 2008. The OECD Indicators of Product Market Regulation (PMR) are a comprehensive and internationally-comparable set of indicators that measure the degree to which policies promote or inhibit competition. These indicators cover formal regulations in the following areas: state control of the economy; legal and administrative barriers to entrepreneurship; barriers to international trade and investment. For further information: *www.oecd.org/eco/growth/indicatorsofproductmarketregulation homepage.htm#indicators.*

Source: OECD *Product Market Regulation* (PMR) Database.

StatLink http://dx.doi.org/10.1787/888933421301

High participation in tertiary education co-exists with weak vocational and entrepreneurship skills

Some 49% of adults had participated in tertiary education in 2014, 16 percentage points above the OECD average. The high proportion of highly-skilled workers is one of the major assets underpinning Israel's strong high-technology performance. At the same time, however, graduate employment in SMEs is limited by the lack of demand from SMEs. In addition, there are weaknesses in the vocational education system, which is poorly attended and mainly classroom (rather than enterprise) based. These are exacerbated by poor learning outcomes in secondary education. For example, the performance of Israeli upper-secondary level students on OECD Programme of International Student Assessment (PISA) tests is below the OECD average (Figure 1.8).

There are several examples of good practice in entrepreneurship education at the primary, secondary and tertiary levels in Israel, but the initiatives are not mainstreamed. For example, only one-half of Higher Education Institutions (HEI) offer entrepreneurship

Figure 1.8. **Israeli student performance in mathematics, science, reading and financial literacy, 2012**

Mean scores

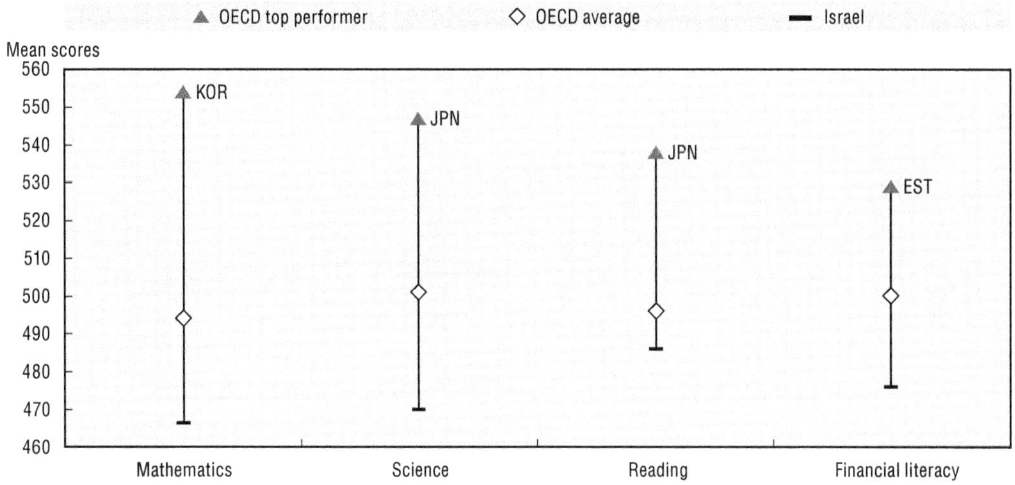

Note: Data on financial literacy are only available for 13 OECD countries.

Source: OECD based on OECD (2013b), *PISA 2012 Assessment and Analytical Framework: Mathematics, Reading, Science, Problem Solving and Financial Literacy*, OECD Publishing, Paris.

StatLink http://dx.doi.org/10.1787/888933421312

education to undergraduates. Moreover, entrepreneurship is usually an optional rather than a compulsory subject. Israel has no national entrepreneurship education strategy unlike some OECD countries such as Finland, Sweden and Spain (European Commission/EACEA/Eurydice, 2016; European Commission, 2014).

Israel's innovation system is strong, but weighted to R&D

Israel had the highest proportion of researchers in relation to total employment among OECD countries in 2013 (OECD, 2015b). Furthermore, its R&D expenditure amounted to 3.9% of national GDP, the second highest value among OECD countries. More than 80% of this is business expenditure on R&D (Figure 1.9) and as much as 7% of higher education R&D is financed by industry. However, public subsidies for innovation are strongly focused on R&D activities, with less support for non-technological innovation in SMEs.

Israel boasts a very strong equity market, but gaps in loan finance persist

The share of venture capital investment in GDP in Israel is the largest in the OECD area, and is more strongly weighted towards seed and early-stage investment stages than in most other countries (Figure 1.10). This makes for an exceptional flow of seed and early-stage investment to technology-based start-ups, although angel investment is still relatively limited in Israel. On the other hand, the typical SME reports problems in obtaining credit. The ratio of bank credit to bank deposits is much smaller for SMEs than for larger firms (OECD, 2014b). Furthermore, the terms of bank credit for SMEs are relatively unfavourable given a relatively large interest rate spread between SMEs and large firms and limited availability of longer term loans (OECD, 2016). One of the causes is that 95% of total bank credit is supplied by the five largest banks. Competition is held back by restrictive regulations, such as on procedures to change banks, establishment of new bank and non-bank financial institutions, and sharing of credit information on customers. Recent government measures have been taken to address this issue, including streamlined

Figure 1.9. **R&D expenditure by performing sector, 2013**

Percentage of gross domestic expenditures on GDP

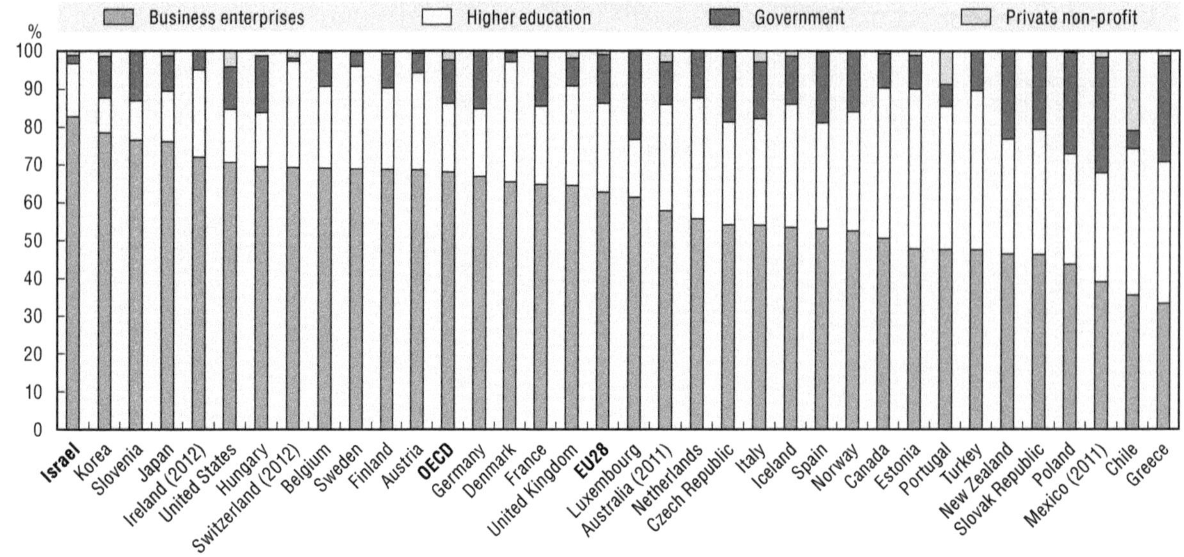

Source: OECD based on OECD (2015b), *OECD Science, Technology and Industry Scoreboard 2015*, OECD Publishing, Paris.

StatLink http://dx.doi.org/10.1787/888933421320

Figure 1.10. **Top ten OECD countries for venture capital investments, 2014**

Percentage of GDP

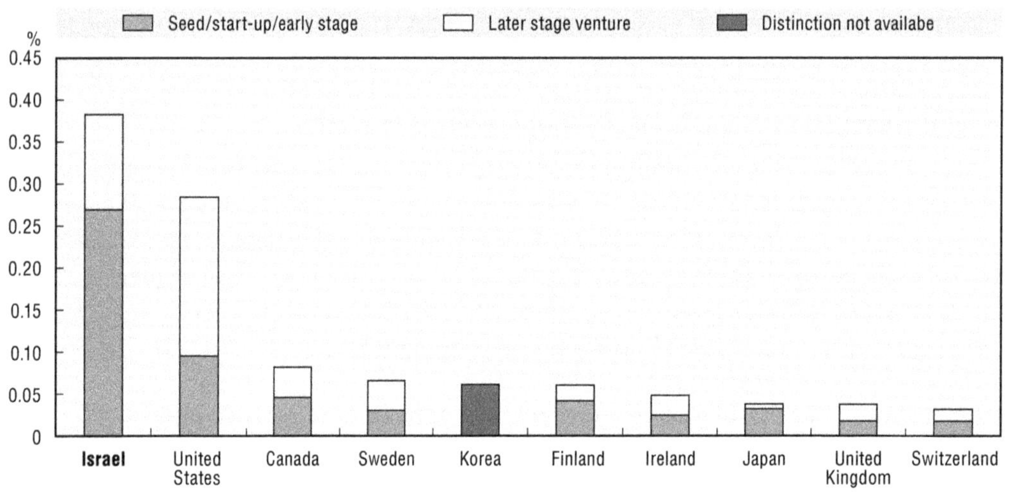

Source: OECD (2015a), *Entrepreneurship at a Glance 2015*, OECD Publishing, Paris.

StatLink http://dx.doi.org/10.1787/888933421334

procedures for customers to change bank accounts and a legal framework for the establishment of credit unions and online banking. However, other mooted measures have not yet been adopted, such as opening up small business lending to insurance companies and pension funds and treating the smallest businesses as retail customers.

The tax environment is favourable, particularly for large, R&D-intensive companies

Israel's corporate income tax rate stands at 26.5%. This is a relatively high headline rate, although the overall tax burden on SMEs and entrepreneurship is mitigated by low personal income taxation. There are extensive subsidies on corporate income tax for export-oriented companies, R&D-based companies and companies located in priority regions, which are accessed disproportionately by large, high-technology companies. The typical SME therefore bears some of the burden of tax relief for high-technology activities, which may discourage growth and encourage informality. Furthermore, there may be significant tax subsidisation of activities that would in any case go ahead (OECD, 2013c). A redistribution of some of these tax expenditures towards more direct support for broader-based innovation in typical SMEs would enable better targeting of public resources to where impacts are greatest.

Inward foreign direct investment is weighted to R&D in ICT

Israel performs well in attracting inward foreign direct investment (FDI), but it is highly concentrated. For example, of the 489 foreign affiliates in Israel at the end of 2009, 286 were ICT (Information and Communications Technologies) R&D centres for larger parent companies. The narrow sector spread of inward FDI limits the opportunities for positive spill overs for market and technology development across the economy as a whole. In addition, a significant proportion of FDI involves small-value acquisitions of Israeli companies (Aahroni, 2009). There is therefore a possibility that some promising high-technology start-ups may be being sold prematurely.

Key recommendations on business environment and framework conditions for SMEs and entrepreneurship

- Strengthen product market competition by rapid implementation of the 2013 Concentration Law and granting more powers to the Anti-Trust Authority, including the ability to apply financial sanctions to companies abusing their market power.
- Simplify the business licensing and permit system through increased monitoring by SMBA of difficulties SMEs and entrepreneurs face with permits and licenses and communication to the relevant authorities, digitalisation of the business license and permit system, and creation of a national online portal that provides comprehensive information on licensing and permit requirements across the country.
- Strengthen Regulatory Impact Assessment (RIA) of new legislation affecting SMEs and entrepreneurship by SMBA by replacing informal consultations with business associations with more rigorous RIA methodologies such as the Standard Cost Model.
- Improve bridging between the supply of higher education graduates and their employment in SMEs by increasing SME participation in curriculum design, teaching and student placements, and providing support for upgrading productivity and management practices in SMEs to increase their demand for higher skilled workers.
- Strengthen the capacity of the Vocational Education and Training (VET) system to supply appropriately skilled workers to SMEs by increasing the share of work-based learning in SMEs (including apprenticeships, work placements and internships) as part of VET studies, experimenting with new approaches to involving employers in VET programme design and take up, experimenting with "associate degree" qualifications, developing a better labour market information system to identify industry skill needs, and promoting national training standards for VET teaching. This could all be part of a national VET strategy jointly designed by the government and industry leaders.

Key recommendations on business environment and framework conditions for SMEs and entrepreneurship *(cont.)*

- Introduce a national entrepreneurship education strategy that makes entrepreneurship a mandatory and integral part of the curriculum. To support this effort, develop steering documents (e.g. curricula and syllabi) and evaluation plans, provide training and incentives to entrepreneurship teachers, and develop an online web portal offering guidelines, information and teaching resources for entrepreneurship education.
- Broaden the targeting of government expenditures on business innovation to cover more non R&D expenditures and support greater numbers of SMEs, including in low-technology manufacturing.
- Reinforce competition in the banking sector by offering training to qualified financial or economic organisations interested in setting up credit unions and by fully implementing the recommendations of the National Committee to Increase the Competitiveness of the Banking Sector (in particular easing access to loans by very small businesses by applying regulations for retail loans rather than business loans).
- Amend regulations to enable disclosure of positive credit history information for entrepreneurs and support credit bureaus in building credit rating information through standardised computation methodologies and disclosure requirements.
- Investigate potential regulatory barriers to domestic institutional investors taking part in the venture capital market and consider tax incentives for investors making equity investments in in firms outside of high-technology sectors.
- Encourage business formalisation through both demand- and supply-side strategies, such as wider availability of the earned income tax credit and voucher schemes in sectors where informality is widespread.
- Develop an FDI attraction strategy that goes beyond high-technology sectors and supports the development of business linkages between FDI affiliates and SME suppliers.

3. Strategic framework and policy delivery system

The creation of the SMBA has strengthened Israel's SME and entrepreneurship policy

The Small and Medium Business Agency (SMBA) was established in 2010 as the government agency for SME and entrepreneurship promotion housed within the Ministry of Economy and Industry. It replaced the former Israel Small and Medium Enterprises Authority, which had delivered government-funded business advice and assistance through a loose group of Non-Governmental Organisations (NGO). The SMBA has four main functions: delivering business development services to SMEs and entrepreneurs; delivering the national loan guarantee programme; reviewing government legislation for impacts on SMEs; and co-ordinating SME and entrepreneurship policy across government.

The SMBA has considerably upgraded Israel's SME and entrepreneurship policy since its creation but more could be done. It has transformed local business development services centres into a higher quality, nationally co-ordinated network of one-stop shop business development services centres, known as MAOF centres, with a better spread across the country. It has also supported the scale up and restructuring of the national loan guarantee programme and implemented systematic reviews of the burden of new legislation on SMEs for the first time.

The SMBA manages its key support services through intermediary organisations

The SMBA manages its two major direct support programmes for SMEs and entrepreneurs by contracting with intermediary organisations. The MAOF business development service centres are operated by five private companies operating in different regions of the country, while the screening and selection of applicants to the national loan guarantee fund are undertaken by two private companies. This relieves SMBA of burdensome administration and management tasks. The service contracts are awarded through a competitive tender process. The control of quality and impact is supported by monitoring systems and an ongoing evaluation of the loan guarantee scheme. The approach could be strengthened further by introducing a system to evaluate the impact of each MAOF centre and provider and make appropriate adjustments. It could also be strengthened by providing more training for MAOF staff and consultants in business diagnosis and referral to appropriate services and advisers.

SMBA has an important role to play in policy co-ordination

Several ministries and agencies are involved in SME and entrepreneurship support in Israel alongside SMBA. R&D activity is supported by the Israel Innovation Authority (IIA), (formerly the Office of the Chief Scientist), minority entrepreneur populations by the Authority for Economic Development of the Minority Sectors (MEDA), exporters by Foreign Trade Administration (FTA) and the Israel Export Institute (IEI), new immigrants and returning residents by the Ministry of Immigrant Absorption, while the Ministry of Education is involved in spreading entrepreneurship education for example. The SMBA helps to steer, prioritise and co-ordinate the various interventions by consulting with businesses, co-operating with other government players on the delivery of certain specific programmes, and providing an entry point to the range of government programmes through the MAOF centre diagnostic and referral work. On the other hand, its ability to co-ordinate policy further is limited by lack of authority to convene other ministries, lack of structures to support co-ordination such as inter-ministerial bodies or an agreed inter-ministerial strategy, and lack of human and financial resources for monitoring and evaluating policy and policy needs and communicating with government and private sector stakeholders.

A national strategy document and an inter-ministerial committee and working group would help

Unlike other Organisation for Economic and Co-operation Development (OECD) countries such as Estonia, Ireland, Portugal and Turkey, Israel has no integrated SME and entrepreneurship policy strategy document setting out the policy objectives and actions expected from each government department and agency. Although the SMBA has its own strategy, this is not a government-wide framework. The creation of a government-wide strategy would increase the incentive for government bodies to support SME and entrepreneurship actions, shape the overall direction of the policy, identify the policy gaps and how they can be filled, and offer a framework for policy monitoring and evaluation.

In contrast to national SME agencies in many other countries, the SMBA does not report to a formal inter-ministerial committee on SME and entrepreneurship policy or animate a corresponding working group on SME and entrepreneurship policy at operational level across ministries. Such bodies would greatly assist its co-ordination function. Inter-ministerial co-ordination is also hampered by the SMBA's status as a department of the Ministry of Economy and Industry rather than a full-authority SME agency. This limits its legitimacy with other government offices. Furthermore, rather than receiving a stable multi-annual budget that would allow for forward planning, the SMBA instead relies on an annual budget allocation from the Ministry of Economy and Industry. Co-ordination is also hampered by the small staff and financial resources at SMBA's disposal. As of 2016, it has only 20 staff including only 6 professionals, with only one professional is dedicated to reviewing regulation.

The monitoring and evaluation work that SMBA is introducing for its own programmes should also be extended across all of the government bodies involved in SME and entrepreneurship support to establish the take-up of policy measures and their impacts. SMBA could play an important role in championing a more evidence-based approach to policy making across government in this field.

The strategy document, inter-ministerial co-ordination arrangements and extended monitoring and evaluation system could be used to rebalance programme expenditures towards priority areas that are currently under-emphasised in the SME and entrepreneurship policy support of the Israeli government. While Israel currently has well-developed support to high-technology businesses, its support for start-up, growth and innovation in non-technology based SMEs is relatively weak. This is reflected in a relatively small scale of programme support for non-R&D based innovation, new business creation outside of high technology fields, growing traditional SMEs, supporting young entrepreneurs and promoting entrepreneurship in the education system. A shift towards more support to more non-high technology SMEs and entrepreneurship should be informed by assessments of the current distribution of expenditures across types of programme intervention and target groups and assessments of the relative merits of the different interventions.

Key recommendations on the strategic framework and policy delivery system

- Prepare an overarching medium-term national SME and entrepreneurship strategic policy, presented in a stand-alone document, which outlines the vision, objectives, priority pillars, target groups, and lines of action across government.
- Create an inter-ministerial SME and Entrepreneurship Policy Committee, with SMBA as its secretariat, and an inter-ministerial Working Group on SME and Entrepreneurship Policy, led by the SMBA and consisting of SME focal points from relevant ministries and agencies.
- Set up a framework of formal consultation forums with SMEs and entrepreneurs, co-ordinated by the SMBA, to solicit their opinions and input on government regulations and policies.
- Conduct an analysis of the current and future staffing and budget requirements of the SMBA and consider strengthening its resources. Strengthen the legal authority of the SMBA by making it a full-authority SME agency.
- Match the SMBA's three-year strategies with a multi-year funding commitment from the Ministry of Finance.
- Ensure that MAOF staff members are fully trained in providing diagnostic and referral services, including deep familiarisation with support programmes offered by other government departments and agencies and the competencies of consultants in the SMBA database.
- Implement a system for regular monitoring of the quality of services being delivered by each MAOF centre and their adherence to specified performance standards. Carry out evaluations of the impact of MAOF services on performance outcomes of clients using robust control group methodologies.

Key recommendations on the strategic framework and policy delivery system *(cont.)*

- Implement an evaluation system for monitoring the take-up by SMEs and entrepreneurs of policy measures across government entities, identifying performance indicators for each support device, and measuring the impact of each policy measure against these performance indicators.
- Establish a co-ordination mechanism for policy support structures, led by the SMBA, to foster communication and exchange among all entities delivering SME and entrepreneurship supports for the purpose of achieving greater collaboration and economies of scale. This could be done within the framework of a Working Group on SME and Entrepreneurship Policy.
- Undertake an assessment of the mix of the portfolio of SME and entrepreneurship programmes by programme type and enterprise target group, including contrasting expenditures and outcomes by technology and non-technology entrepreneurship. Based on the results of this assessment, increase programme support for traditional start-ups and SMEs, including programmes for non-R&D based innovation, new business creation in non-technology fields, promoting the growth of traditional SMEs, supporting young entrepreneurs and promoting entrepreneurship in the education system.

4. National programmes for SMEs and entrepreneurship

The government has made important interventions to foster SME and entrepreneurship finance, but gaps remain

The government loan guarantee programme, the Small and Medium Business Fund (SMBF), plays a fundamental role in improving SME access to bank loans in Israel. The system was reinforced in 2012 through an increase in the state resources committed, merger of three guarantee funds into one, and streamlining of the administrative procedures involved for SMEs and banks. A new four year round of support started in 2016, which involved a number of further improvements: institutional investors can now participate with banks in making guaranteed loans, the one-time administration fee has been increased to help increase the sustainability of the fund, a new option has been created to guarantee loans of up to 5 years for export activity, and the maximum guaranteed loan term has been increased from 5 years to 12 years for industrial capital, including R&D. On the other hand, the SMBF has a high rate of rejection of loan guarantee applications, which stands at approximately 45%. This is despite loan default rates that are not significantly higher than international norms. It suggests the need for increases in coverage ratios and more financial literacy training for SME managers to increase the quantity of loan applications.

The government is also providing financial resources to microfinance institutions to boost small business lending. In particular, significant resources are provided to one of the largest microfinance institutions, the Koret Israel Economic Development Fund, which is very active in lending to women entrepreneurs. There is nevertheless a need to further increase the scale of microfinance for entrepreneurs. In addition, entrepreneurship training and business advisory services should be attached to micro loans more frequently.

The government has been very successful in securing the development of a healthy early-stage venture capital sector. One of the triggers was the creation of 10 YOZMA venture capital funds in the 1990s, which are now entirely private. The government today is seeking to extend equity finance to smaller investment sizes through supporting the establishment of two new private equity funds for SMEs that will start operation in 2016. On the other hand, business angel finance for non-high-technology SMEs is limited. At the same time, new support for financial innovations such as loan securitisation and business development companies could increase the flow of institutional funds to SME lending.

R&D programmes are successful, but more emphasis is needed on other types of innovation

The Israel Innovation Agency (IIA) operates several successful R&D support programmes that are open to SMEs including the R&D Competition Fund, the MAGNET programme for collaborative R&D and the Technological Incubator Programme. However, Israel lags behind other OECD countries in supporting innovation that is not based on R&D, such as innovations in design, introduction of digital technologies, new forms of marketing and new management techniques. The SMBA could support non-technological innovation through an extended consultancy support offer for SME innovation in its MAOF centres.

More support is needed for new and small exporters

The FTA and IEI run several export programmes that are open to SMEs. However, the main funding programme tends to focus on large exporters. Furthermore, whilst some training, consulting and guidance is available for first-time and small exporters through the IEI School for Exporters, it tends to be in the form of one-off courses and seminars rather than more intensive support and longer-term mentoring. The latter types of support are common for high-growth potential SMEs across a range of OECD countries such as Canada, the United Kingdom and Denmark (OECD, 2013d).

There are no major programmes for developing skills in existing SME workforces

Israel offers little policy support for upgrading the skills of existing SME workforces. Common approaches to in-situ SME workforce development include financial incentives for employees or employers to undertake training and the provision of training courses to SMEs and networks of SMEs in other OECD countries such as Korea, France and Ireland. The MAOF centres offer a few business studies courses for existing SME employees, but their role in SME workforce skills development is essentially limited to helping SME managers identify the training needs of their employees as part of their wider diagnostic services. There are few public on-the-job training programmes available to help meet these needs. The MAOF centres are currently piloting a programme that offers training in digital technology to SME employees, but it is very small in scale and narrow in focus, since it is designed as part of a broader programme to upgrade SME productivity rather than a dedicated effort to strengthen SME skills. A much larger scale in-company workforce training programme is called for, which could make use of MAOF centre visibility, networks and facilities to reach SMEs and networks of SMEs.

MAOF centres are building up business development services, but could go further

The SMBA operates 35 MAOF local business development services centres across Israel. They provide client SMEs with a diagnostic analysis that helps them to identify their development needs and can refer them to appropriate subsidised consultancy from a network of MAOF-approved external consultants. There are two major challenges for the network; providing more tailored consultancy and mentoring to SMEs with strong growth potential and expanding the range of services offered to cover significant niche areas that currently do not get adequate attention, such as assistance in business restructuring, dedicated consultancy for women entrepreneurs, and support for peer learning networks. This will require incremental expansion of budgets for the MAOF centres.

Public procurement can be better tapped as a driver of SME growth and innovation

Israeli SMEs have free access to information on public tenders from newspapers and websites. Provisions for cutting tenders into smaller lots further reinforce their chances of winning public contracts as a means of increasing their capacities. However, Israel does not yet have a well-developed system of e-procurement or set-aside provisions for SMEs. Public procurement from SMEs could further be boosted by disseminating guidance to SMEs on how to access public procurement opportunities and providing training for public procurement officers on how to facilitate access by SMEs.

Support for entrepreneurship in disadvantaged social groups is limited

With the exception of Arab Israeli minority programmes, Israel's main support for entrepreneurship in disadvantaged and under-represented groups is the "Initiating a Business" initiative delivered by the MAOF centres. Approximately 7 000 individuals received training and mentoring through the programme in 2013, from groups such as the unemployed, seniors, Ultraorthodox Jews, the disabled and immigrants. In addition, the Ministry of Immigrant Absorption offers training and loans for immigrant entrepreneurship, the IIA offers loans and subsidised mentoring to Ultraorthodox Jews looking to develop an R&D-based business, and there are a few support programmes targeted at young people. However, the numbers of participants are generally small compared with the size of the target groups. Furthermore, the programmes tend to concentrate on start-up, whereas there is also a need to support the sustainability of the businesses created by combining the entrepreneurship training that is offered with business advice and financial support and prolonging assistance after the businesses have begun operations.

Key recommendations on national programmes

Finance programmes

- Increase the share of the SMBF resources allocated to loans for new businesses through introduction of quotas, adjustment of coverage ratios for new businesses and training and financial literacy work with start-ups to increase the quality of their proposals.
- Introduce greater flexibility in the SMBF to facilitate a more staged approach to lending whereby the loan size increases and the interest rate decreases as the bank and the SME client develop a relationship of mutual knowledge and trust.
- Reinforce the provision of microfinance and associated soft support such as training and business advice by fostering the expansion of NGOs currently active in this market and/or creating a government micro-enterprise loan fund combined with training and business advice.
- Provide additional incentives for venture capital funds and private equity firms to invest in non-high-technology growth-oriented enterprises or, alternatively, supply the initial capitalisation for a new seed/venture fund for this purpose based on the principle of matching public and private sector funding. The two private equity funds that will start operations in 2016 are good models for a broader intervention.

Key recommendations on national programmes *(cont.)*

- Encourage business angel investment through the development of regional business angel networks, support of investment-readiness programmes for new entrepreneurs who could benefit from angel investment, and launching a state matching fund to stimulate angel investment in non-R&D based start-ups and early-stage SMEs.
- Support the diversification of finance sources and instruments for SMEs and entrepreneurship, including through setting up alternative finance mechanisms such as Business Development Companies and legal and support frameworks for SME loan securitisation by which institutional actors such as pension funds and insurance companies can invest in SMEs. Design incentives so that institutional investments are channelled to SMEs in traditional industries as well as high-technology enterprises.
- Boost MAOF centre activities for strengthening the financial literacy skills of SME owners, such as offering referrals to financial consultants in the MAOF centre database, focusing on their ability to prepare bankable proposals and understand credit access practices.

Innovation programmes

- Facilitate the transfer of technology developed by Israeli high-technology companies and R&D centres to domestic SMEs to improve their productivity. This could be achieved by the creation of intermediate technology institutes that make technical expertise and facilities available to SMEs that do not have the resources to develop in-house R&D, creating exchange forums to share knowledge on the high-technology developments coming out of Israel and their application in traditional SMEs, or engaging consultants to work with traditional SMEs in sector clusters to examine how these relevant new technologies could improve their production, operational and managerial processes.
- Create a fast-track lane in the IIA R&D Fund to simplify the application process for SMEs with smaller R&D projects.
- Establish closer co-operation between the IIA and the SMBA so that the MAOF centres, which are managed by the SMBA, can become local entry-points for SMEs interested in using the R&D incentives of the IIA. This could include MAOF support to SME consortia to develop an innovation mind set and identify projects that could be supported by the IIA R&D Fund.
- Encourage the Israel Investment Centre to increase the share of its budget for capital investment in SME-led projects by reducing eligibility requirements as to export and turnover thresholds for its subsidies.
- Establish incubators and accelerators for more traditional start-ups and existing SMEs in the manufacturing and service sectors that are not necessarily R&D-driven, but which are nonetheless innovative in other ways.
- Provide more funding and technical assistance (awareness raising, mentoring, counselling, etc.) for non-technological innovation (e.g. design, marketing, organisational approaches, and innovation management) in SMEs.
- Strengthen the MAOF centre advice on innovation management to SMEs by hiring specialised innovation agents.
- Expand support for collaborative innovation in small non R&D-based firms by supporting networks of SMEs for innovation activity.
- Continue support for the greening of the economy by encouraging more SMEs to join the natural gas grid and re-launching the Investment Centre's greenhouse gas reduction programmes.

Key recommendations on national programmes *(cont.)*

Internationalisation programmes

- Design a more comprehensive approach to export training and advice for SMEs including awareness-raising events among SMEs potentially interested in exporting, export-readiness courses to instruct new and occasional exporters on how to export for the first time or expand export volumes, and advanced tailored advice for more experienced exporters.
- Adjust eligibility criteria for export programmes to facilitate participation by new and small firms with exports worth less than NIS 1 million (approximately USD 250 000) and make travel costs eligible for new and young firms to attend international trade fairs, explore international markets or meet international buyers.
- Launch a new dedicated programme for SME export promotion combining financial support with advice on exporting, export logistics management and adoption of digital infrastructures conducive to e-commerce.
- Keep the MAOF centres up-to-date about the various export promotion tools that the government provides through the FTA and the IEI and ensure that MAOF centres hire experts in exporting among their consultants and mentors.
- Introduce a more formal approach to backing the creation, operation and expansion of export consortia in Israel in order to spread the benefits of government funding among larger numbers of exporting firms and to foster the transfer of export-related knowledge among consortia members.
- Designate "export financing" as a specific loan category under the SMBF to ensure that firms can use state-backed loan guarantees when applying for bank loans to finance their export activity.

Workforce skills development programmes

- Set up a publicly-funded advice and brokerage service to increase the awareness of SME managers about the advantages of workforce training, develop training plans for SMEs, and refer SMEs to appropriate training providers, potentially as part of MAOF centre activities.
- Pilot a financial incentive scheme (such as a voucher, grant or tax subsidy) to assist SMEs in engaging professional training providers for workplace-based training.
- Expand the support offered by MAOF centres to include organisation of in-company workforce training packages for SMEs.
- Promote national training standards that recognise the continuing professional development undertaken by employees.
- Support networking and clustering arrangements to allow SMEs to work collaboratively with suppliers, customers, training providers and the public sector in developing and implementing appropriate training provision.
- Pilot an approach to peer learning in SME management development by setting up private-led "communities of practice" brokered and supported by MAOF centres, based on the idea of SME learning circles through which SME managers can advise and mentor peers.

Business diagnosis, advice and consultancy programmes

- Scale up the budget and activities of the MAOF centres for business diagnosis, advice and consultancy services with a particular emphasis on providing more support to SMEs with strong growth potential and expanding the range of services offered to cover significant niche areas that do not get adequate attention.

Key recommendations on national programmes (*cont.*)

- Introduce dedicated and tailored coaching and consultancy services for growth-orientated businesses in MAOF centre activities.
- Introduce a management advice and support programme to help companies requiring business restructuring either to turn around or to close down in a way that reduces social and economic costs for the entrepreneurs and their customers.
- Consider strengthening the specialisation of MAOF staff by creating two tracks, one for manufacturing and one for services firms, reflecting the different development challenges of these two types of SMEs.
- Better link the managerial support of the MAOF centres with the financial assistance available from other public programmes. As part of this, ensure that those SMEs that do not receive loan guarantee assistance from the SMBF are automatically re-directed towards alternative support from the business consulting and signposting services offered by MAOF centres.

Public procurement programmes

- Develop online guidelines for SMEs in the form of a step-by-step guide for contracting with the government.
- Implement a national e-procurement system in order to simplify administrative procedures for businesses to reduce the comparative disadvantage of SMEs in accessing procurement opportunities.
- Collect data on the number and volume of public procurement contracts awarded to SMEs to ascertain whether SMEs have fair access to public procurement, making use of set-aside quotas or targets for the value of contracts from SMEs if they are found to experience discrimination.
- Provide training and support to government procurement officers in how to ensure that their procurement processes are open to SMEs.

Programmes to support entrepreneurship in specific social target groups

- Launch additional specialised support programmes for self-employment and entrepreneurship for people from disadvantaged and under-represented social groups in entrepreneurship, including youth, women, Arab Israelis, and Ultraorthodox Jews.
- Develop more comprehensive interventions for these groups, which integrate training and business advice with financial assistance and offer some follow-on support after the immediate start-up event.

5. The local dimension

There is no regional level of government in Israel, and local government action for SMEs is limited

Most SME and entrepreneurship policy actions in Israel are developed by national government ministries and agencies. Given its small size, there are no regional governments or regional development agencies, and the ability of local governments to introduce their own support measures is constrained by their frequently small sizes and professional capacities. Only 28 of the 232 local authorities in Israel have populations of more than 50 000, although there are 6 cities with populations of more than 200 000. Apart from the largest local authorities, most have not developed any specific support programmes for SMEs and entrepreneurship, and in general the local authorities do not even carry out the role of information provider to SMEs on issues such as local premises availability, public procurement opportunities and business regulations.

Local actions could be a useful complement to national government policies and programmes, particularly for building local supply chains and clusters and financing, developing and marketing sites and premises for SMEs. This could be encouraged by national government capacity building support for local authorities in these areas, for example through offering professional training and guidelines. It could also be encouraged by brokering and incentivising co-operation projects among local authorities. There are a few examples of local authority co-operation projects for regional cluster development and for joint industrial sites, but such co-operation is currently limited.

Local authorities can improve their business licensing, procurement, planning and property development activities for SMEs

Local authorities have some important areas of responsibility that affect SMEs and entrepreneurship in business licensing, procurement, planning decisions and property development. Business licensing procedures are often quite burdensome for businesses, hampering formal business activity and expansion. In response, some local authorities have taken actions to streamline their licensing procedures. More could be done to exchange information across local authorities on good practices in business licensing. There are significant public procurement opportunities from local governments and participation of local authorities in national efforts to open up public procurement to SMEs should be considered, for example in simplified procurement procedures for SMEs, training for officials in good practice procurement methods and participation in a national e-procurement system or SME set-aside system. In addition, the availability of sites and premises for SMEs is often constrained by poorly defined local land use plans and slow planning procedures and lack of financial and professional capacities to support industrial site provision. National government support could be considered for local authorities to help address this issue.

National enterprise and regional policy include limited emphasis on building local supply chains and clusters

There is a strong regional economic development divide in Israel between a dynamic core and an underdeveloped northern (Galilee) and southern (Negev) periphery. The current pattern of SME and entrepreneurship activity is contributing to that divide. For example, only 3% of adults were involved in early-stage entrepreneurial activity in the Negev region in 2010, compared with an average of 5% in Israel as a whole (Menipaz et al., 2011). Although there is a clear political objective in Israel to develop the periphery, the main regional policy tools are infrastructure investment and subsidies for mobile capital and individuals. This contrasts with regional development approaches in other OECD countries, which tend to focus on building regional competitiveness through a range of support for innovation and entrepreneurship, such as activities for innovation networks, cluster building and new firm formation.

Most enterprise policies operated by national government ministries and agencies are "spatially blind" in that they offer standardised support across the country, rather than seek to identify locally-specific barriers and opportunities for SME and entrepreneurship development. More could be done to integrate measures to support local supply chains and clusters in both national enterprise and regional policy. Furthermore, existing SME and entrepreneurship development measures in the development programme for the Negev could be extended to the Galilee region, including actions to support peripheral SMEs to introduce digital technologies for sales to non-local markets and supplier chain development actions to help peripheral firms win subcontracting orders with large firms and government organisations.

Key recommendations on the local dimension of SME and entrepreneurship policy

- Provide capacity-building support to local government authorities on local actions for streamlining local business licensing procedures and assisting entrepreneurs through the process of obtaining licenses, making the local planning system more effective and opening up local public procurement to SMEs. This could take the form of professional training, preparation of guidelines and disseminating information on the practices of the best performing local authorities as examples for others to follow.
- Encourage participation of local authorities in national efforts to open up public procurement to SMEs, including simplification of procurement procedures for SMEs, training for officials in good practice procurement methods and participation in a national e-procurement system or SME set-aside system if introduced.
- Offer funding and brokerage for co-operation projects amongst groups of smaller local authorities for joint SME actions. These can include joint projects for property development, business licensing simplification, local public procurement from SMEs, and local cluster and supply chain development.
- Expand support for SME and entrepreneurship development in the regional development programme for the southern periphery and develop a relevant set of SME support actions for development in the northern periphery.

6. SMEs and entrepreneurship in the Arab Israeli population

Expansion, diversification and upgrading of Arab-owned SMEs is required for national growth and equity

Economic outcomes for the 20% of the population that are Arab Israelis are much poorer than the average (CBS, 2014; OECD, 2009). Approximately one-half live below the poverty threshold and less than one-half of adults are active in the labour force. Arab Israeli women suffer the highest unemployment rate of any social group in Israel. These inequalities are a key factor in Israel's relatively poor national performance on productivity and social cohesion measures.

Much of the problem stems from poor employment opportunities in Arab-owned SMEs and poor entrepreneurship outcomes. First, Arab-owned SMEs are relatively small. Arab-owned employer businesses make up 11.5% of businesses with less than 5 employees but only 3.1% of businesses with at least 50 employees (Table 1.2). Their average employment is 5.4 compared with 13.6 in Jewish businesses. Second, Arab-owned SMEs have relatively low productivity. They are concentrated in low value-added sectors and under-represented in high-technology manufacturing knowledge-based services. They also accounted for only 0.1% of total Israeli exports in 2011. Third, entrepreneurship outcomes are relatively poor for the Arab Israeli community (Menipaz et al., 2013). Only, 8.5% of Arab Israeli adults and 4.0%

Table 1.2. **Distribution of Arab- and Jewish-owned employer businesses by enterprise size, 2014**

Firm size (by no. employees)	Arab-owned		Jewish-owned		Total	
	No. (thousands)	Per cent	No. (thousands)	Per cent	No. (thousands)	Arab share
1-5	15.5	77.2	118.6	68.1	134.1	11.5
6-19	3.7	18.6	38.7	22.2	42.4	8.8
20-49	0.6	3.2	10.7	6.1	11.3	5.6
50+	0.2	1.0	6.2	3.6	6.4	3.1
Total	20.0	100.0	174.2	110.0	194.2	10.3

Note: Data are drawn from the Ministry of Economy and Industry register of includes businesses with at least one employee. Arab-owned businesses are defined as those in which 50% or more of owners are Arab or Druze. Discrepancies are due to rounding.
Source: Minorities Economic Development Authority (MEDA), Note supplied to the OECD secretariat.

StatLink http://dx.doi.org/10.1787/888933421364

of Arab Israeli women were involved in setting up or running a new business compared with an average of 10.0% for all adults in 2013. Furthermore, only 28% of Arab Israeli female entrepreneurs and 66% of Arab Israeli male entrepreneurs were opportunity-driven, which compares with 84% of Jewish male entrepreneurs and 94% of Jewish female entrepreneurs.

Access to finance is an obstacle

Whilst internal financing is limited by low incomes and savings, a lack of collateral constrains access to bank credit. The Authority for the Economic Development of the Minorities Sectors (MEDA) is active in improving the supply of finance. Its key initiatives are support to the Koret SAWA microfinance programme, additional funding to the state guarantee loan fund for loans to Arab-owned businesses and commitment of NIS 50 million towards the establishment of the Al Bawader venture capital fund. However, additional supply-side actions can be envisaged to expand the number of financial institutions addressing Arab-owned SMEs and the range of financial instruments available to them. The measures could include additional support for angel investment and crowdfunding, demand side actions to promote financial literacy for business managers, and better linkages between finance programmes for Arab Israeli entrepreneurs and mainstream business development support services for the population as a whole.

SMEs lack suitable premises

Large numbers of Arab-owned SMEs have to operate from constrained and inefficient premises. Only 3.5% of purpose-built modern premises in designated industrial zones are within or adjacent to Arab-dominated settlements, although Arab communities make up 20% of the national population. MEDA is allocating a substantial budget to developing industrial zones for Arab-owned businesses. However, property development by the private sector and by local authorities in Arab areas is held back by several problems. These involve a lack of detailed local authority land use plans and associated difficulties in obtaining planning permissions and difficulties in obtaining leases to use state-owned land. Furthermore, Arab-dominated local authorities tend to have very limited tax revenues, budgets and professional capacities for industrial zone development. Continued central government financing for zone construction in Arab-dominated areas will be important. Additional national support measures that should help include training in zone development for local authorities operating in Arab areas and better planning guidance.

Co-operations could also be encouraged among Jewish and Arab dominated local authorities for the development of zones, including mechanisms to redistribute taxes collected on the zones across the local authorities involved. MEDA has recently created a pilot project of this kind that could form the template for further co-operations.

Workforce skills and management practices should be strengthened

Lack of workforce and management skills is a further problem for Arab-owned SMEs. Low workforce skill levels link back to low educational attainment rates (only 20% of Arab Israeli adults have had tertiary education) and a lack of opportunities to build skills on the job (given low Arab Israeli labour force participation rates and low productivity in existing Arab-owned SMEs) (OECD, 2011, CBS, 2014b). A 'skills drain' is also in operation as some of the most skilled Arab Israeli workers migrate and commute to mainly Jewish labour market areas. New Employment Orientation Centres in Arab-dominated local labour market areas are having a welcome impact by offering vocational guidance, soft skills coaching, work placements, training and retraining services to Arab Israeli job seekers (OECD, 2015c). However, there is little policy support for training existing workforces in Arab-owned SMEs.

Traditional family business management practices are especially dominant in Arab-owned SMEs and are often not appropriate for business growth and diversification (Drori and Lerner, 2002). MAOF centres are the main players in offering management development support to Arab-owned businesses, although there are also two incubators and a business accelerator for high-potential Arab-owned SMEs. However, the MAOF centre support is not tailored specifically to the issues faced by Arab business owners and there is no additional budget allocation for responding to the greater needs of Arab-owned SMEs. A major programme for business management upgrading in SMEs should be considered. Arab Israeli women entrepreneurs in particular recognise a need for management skills support and may be better served by dedicated programmes. An important accompaniment to these management skills development programmes would be a dedicated financial support programme for business diversification, innovation and productivity upgrading in Arab-owned businesses. At the same time, there are increasing numbers of young talented Arab Israeli potential entrepreneurs in universities, and university incubator and entrepreneurship education initiatives should be sure to reach them.

Addressing these problems, and a public procurement stimulus, can tackle the market demand constraint

Lack of market demand is a further constraint to the growth and improvement of Arab-owned SMEs in Israel. To a large extent this reflects their concentration in sectors with low entry costs, low demand growth, low levels of exports and limited participation in national and international supply chains. Addressing the market demand constraint is likely to require actions to provide advice, training, consultancy and investment finance to Arab-owned SMEs and entrepreneurs that help them to diversify their businesses and to set up in new sectors and target markets. An additional stimulus could nevertheless come from a dedicated public procurement programme for Arab-owned SMEs. While such public procurement programmes for minority-owned businesses are common in OECD countries there is currently none in Israel. Typical approaches involve targets for direct procurement from minority enterprises, favouring contractors that sub-contract to minority businesses, enabling bids by consortiums of minority-owned SMEs, and offering consultancy, training and other support to prepare minority firms to submit successful bids.

Further investment in MEDA will be crucial

MEDA was created in 2007 to boost policy support for Arab Israelis. Together with SMBA, it has been charged with implementing expenditure programmes for Arab SMEs and entrepreneurship worth approximately NIS 1.5 billion since 2010. It has also had oversight of a further NIS 0.5 billion of programmes managed by line ministries. This has enabled the development of many important interventions for industrial zone development, financing, export promotion, business plan guidance, management training, business incubators, and tourism development. The support has been further strengthened by Government Decision 922 of January 2016, which gives MEDA the role of co-ordinating a new cross-government 5-year economic development plan for the Arab sector.

In implementing the new 5-year plan for the Arab sector, MEDA could play a key role in helping increase the coherence and prioritisation of intervention by the various ministries and agencies concerned based on more systematic monitoring and evaluation of programmes and establishment of better data on the Arab SME and entrepreneurship population. However, with only approximately 13 senior professional staff and an operational budget of NIS 21 million in 2014, MEDA is small compared with other minority business development agencies internationally and this does not match with the government's ambition to reduce the gap in Arab Israeli business participation. Additional staff and budget are needed both for policy co-ordination and to expand the scale of MEDA's most effective direct initiatives for Arab Israeli SMEs and entrepreneurs, particularly women.

Key recommendations on SMEs and entrepreneurship in the Arab Israeli population

Open up public procurement to Arab Israeli businesses

- Introduce public procurement measures dedicated to Arab-owned SMEs and start-ups, through setting a quota or target for the share of contracts or volume of business for Arab-owned enterprises, supporting the development of bidding consortia among Arab-owned enterprises and requiring prime contractors to offer a proportion of subcontracts to Arab-owned businesses.

Build workforce and management skills

- Introduce incentives for Arab-owned SMEs to undertake in-company workforce training and offer in-company workforce training programmes for networks of Arab-owned SMEs.
- Expand dedicated management development programmes for Arab Israeli SMEs and entrepreneurs offering advice, consultancy and mentoring on business innovation, upgrading of equipment and technology, expanding markets and participating in local and international supply chains.
- Ensure that university business incubator programmes across the country give support to Arab Israeli students and staff in proportion to their numbers and needs by setting target quotas for Arab Israeli participants and/or creating a specific university incubation programme for Arab Israeli entrepreneurs.

Introduce a dedicated financial incentive programme for investment and innovation

- Launch a time-limited, 'challenge fund' type programme of subsidies for capital investment, R&D, product and marketing development and meeting international quality standards in Arab-owned SMEs, both in traditional manufacturing and tourism sectors and emerging knowledge-intensive business services.

Key recommendations on SMEs and entrepreneurship in the Arab Israeli population *(cont.)*

Improve access to finance

- Include special provisions such as quotas for Arab businesses within financial competition reforms.
- Provide financial and technical support to existing microfinance institutions, credit unions and cooperative banks serving the Arab Israeli business community to help them expand their operations.
- Develop a graduation facility for the MEDA microcredit programmes whereby entrepreneurs with growth ambitions for their enterprises can be accompanied into mainstream business development support services.
- Promote the development of business angel networks targeting investments in Arab-owned enterprises.
- Explore the potential for equity and loan crowdfunding based within – but open to expansion beyond – the Arab Israeli community.

Provide industrial sites and premises

- Continue central government investment in the creation of industrial zones in and around Arab-dominated local authority areas at such a scale as to ensure that there is an adequate supply of local premises for Arab-owned businesses.
- Make regulations and land use planning decisions more favourable to the establishment of industrial zones and business premises in and around Arab-dominated local authority areas, in particular by streamlining the decision-making of planning authorities, establishing planning authorities for individual Arab-dominated areas where possible, and providing planning policy guidance notes supportive of SME development.
- Produce and disseminate guiding principles on sharing of business tax revenues between Jewish- and Arab-dominated municipalities in the case of joint industrial zones and broker partnerships among local authorities for joint industrial zone development.
- Provide training and guidance to professionals in Arab-dominated local authorities to increase their ability to finance, develop, manage and market industrial zones.

Improve policy co-ordination and outreach

- Transfer responsibility for economic development support of Druze municipalities to the MEDA.
- Organise periodic in-depth surveys of Arab Israeli business development trends and issues and introduce more systematic monitoring and evaluation of policy activities implemented for minority businesses. Establish a unit within the MEDA for research and evaluation to assist in particular in scaling up successful experimental projects, making the case for increased funding for the MEDA and securing the greatest impacts from this funding.
- Create and manage through the MEDA a single, integrated information portal on business support for Arab Israeli SMEs and entrepreneurs.
- Apply gender targets consistently for participation in public programmes for Arab Israeli SMEs and entrepreneurship, establishing rolling targets that they are feasible at the outset and increase over time as expectations and awareness are raised.

Key recommendations on SMEs and entrepreneurship in the Arab Israeli population *(cont.)*

- Strengthen gender-targeted measures for Arab Israeli women entrepreneurs, e.g. creation of women's cooperatives and sponsorship of women's business organisations, networks and mentoring (including by senior Jewish businesswomen).
- Increase funding for the MEDA in order to enable it to co-ordinate policy across government and develop the necessary statistical and evaluation base as well as to scale up its direct interventions for Arab Israeli SMEs and entrepreneurs that have the greatest net benefits.

7. Medium-Sized Enterprises

Israel's medium-sized enterprises have relatively weak productivity performance

Israel's medium-sized enterprises (MSEs) are defined by SMBA as those with between 20 and 99 employees. These firms make up 6.5% of employer enterprises and one-fifth of private sector employment in Israel. Figure 1.11 shows that there is an important productivity gap between MSEs and larger firms in manufacturing in Israel, a gap which is greater in Israel than in many other OECD countries. The gap is not found in services sectors. One of the reasons for the productivity gap in manufacturing MSEs is limited a low share of manufacturing MSEs in R&D activity and a large gap between manufacturing MSEs and large manufacturing firms in new-to-market technological innovation and product innovation.

Figure 1.11. **Labour productivity by enterprise size, manufacturing**

Value added per person employed, index 250+ = 100, 2013 or latest available year

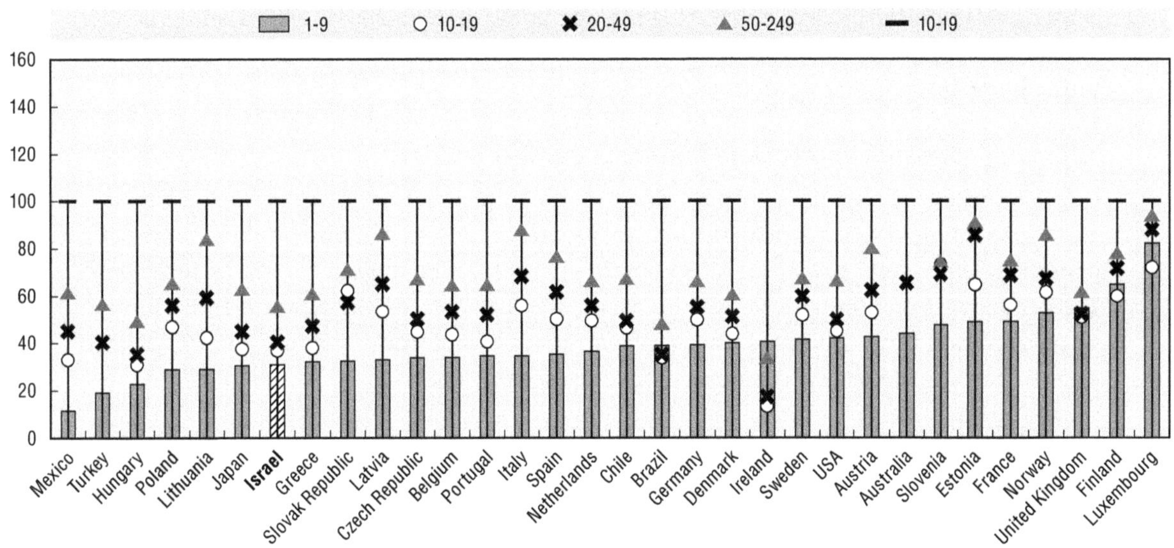

Note: Data for the United States on labour productivity are constructed as value added per employee. Data for Mexico refer to 2014, data for Ireland refer to 2011, and data for Israel refer to 2012. The size-class classification for Mexico is based on establishments.

Source: OECD (2016b, forthcoming) *Entrepreneurship at a Glance 2016*, based on OECD Structural and Demographic Business Statistics (database).

StatLink http://dx.doi.org/10.1787/888933421341

Supporting MSE productivity, innovation and growth would have an important impact on improving national economic performance and reducing duality in the Israeli economy.

MSEs comprise a stable part of the economy and have organisational systems in place that can be built on for growth. They can also play the role of anchor firms, cluster enablers, magnets for supply and service firms, orchestrators of networks, and a generator of positive spill-overs.

There are few opportunities for workforce training in medium-sized firms

Israel's vocational training system is not working well for MSEs, reflecting small numbers of participants in engineering and technical training, limited sector-specific training and a mix of courses that does not match key skill needs. The design of more relevant training courses in vocational training colleges could be supported by a national training needs analysis for MSEs and by inviting MSEs to work more often with local colleges in helping to design specific local continuing professional development courses and tertiary level vocational training programmes. The MAOF centres are providing some relevant training support to MSEs in the form of specialist workshops and short courses where there is a demand for them from companies. This function could be encouraged further with more diagnostic analysis of MSE training needs by the MAOF centres accompanied by a targeted offer of subsidised courses and longer courses.

Management skills and practices need upgrading

Management skills and practices are often weak or poorly adapted in Israeli MSEs. There is no national programme for management skills development in MSEs or dedicated management and leadership programme for high-growth potential MSEs. At the same time, there are several good practice examples of innovation management training in universities that could be extended, including the Technion University programmes offering networking and mentoring for senior managers. In parallel, the MAOF centres are playing an important role in supporting the upgrading of management skills and practices through their consultancy support, but MSE users often report that these services are not sufficiently specialised or intensive for their needs.

Difficulty accessing appropriate finance is another barrier

MSEs have difficulties in obtaining loans from banks of appropriate sizes and durations for growth and restructuring. State loan guarantees can play a role in increasing access to loans, but only 7% of MSEs obtain guarantees, compared to 18% of firms with 6-10 employees and 9% with 11-20 employees. Moreover, state loan guarantees are limited to a maximum term of 5 years. Factoring can provide important working capital for MSE growth, but the industry is currently still at a nascent stage.

Equity finance is a further option but although Israel has a very strong private equity industry, the majority of investments go to the high technology sector. Building up angel investments outside of high technology sectors could help address the gap for traditional manufacturing MSEs. Business crowdfunding for MSEs is currently held back in Israel by an unfavourable regulatory environment that offers excessive protection to consumers. Current legislation requires firms to issue a prospectus in order to offer shares to more than 35 offerees and forbids offers to a large number of non-accredited investors. Although new legislation is proposed that will loosen requirements for SMEs and new firms wishing to raise funds from the crowd whilst protecting consumers through restricting the scale of individual investments that can be made under this regime, it will not do much to address the MSE problem, since it plans to restrict crowdfunding issues to R&D active firms (Shenhav & Co, 2014).

There is no major supply chain development programme

Although Israel's innovation policies have been very successful in developing the ICT sector, Israel has not done as well in developing innovative clusters in other sectors such as water, energy, health and biotechnology, in which there are nascent R&D and start-up activities but not full cluster ecosystems. An explicit strategy of supply chain development could help build these clusters as well as promote productive efficiency, technology diffusion, and responsiveness to changing market conditions and customer needs in traditional MSEs. Although there are some private supply chain development actions in place by large companies and business associations, there is no major national public supply chain development programme.

Opening up of public procurement could have important benefits for MSE growth

MSEs are more likely than smaller firms to have the ambitions, technologies, access to capital and management practices necessary for upscaling, and hence are well placed to translate opening up of public procurement into growth. However, participation of MSEs in public procurement remains weak (Adalya Economic Consulting, 2011). The problems could be addressed by subsidised training for MSEs in accessing public procurement, delivered online or with support from local MAOF advisors. Defence procurement could also be opened up further to MSEs.

There is only limited innovation support for traditional manufacturing MSEs

The IIA offers significant policy support for R&D activity that is accessible to MSEs. Furthermore, a special track has been created for R&D grants for Traditional Industries within the R&D Fund. However, this support has limited relevance to traditional manufacturing MSEs without formal R&D activities. In order to introduce necessary incremental improvements to their processes and organisational and marketing innovations, traditional manufacturing MSEs require dedicated consultancy and mentoring support and funding for developing and implementing innovation strategies.

Key recommendations on medium-sized enterprises

- Develop a specific MSE component in the new national strategy document proposed in this report for SME and entrepreneurship policy.
- Undertake a national training needs analysis for MSEs in collaboration with the Ministry of Education, the Ministry of Economy and Industry, universities, colleges, unions and MSE employers and adapt VET programmes and MAOF centre short courses in line with the findings.
- Introduce additional management development programmes for MSEs in selected universities based on good practices developed by Technion University, including a management and leadership programme for existing high-potential MSEs.
- Introduce a dedicated consultancy track for MSEs in MAOF centres with more specialised consultants and more intensive diagnosis, consultancy and mentoring.
- Extend the maximum term of SMBF loan guarantees to repayment periods of 10-15 years and ensure that MSEs have the same access to these guarantees as smaller enterprises, introduce tax incentives for angel investments in non-R&D based MSEs, and make further improvements to the regulatory environment for crowdfunding.

Key recommendations on medium-sized enterprises *(cont.)*

- Introduce a national supply chain development programme for MSEs involving brokering relationships among potential supply chain partners, developing marketing and marketing platforms, targeted training and mentoring, and support for introduction of supply chain management software and management procedures.
- Open up defence procurement to MSEs in traditional industries and set up an information portal where details of how to apply are placed and other support offered to potential bidders in co-operation between the Ministry of Defence and the Ministry of Economy and Industry.
- Introduce a programme to stimulate non-R&D based innovation in traditional manufacturing MSEs involving knowledge transfer partnerships between MSEs, college-based researchers, and college graduates.

References

Aahroni, Y. (2009), *Inward FDI in Israel and Its Policy Context*, Columbia FDI Profiles, New York.

Adalya Economic Consulting l.T.D (2011), *Strategic Report of Israeli Governmental Assistance to Small and Medium Businesses – Phase A, http://adalya.co.il/en/adalya-economic-consulting.*

CBS (2014), *Statistical Abstract of Israel*, Central Bureau of Statistics, Jerusalem.

CBS (2013), Business Demography: A Collection of Statistical Data from the Business Register: 2003-11, Publication No. 1541, Jerusalem.

Drori, I. and M. Lerner (2002), "The Dynamics of Limited Breaking Out: The Case of the Arab Manufacturing Businesses in Israel", *Entrepreneurship and Regional Development: An International Journal*, 14.2, 135-154.

European Commission (2014), *Thematic Working Group on Entrepreneurship Education Final Report*, European Commission Directorate-General Education and Culture.

European Commission/EACEA/Eurydice (2016), *Entrepreneurship Education at School in Europe, Eurydice Report*, Luxembourg, Publications Office of the European Union OECD (2015a), *Entrepreneurship at a Glance 2015*, OECD Publishing, Paris.

Menipaz, E., Y. Avrahami and M. Lerner (2013), *National Report for Israel by the Global Entrepreneurship Monitor 2013*, Ira Center for Business Technology and Society, Ben Gurion University.

Menipaz, E., Y. Avrahami and M. Lerner (2011), *GEM 2010 Israel National Entrepreneurship Report*, Ben Gurion University of the Nagev, Beer Sheva, *www.gemconsortium.org/docs/2290/gem-israel-2010-report.*

OECD (2016a), *Financing SMEs and Entrepreneurs 2016: An OECD Scoreboard*, OECD Publishing, Paris, *http://dx.doi.org/10.1787/fin_sme_ent-2016-en.*

OECD (2016b, forthcoming) *Entrepreneurship at a Glance 2016*, OECD Publishing, Paris.

OECD (2015a), *Entrepreneurship at a Glance 2015*, OECD Publishing, Paris, *http://dx.doi.org/10.1787/entrepreneur_aag-2015-en.*

OECD (2015b), *OECD Science, Technology and Industry Scoreboard 2015*, OECD Publishing, Paris, *http://dx.doi.org/10.1787/sti_scoreboard-2015-en.*

OECD (2015c), *Employment and Skills Strategies in Israel*, OECD Publishing, Paris, *http://dx.doi.org/10.1787/9789264232969-en.*

OECD (2014a), *Entrepreneurship at a Glance 2014*, OECD Publishing, Paris, *http://dx.doi.org/10.1787/entrepreneur_aag-2014-en.*

OECD (2014b), *Financing SMEs and Entrepreneurs 2014: An OECD Scoreboard*, OECD Publishing, Paris, *http://dx.doi.org/10.1787/fin_sme_ent-2014-en.*

OECD (2013a), *Entrepreneurship at a Glance, 2013*, OECD Publishing, Paris, *http://dx.doi.org/10.1787/entrepreneur_aag-2013-en.*

OECD (2013b), *PISA 2012 Assessment and Analytical Framework: Mathematics, Reading, Science, Problem Solving and Financial Literacy*, OECD Publishing, Paris, *http://dx.doi.org/10.1787/9789264190511-en*.

OECD (2013c), *OECD Economic Surveys: Israel – December 2013*, OECD Publishing, *http://dx.doi.org/10.1787/eco_surveys-isr-2013-en*.

OECD (2013d), *An International Benchmarking Analysis of Public Programmes for High-Growth Firms*, OECD LEED Programme, Paris, *www.oecd.org/industry/high-growthreport.htm*.

OECD (2011), *Higher Education in Regional and City Development*, The Galilee, Israel, OECD, Paris, *http://dx.doi.org/10.1787/9789264088986-en*.

OECD (2009), *OECD Economic Surveys: Israel 2009*, Volume 2009/21– January 2010, Supplement No. 3, OECD Publishing, Paris, *http://dx.doi.org/10.1787/eco_surveys-isr-2009-en*.

Schneider, F. (undated), "Size and Development of the Shadow Economy of 31 European and 5 other OECD Countries from 2003 to 2012: Some New Facts", *www.econ.jku.at/schneider*.

Schneider, F., A. Buehn and C. Montenegro (2010), "New Estimates for the Shadow Economies all Over the World", *International Economic Journal*, 24, 443-461.

Shenhav & Co (2014), *Crowdfunding – Current Status and Proposed Changes www.shenhavlaw.com/wp-content/uploads/2014/06/Crowd-Funding-Presentation.pdf*.

Chapter 2

SME and entrepreneurship performance in Israel

This chapter investigates SME and entrepreneurship characteristics and performance in Israel in comparison with other OECD countries. It presents the numbers of SMEs, their employment and value-added contributions to the economy, and their export and innovation levels and shows breakdowns by SME sectors and size bands. It also explores entrepreneurship behaviours and attitudes in Israel by population group. There are several clear areas of excellence in Israel's SME and entrepreneurship activity, including a high business creation rate and a large share of high-impact enterprises. At the same time, there are relatively low numbers of SMEs and low levels of SME productivity, particularly in manufacturing. There is also a strong dualism whereby very productive high-technology SMEs and start-ups operate alongside a much less efficient and relatively underdeveloped traditional SME sector. Entrepreneurship rates are also much higher among men than women.

The statistical data for Israel are supplied by and under the responsibility of the relevant Israeli authorities. The use of such data by the OECD is without prejudice to the status of the Golan Heights, East Jerusalem and Israeli settlements in the West Bank under the terms of international law.
This document and any map included herein are without prejudice to the status of or sovereignty over any territory, to the delimitation of international frontiers and boundaries and to the name of any territory, city or area.

The size and structure of the SME sector[1]

The size analysis

Small and medium-sized enterprises (SMEs) constitute 99.8% of Israel's business enterprises (Figure 2.1). Only 0.2% of Israeli employer businesses have more than 250 workers, i.e. around 500 companies. The predominance of SMEs in the business population is common to all OECD countries, although the proportion of enterprises that are SMEs in Israel is slightly above the OECD average. Micro-enterprises (1-9 employees) account for 92.3% of all businesses in Israel compared with an OECD average of 90.0%, small enterprises (10-49 employees) account for 6.3% of businesses compared with an OECD average of 8.3% and medium-sized enterprises (50-249 employees) account for 1.5% of businesses compared with an OECD average of 0.7%. Thus, compared to the OECD average, the Israeli SME economy is weighted towards the micro-enterprise segment.

Figure 2.1. **Enterprises by business size class, total business economy, 2012 or latest available year**

Percentage of total number of enterprises

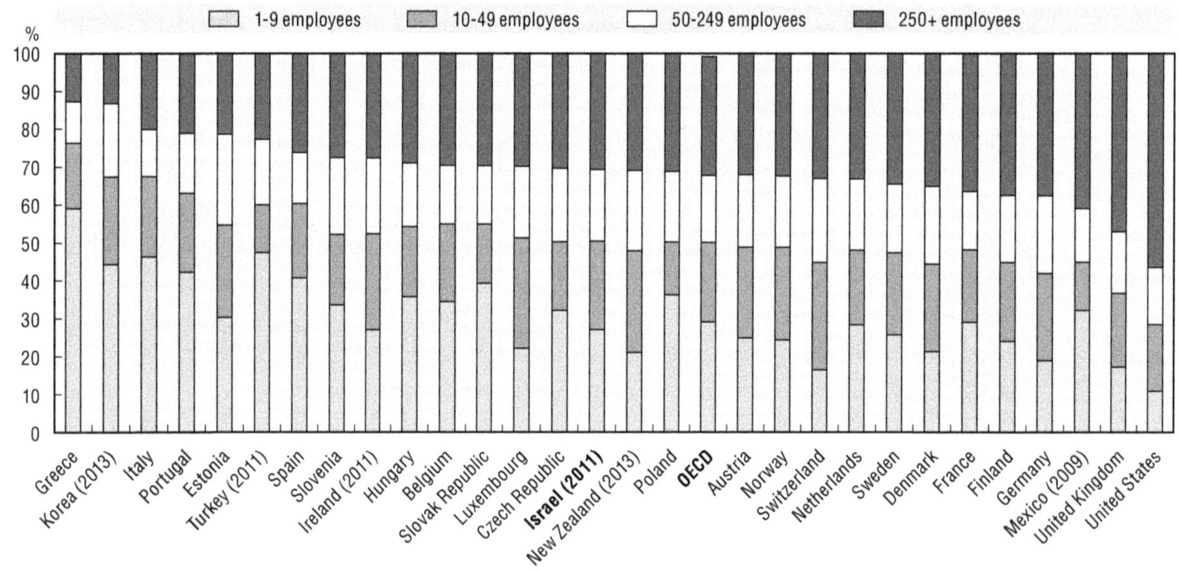

Note: Countries are presented in descending order, from the country where SMEs (up to 249 employees) are the biggest share of the total business population to the country where they are the smallest share. All countries present information using the enterprise as the statistical unit except Korea and Mexico which use establishment. For Canada and the United States, data do not include non-employer enterprises. Data for Korea include financial services. Different size classes apply to Australia (1-19; 20-199; 200+), Korea (1-9; 10-49; 50-299; 300+), Mexico (1-10; 11-50; 51-250; 251+), Turkey (1-19; 20-49; 50-249; 250+).

Source: OECD based on OECD (2015a), *Entrepreneurship at a Glance 2015*, OECD Publishing, Paris.

StatLink http://dx.doi.org/10.1787/888933421377

Some 69.3% of the business sector workforce is employed by an SME in Israel, which is slightly greater than the OECD average of 68.7% (Figure 1.1 reproduced below). Medium-sized firms (50-249 employees) account for 18.9% of national business employment compared with the OECD average of 17.7% and small companies (10-49 employees) account for 23.4% of the business workforce compared to an OECD average of 21.0%. On the other hand, only 27.0% of the employed labour force in the business economy is engaged in a micro-enterprise in Israel, which is below the OECD average of 29.1%. Given the above average share of micro enterprises in business numbers, this suggests that micro firms are relatively small in Israel compared with other OECD countries.

Employment by enterprise class size, total business economy, 2012 or latest available year

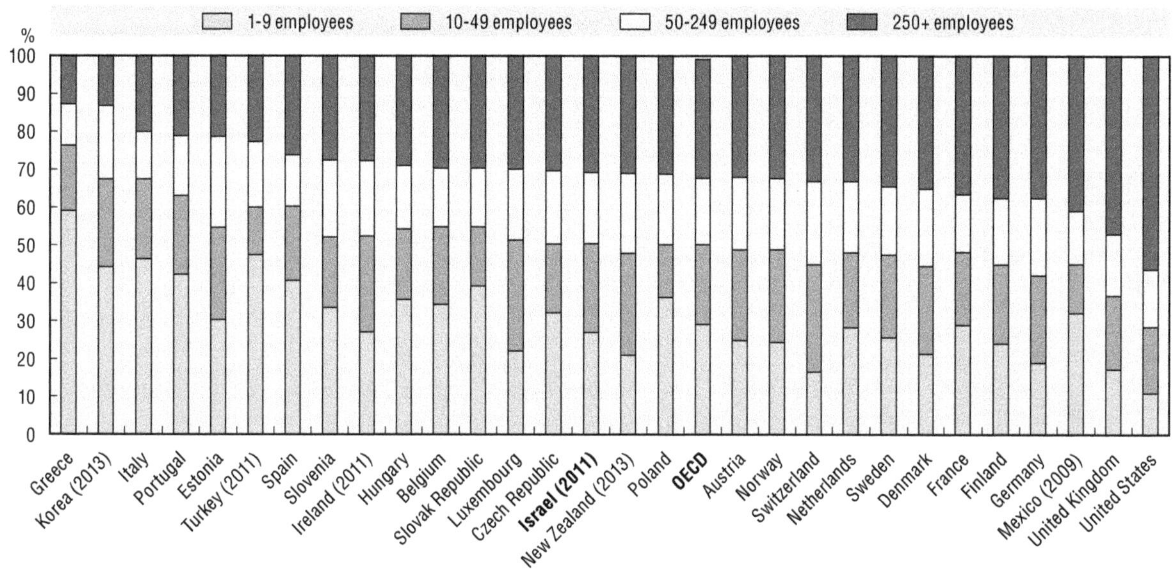

Note: Countries are presented in descending order, from the country where the SME sector as a whole (up to 249 employees) accounts for the largest share of national employment to the country where it explains the smallest share. All countries present information using the enterprise as the statistical unit except Korea and Mexico which use establishment. For Canada and the United States, data do not include non-employer enterprises. Data for Korea include financial services. Different size classes apply to Australia (1-19; 20-199; 200+), Korea (1-9; 10-49; 50-299; 300+), Mexico (1-10; 11-50; 51-250; 251+), Turkey (1-19; 20-49; 50-249; 250+). This Figure appears as Figure 1.1 in this report.
Source: OECD based on OECD (2015a), *Entrepreneurship at a Glance 2015*, OECD Publishing, Paris.

SMEs make up the vast majority of enterprises in Israel in both manufacturing and services, but their share of total business employment is greater in services (69%) than in manufacturing (60%). The SME employment shares within these two sectors are slightly below the OECD averages, respectively 71% and 62%. Whereas the employment shares of micro and small firms in manufacturing and micro firms in services are smaller than the OECD averages, the employment shares of medium-sized firms in manufacturing and medium and small firms in services are greater than the OECD averages (Figure 2.2). These results stem from relatively small sizes of Israeli small manufacturing and micro services enterprises and a relative dearth in both numbers and employment in Israeli micro manufacturing firms.

SMEs generate 62.3% of business economy value added in Israel, which is above the OECD average of 57.9%. Each of the main SME size bands in Israel contributes a greater share of national business value added than the OECD average (Figure 2.3).

High-impact SMEs

Israel performs quite well among OECD countries in generating high-impact SMEs in services, although its performance is not exceptional in manufacturing (Figure 2.4).

Figure 2.2. **Enterprise and employment distribution by enterprise size class and industry, 2013 or latest available year**

Percentage contribution to total number of firms and total employment

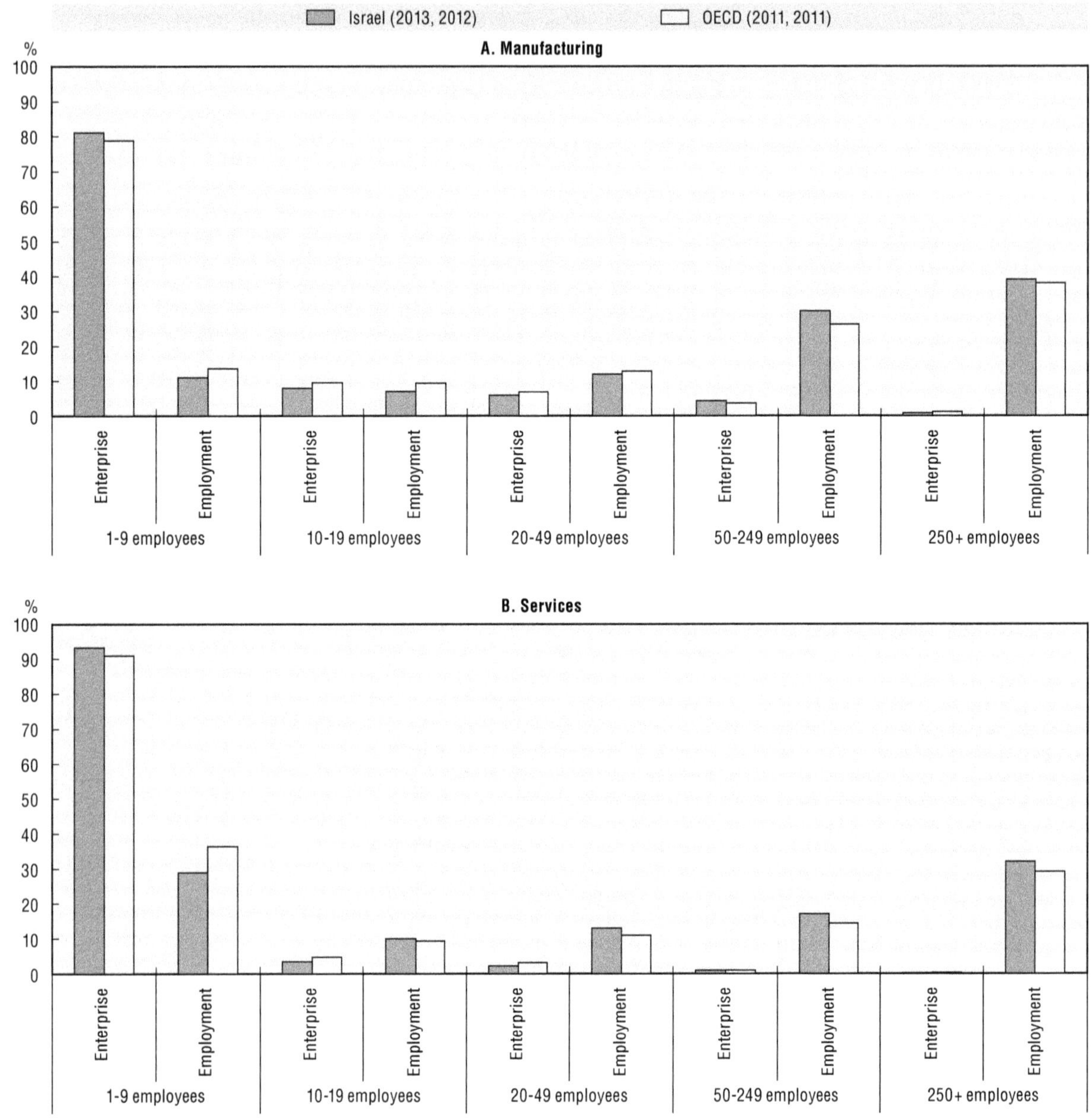

Source: OECD based on OECD (2015a), *Entrepreneurship at a Glance 2015*, OECD Publishing, and OECD (2014), *Entrepreneurship at a Glance 2014*, OECD Publishing, Paris.

StatLink http://dx.doi.org/10.1787/888933421387

High-growth firms, i.e. firms that are able to grow rapidly over a short period of time, made up 3.1% of the total in industry, 4.4% in services and 5.0% in construction in Israel in 2013. Such firms tend to account for a substantial proportion of new job creation in a country, for example, Henrekson and Johansson (2010) found that around 4-6% of the fastest growing firms produced half-to-three quarters of new jobs across a range of OECD countries. In addition, high-impact SMEs tend to generate positive knowledge spillovers and often become role models for budding entrepreneurs.

Figure 2.3. **Value added by enterprise size class, 2012 or latest available year**

Percentage contribution to total national value added

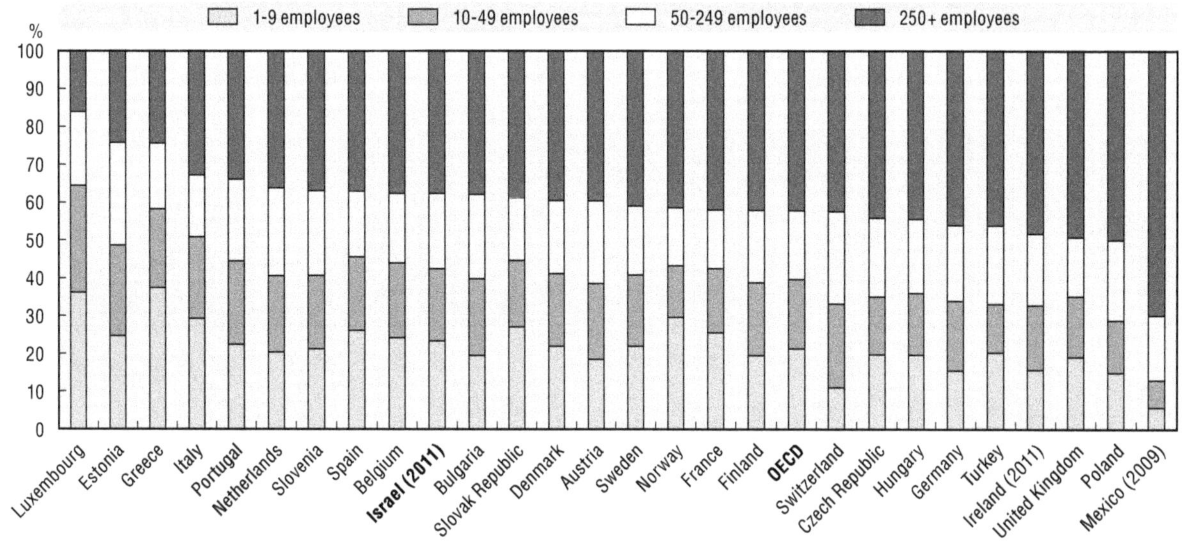

Note: Countries are presented in descending order, from the country where the SME sector as a whole (up to 249 employees) accounts for the largest share of national employment to the country where it explains the smallest share. The same country-specific considerations of Figure 2.1 apply to Figure 2.4.

Source: OECD based on OECD (OECD, 2015a), *OECD Entrepreneurship at a Glance 2015*, OECD Publishing, Paris.

StatLink http://dx.doi.org/10.1787/888933421398

Gazelles are a sub-set of high-growth firms, in that they are high-growth firms that are start-ups or that have been recently established. Gazelles represent 0.3% of all firms in industry, 2.1% in services and 0.9% in construction, which, with the exception of industry, are values significantly higher than those in the other benchmarked countries. It is this type of performance that has given rise to the image of Israel as a "start-up nation" where growth-oriented entrepreneurship can thrive.[2]

Relative to 2008, the proportion of high-growth firms in the economy has decreased in manufacturing and services. This is partly related to lower economic growth rates in the period immediately following the global economic crisis but is also the statistical outcome of a continued surge in the total number of firms in the national economy, most of which do not achieve high-growth status.

Self-employment

On average, 51% of active businesses in Israel are run by solo entrepreneurs, which is slightly below the average in international terms (Figure 2.5), although the range of values is large and affected by the legal and statistical definitions of what constitutes a business enterprise across countries. Labour Force Survey information confirms the finding that the self-employment rate is comparatively low in Israel (Figure 2.6). Moreover it declined somewhat from 14.2% in 2000 to 12.6% in 2013.

Informal economy

The scale of informal economic activities (i.e. the production of legal products and services in partial or total noncompliance with tax and labour regulations) has recently been estimated at 22% of Israeli GDP, five percentage points above the OECD average (Figure 2.7). In most countries informality is concentrated in micro firms, where it is often

Figure 2.4. **Share of high-growth firms and gazelles in OECD countries, 2012 and 2008 (or latest available years)**

Percentage of employer firms with at least 10 employees, employment definition

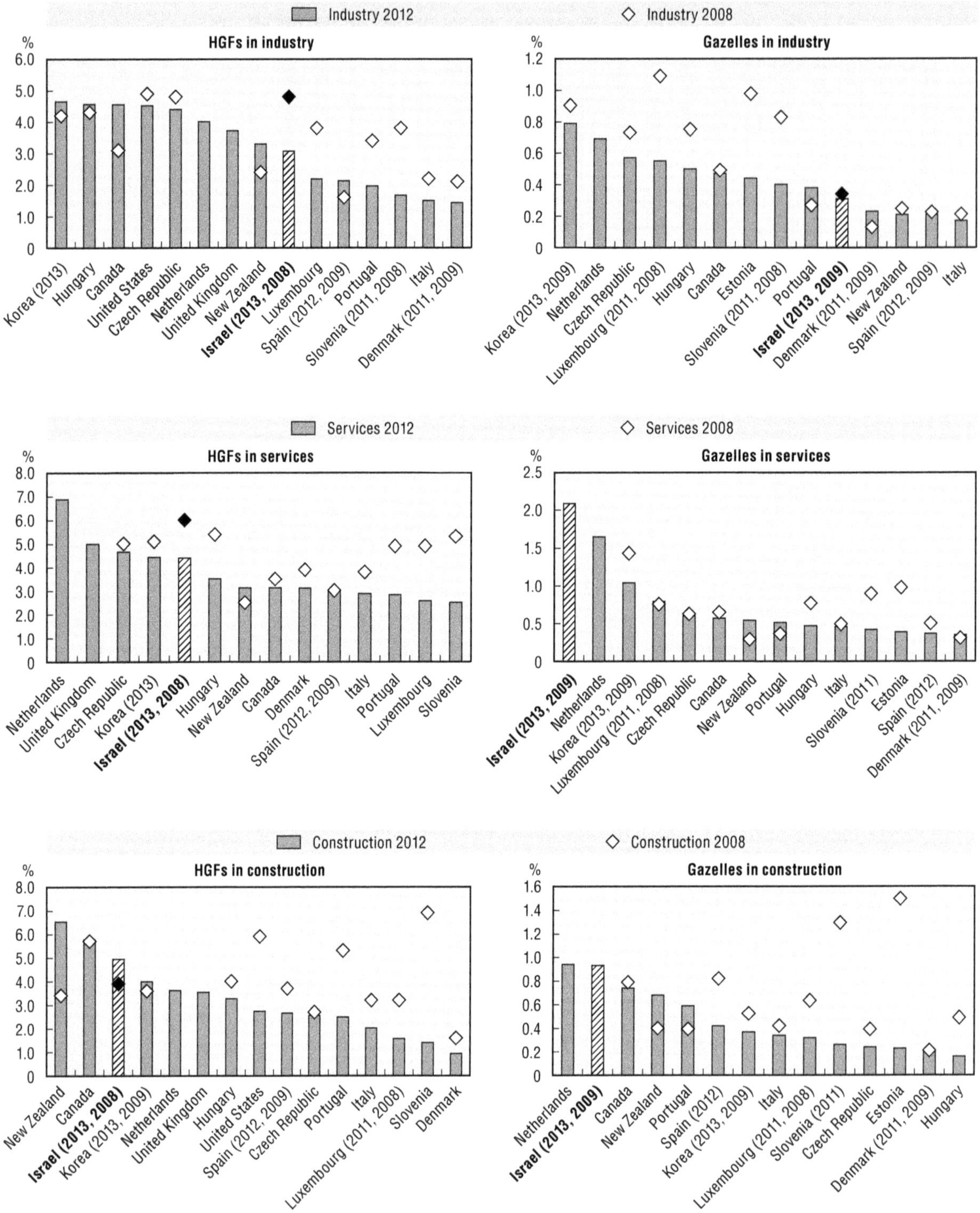

Note: The OECD defines high-growth firms, from an employment point of view, as firms with average annualised growth in employees greater than 20% a year, over a three-year period, and with ten or more employees at the beginning of the observation period, while gazelles are high-growth firms which have been employers for a period up to five years.

Source: OECD based on OECD (2015a), *Entrepreneurship at a Glance 2015*, OECD Publishing.

StatLink http://dx.doi.org/10.1787/888933421401

Figure 2.5. **Share of non-employer enterprises in OECD countries, 2012 or latest available year**

Percentage of total business population

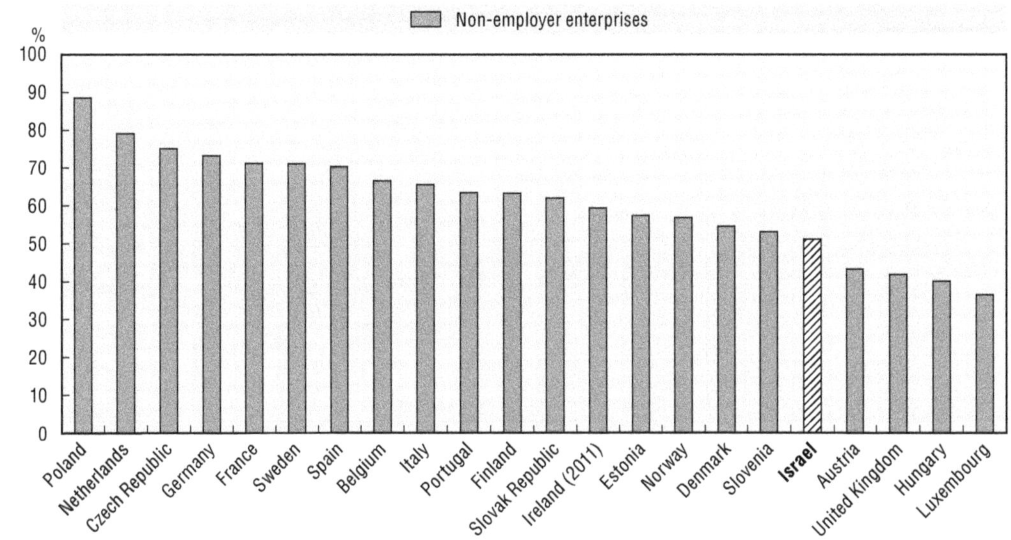

Source: OECD based on OECD (2015a), *Entrepreneurship at a Glance 2015*, OECD Publishing, Paris.

StatLink http://dx.doi.org/10.1787/888933421414

Figure 2.6. **Self-employment rate in selected OECD countries, 2010**

Percentage of total employment

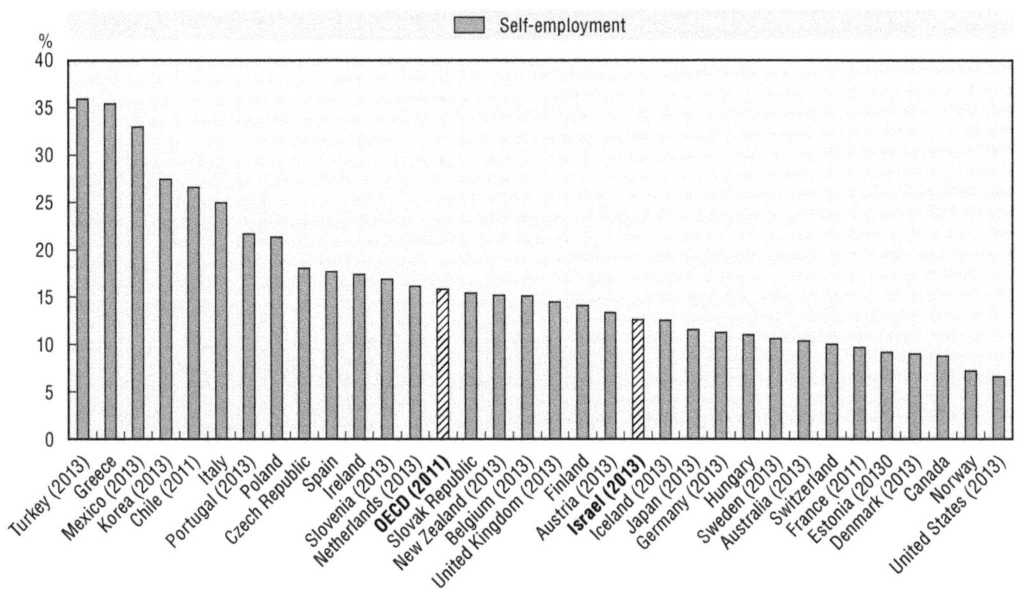

Note: The self-employment rate is given by the number of employers, workers who work for themselves, members of producers' cooperatives, and unpaid family workers out of the total employed population.
Source: OECD based on OECD Labour Force Statistics Database.

StatLink http://dx.doi.org/10.1787/888933421421

easier for business owners to hide part of their activities from government authorities. A large informal sector is a problem for the economy, not just because of the adverse impact on government tax revenues and spending capability, but also because informal enterprises tend to have lower average labour productivity, worker wages and growth rates than formal

Figure 2.7. **Estimates of the size of the informal economy in OECD countries, 2011**
Percentage of national GDP

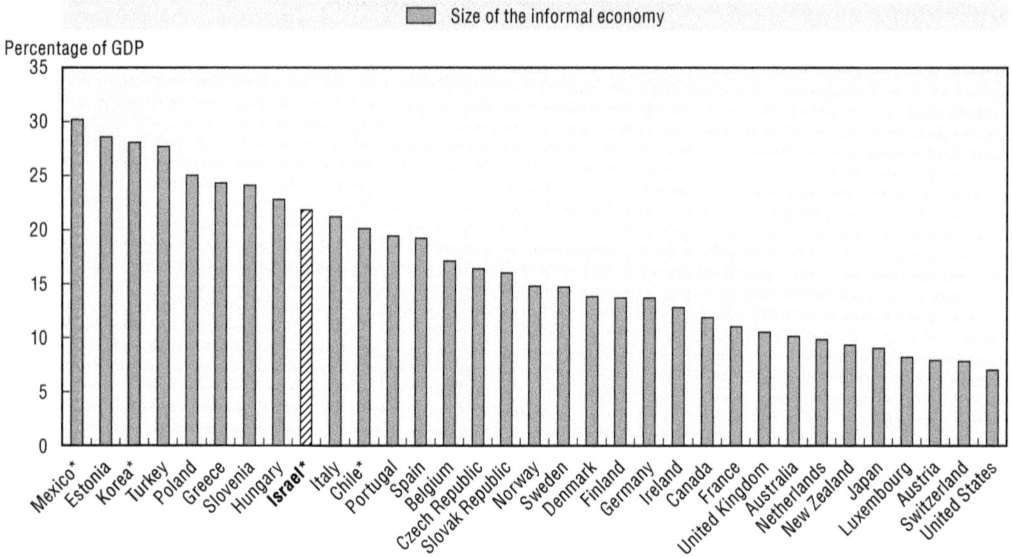

Note: Estimates for most countries are based on the first article reported in the sources. For countries with (*), estimates are from the second article and refer to average values for the period 1999-2007.
Source: OECD based on Schneider F. (undated), "Size and Development of the Shadow Economy of 31 European and 5 other OECD Countries from 2003 to 2012: Some New Facts", *www.econ.jku.at/schneider* and Schneider, F., A. Buehn and C. Montenegro (2010), "New Estimates for the Shadow Economies all Over the World", *International Economic Journal*, 24, 443-461.

StatLink http://dx.doi.org/10.1787/888933421438

enterprises. This may be linked to more limited market opportunities for businesses that work informally and possible self-imposed restrictions on growth in order to limit exposure to control by public authorities.

Business demography

Business births and change in stock

Employer and non-employer enterprises

The number of businesses in the Israeli economy has grown steadily in recent years (Figure 1.3 reproduced below), which reflects sustained economic growth rates. Including both employer and non-employer businesses, there were nearly 500 000 private sector companies across all sectors of the economy in 2011. This represents an increase of one-quarter compared with 2003, and an annual growth rate of 3% in the number of businesses in this period, despite the global economic and financial crisis.

This sustained net business creation has underpinned private sector employment growth and contributed to the decline of the official unemployment rate in the wider economy, which touched the low of 5.6% in 2011 from nearly twice that rate in 2003 (10.7%). The number of private sector jobs increased by nearly 30% from 2003 to 2011, from less than 2.5 million to nearly 3.2 million, an annual compounded growth rate of 3.4% (Figure 2.8).

At sector level, net business creation has been positive across all sectors of the economy except manufacturing (Figure 2.9). The most dramatic increase in firm numbers was in real estate activities (+51.7%), while the greatest increase in job numbers has been in "accommodation services and restaurants" (+69.5%) and "community and personal services"

Number of enterprises in Israel, 2004-11

Absolute numbers and annual percentage growth rate

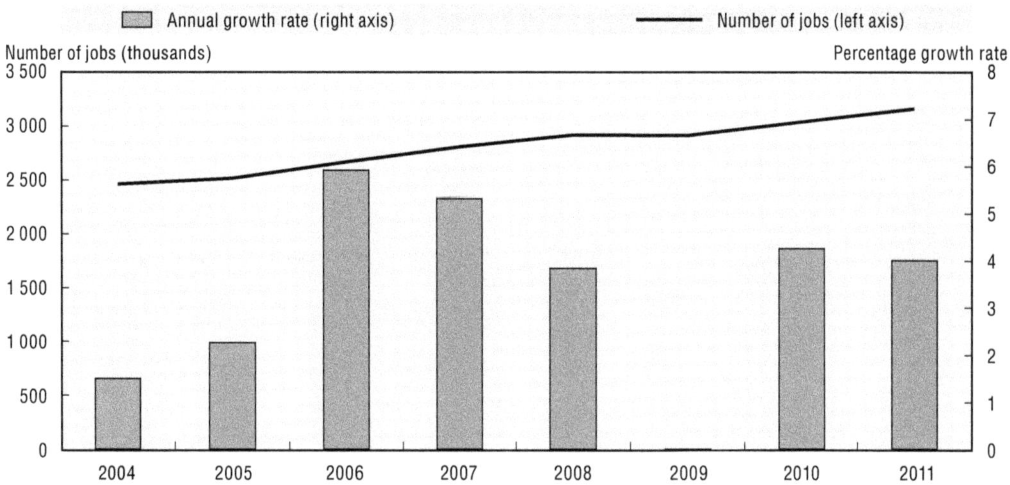

Note: Data also include non-employer firms. This Figure appears as Figure 1.3 in this report.

Source: OECD based on CBS (2013), Business Demography: A Collection of Statistical Data from the Business Register: 2003-2011, Publication No. 1541, Jerusalem.

Figure 2.8. **Number of business sector jobs in Israel, 2003-11**

Absolute numbers (thousands) and annual percentage growth rate

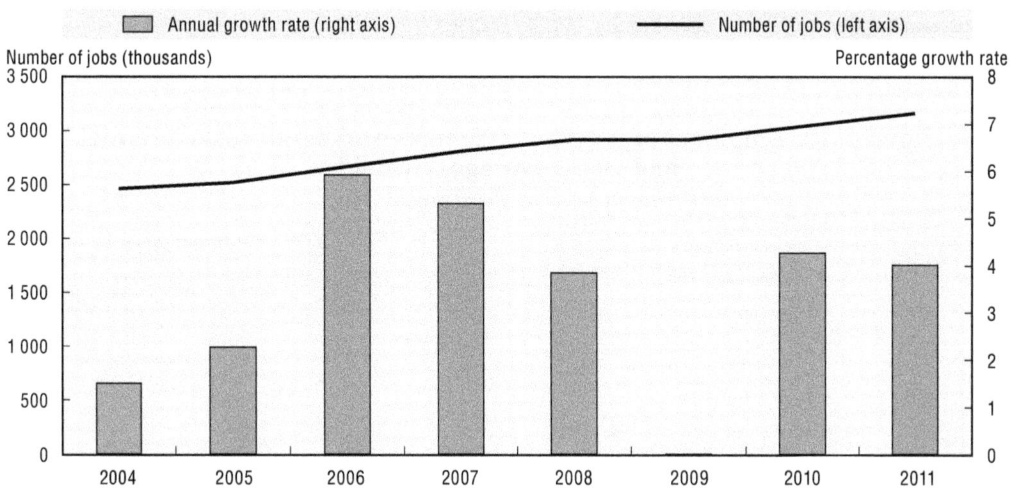

Source: OECD based on CBS (2013), Business Demography: A Collection of Statistical Data from the Business Register: 2003-2011, Publication No. 1541, Jerusalem.

StatLink http://dx.doi.org/10.1787/888933421445

(+39.6%). Jobs in low value-added services have, therefore, increased more proportionally than jobs in manufacturing, which has contributed to a structural change in the economy whereby labour productivity growth has not kept up with employment growth.

Employer enterprises

Data are also available on business birth rates and change in business stock for employer enterprises as a separate category. This is interesting because employer firms tend to make greater proportional contributions to output and employment and have higher productivity levels than sole self-employed enterprises. As shown in Figure 2.10, Israel's employer

Figure 2.9. **Growth in number of firms and number of jobs by sector in Israel, 2003-11**

Percentage growth

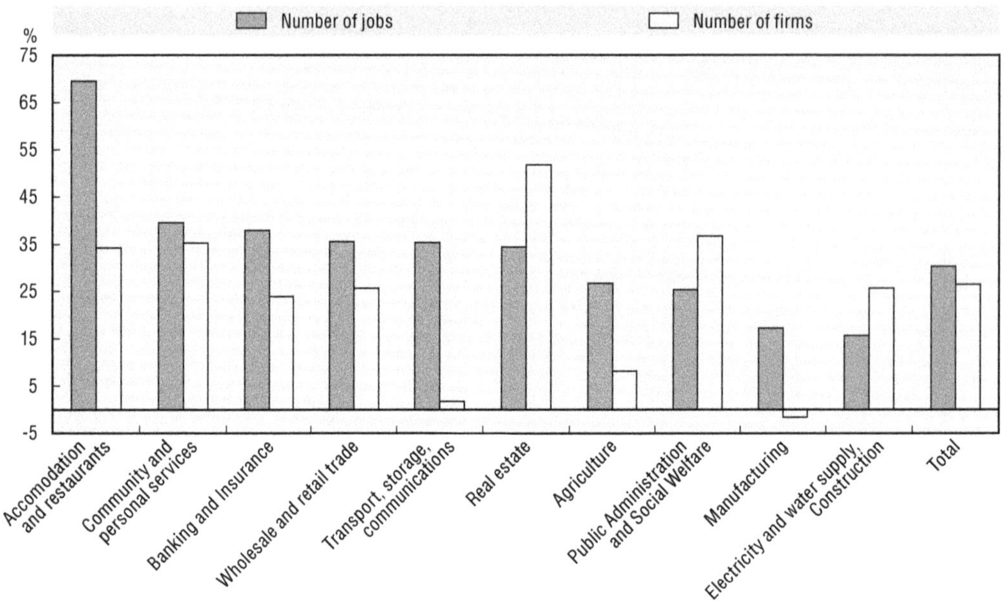

Note: Data also include non-employer firms.

Source: OECD based on Central Bureau of Statistics (2013), Business Demography: A Collection of Statistical Data from the Business Register: 2003-2011, Publication No. 1541, Jerusalem.

StatLink http://dx.doi.org/10.1787/888933421459

Figure 2.10. **Employer enterprise birth rates and death rates in Israel and OECD average, 2006-13**

Percentage of employer enterprises

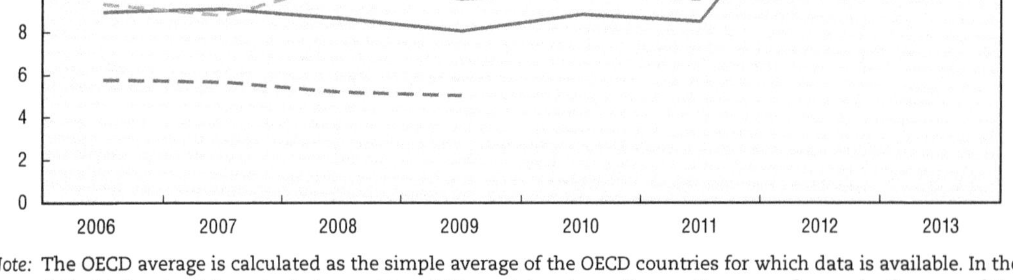

Note: The OECD average is calculated as the simple average of the OECD countries for which data is available. In the case of the birth rate, this varies between 14 and 24 countries, depending on the year, whereas in the case of the death rate it ranges between 14 and 18 countries.

Source: OECD based on OECD (2015a), *Entrepreneurship at a Glance 2015*, OECD Publishing, Paris.

StatLink http://dx.doi.org/10.1787/888933421464

business birth rates exceeded its employer business death rates in the period 2006-11, leading to growth in the stock of employer enterprises. This indicates that the positive net business creation rate in the range of 3% per year applies to employer as well as non-employer firms. The Figure also shows that there was a substantial increase in the business birth rate in Israel in 2012 and 2013, although data on the death rate in those years are not yet available.

A more disaggregated analysis (Figure 2.11) shows that business birth rates are higher in construction and services than manufacturing, a trend which is common to most other countries and which parallels higher business death rates in these sectors as well. The Figure also shows that business birth rates are higher in smaller enterprise size bands, with differences between smaller and larger size bands especially relevant in industry and services.

Figure 2.11. **Annual employer enterprise birth rates by sector and size classes in Israel, 2013**

Enterprise births as a percentage of employer enterprises in each sector and size class

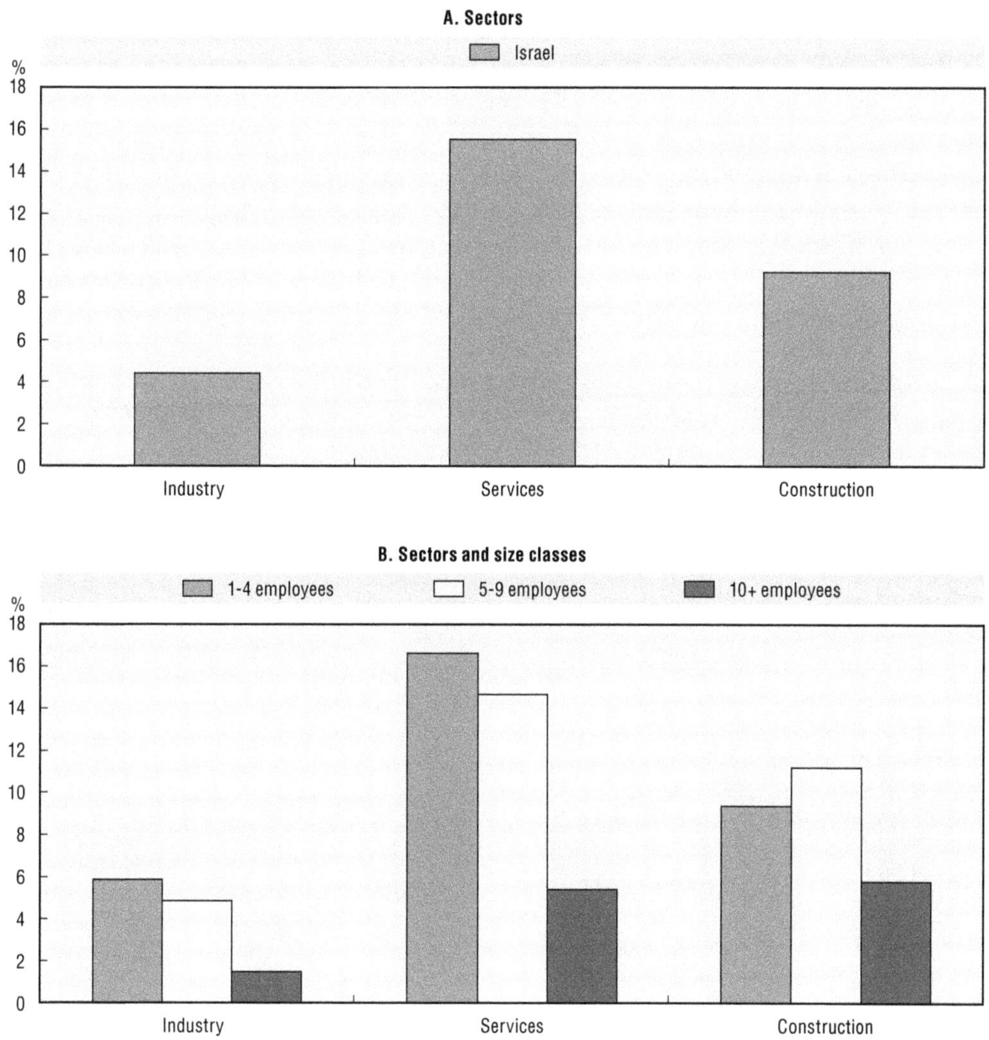

Source: OECD based on OECD (2015a), *Entrepreneurship at a Glance 2015*, OECD Publishing, Paris.

StatLink http://dx.doi.org/10.1787/888933421470

Table 2.1 shows that during the time period 2005-09, job generation out of net creation of employer businesses was equally shared across the four business size classes for which national data were available, although the highest numbers are found in the smallest (1-4 employees) and largest (+20 employees) size bands.

Table 2.1. **Annual job creation by business births and job destruction by business deaths in Israel, 2005-09**

Thousands of jobs

Size classes	Job creation by business births					Job destruction by business deaths					Net job creation				
	2005	2006	2007	2008	2009	2005	2006	2007	2008	2009	2005	2006	2007	2008	2009
1-4 employees	23.5	24.2	26	25.2	24	15.8	15.9	16.4	15.7	15.4	7.7	8.3	9.6	9.5	8.6
5-9 employees	16	16.1	17.5	17.2	15.7	10	9.5	9.8	8.9	8.7	6	6.6	7.7	8.3	7
10-19 employees	15.4	16.4	17	17.1	15.1	9.1	8.7	9.9	8.8	8.3	6.3	7.7	7.1	8.3	6.8
20+ employees	27.5	28.6	23	24.5	22.1	17.9	29.3	12.6	15.8	12.8	9.6	-0.7	10.4	8.7	9.3
Total	82.4	85.3	83.5	84	76.9	52.8	63.3	48.7	49.2	45.1	29.6	22	34.8	34.8	31.8

Source: Israel's Central Bureau of Statistics.

StatLink http://dx.doi.org/10.1787/888933421610

The rate of churn of employer enterprises

Although the stock of enterprises has been growing because of an excess of business births over business deaths, Israel's rate of churn of employer enterprises (business births plus business deaths) is only average (Figure 1.4 reproduced below). The churn rate is important because it represents a proxy for the process of entrepreneurial creative destruction, which is in turn linked to productivity growth in the economy. The main cause of Israel's low churn rate is its low business death rate, i.e. the low rate of firms which exit the market. This is generally the result of high protection of incumbents and is likely to lead to a

Annual employer enterprise birth rates, death rates and churn rates across selected countries and Israel, 2012 or latest available year

Percentage of employer enterprises

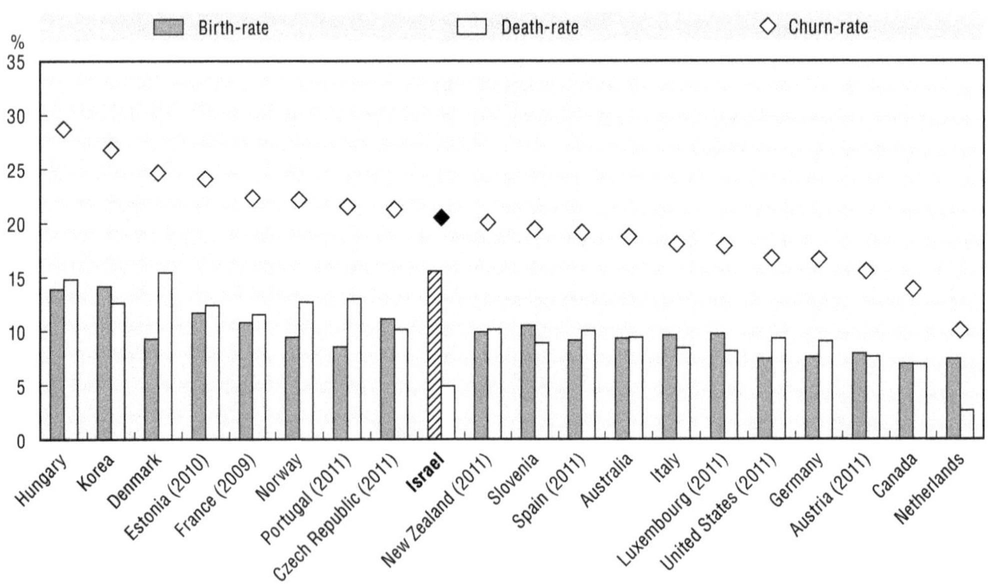

Note: The business churn rate is the sum of the business birth rate and the business death rate. This Figure appears as Figure 1.4 in this report.

Source: OECD based on OECD (2015a), *Entrepreneurship at a Glance 2015*, OECD Publishing, Paris.

Figure 2.12. **Share of young firms (aged 3 years or less) in industry and services, 2012 or latest available year**

Percentage of total employer enterprises

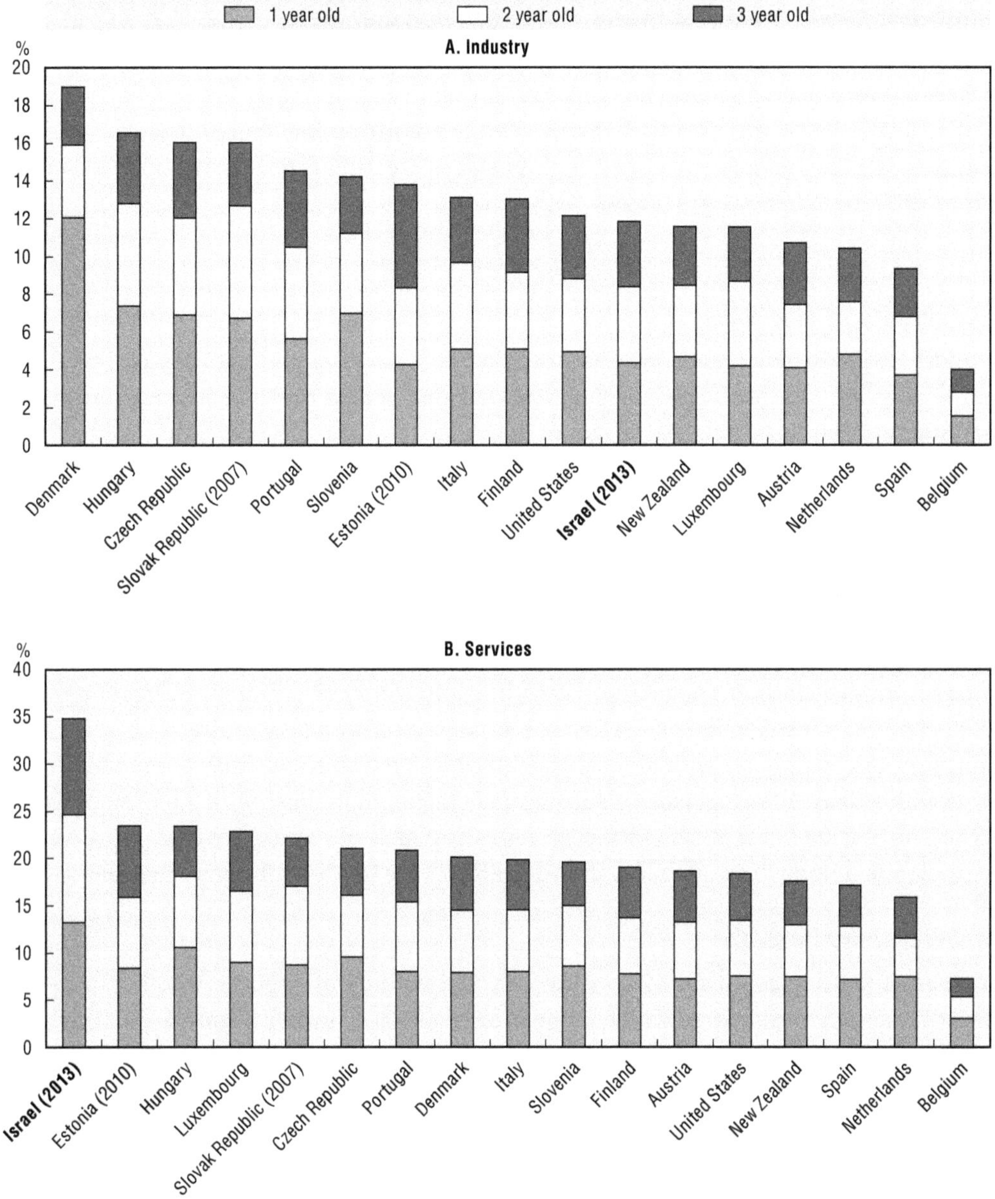

Source: OECD based on OECD (2015a), *Entrepreneurship at a Glance 2015*, OECD Publishing, Paris.

StatLink http://dx.doi.org/10.1787/888933421480

high proportion of old SMEs which neither grow nor contract and whose contribution to growth is typically marginal. These findings suggest that there may be a weakness in Israel's entrepreneurial economy related to low replacement of incumbents by young and dynamic firms. Reducing protection of long-established, low-productivity incumbents could stimulate the introduction of young and dynamic firms even further than is the case at present, and is likely to become an increasing concern in future years when the scope for business births to exceed deaths starts to dwindle.

Share of young firms

Young firms are generally a major source of productivity growth and job creation in the economy. It has been shown, for example, that firms less than five years old made up about 20% of non-financial business sector employment over the past decade, and spawned nearly half of all new jobs (OECD, 2013a). In Israel, the share of young firms of up to three years old is 12% in industry and 35% in services, which are respectively below and significantly above the averages for the OECD countries for which data are available (Figure 2.12). This reflects sustained high business creation rates, particularly in services rather than manufacturing.

SME productivity, innovation and exporting

Productivity by size class

Labour productivity tends to be higher in larger companies thanks to greater investment and economies of scale. Figure 2.13 shows that this is also the case in Israel, at least in manufacturing sectors. Indeed, the labour productivity gap between SMEs and large firms is wider in Israel than for most other OECD countries. On the other hand, SME labour productivity levels in the Israeli services sector are fairly similar to large firm levels. This evidence points to particular scope for improving Israel's SME productivity performance in the manufacturing sector, especially among firms in the 10-19 and 20-49 employee size classes in this sector, where the gap to large firm productivity is especially marked.

Table 2.2 contrasts labour productivity in capital-intensive and labour-intensive sectors in Israel by size class. It shows that firms in capital-intensive sectors in Israel are more productive than firms in labour-intensive sectors only within larger enterprise size classes (starting from companies with at least 20 employees). It also shows that the productivity of firms with at least 100 employees is substantially higher than those with 20-99 employees in capital-intensive sectors. This may be revealing lack of capital investment and poor technologies among firms with less than 100 employees in capital-intensive sectors.

Export activity in SMEs

Israeli SMEs account for 42% of the national volume of exports, which is a median performance when compared with a range of other OECD countries (Figure 2.14). Israel has a small domestic market, which means that firms tend to be relatively reliant on accessing international markets for expansion and this is likely to be a driver of this export performance, as well as the slightly greater weight of SMEs in value added in Israel than the OECD as a whole. At the same time, however, only 15% of Israeli SMEs are involved in exporting, according to SMBA data, and micro-enterprises produce less than 10% of total export volumes, which is low by OECD standards. One of the obstacles is that Israel is surrounded by neighbouring countries with which trade relationships are limited, if not absent, and that firms therefore need the capacity and financial means to export to relatively far-off markets such as the EU and the USA, the two major destinations for Israeli exports.

Innovation activity in SMEs

Israel has high levels of business innovation. Business Expenditure on R&D (BERD) amounts to 3.3% of national GDP, by far the highest value in the OECD area and more than twice the OECD average of 1.6% (Figure 2.15). Israel's high BERD is influenced by its many R&D centres, often linked to foreign multinational enterprises, which are the result of the

Figure 2.13. **Labour productivity by business size classes and sector, 2012 or latest available year**

Percentage of labour productivity in large firms (250+ = 100)

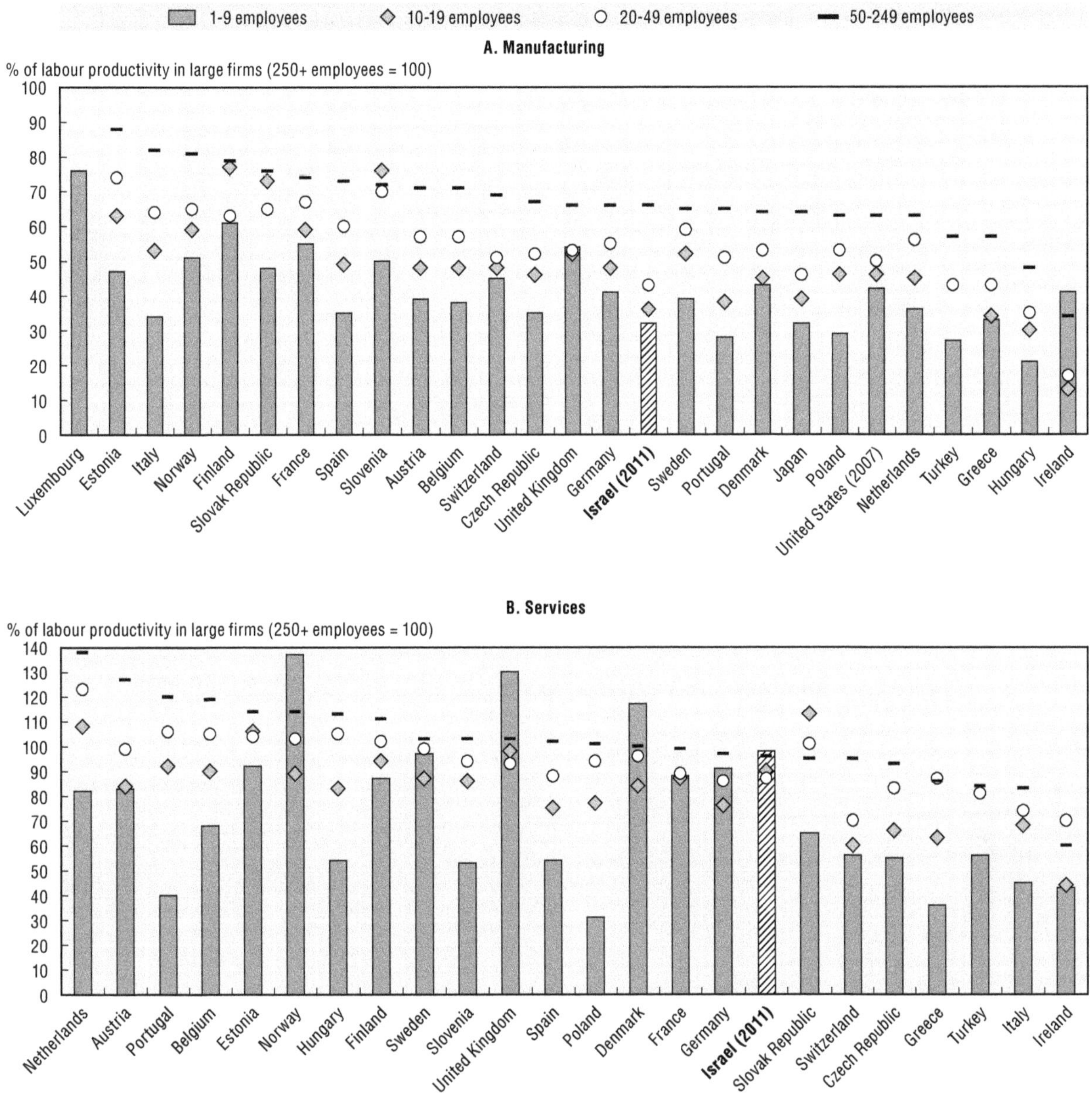

Note: Labour productivity is measured as the current price, gross value added per person employed. Data are presented for each country as percentage of labour productivity in large firms (i.e. index 250+ = 100). Financial services activities are not included in the services sector. Data are presented in descending order from the country where the gap between firms with 50-249 employees and large firms (250+) is the smallest.

Source: OECD, based on OECD (2015a), *Entrepreneurship at a Glance 2015*, OECD Publishing, Paris.

StatLink http://dx.doi.org/10.1787/888933421292

Table 2.2. **Labour productivity by enterprise size and type of industry, 2010**

Israeli New Sheqel (NIS) per worker

	1-4 employees	5-19 employees	20-99 employees	100-249 employees	250+ employees
Capital-intensive	139,522	129,526	198,762	346,751	399,479
Labour-intensive	162,545	159,734	155,891	177,189	178,596

Source: OECD based on data supplied by the Israeli Small and Medium Business Agency.

StatLink http://dx.doi.org/10.1787/888933421628

Figure 2.14. **Exports by enterprise size in selected OECD countries, 2011 or latest available year**

Percentage of total export volume

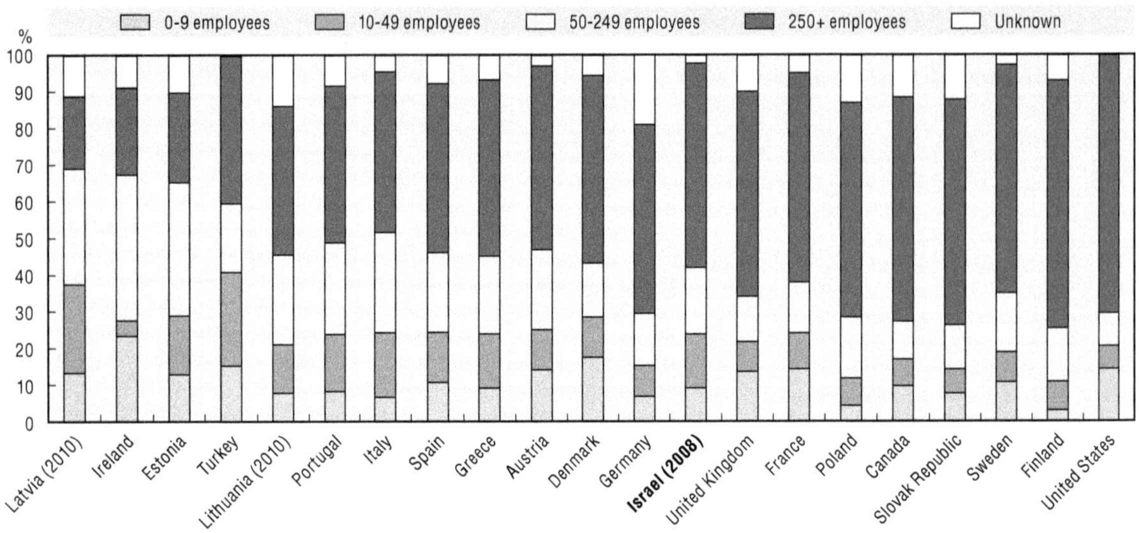

Note: Data are presented in descending order from the country where the largest share of export is accounted for by SMEs (0-249) to the country with the smallest equivalent share. For seven countries, more than 10% of export volume cannot be securely ascribed to a specific firm size class. Countries where more than 20% of export volume could not be attributed to a specific firm size class have not been included in the graph.

Source: OECD based on OECD (2014), *Entrepreneurship at a Glance 2014*, OECD Publishing, Paris.

StatLink http://dx.doi.org/10.1787/888933421497

Figure 2.15. **Business enterprise spending in R&D (BERD), 2012 and 2002**

Percentage of GDP

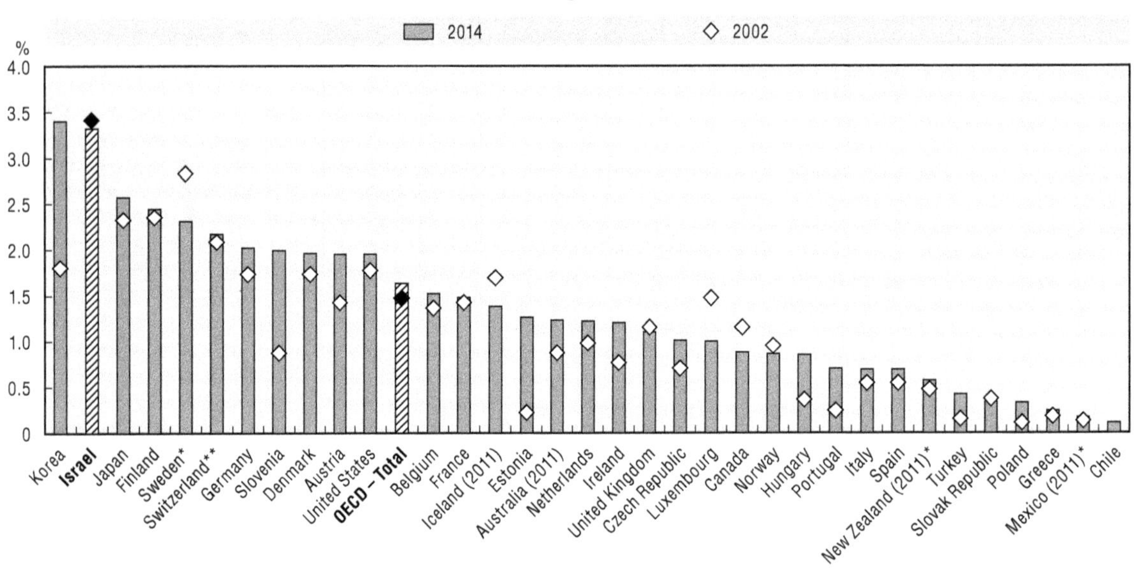

Note: For countries with (*), 2002 data refers to 2003. For countries with (**), 2002 data refers to 2004.

Source: OECD based on *OECD Science, Technology and Industry Outlook 2014 Database*.

StatLink http://dx.doi.org/10.1787/888933421507

country's success in generating a high-skilled labour force, but which are sometimes perceived to be disconnected from the rest of the economy. Nonetheless, even excluding foreign-affiliated R&D centres, Israel's BERD is still 2% of the national GDP, higher than most other OECD countries.[3]

Against this backdrop, 27% of national BERD is performed by SMEs employing less than 250 employees (Figure 2.16). This is below the OECD average (34.5%). However, this figure is also affected by the R&D intensity of the national large corporate sector, as shown by the fact that advanced economies such as the United States, Japan and Germany also feature very low proportions of BERD undertaken by SMEs.

Figure 2.16. **Share of BERD undertaken by small firms, 2013 or latest available year**

Percentage of total national BERD

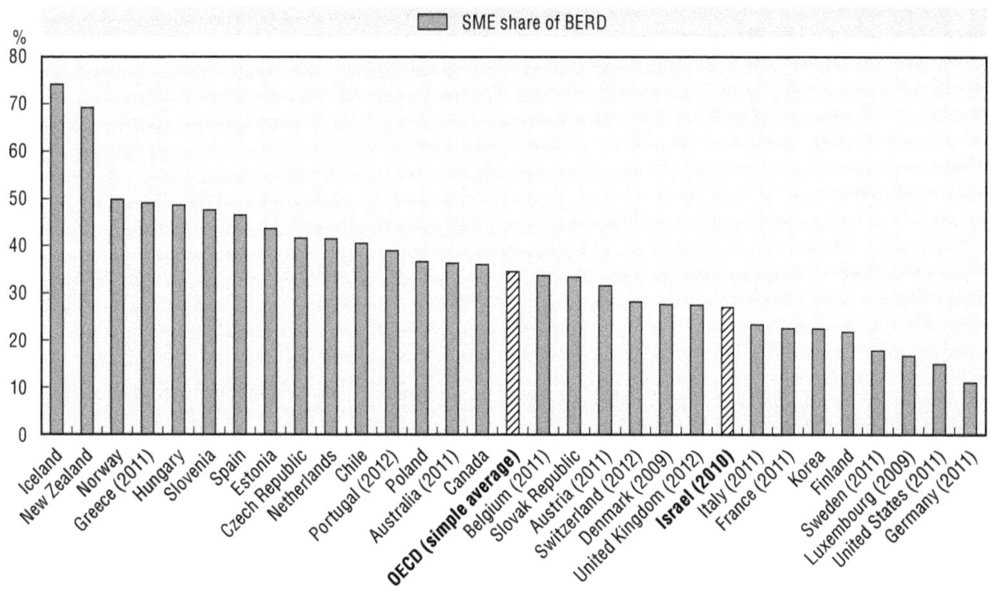

Note: The figure for Israel (27%) has been supplied by the Israeli Central Bureau of Statistics (CBS) and, as such, might not be fully comparable with the other OECD countries for which data have been harmonised. The OECD average is the simple mean of the 30 OECD countries, excluded Israel, for which data is available.

Source: OECD based on OECD (2015b), *OECD Science, Technology and Industry Scoreboard 2015*, OECD Publishing, Paris and data supplied by the Israeli Central Bureau of Statistics.

StatLink http://dx.doi.org/10.1787/888933421513

Relatively weak SME innovation performance is also illustrated by evidence that less than one-half of Israeli SMEs engage in some form of innovation, whether this is of technological or non-technological nature. This is only the nineteenth highest value among OECD countries, nearly 30 percentage points less than the equivalent proportion of innovative large firms (Figure 1.5 reproduced below). In addition, only 20% have undertaken technological (i.e. product or process) and non-technological (i.e. marketing and organisational) innovation together, which may hinder the exploitation of complementarity between the two modes of innovation (e.g. new organisational methods could support the implementation of a new production process or new processes could call for new ways of organising work). Finally, Israel has both the highest share of SMEs that exclusively perform non-technological innovation and the lowest share of SMEs that only carry out technological innovation, which may point to ongoing diversification of innovation strategies among existing SMEs and a growing role of the services industry in innovation.

The Israeli SMEs which innovate are, on average, quite collaboration-oriented in the way they undertake innovation. This can facilitate their involvement in open innovation processes and help compensate for lack of internal innovation resources. About 17% of

Innovation in SMEs by type of innovation and compared to large firms (total innovation), 2010-12

Percentage of all SMEs and large firms covered by national innovation surveys

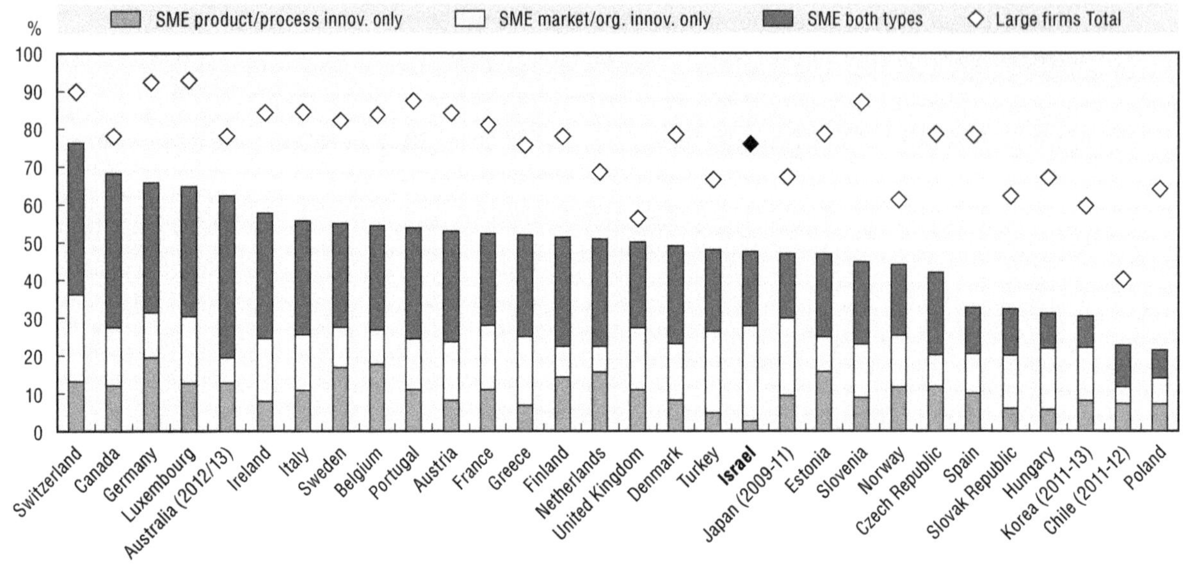

Note: International comparability may be limited due to differences in innovation survey methodologies and country-specific response patterns. This Figure appears as Figure 1.5 in the report.

Source: OECD based on OECD (2015b), *OECD Science, Technology and Industry Scoreboard 2015*, OECD Publishing, Paris.

SMEs that undertake product or process innovation partake in innovative projects with suppliers, while 15% collaborate on innovation with clients. Moreover, approximately 10% of innovative SMEs collaborate with public research institutions, while 16% collaborate with international partners (Figure 2.17). These results suggest that there may be scope for even greater collaboration between SMEs and public research institutions, given the high levels of government investment in R&D, and to increase innovation collaboration with suppliers and clients, given the importance of integration in global and national supply chains for further SME development.

Larger SMEs are generally more likely than smaller ones to engage in innovation in general (Table 2.3) and technological innovation in particular (Table 2.4). High-technology SMEs are also more frequently involved in innovation than lower technology SMEs. However, only between 9% and 17% of Israeli SMEs, depending on the size class, have introduced "new-to-market" innovations, i.e. the most radical innovations with greatest impacts on productivity growth. There is scope for government measures to encourage more radical innovation to bridge labour productivity gaps, especially in manufacturing where the productivity gap is relatively large.

Entrepreneurship: attitudes and performance

Attitudes towards entrepreneurship

Data from the Global Entrepreneurship Monitor (GEM) suggest that attitudes to entrepreneurship are generally positive in Israel. As shown in Figure 2.18, 80% of the Israeli population believes that successful entrepreneurs receive high status in society and 60% consider that entrepreneurship is a desirable career choice, both of which compare favourably within the OECD area. Furthermore, nearly one-quarter of Israelis express an intention to set up a business within the next three years, ten percentage points above the

Figure 2.17. **Firms collaborating on innovation by firm size and by type of collaboration, 2010-12**

Percentage of product and/or process-innovating firms in each size category

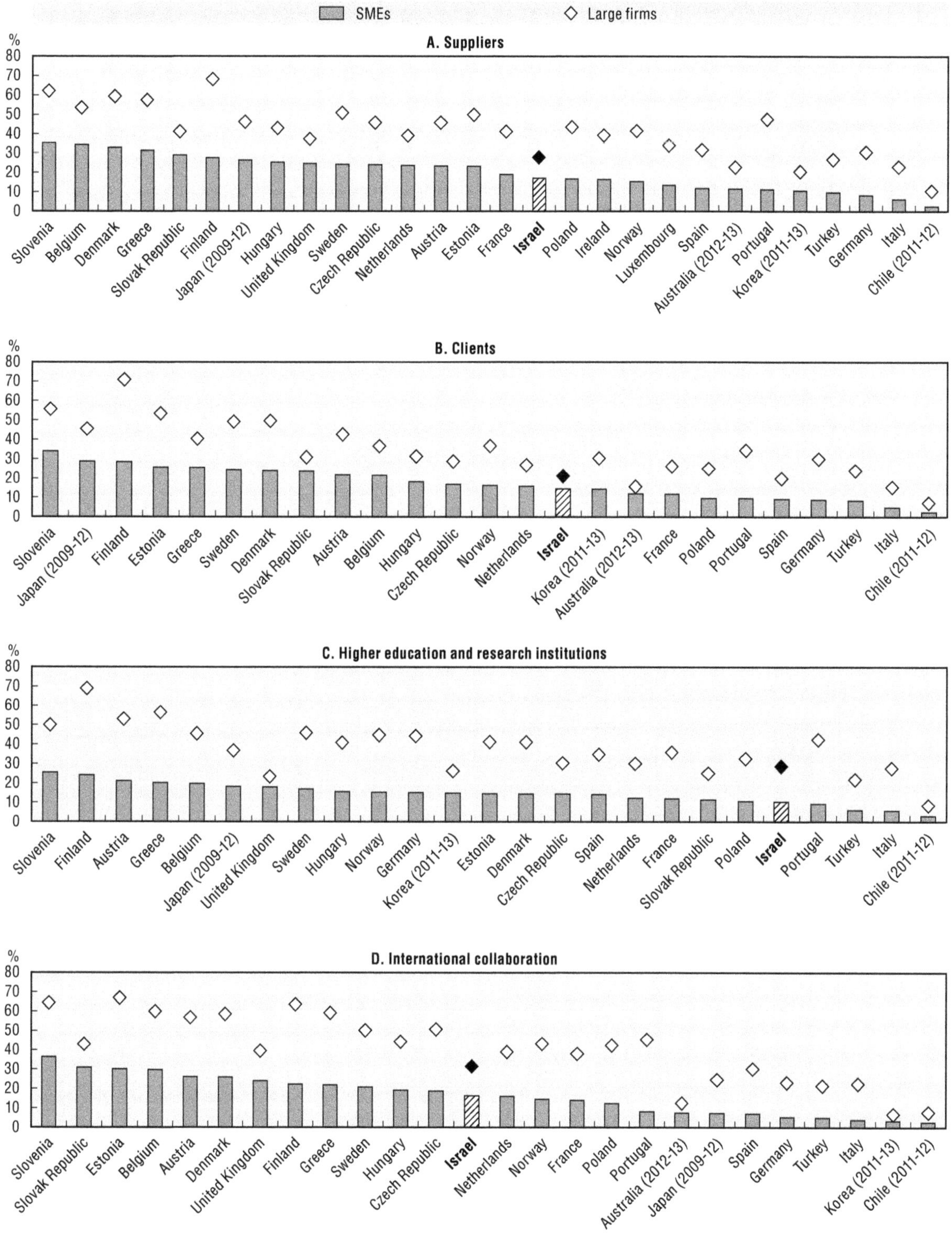

Note: International comparability may be limited due to differences in innovation survey methodologies and country-specific response patterns.

Source: OECD based on OECD (2015b), *OECD Science, Technology and Industry Scoreboard 2015*, OECD Publishing, Paris.

StatLink http://dx.doi.org/10.1787/888933421521

Table 2.3. **SMEs active in innovation, Israel, 2006-08**

Percentage of companies in size group

	10-50 employees	51-100 employees	101-250 employees
Total firms	30	33	51
Manufacturing (total)	32	63	59
High-tech	46	80	68
Medium-high	32	36	55
Medium-low	33	74	61
Low	30	59	54

Source: Data supplied by the Israeli Central Bureau of Statistics.

StatLink http://dx.doi.org/10.1787/888933421638

Table 2.4. **SMEs active in technological innovation by size class and type of innovation, 2006-08**

Percentage values of companies in size group

	10-19 employees	20-49 employees	50-249 employees
Technological innovation – total	23	35	44
Of which, new to market	*9*	*16*	*17*
Production innovation	16	29	38
Process innovation	16	23	29
Product and process innovation	9	17	24

Source: Data supplied by the Israeli Central Bureau of Statistics.

StatLink http://dx.doi.org/10.1787/888933421640

Figure 2.18. **Entrepreneurial attitudes in Israel compared to the OECD average, 2013**

Percentage values

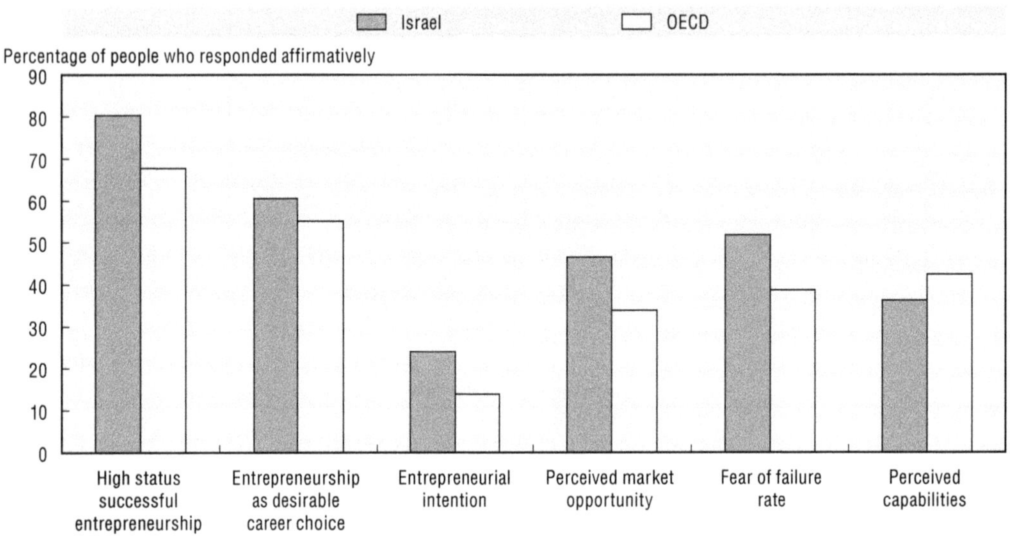

Note: The OECD average is the simple mean of the values of the OECD countries for which information is available (between 28 and 30 countries, depending on the indicator). Percentage values are out of the total adult population (18-64), except for "fear of failure" which is out of those who "perceive a market opportunity". The exact definition for each indicator presented is: i) High status of successful entrepreneurship: Percentage of 18-64 population who agree with the statement that in their country, successful entrepreneurs receive high status; ii) Entrepreneurship as a desirable career choice: Percentage of 18-64 population who agree with the statement that in their country, most people consider starting a business as a desirable career choice; iii) Intention to start a business: Percentage of 18-64 population (individuals involved in any stage of entrepreneurial activity excluded) who intend to start a business within three years; iv) Perceived market opportunity: Percentage of 18-64 who see good opportunities to start a firm in the area where they live; v) Fear of failure: Percentage of 18-64 population with positive perceived opportunities who indicate that fear of failure would prevent them from setting up a business; vi) Perceived capabilities: Percentage of 18-64 population who believe to have the required skills and knowledge to start a business.

Source: OECD based on the Global Entrepreneurship Monitor (GEM) database, *www.gemconsortium.org/key-indicators*.

StatLink http://dx.doi.org/10.1787/888933421532

OECD average. In addition, nearly one-half of Israelis (47%) see good opportunities to start up a business in the area where they live.

There are, however, two weak points in the picture. Firstly, more than one-half (52%) of those who perceive existing opportunities for entrepreneurship maintain that "fear of failure" could prevent them from taking concrete steps towards establishing an enterprise. This is high by international standards and may signal both a lack of risk-taking at the individual level and stigma of business failure at the societal level. The finding is confirmed by a Eurobarometer survey, which reveals that in comparative terms Israelis are more likely to be afraid of personal failures than in other countries when they ponder starting an enterprise (European Commission, 2013). Secondly, only 36% of Israelis report having the right skills set to succeed in business, which compares unfavourably with a large majority of OECD economies and points to a problem of lack of confidence or lack of adequate entrepreneurship and business management skills in the population.

As shown in Figure 2.19, attitudes to entrepreneurship have generally improved in Israel in recent years, and the proportion with entrepreneurial intentions has nearly doubled since 2007. However, as more Israelis have become interested in exploring a business opportunity, a greater number have also become afraid of failure (+8 percentage points) while there was a further small decline in the already low proportion of people who feel they have "adequate skills" to succeed in business. This evidence suggests the value of interventions to strengthen entrepreneurship and business management skills in the population.

Figure 2.19. **Evolution of entrepreneurial attitudes in Israel, 2007-13**

Percentage values

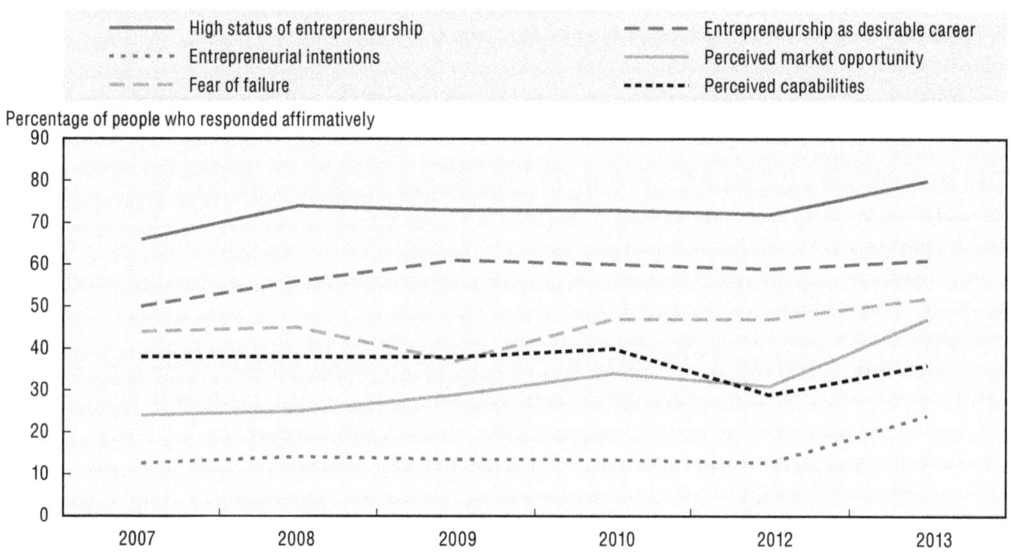

Note: Percentage values are out of the total population, except for "fear of failure" which is out of those who "perceive a market opportunity". Data for 2011 is not available for Israel.

Source: OECD based on the Global Entrepreneurship Monitor (GEM) database, *www.gemconsortium.org/key-indicators*.

StatLink http://dx.doi.org/10.1787/888933421541

From intentions to action: early-stage entrepreneurial activity

According to the GEM survey, one-in-ten working age adults are actively engaged in early-stage entrepreneurial activity in Israel (i.e. are involved in a start-up process or own a newly-established business). This compares favourably with many other OECD countries

(Figure 1.2 reproduced below). Furthermore, Israel's early-stage entrepreneurship rate has grown by more than three percentage points since 2004.

Total Entrepreneurial Activity (TEA) rate across OECD countries, 2013

Percentage of adult population (18-64 years old)

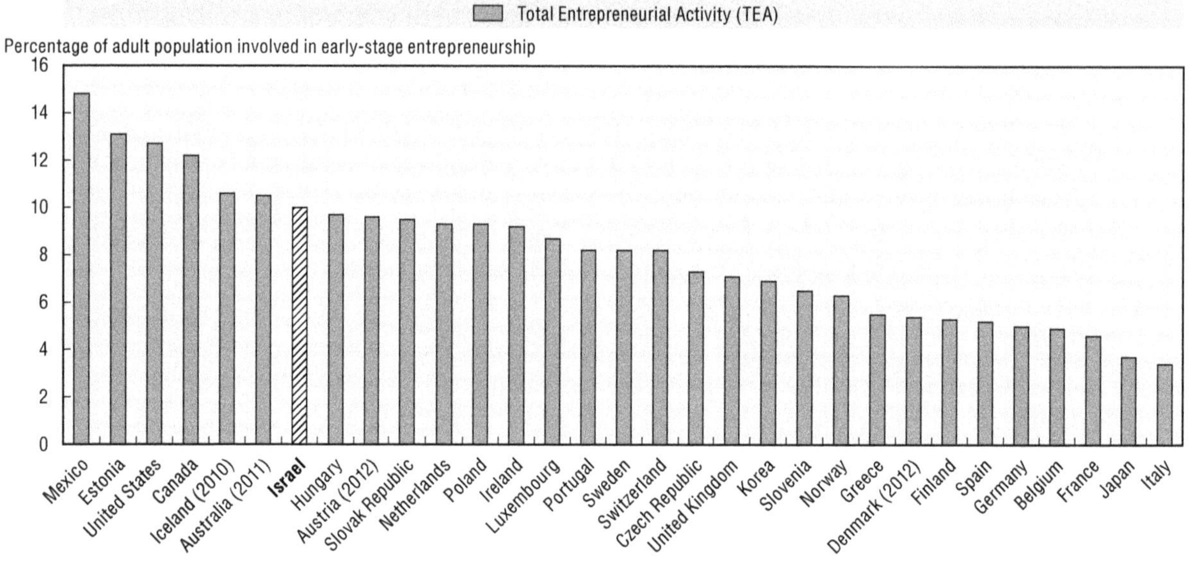

Note: TEA rate: Percentage of 18-64 population who are either a nascent entrepreneur (i.e. actively involved in setting up a business he/she will own or co-own; this business has not paid salaries, wages, or any other payments to the owners for more than three months) or owner-manager of a new business (i.e. owning and managing a running business that has paid salaries, wages, or any other payments to the owners for more than three months, but not more than 42 months). This Figure appears as Figure 1.2 in this report.
Source: OECD based on the Global Entrepreneurship Monitor (GEM) database, *www.gemconsortium.org/key-indicators*.

Both the proportion of early-stage entrepreneurs with rapid growth expectations (i.e. new entrepreneurs who plan to hire at least five workers in the following five years) and with international orientations are above the OECD averages, although both have fallen substantially since the global economic and financial crisis, from 47% and 32% respectively in 2007 to 30% and 24% respectively in 2013. This suggests there is room for public intervention to refuel growth-oriented entrepreneurship as economic conditions improve.

The information on the motivations for early-stage entrepreneurship in Israel is ambivalent (Figure 2.20). On the one hand, the proportion of Israeli early-stage entrepreneurial activity that is opportunity driven (i.e. driven by existing market opportunities and the entrepreneur's desire to improve one's own income and/or independence) is less than in most other OECD countries. On the other hand, the proportion of necessity-driven entrepreneurship is also relatively low. Correspondingly, the proportion of Israeli entrepreneurs stating neither opportunity nor necessity motivations is relatively high.

Social target groups

It is generally the case across OECD countries that business creation and business ownership are not equally distributed across the population. Women tend to be less likely than men to start a business, young people, immigrants and ethnic minorities often set up businesses with lower growth and survival prospects than the average, and although seniors often remain active through entrepreneurship many more inactive seniors could

Figure 2.20. **Characteristics of early-stage entrepreneurship, 2013**

Percentage of total TEA rate

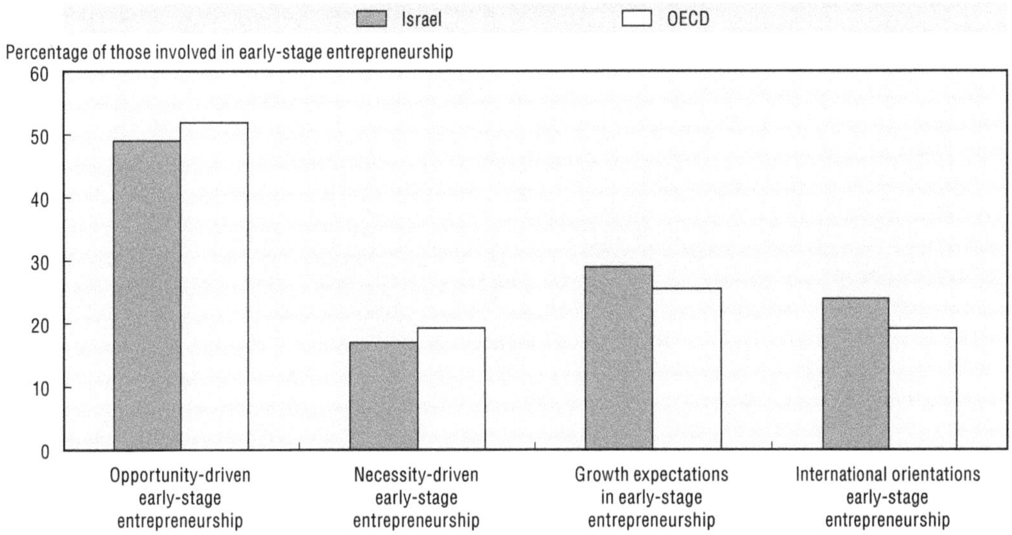

Note: i) Opportunity-driven TEA: Percentage of those involved in TEA who i) claim to be driven by opportunity as opposed to finding no other option for work; and ii) who indicate the main driver for being involved in this opportunity is being independent or increasing their income, rather than just maintaining their income; ii) Necessity-driven TEA: Percentage of those involved in TEA who are involved in entrepreneurship because they had no other option for work; iii) Growth expectations: Percentage of TEA who expects to employ at least five employees five years from now; iv) International orientations: Percentage of TEA who indicates that at least 25% of the customers come from other countries. The OECD average is the simple mean of the values of the OECD countries for which information is available (32-33 countries, depending on the indicator).

Source: OECD based on the Global Entrepreneurship Monitor (GEM) database, *www.gemconsortium.org/key-indicators*.

StatLink http://dx.doi.org/10.1787/888933421553

benefit. All of these social groups face a number of specific or heightened obstacles to entrepreneurship compared to the rest of the population (OECD/European Union, 2015).

Israel is a very heterogeneous country where divisions along the traditional gender and age lines are crossed by country-specific divisions which reflect the ethnic and religious backgrounds of the population. Two segments of the Israeli society are often reported to be on the edge of the labour market, including entrepreneurship and self-employment: Arab Israeli women and Jewish Ultraorthodox (i.e. Haredi) men, who together make up approximately 15% of the total population. In addition, in the early 1990s, Israel became the new home for nearly one million new Jewish immigrants who migrated from a range of countries, notably countries that were part of the former Soviet Union, which makes foreign-born entrepreneurship a substantial phenomenon in the country.

Female entrepreneurship

Israel's female total early-stage entrepreneurship rate is relatively high and places the country in the top half of a comparative international ranking on this measure (Figure 2.21). At the same time, however, the gender gap between men and women early-stage entrepreneurs is the second-highest among OECD members, given the high rate of male early-stage entrepreneurship in Israel. This gender gap points to an untapped entrepreneurial potential in the female population. A further disaggregation shows that the total early-stage entrepreneurship rate in the period 2009-10 was especially low in the subgroup of female Russian immigrants (2.1%), compared to Jewish females (3.6%) and Arab Israeli females (5.7%) (Menipaz et al., 2011).

Figure 2.21. **Female total early-stage entrepreneurial activity rate and gender gap, 2013**

Percentage of female adult population (18-64)

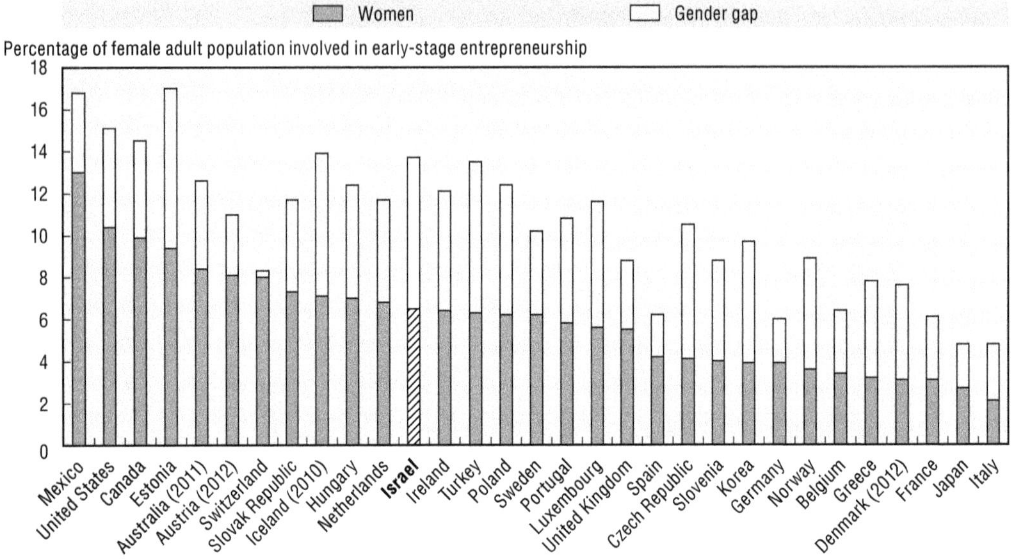

Note: The female early-stage entrepreneurship rate is the proportion of adult women (18-64 years) who are either starting a business or have managed one for less than three-and-a-half years. More specifically, the proportion of adult women who are either a nascent entrepreneur (i.e. actively involved in setting up a business she will own or co-own; this business has not paid salaries, wages, or any other payments to the owners for more than three months) or owner-manager of a new business (i.e. owning and managing a running business that has paid salaries, wages, or any other payments to the owners for more than three months, but not more than 42 months).

Source: OECD based on the Global Entrepreneurship Monitor (GEM) database, *www.gemconsortium.org/key-indicators*.

StatLink http://dx.doi.org/10.1787/888933421568

On the measure of self-employment, Israel's women's self-employment rate is nearly three percentage points below the OECD average, i.e. 7.6% versus 10.4%, while there is also an Israeli gender gap in self-employment participation, which is similar in scale to that of the OECD as a whole (around 8 percentage points) (Figure 2.22).[4]

The gender gap in entrepreneurship and self-employment in Israel appears to be related to women's lower interest and self-confidence in this career option. For example, only 29% of Israeli women say that they have the skills needed to start a business compared with 49% of Israeli men (Menipaz et al., 2011). One area for possible government intervention therefore concerns the development of the skills and competences to a start and run a business among the female population in Israel.

Youth and senior entrepreneurship

Israel's youth self-employment rates (people aged 15-24 years) for both men (5%) and women (2%) are significantly below the OECD averages (respectively, 7% and 4%). While these values are similar to those in economies such as Ireland, Germany and Austria, it should be taken into account that young people in Israel generally serve in the army for periods of two years for women and three years for men, which delays their entry into the labour market (Figure 2.23).

The self-employment rate for seniors (aged 65 or more) is also relatively low compared with the equivalent age group in other OECD countries (Figure 2.24). In the context of an Israeli society in which the elderly population is growing fast (OECD, 2013a), greater

Figure 2.22. **Female self-employment rate and gender gap, 2013**

Percentage of female employed population

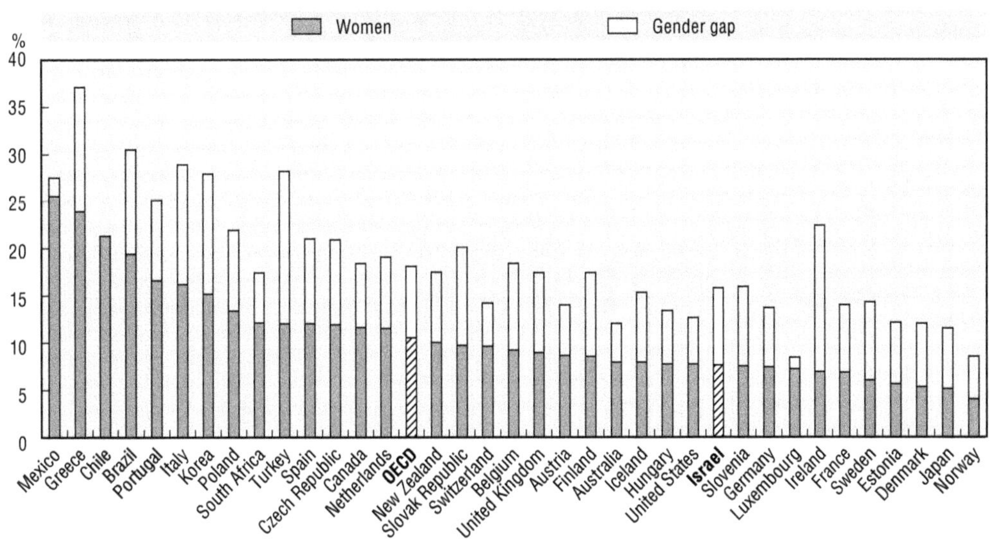

Source: OECD based on OECD (2015a), *Entrepreneurship at a Glance*, 2015, OECD Publishing, Paris.

StatLink http://dx.doi.org/10.1787/888933421572

Figure 2.23. **Youth (15-24) self-employment rates, men and women, 2013**

Percentage of the employed aged 15-24 who are self-employed

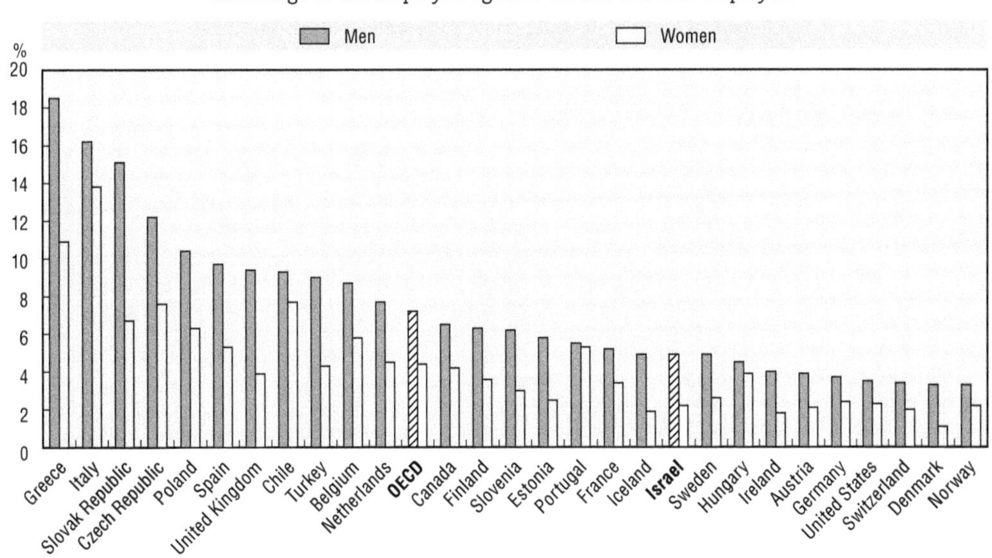

Source: OECD based on OECD (2015a), *Entrepreneurship at a Glance*, 2015, OECD Publishing, Paris.

StatLink http://dx.doi.org/10.1787/888933421588

participation in self-employment could be encouraged among older people to help those who wish to remain socially and economically active.

Despite relatively low levels of youth self-employment, total early-stage entrepreneurial activity, i.e. the rate of nascent and new business ownership, is high for youth (Figure 2.25). Indeed the highest rates of total entrepreneurial activity are in the age bracket of 25-34 years old both for men and for women (20% and 12% respectively). On the other hand, total early-stage entrepreneurial activity is very low for senior women (55 to 64 years old).

Figure 2.24. **The self-employment rate of seniors (65+), average 2009-11**

Percentage of employed people aged 65 or older who are self-employed

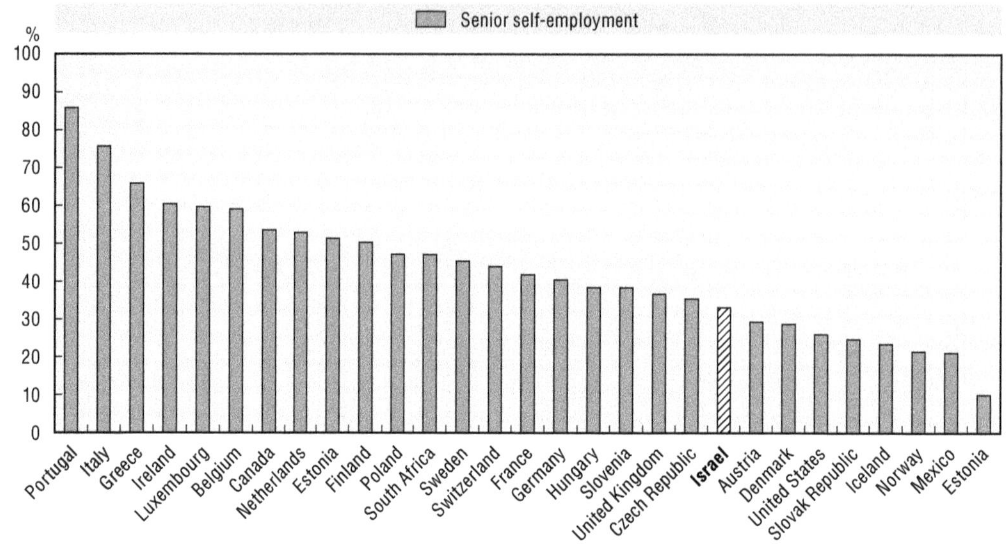

Source: OECD based on OECD (2013b), *Entrepreneurship at a Glance, 2013*, OECD Publishing, Paris.

StatLink http://dx.doi.org/10.1787/888933421597

Figure 2.25. **Total early-stage entrepreneurial activity rate by gender and age group, Israel, 2010**

Percentage of adult male and female population in each age group

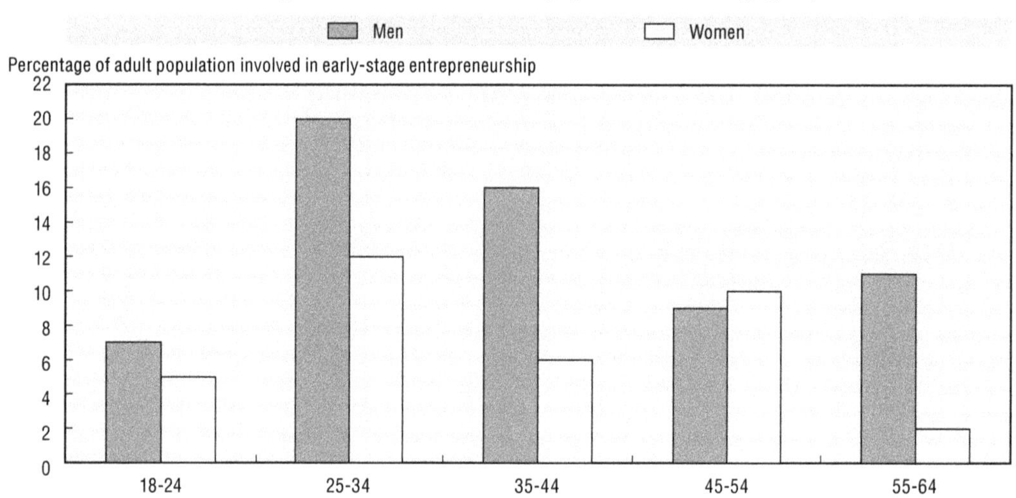

Source: Menipaz, E. et al. (2011), *GEM 2010 Israel National Entrepreneurship Report*, Ben Gurion University of the Nagev, Beer Sheva, *www.gemconsortium.org/docs/2290/gem-israel-2010-report*.

StatLink http://dx.doi.org/10.1787/888933421605

Entrepreneurship by religious and ethnic background

As shown in Table 1.1 (reproduced below), GEM data for the period 2009-10 suggest that total early-stage entrepreneurship is highest among Arab Israelis (6.9%), followed by the Jewish Israelis (5.6%) and Russian Jewish immigrants (3.5%). Russian immigrants are also the most sceptical about a possible future career as entrepreneurs. Only 21% of them see a "market opportunity" to set up an enterprise within the next six months compared with an average of approximately 34% in Israel as a whole.

Total early-stage entrepreneurial activity by ethnic background, 2009-10

Percentage values of adult population (18-64) in each group

	2009	2010	2009-10 (unweighted average)
Jewish Israelis	6.3	5	*5.7*
Male	8.2	7.9	8.1
Female	4.6	2.6	3.6
Arab Israelis	7.3	6.5	*6.9*
Male	9.4	6.5	8.0
Female	4.9	6.5	5.7
Russian Jewish immigrants	4.2	2.8	*3.5*
Male	5.8	3.3	4.6
Female	1.8	2.4	2.1
Israel (total mean)	6.1	5	*5.6*

Note: This Table appears as Table 1.1 in this report.

Source: OECD based on Menipaz, E. et al., (2011), *GEM 2010 Israel National Entrepreneurship Report*, Ben Gurion University of the Nagev, Beer Sheva, *www.gemconsortium.org/docs/2290/gem-israel-2010-report*.

Although Arab Israelis are the most actively involved in early-stage entrepreneurship, their growth expectations are extremely low. Only 8% of those who are starting a business or have owned one for less than three-and-a-half years expected to employ at least five workers in the following five years, as against 15% of Israeli Jews and 25% of Jewish Russian immigrants.

Within the Jewish population, Ultraorthodox Jews have labour market participation rates that are far lower than the rest of the population, and this is also reflected in low participation in entrepreneurship. In 2010, they only accounted for 6.1% of total early stage entrepreneurial activity, far from the 11% of the total Israeli population that they represent.

Conclusions and policy recommendations

This chapter highlights several features of the structure and performance of SMEs and entrepreneurship in Israel that have important implications for public policy objectives in the country.

Among the key characteristics of SMEs and entrepreneurship that need to be taken into account are the large weight of SMEs in the economy and their positive growth and development trends. SMEs represent a large share of all enterprises, employment and value added in the Israeli business economy, in line with many other OECD countries. The stock of businesses in the economy has been growing significantly, at a rate of approximately 3% per year, which has also contributed to strong private sector employment growth. There is a high rate of early-stage entrepreneurial activity, and a high proportion of new entrepreneurs with high growth aspirations, although growth ambitions have fallen since the crisis. Israel's performance in high-impact entrepreneurship is also strong in international terms, in the sense of generating high-growth SMEs and gazelles, especially in the services and construction sectors.

On the other hand, Israel has a relatively large proportion of enterprises and entrepreneurs that operate in the informal economy, a low rate of entrepreneurial churning, and a growth in business numbers that has been weighted to lower value-added sectors such as construction and transport. All these features of the economy tend to be associated with poor productivity performance. Moreover, there appears to be a significant productivity gap between SMEs and large firms in the manufacturing sector in Israel. There is reasonable SME export performance, although only 15% of SMEs export, while SME innovation performance could be stronger.

Furthermore, although there are positive attitudes and activity rates overall in the population with respect to entrepreneurship, there are also certain weaknesses. There are relatively high proportions of adults who express a fear of failure in entrepreneurship and a lack of the necessary skills and competences. There are also lower rates of entrepreneurship activity among women, seniors and Russian Jewish immigrants than the population as a whole, and very low growth aspirations among Arab Israeli entrepreneurs.

There is also an important dualism in the Israeli economy between a narrow but very strong export-oriented high-technology sector and a broad traditional SME economy where informality is common and average labour productivity is low.

These characteristics of SMEs and entrepreneurship in Israel suggest that there are four major challenges for Israeli SME and entrepreneurship policy, namely to:

1. Increase the rate of SME productivity and innovation, particularly among low-technology firms and SMEs in manufacturing.
2. Increase the rate of entrepreneurial churn in the economy and the share of young firms, by continuing to generate start-up companies and improving their success in the early years.
3. Increase entrepreneurial skills and competences in the population.
4. Address weaknesses in entrepreneurship activity among women, seniors, recent immigrants and Arab Israeli entrepreneurs.

The following specific recommendations are offered to address this agenda:

Key recommendations on SME and entrepreneurship performance

- Adopt measures aimed at increasing the sustainability and growth of small businesses and young businesses.
- Take measures to increase the innovation activities of the bulk of SMEs in services and traditional non-R&D based manufacturing.
- Increase policy attention to productivity upgrading in medium-sized manufacturing enterprises.
- Reduce the scale of the informal economy through a review of tax and regulatory measures that may discourage formality.
- Expand entrepreneurship training for new and potential entrepreneurs, particularly among under-represented groups in growth-oriented entrepreneurship, including women, seniors, recent immigrants and Arab Israelis.

Notes

1. In this chapter, unless otherwise specified, the OECD definition of micro (1-9 employees), small (10-49 employees) and medium (50-249 employees) enterprises is used. The category of small enterprises is also sometimes split into two further groups: lower-small enterprises (10-19 employees) and upper-small enterprises (20-49 employees). In Israel, there is not a standard definition of SMEs, although the Small and Medium Business Agency (SMBA) considers micro enterprises those with between 1 and 4 employees, small those with 5-20 employees, and medium enterprises those with 21-99 employees.

2. "The Start-up Nation" is the title of a bestseller narrative book dedicated to the innovation-driven growth of Israel since its foundation.
3. Data on BERD undertaken by research centres were supplied by the Israeli Central Bureau of Statistics (CBS).
4. While covering business owners who employ themselves, self-employment measures tend to exclude business owners and managers who are employees of their own businesses. They include people who see themselves as workers who employ themselves rather than entrepreneurs and people operating business that have been operating for some time.

References

Central Bureau of Statistics (2013), *Business Demography: A Collection of Statistical Data from the Business Register*, 2003-2011, Publication No. 1541, Jerusalem.

European Commission (2013), *Entrepreneurship in the EU and Beyond*, Flash Eurobarometer No. 354, Brussels.

Menipaz E., Y. Avrahami and M. Lerner (2011), *GEM 2010 Israel National Entrepreneurship Report*, Ben Gurion University of the Nagev, Beer Sheva, *www.gemconsortium.org/docs/2290/gem-israel-2010-report*.

OECD (2015a), *Entrepreneurship at a Glance 2015*, OECD Publishing, Paris, *http://dx.doi.org/10.1787/entrepreneur_aag-2015-en*.

OECD (2015b), *OECD Science, Technology and Industry Scoreboard 2015*, OECD Publishing, Paris, *http://dx.doi.org/10.1787/sti_scoreboard-2015-en*.

OECD (2014), *Entrepreneurship at a Glance 2014*, OECD Publishing, Paris, *http://dx.doi.org/10.1787/entrepreneur_aag-2014-en*.

OECD (2013a), *OECD Economic Surveys: Israel*, OECD Publishing, Paris, *http://dx.doi.org/10.1787/eco_surveys-isr-2013-en*.

OECD (2013b), *Entrepreneurship at a Glance 2013*, OECD Publishing, Paris, *http://dx.doi.org/10.1787/entrepreneur_aag-2013-en*.

OECD (2011), *OECD Economic Surveys: Israel*, December 2011, OECD Publishing, Paris, *http://dx.doi.org/10.1787/eco_surveys-isr-2011-en*.

OECD/European Union (2015), *The Missing Entrepreneurs 2015: Policies for Self-Employment and Entrepreneurship*, OECD Publishing, Paris, *http://dx.doi.org/10.1787/9789264226418-en*.

Schneider F. (undated), *Size and Development of the Shadow Economy of 31 European and 5 other OECD Countries from 2003 to 2012: Some New Facts*, *www.econ.jku.at/schneider*.

Schneider, F., A. Buehn and C. Montenegro (2010), "New Estimates for the Shadow Economies all Over the World", *International Economic Journal*, 24, 443-461.

OECD Studies on SMEs and Entrepreneurship
SME and Entrepreneurship Policy in Israel 2016

Chapter 3

Business environment and framework conditions in Israel

This chapter examines the framework conditions influencing SME and entrepreneurship development in Israel. It covers macroeconomic conditions, product market regulations and the ease of doing business, human resources, the innovation system, access to finance, business taxation and foreign direct investment. Israel has experienced strong economic growth in recent years thanks to major assets such as high rates of participation in tertiary education, strong R&D expenditure, well-developed equity finance, and favourable business taxation. This has offered favourable conditions for Israel's successful high-technology entrepreneurial ecosystem. Nonetheless, improvements can still be made to framework conditions for SME and entrepreneurship development more generally, including addressing barriers to product market competition, inadequate vocational skills and training, limited access to loan finance, limited support for non-R&D based innovation and limited FDI-SME linkages. Tackling these issues can help reduce the dualism of the Israeli economy between an internationally advanced high-technology sector and a lagging traditional manufacturing and services sector.

Macroeconomic conditions

GDP growth

SMEs and entrepreneurship have benefited from the strong growth of the Israeli economy in recent years in terms of growing market and other opportunities. Israel's GDP growth rates were positive throughout the decade 2003-13, despite the global recession, although they have recently slowed (Figure 3.1). OECD estimates set them at 3.2% and 3.5% for 2014 and 2015.[1] The economy appears to be close to potential and there are relatively few areas of spare capacity (OECD, 2013a). As a result, GDP growth in the future will have to stem more and more from increased productivity, which is a challenge for SME and entrepreneurship policy as well as other government policy areas.

Figure 3.1. **Annual GDP growth rates (volume), 2001-16**

Year-on-year growth rates

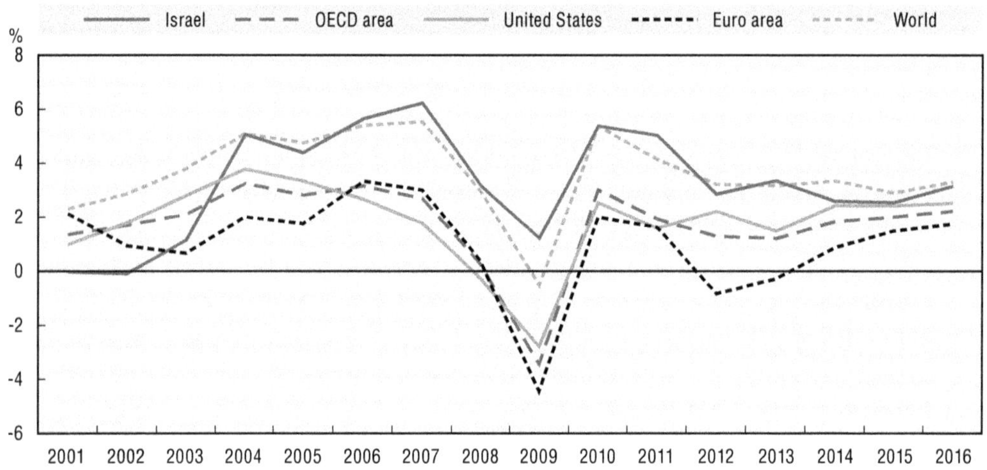

Note: Data for 2015 and 2016 are estimates.
Source: *OECD Economic Outlook Database.*

StatLink http://dx.doi.org/10.1787/888933421653

Labour market trends

As a result of sustained recent economic growth, labour market performance has reached record highs. In 2013, Israel outperformed the OECD average on the labour market participation rate, the employment rate and the unemployment rate. Israel's labour force participation rate and employment rate are close to 70%, whereas the unemployment rate stood at approximately 6% in 2013 (Figure 3.2).

Figure 3.3 shows employment rates by population group in Israel for men and women. It shows that although the general context is one of high labour utilisation, there are two particular segments of the population – Ultraorthodox Jewish men and Arab Israeli women – whose participation in the labour market is significantly below that of the total population.

Figure 3.2. **Evolution of main labour market indicators, Israel, 2001-13**

Percentage values

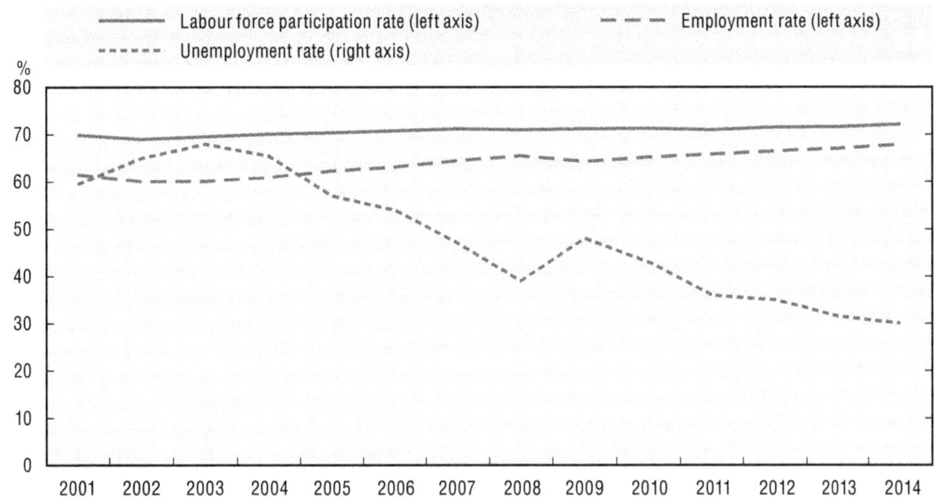

Source: *OECD Labour Force Statistics Database.*

StatLink http://dx.doi.org/10.1787/888933421661

Figure 3.3. **Main labour market indicators in Israel and OECD countries, total and by sex, 2014**

Percentage values

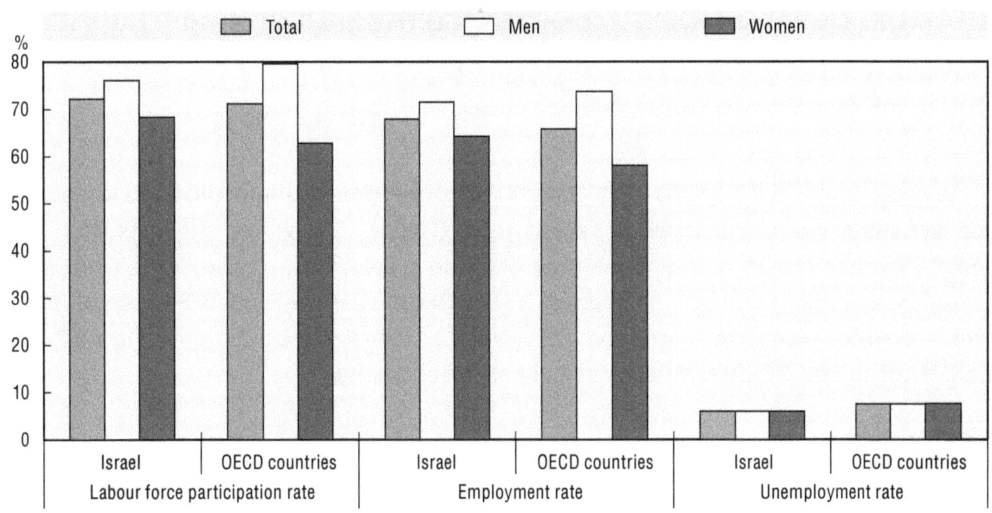

Source: *OECD Labour Force Statistics Database.*

StatLink http://dx.doi.org/10.1787/888933421670

In addition, there is a smaller gap between the Arab Israeli male participation rate and that of all males than between the participation rate of Ultraorthodox Jewish women and that of all females. The support offered to these groups to increase their labour market participation could include encouragement for self-employment in the formal sector.

Growing labour market participation and job creation in new and small enterprises have been facilitated by a flexible labour market. OECD employment protection legislation (EPL) indicators show the Israeli labour market to be less rigid than the OECD average with respect to both regulations on dismissals against regular workers and regulations on temporary contracts (Figure 3.4). This is likely to make new and small business owners less reluctant to hire workers in periods of economic expansion for fear of being unable to reduce their labour force when the economy slows down.

Figure 3.4. **Employment protection legislation across OECD countries, 2013**

Scale from 0 (least restrictive) to 6 (most restrictive)

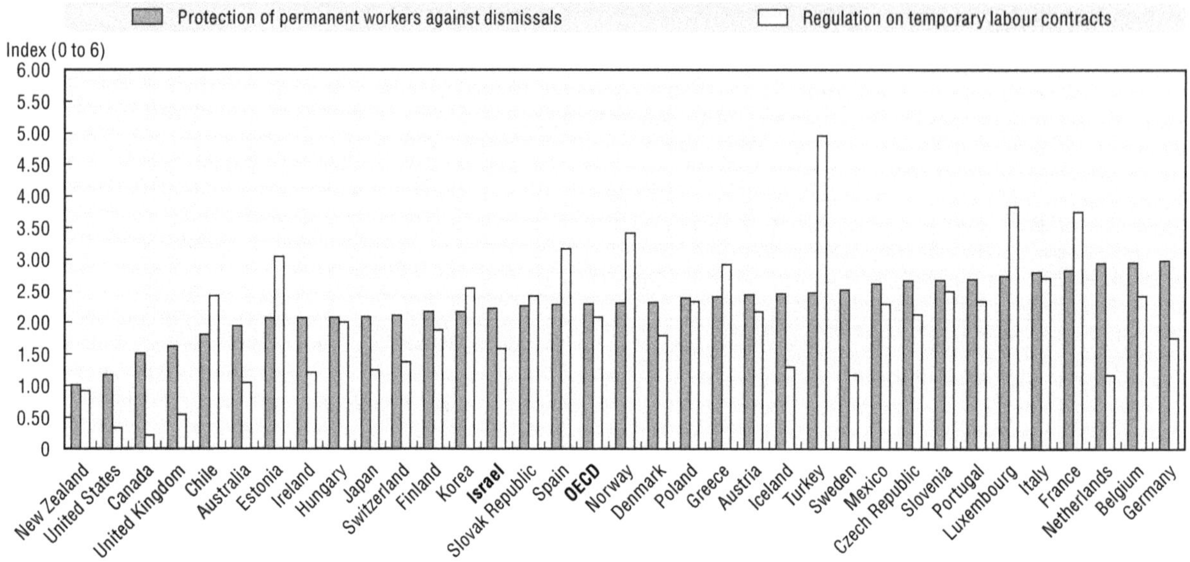

Note: The OECD indicators of employment protection legislation measure the procedures and costs involved in dismissing individuals or groups of workers and the procedures involved in hiring workers on fixed-term or temporary work agency contracts. For further information: *www.oecd.org/employment/emp/oecdindicatorsofemploymentprotection.htm.*

Source: OECD Employment Protection Legislation Database.

StatLink http://dx.doi.org/10.1787/888933421685

Wages growth has significantly trailed GDP growth and labour productivity growth (GDP per hour worked) in Israel in recent years (Figure 3.5),[2] which suggests that wage moderation has played a role in helping SMEs to create jobs. At the same time, wage inequality in Israel is the second-highest in the OECD after the United States, calling for increased policy attention to improve the quality of low-end jobs, including in SMEs and micro firms in non-high-technology sectors of the economy.

Labour productivity

Israel's labour productivity growth has not kept pace with the Euro area, the OECD area or the United States (Figure 3.6) over the last fifteen years. Further measures are needed to address this productivity gap, which would include facilitating business entry and dynamism and increasing productivity in established SMEs and micro firms in traditional sectors, where productivity levels are low. Productivity growth in established SMEs is primarily supported through technology development, notably through the incentives of the Law for the Encouragement of Capital Investment. However, the incentives of this Law are mainly used by larger and R&D-based SMEs, whereas fostering productivity in existing non-high-technology SMEs is likely to require a different set of policies that include, among others, business management skills upgrading and improved integration in national and global supply chains.

Figure 3.5. **GDP, labour productivity and average wage growth in Israel, 2006-14**

Annual growth rates in GDP per capita, GDP per hour worked and average wage

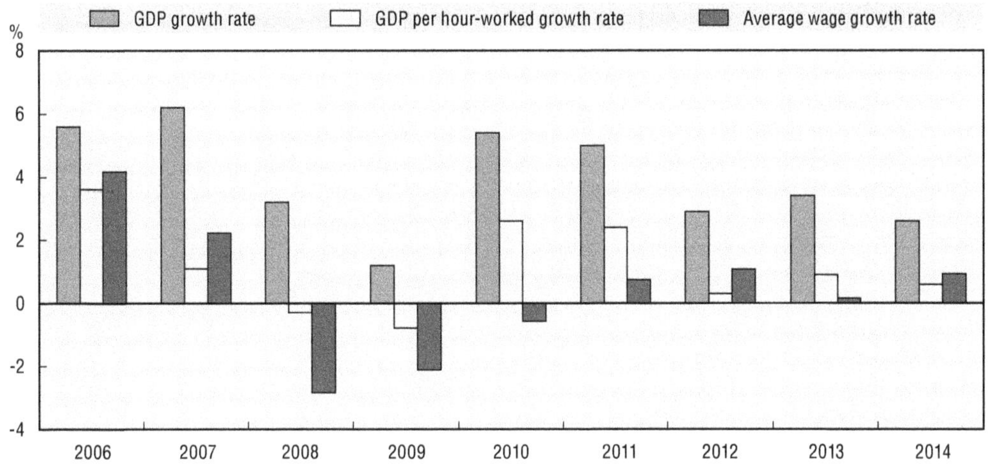

Source: OECD based on OECD *Earnings database*, *Productivity database* and *Economic Outlook database*.

StatLink http://dx.doi.org/10.1787/888933421699

Monetary and fiscal policy

The Bank of Israel has undertaken a long series of interest-rate cuts that brought the base rate to a historic low of 0.1% in June 2016. This policy aims to boost investment as the economy starts to show some signs of slowdown and to reduce the appreciation of the national currency thus mitigating a recent decline in exports. These measures should maintain a positive climate for SME investment and market access. Although there are no signs of inflationary pressures in the economy, with the significant exception of the housing market, it will be important to continue gradual adjustment of interest rates to prevent potential inflationary shocks that could harm the ability of SMEs to invest or export.

Israel has a "small government" approach to fiscal policy, where low taxation is coupled with low government spending.[3] There has been slow fiscal consolidation in the last ten years, during which public debt has fallen by one-fifth in relation to GDP, from 98% in 2004 to 79% in 2014. The government deficit has been low, although the global economic crisis led it to increase to between 3.5% and 6% of GDP during the period 2009-14. With renewed growth and a reduced government deficit, there should be room for moderate fiscal expenditures on SME and entrepreneurship policy.

Product market regulations and the ease of doing business

Competitive product markets support the productivity-enhancing role of entrepreneurship in the economy. Israel trails only Turkey in the overall restrictiveness of its product market regulations, based on the OECD Product Market Regulation (PMR) index (Figure 1.7, reproduced below). In particular, Israel lags behind most other OECD countries in all three main areas covered by this index: state control of the economy, barriers to entrepreneurship and barriers to trade and investment.

Progress in reducing regulatory burdens has also been slow in relation to other OECD countries, despite some recent pro-competition reforms such as the new Concentration Law and the new powers granted to the Israel Anti-trust Authority that have not yet generated their full intended benefits. More generally, this also suggests the importance of reviewing regulations and their impact on SMEs and entrepreneurship, something which

Figure 3.6. **Labour productivity in Israel compared with main economic areas, 2000-15**

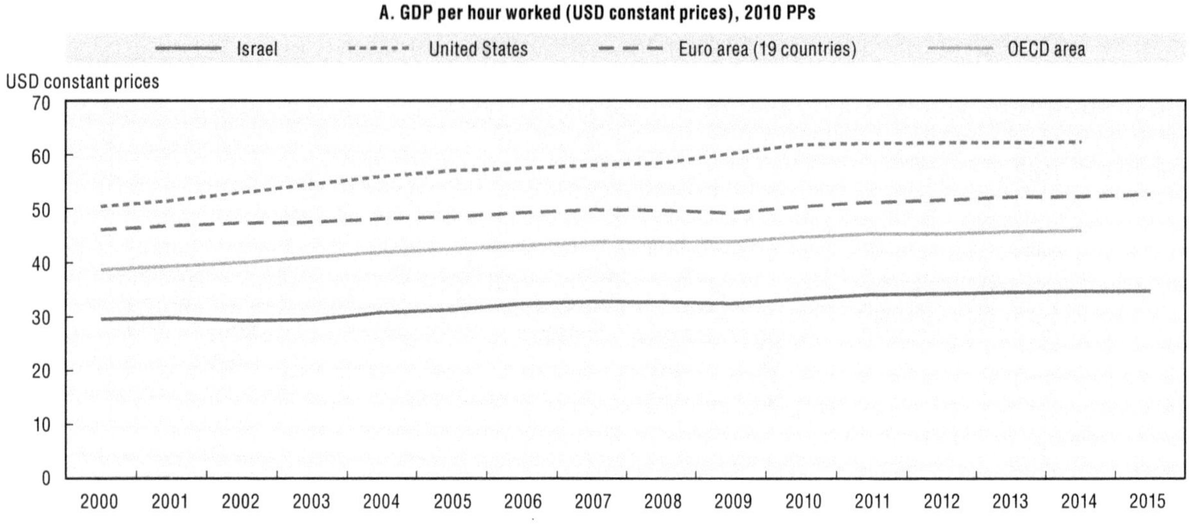

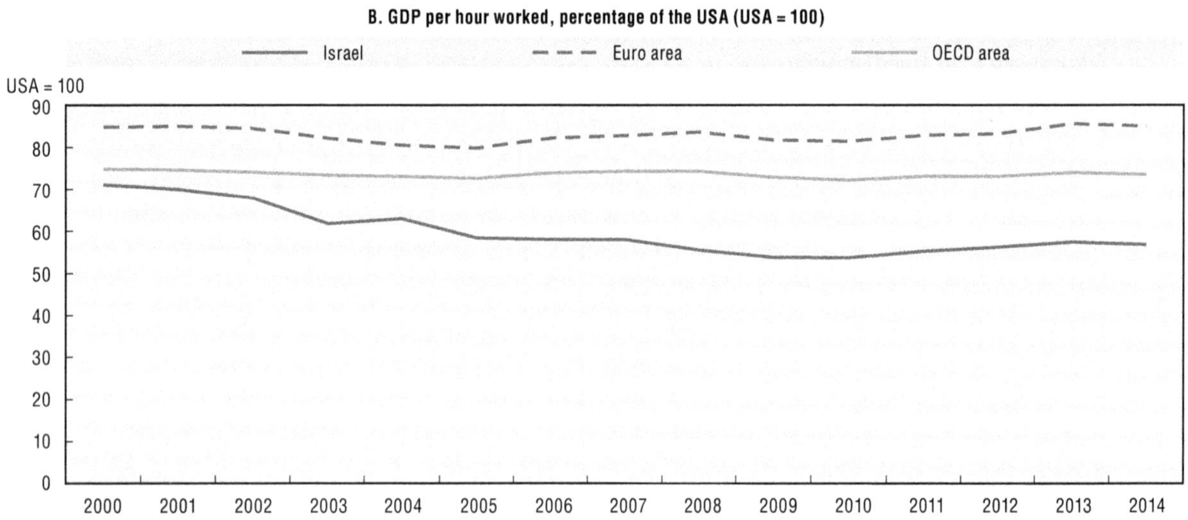

Source: OECD Productivity database.

StatLink http://dx.doi.org/10.1787/888933421700

the SMBA has started to do mainly through an informal process of consultation with private-sector business associations and chambers of commerce. In the future, the use of more standard regulatory impact assessment methodologies such as the Standard Cost Model would enable the SMBA to assess the impact of new regulations on SMEs in a more rigorous way.[4]

A disaggregated analysis of the PMR index shows that Israel lags behind most OECD countries in each of the three covered areas (Figure 3.7). Progress in reducing regulatory burdens has also been slow in relation to other OECD countries. This suggests the importance of reviewing regulations and their impact on SMEs and entrepreneurship.

The World Bank's Doing Business Survey offers results substantially in line with those of the OECD PMR index (Table 3.1). The most problematic areas identified by this survey are those which involve licenses and permits, such as obtaining a construction permit, registering property or getting electricity for a new business premise. Similarly, the survey

Product market regulations across OECD countries, 2003 and 2013

From 0 (least restrictive) to 6 (most restrictive)

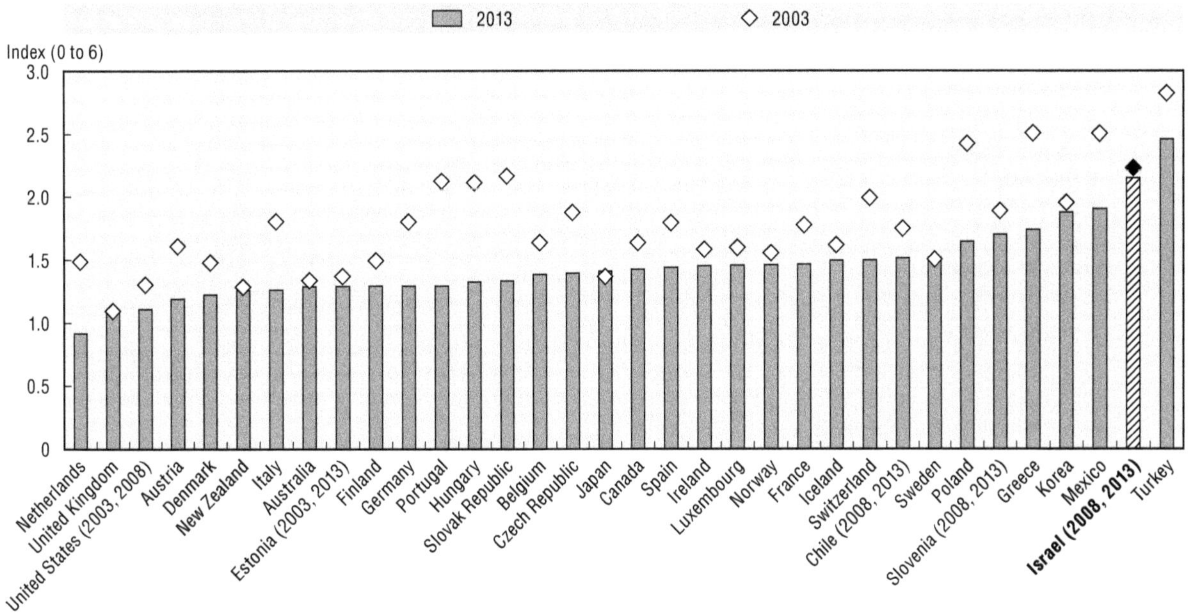

Note: For Israel, data refer to 2013 and 2008. The OECD Indicators of Product Market Regulation (PMR) are a comprehensive and internationally-comparable set of indicators that measure the degree to which policies promote or inhibit competition. These indicators cover formal regulations in the following areas: state control of the economy; legal and administrative barriers to entrepreneurship; barriers to international trade and investment. For further information: *www.oecd.org/eco/growth/indicatorsofproductmarketregulationhomepage.htm#indicators*. This Figure appears as Figure 1.7 in this report.

Source: OECD Product Market Regulation (PMR) Database.

Figure 3.7. **Product market regulations by main area in Israel, 2008 and 2013**

From 0 (least restrictive) to 6 (most restrictive)

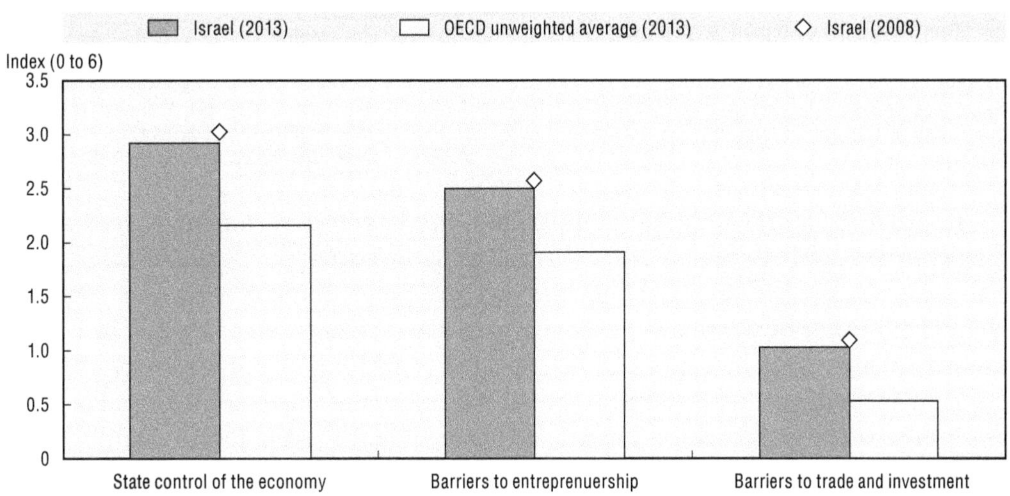

Note: "State control" refers to public ownership (e.g. scope and governance of state-owned enterprises, government involvement in network sectors, etc.) and involvement in business operations (e.g. price controls); "barriers to entrepreneurship" include complexity of rules and procedures (e.g. the license and permit system), administrative burdens on start-ups (i.e. for both corporation and sole proprietor firms) and regulatory protection of incumbents (e.g. legal barriers to entry and anti-trust exemptions); "barriers to trade and investment" encompass explicit barriers (e.g. tariffs) and non-explicit barriers (e.g. different treatment of foreign suppliers").

Source: OECD based on *Product Market Regulations (PMR) Database.*

StatLink http://dx.doi.org/10.1787/888933421719

Table 3.1. **Israel's profile in the World Bank's Doing Business Survey, 2016**

Rank and distance to the frontier (DTF)

	Rank	Distance to the frontier (%)
Starting a business	56	90.55
Dealing with construction permits	96	68.2
Getting electricity	91	68.96
Registering property	127	52.84
Getting credit	42	65
Protecting minority investors	8	73.33
Paying taxes	103	71.65
Trading across borders	58	82.85
Enforcing contracts	77	59.78
Resolving insolvency	29	72.47

Note: Countries are ranked from 1-189. The distance to frontier (DTF) measures the distance of Israel to the leading country in the respective topic. An economy's distance to frontier is indicated on a scale from 0 to 100, where 0 represents the lowest performance and 100 the frontier.

Source: The World Bank's Doing Business database, *www.doingbusiness.org/data/exploreeconomies/israel*.

StatLink http://dx.doi.org/10.1787/888933421859

highlights the complexity of the tax and judicial systems for businesses. On the other hand, "starting a business" in Israel is no more difficult than across most OECD countries; in fact, setting up a limited company in Israel takes the same number of procedures but slightly more time than the OECD high-income country average (Table 3.2).[5]

Table 3.2. **Starting a business in Israel, 2016**

Number of procedures, number of days and cost

	Israel	OECD high-income
Procedures (number)	5	4.7
Time (days)	13	8.3
Cost (% of income per capita)	3.4	3.2

Note: The World Bank definition of "OECD high-income" includes all 34 OECD countries, except Mexico and Turkey, which in the World-Bank income classification fall under the upper-middle income category. Further information on the definitions of procedures, time and cost is available in the World Bank's Doing Business website: *www.doingbusiness.org/data/exploreeconomies/israel#starting-a-business*.

Source: The World Bank's Doing Business database, *www.doingbusiness.org/data/exploreeconomies/israel*.

StatLink http://dx.doi.org/10.1787/888933421868

In order to improve market competition, the Israeli government passed a new Concentration Law in December 2013. This will oblige industrial conglomerates to separate their financial and non-financial branches and make more difficult the use of corporate pyramid structures by which one public company can retain control of another by holding minority shares. This measure can be expected to facilitate business entry and SME development among other benefits. However, the law will be implemented over six years, which may reduce its immediate impact and expose it to the risk of future changes.

The government has also strengthened the functions of the Israeli Anti-trust Authority (IAA). In food retailing, for example, the IAA has encouraged price transparency by publicising "exclusivity agreements" between suppliers and retailers, while in network services small electricity and gas suppliers have been allowed to connect to the national grid and sell energy services to the market. Nonetheless, there is a risk that other existing rules prevent prices from dropping in the immediate future, such as guaranteed producer prices in agriculture (OECD, 2013a), while state-owned companies are still core producers and distributors of electricity and gas in Israel, leading to higher utility costs for SMEs.

More generally, the approach of the IAA has been to propose solutions to restore competition in markets where this is at risk, whereas greater powers, including the ability to impose financial sanctions on wrongdoers, would help the IAA to undertake its task more effectively (OECD, 2011a).

A complex license and permit system, largely managed at the local level by municipalities, is another major regulatory barrier to entrepreneurship and SME development in Israel. Approximately 40% of companies need a license in Israel, but one-quarter of them does not have one. Key problems include lack of information to businesses about the process to follow to obtain the permit, long delays in receiving a response, and poor standardisation of procedures across different municipalities. To tackle these problems a law has been proposed, but not yet approved, that aims to harmonise license requirements across the country, make it more difficult for municipalities to add extra local requirements on top of the national ones, and reduce delays to obtain licenses especially in trades that pose no environmental risks. As part of its SME advocacy function, SMBA could help identify difficulties in permits and licenses and encourage their simplification with the relevant authorities. Digitalisation is another approach that many OECD governments have pursued to modernise their business license and permit system that could also be applied in Israel (see Box 3.1).

Box 3.1. **The Canadian online service for business permit and licensing**

Description of the approach

BizPaL is an online government service, launched in 2005, for streamlining business permit and licensing procedures and reducing the amount of red-tape for new entrepreneurs and SMEs (*www.bizpal.ca*). BizPaL receives CAD 3 million annually (EUR 2.1 million) in federal funding to support its maintenance, continued expansion and service improvements. Through BizPaL, the three levels of government work collaboratively to help SMEs comply with government requirements. To date, over 34 federal departments/agencies and all 12 provinces/territories are participating in BizPaL together with about 700 municipalities.

Accessing BizPaL allows SMEs and entrepreneurs to identify which permits and licenses they require and how to obtain them. From the website, they select the business activities they plan to undertake (and in which sectors) and BizPaL automatically generates a list of all required permits and licenses from all levels of government (federal, provincial/territorial and municipal), along with basic information on each with links to the specific government sites where the entrepreneur can learn more and, in some cases, apply online. By using this portal, less time is needed to search for information about which permits and licenses are needed, which also improves business planning because entrepreneurs are able to "get it right the first time".

In developing the BizPaL tool, the federal government (Innovation, Science and Economic Development Canada, or ISED Canada) was responsible for securing the participation of provincial/territorial governments, which were responsible for securing the participation of municipal governments. ISED Canada manages the project but each jurisdiction is responsible for maintaining its own data within the system. BizPaL data is housed in a central database. Information is entered into this database using the BizPaL Administration Module, a secure web-based application. The database contains the permit and license information from all participating jurisdictions and the questions that link a business activity to the permit or license required for that activity.

BizPaL receives CAD 3 million annually (EUR 2.1 million) in federal funding to support its maintenance, continued expansion and service improvements.

Box 3.1. The Canadian online service for business permit and licensing *(cont.)*

Factors for success

Success was dependent on three main factors:

- Establishing a national coordinating body (a role assumed by ISED Canada) to provide a secretariat function to support the partnership and oversee the technology infrastructure, and a Steering Committee consisting of federal, provincial/territorial and local governments, which cemented the partnership approach.
- Providing training and technical support, business process mapping tools and other assistance to federal, provincial/territorial, and municipal partners so they could participate in BizPal.
- Recognition and endorsement of the project by the Canadian Federation of Independent Business, the largest SME membership association in Canada.

Obstacles and responses

It was more difficult than initially expected to bring municipalities into the project, especially those in smaller and more remote locations, because they lacked staff and capacity to participate. When the project was piloted in 2006, only 13 municipalities were part of the project. Two years later, 454 had joined and another 136 were in the process of joining. Together, this represented 16% of the 3647 municipalities Canada. The BizPal team realised that their target objectives for municipality participation were too ambitious and that much more intensive involvement with municipalities was needed to bring them on board. For example, provincial/territorial governments had to spend considerably more time process uploading information on behalf of the local governments than they had originally thought.

Moreover, the awareness of the BizPal service among SMEs was low, even two years after launch. BizPal therefore undertook a national marketing campaign to increase awareness and interest among potential users. The specific objectives of the marketing campaign were to improve client awareness and usage of the BizPaL service and increase BizPaL recognition through cohesive and consistent marketing communication, activities and messaging, which included ads and banners on search engines.

Finally, there was uncertainty with respect to securing ongoing resources from federal and provincial governments, which was alleviated by the decision by the federal government to allocate CAD 3 million annually to the BizPal project as part of A-base funding.

Relevance for Israel

Complexities in obtaining business licenses and permits are a significant obstacle for SMEs and entrepreneurs in Israel.

Implementing a BiZPal-like online portal in Israel would reduce learning costs for SMEs and entrepreneurs and increase transparency of municipal requirements. It would provide an important complement to the reforms currently underway to expedite the licensing process and would also be in line with the "Digital Israel" Initiative, which includes a transition towards e-government services.

Sources for further information

- The website can be consulted and reviewed at: *www.bizpal.ca*.
- Further information can be obtained from the Small Business Policy Branch, ISED Canada, Ottawa, Canada (+1 613 954 5489).
- Reference can also be made to the evaluation report on the BizPal project, "Evaluation of Industry Canada's BizPaL Service" (2011), available online at: *www.ic.gc.ca/eic/site/ae-ve.nsf/eng/h_03356.html/*.

Human resources

Tertiary education

During the last twenty-five years, the proportion of people enrolled in tertiary education (expressed as a percentage of the total population of the five-year age group following on from secondary school leaving) has nearly doubled, from 34% in 1990 to 66% in 2015. As a result, in 2014, 48.5% of the Israelis aged 15-64 had received tertiary-level education, a proportion second only to Canada among OECD countries and 16 percentage points above the OECD average (Figure 3.8). These high skills are a major asset of the Israeli economy and help support SME and entrepreneurship activity by increasing labour productivity in SMEs and by improving the growth-orientation of entrepreneurs.

Figure 3.8. **Percentage of adults who have attained tertiary education across OECD countries, 2014**

Percentage of adult population (aged 25-64)

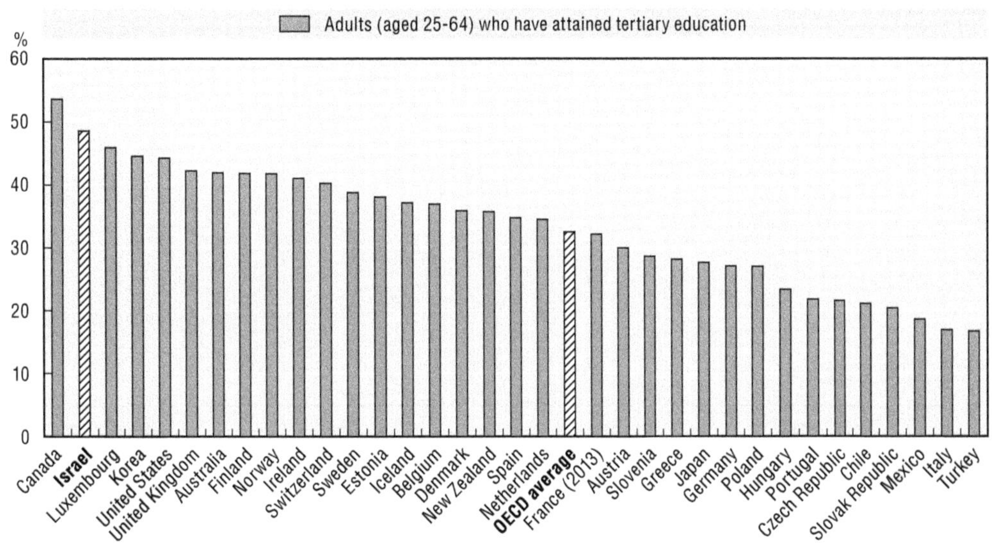

Source: OECD based on OECD (2015a), *Education at a Glance 2015: OECD Indicators*, OECD Publishing, Paris.

StatLink http://dx.doi.org/10.1787/888933421724

At the same time there is a skills mismatch in the economy, and many highly-educated workers are under-employed in low-productivity jobs. This implies a need to improve the bridging process between the supply of graduates from the university system and the demand for graduates in existing SMEs. Options for intervention in these areas include increasing employer participation in curriculum design and increasing placements offered to higher education students in SMEs in order to increase the probability of matching the student to an employment that requires their skills. In addition, it implies a need for consultancy and advice to SMEs that upgrades their management and working practices so that they can make better use of the skills that graduates offer.

Secondary education

Secondary education completion rates in Israel are above the OECD average (87% vs. 84%). However, results from the OECD Programme for International Student Assessment (PISA) survey reveal an under-performance in the learning outcomes of Israeli upper-secondary students (aged 15 years) in maths and science compared with the OECD average (Figure 1.8

reproduced below). Israeli students also perform poorly in financial literacy skills, which are particularly relevant for those who will undertake an entrepreneurial career in the future (nearly one-quarter of Israeli students are in the two lowest performance brackets). Furthermore, certain segments of the population such as Arab Israelis and Ultraorthodox Jews perform particularly poorly in secondary education, which has negative consequences on their ability to enrol in university and on their career prospects. Only 12% of Arab Israelis enrol in university, while Ultraorthodox Jewish students tend to attend religious schools which lack a strong curriculum in secular subjects such as mathematics and foreign languages.

Israeli student performance in mathematics, science, reading and financial literacy, 2012

Mean scores

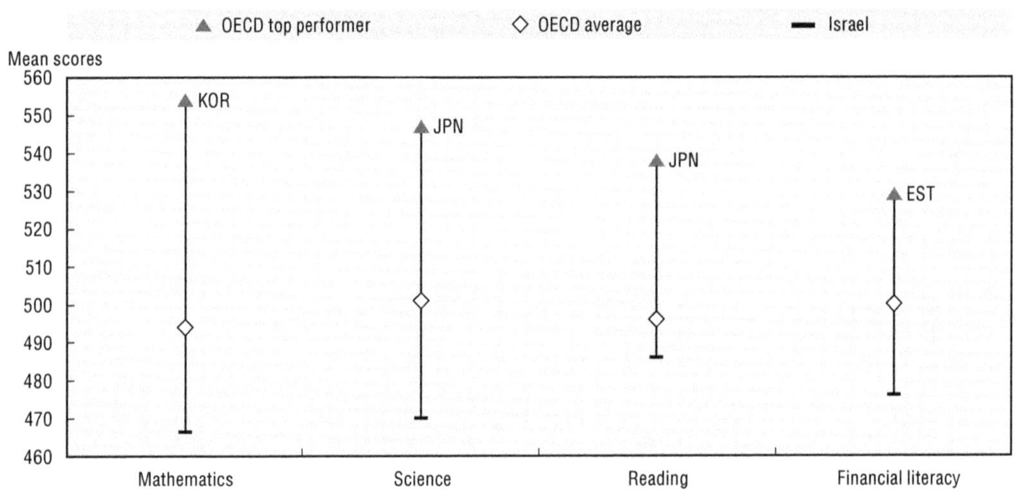

Note: Data on financial literacy are only available for 13 OECD countries. This Figure appears as Figure 1.8 in this report.
Source: OECD based on OECD (2013b), *PISA 2012 Assessment and Analytical Framework: Mathematics, Reading, Science, Problem Solving and Financial Literacy*, OECD Publishing, Paris.

Strengthening core skills achievement and participation by under-represented groups in secondary education will be important to improving the quality of labour available to SMEs. In addition, secondary schools need greater support to build educational links with local enterprises, such as for short-term work placements, company visits and case study exercises related to real-world business problems.

The vocational education and training school system

Adult VET is primarily available through a nationwide system of occupational certifications delivered by local technical colleges and covering more than 100 different professions with approximately 70 000 people qualifying each year (MOITAL, 2012). Both the Ministry of Economy and Industry and the Ministry of Education are involved, which operate two distinct VET school systems.

The Ministry of Education is responsible for the vast bulk of schools (around 1 700), which are divided along religious and ethnic lines (schools for secular Jews, religious Jews, Ultraorthodox Jews and Arab Israelis). Some 60% of students in these schools work towards the high-school graduation certificate, i.e. the *Bagrut* certificate. The other 40% (around 137 000 students) follow a technical and vocational route, which is divided into three tracks: science and engineering (around 46 000 students); technical studies (around 49 000 students); and vocational studies (around 42 000 students) (European Training Foundation, 2014). Numbers in the VET school system have been on the decline since the peak of the 1980 when 53% of all high school students were enrolled in the VET system (Natanzon and Levi, 2010).

The Ministry of Education VET school system is implemented through a range of partner organisations, the most notable being the ORT (the Society for Trades and Agricultural Labour) and AMAL Educational Network. The ORT manages a network of 205 schools, 16 of which are vocational high-schools, with approximately 100 000 students and 7 500 staff across Israel. AMAL is a smaller network of 128 schools with an enrolment of around 40 000 students. In total, about 40% of vocational students are enrolled in ORT and AMAL programmes (European Training Foundation, 2014). There is some involvement from business support organisations such as the Manufacturer's Association of Israel on the identification of training needs and design of curricula, while municipalities also play an important role in the system by providing additional funding and helping to tailor national curricula in ways that meet local needs.

The Ministry of Economy and Industry operates around 70 schools, attended by about 13 000 students (Yair et al., 2013; European Training Foundation, 2014). The major programme addresses upper-secondary-level students who take practical courses of three-to-four years during which, depending on the year of the curriculum, they spend one or two days practising in an enterprise with the rest of the time spent in traditional classroom activities. These schools absorb 60% of the drop-outs from the schools of the Ministry of Education. The emphasis is therefore on reintegrating students back into society through a curriculum that is more vocationally orientated. In particular, three options are offered:

- "industrial schools", where students mainly work with large firms or the Israeli Defence Force and receive a mix of practical and vocational training;
- "apprenticeship schools", where students primarily work with small firms and study between one and three days per week; and
- "work groups/courses", which are designed for students who are neither studying nor working elsewhere.

The fact that Israel operates two parallel VET school systems is associated with a number of problems. Yair et al. (2013) identify a number of examples of duplicated VET provision. For example, within the Ministry of Economy, MAHAT (the National Institute for Technical Training) accredits colleges and set examinations. In parallel, the Ministry of Education and the Science and Technology Administration oversee separate programmes. Another challenge is that VET students are often stigmatised, reflecting the wider association between vocational education and poor social outcomes (Neuman and Ziderman, 1999; 2003). For example, VET students often do not take enough credits to matriculate, which stymies their ability to progress onto higher education. This magnifies the cultural stigma associated with VET and makes it difficult for SMEs to attract talented individuals. Despite attempts to challenge the stigma (see Box 3.2), one disadvantage of not having a visible and well-defined VET pathway structure in schools and colleges (e.g. TAFE institutions in Australia, community colleges in the US, Fachschulen in Germany) is that it is difficult for SME employers to trust that VET schools are likely to produce high quality students to meet their needs. Employer engagement is further impeded by the fact that

Box 3.2. **The Zur Lavon Training Centre, Israel**

Founded by the philanthropist, Stef Wertheimer, the Zur Lavon training centre delivers a range of vocational education programmes that aim to offer both Jewish Israelis and Arab Israelis the opportunity to develop key workforce skills. One strand of this training is working in with other stakeholders (the local municipality, the Ministry of Economy, and the Israel Defence Forces) to provide vocational education to upper secondary students in the Negev and the Galilee. This training mixes vocational, academic and soft skill development to build professional skills. Another activity of the center is to train post-secondary students in plastic injection and metal casting. This course last around 10 months (1 430 hours) and leads to a nationally-accredited certificate. In addition, working with the Ministry of the Economy and with the state of Baden-Wurttemberg in Germany, the center also offers a teachers training programme that leads to "the Kammer" which is a nationally recognised qualification for those who wish to be professional instructors. The training lasts eighteen months with the first half being class room based with the second half being a mix of work and study based training.

Source: www.zur.co.il.

there is no common system and framework of qualifications between the various ministries involved in VET in schools.

The Ministry of Economy and Industry also offers manual and non-manual VET to the unemployed or those with low skill levels. These courses typically run for between 3 and 11 months and give practical and theoretical training delivered by external providers. Training vouchers are also available for young unemployed individuals. The two main programmes in this area are "On the Job Training in Industry" (OJT) and "A Class in the Workplace".

The OJT is a scheme where a group of 3-10 new employees participates in a "work-and-study" programme of three months in a company under the responsibility of an in-house instructor. The government pays part of the salary of the new employees (NIS 2 000 per month) and of the instructor (NIS 3 000 per month) on condition that those who complete the programme remain in the company payroll for at least one year. "A Class in the Workplace" is an apprenticeship scheme which gives practical training, backed up by theoretical training in the workplace or in a training institution. Employers are expected to hire or find employment for 65% of those that graduate from the programme. These programmes are usually for unemployed young adults (28-35 year olds) referred by the public employment service, while employers are large companies or larger SMEs who are asked to place the new recruit in the payroll in change of reimbursement of training costs and a wage subsidy.

While survey evidence suggests that some of the programmes (i.e. the voucher scheme) produce good outcomes (MOITAL, 2012), one general limitation consists in the very small number of participants: 7 846 (1.7% of all jobseekers) altogether for the OJT and "A Class in the Workplace" and 1 449 (0.3% of jobseekers) for the voucher programme (figures for 2011). These modest numbers possibly reflect Israel's low spending on active labour market policy, i.e. 0.3% of its GDP, half of the OECD average.

Small-scale sector-specific training is also available in Israel through the Ministry of Tourism (accredited courses in tour guiding), the Ministry of Immigrant Absorption (e.g. targeting Ethiopian immigrants) and the Israeli Defence Forces (IDF), which offer vocational training to a small number of people who are allowed to postpone conscription for two years and then to enter the army in technology-orientated positions.

A significant weakness affecting the ability of Israel's VET school system to supply SMEs with entry workers with intermediate technical skills is that the training provided often lacks close relevance to SME needs. Only around 4% of VET students receive training with employers during their studies (Musset et al., 2014), a much lower proportion than in other OECD countries such as the Netherlands, where about one-third of the study-time of VET students is spent with employers (OECD, 2015b). This leads both to a lack of integration of classroom activities with practice in enterprises and limited opportunities for students to link up with potential employers.

In addition, the design of VET curricula has insufficient input from SMEs. Although organisations such as government ministries, the Israel Defence Forces, Histradut (Israel's trade union federation), the Manufacturing Association and education providers such as AMAT and ORT are all involved in VET design, there is weak formal involvement by SMEs and their trade bodies, and no systematic partnership arrangement to engage industry bodies in the design of VET curricula. To reduce duplication and to ensure a more seamless transition into employment, there is a need for a strategic steering body capable of auditing, mapping and strategically planning VET provision so that it is more responsive to the present and future skill needs of the economy. This will necessitate the rationalisation of the current system where there are large numbers of providers chasing a relatively small number – by international standards – of students. Developing synergies will ease the current fragmentation and make it easier for SME employers to identify and support vocational pathways for their employees.

Formal partnerships with industry bodies are common in other OECD countries such as Switzerland or Germany where employers, ministries and employee representatives work together to determine the national skill strategy and could help to improve the relevance of VET schools to SME skill needs in Israel. An example is the Employer Ownership of Skills pilot programme in the United Kingdom, which asked SMEs to come forward with their own ideas about the training programmes that are needed (see Box 3.3). The risk of a skill mismatch between VET supply and industry demands is exacerbated by the lack of a robust labour market information system in Israel that could help identify skill needs and plan training (ETF, 2014).

Box 3.3. **The Employer Ownership of Skills Pilot, United Kingdom**

Description of the approach

Despite rising funding and uptake of VET in the United Kingdom over the last 10 years, the UK Commission for Employment and Skills (UKCES) – a publicly-funded, industry-led organisation with a mission to provide strategic leadership for UK employment and skills development – identified a need for greater employer ownership of skills if VET were to have a long-term sustainable footing.

UKCES set out five principles for VET design, underlining the importance of greater employer involvement:

1. VET should be employer-owned not government-led.

Box 3.3. **The Employer Ownership of Skills Pilot, United Kingdom** *(cont.)*

2. There should be a single market for skills development. In the UK, as in other OECD countries, there is substantial private sector provision of VET. In parallel, there is a public sector market, which is orientated towards qualification attainment. One downside of these parallel markets is that that many publicly-funded colleges follow state funding incentives rather than business needs.
3. Employer-led partnerships should design skills solutions to ensure that workforce development is relevant and practical.
4. There should be a shift from public grant provision to a system in which employers determine incentives and investments.
5. Public funding should be transparent, simple and less bureaucratic.

To support these principles, UKCES developed the Employment Ownership of Skills (EOS) pilot programme. With GBP 340 million of co-investment funds available over four years, the EOS invited employers, including SMEs, to come forward with innovative employer-led training and recruitment programmes, sensitive to local, regional and sectoral labour market needs.

This was organized through an open call for proposals. The EOS did not define the skills or delivery mechanisms. Instead, it suggested that employers may consider different VET pathways involving delivery of VET to:

- regional industrial clusters;
- large-small firm supply chains;
- partnerships that involve employers currently not investing in skills; or
- networks of SMEs working with local training providers and other stakeholders.

The EOS also asked employers to come forward with new curriculum models and qualifications that would meet future employer needs in their sector or region. By providing an impetus to employer-owned VET, the aim has been to incentivise public sector education colleges to shift away from focusing on government VET targets to become more responsive to business needs.

In the first round of the open competition for EOS co-investment funding, out of 269 bids, 35 employer-led projects won funding. One of these was a consortium bid led by AJ Woods Engineering, an SME that provides shore-based facilities for the construction of wind farms. Concerned with the difficulty of obtaining skilled workers in the locality, AJ Woods successfully bid to EOS to work with other SMEs and further education providers to develop a programme of skills development, shared work experience and support for new entrants to the sector. A bid led by PwC, the professional service practice, was also successful. It involved PwC working with both large and small firms seeking to recruit and upskill professional services (e.g. payroll, project management, legal and tax issues) personnel to manage their access to government funding, provide training or arrange suitable training for them.

Factors for success

This pilot has a number of attractive features that may help contribute to success:

- the funding is contestable, enabling policy-makers to direct funding to the best value and innovative projects;
- employers have the opportunity to shape training to present and expected future labour market needs;

Box 3.3. **The Employer Ownership of Skills Pilot, United Kingdom** *(cont.)*

- the supply of potential training providers may increase due to the ability to work with employers to put forward training bids;
- greater employer contributions may be secured for VET, thereby increasing the potential for sustainable private sector funding and leadership of VET.

Obstacles and responses

The EOS pilot faces a number of challenges. For example, because of public money involved, administrative demands to comply with audit requirements may deter SMEs from applying, either on their own or with other businesses. In addition, for SME employees, the skills and qualifications obtained through the programmes, particularly if they are not portable, may be too specific, thereby inhibiting the willingness of workers to take up the training. Similarly, because employers may be unwilling or unable to fully fund the long-term sustainability of the vocational training, the need for public funding may be on-going. One objective of the second round of the pilot was to address these types of issues.

Relevance for Israel

The EOS pilot shows that there are mechanisms available to shift from government-led to business-owned VET. This type of approach could help Israel to develop vocational training that is more practical and relevant to its SMEs in the future.

Source: UKCES (2011, 2013, 2014).

It is also important to upgrade and support the VET teaching profession. Under both the Ministry of Economy and Education frameworks, VET teachers are required to have practical industry experience before they can teach. However, particularly for Ministry of Education teachers, this requirement is not always followed (MOITAL, 2012). In-service training to upskill teachers is also not mandatory. Alongside a more integrated qualification system for employees, there is a need for a unified system that supports the ongoing professional development of VET teachers. For example, Ireland offers a number of pedagogical qualifications for further education and training teachers and trainers at various levels of the National Framework of Qualifications. Furthermore, a professional development strategy is currently under development which is aimed at all practitioners in the further education and training sector. The implementation of this strategy will provide a unified system for the ongoing pedagogical, subject matter and employer liaison development of further education and training personnel.

Measures that could help address the issue of the relevance of VET school training to SMEs therefore include increasing the share of credit-generating and quality-controlled work-based learning (including apprenticeships, work placements and internships) in SMEs as part of the VET school studies, introducing formal partnership programmes to involve SMEs in the design of VET school curricula, developing a better labour market information system to better identify industry skill needs, and introducing certification of training standards in VET schools.

A further approach to improving the supply of "middle skills" to Israeli SMEs through the formal education system could involve the development of "associate degree" qualifications through VET schools. Associate degrees are typically two-year programmes offered by tertiary education institutions which offer a more practical and applied curriculum. The two years of coursework can often be taken by students either on a full-time or part-time basis, for example students could take the associate degree over four years attending courses for half a day a week during that period. Associate degrees provide a higher level of education than secondary school diplomas but lower than bachelor's degree programmes. This type of qualification has become common in some other OECD countries. For example, in the United States, 10% of workers have an associate degree, which usually implies two years of full-time coursework (Carnevale et al., 2012). Other countries have also expanded associate degree provision such as Japan (the *Jun-gakushi*) and France (the *Brevet de technicien supérieur/Diplôme universitaire de technologie*) (Varghese and Püttmann, 2011).

Entrepreneurial culture and skills

The formal education system can play a significant role in strengthening enterprise culture and increasing people's abilities to exploit business opportunities. However, in Israel only 13% of adults in 2012 reported that their school education promoted entrepreneurial attitudes, in contrast to 22% in the EU27 and even higher figures in countries such as Brazil (57%), Norway (41%) and the United States (27%). Israelis were also less likely to report that their education helped them to understand the role of entrepreneurs in society (13% compared with 20% in the EU27) or equipped them with the skills needed to run a business (12% compared with 18% in the EU27) (European Commission, 2012). Furthermore, only 28% of 18-34 year old Israelis reported that they have the skills and knowledge required to set up a business, compared with 40% in the EU (GEM/YBI, 2013).

Some of Israel's eight universities and more than 70 government and non-government funded colleges have entrepreneurship education initiatives. In particular, the Technion, the Hebrew University of Jerusalem, Tel Aviv University, and the University of Haifa all have dedicated entrepreneurship centres offering courses and modules on entrepreneurship for students from across the institution (see Box 3.4). Others offer various undergraduate and postgraduate modules to certain parts of the student population. For example, the Shamoon College of Engineering runs the Engineer-Entrepreneur programme, which provides engineering undergraduates with an interest in starting businesses with dedicated entrepreneurship teaching modules and business coaching and encourages them to mentor the entrepreneurial aspirations of secondary-level students (Yemini and Haddad, 2010). However, entrepreneurship in Higher Education Institutions (HEIs) is usually taught as an elective rather than a compulsory module, is often only available to postgraduate business school students, and tends to focus mainly on technology-orientated businesses (Almor and Heilbrunn, 2014).

There are also examples of good practice in entrepreneurship education at the primary (see Box 3.5) and secondary education levels in Israel, such as the Network for Teaching Entrepreneurship. Junior Achievement Young Enterprise Europe (JA-YE Europe) is also active in Israel through the Young Entrepreneurs Israel association. The JA-YE Europe Company Programme supports teams of 15-18 year old students to form mini-corporations under the guidance of an education advisor for schools and youth centres and a volunteer business mentor. It also offers an access course to the Company Programme through a 6-hour teaching programme for 14-15 year olds. However, the JA-YE Europe programmes available and the numbers of participants in Israel are more limited than in many other countries, although they have grown significantly since 2013 (JA-Worldwide, 2014).

Despite these examples of good practice in entrepreneurship education in Israel, its patchy nature is a concern, when considering the limited numbers of institutions offering programmes and the limited numbers of students able to access them. A national entrepreneurship education strategy in Israel would help to expand these actions and give them better foundations in terms of funding, inclusion in the curriculum, and teaching training and support.

Box 3.4. **The Bronica Entrepreneurship Centre at Technion, Israel**

The Bronica Entrepreneurship Centre is the central point of contact for entrepreneurship at Technion University. It offers a wide range of support both for its own students and those from other HEIs. For its own students, the Centre offers an undergraduate minor in entrepreneurship, a range of entrepreneurship modules, a dedicated MBA in entrepreneurship, a summer school programme, and mentoring, consultancy and alumni support for its present and former students. It has also set up the *Dream Factory*; an idea-generation scheme that encourages student teams to find novel and innovative solutions to real-world business problems submitted by companies.

The Centre is also responsible for implementing the national BizTEC Entrepreneurship Challenge start-up competition. This has been running since 2004, and is open to all Israeli HEI students. Out of the hundreds of applications that the competition attracts every year, up to 30 teams are selected to attend a dedicated workshop programme supported by faculty and outside professionals. The next stage sees up to 8 of these teams going forward to the business accelerator stage where they receive more intensive assistance from faculty, outside professionals and a dedicated mentor from a relevant field. Five of the teams can win financial assistance and the opportunity to represent Israel in the international Intel Challenge Europe competition.

The Centre offers lessons for other HEIs seeking to develop entrepreneurship education. The 'one-stop shop' service provided by the Centre makes it easier for students at the Technion to find out about entrepreneurial support. In addition, the BizTEC competition offers a means to support students in entrepreneurial ventures through an integrated package of workshops, one-to-one mentoring advice and financial support.

Source: yazamut.technion.ac.il.

Box 3.5. **The Misgave Elementary School, Israel**

Misgave Elementary School provides an example of how entrepreneurship skills can be embedded within the conventional primary school curriculum. Led by the school management team, the school initially piloted the viability of embedding entrepreneurship teaching. Having demonstrated the potential, the Ministry of Education committed extra resources and a mentor to work with the school. All teachers were also offered the opportunity to participate in workshops to build their understanding of the ways in which entrepreneurship could be taught. The school also worked with the local municipality, parents and representatives from industry to establish its entrepreneurship teaching.

Within the school's "entrepreneurial centres", students participated in a weekly two-hour entrepreneurship course embedded within subjects such as mathematics, science, English, ecology, the arts, and community involvement. Students were also asked to use creative techniques, work in teams and follow their ideas through into their implementation. Grade 5 and 6 students had the opportunity to mentor younger students in the entrepreneurial centres while Grade 2 pupils had a weekly creativity lesson. At the end of the school year, products developed by the students (e.g. a bracelet to avoid harassment between students, herbal ice-cream, user-friendly refuse disposal) were presented and sold at a school fair.

Source: Heilbrunn, S. (2010), "Advancing entrepreneurship in an elementary school: A case study", *International Education Studies*, 3(2), page 174.

Some OECD countries have introduced dedicated national strategies for entrepreneurship education that could act as models for Israel, such as Belgium, Denmark, Estonia, Finland, Norway, Spain and Sweden, while several others explicitly set out entrepreneurship education actions as part of broader education policy documents or economic and employment policy documents (European Commission/EACEA/Eurydice, 2016; European Commission, 2014). Typically, these strategies set out definitions of entrepreneurship education, the entrepreneurship education and practical entrepreneurship experiences to be delivered in the curriculum, the teaching and support methods to be used, the arrangements for training entrepreneurship teachers, and the arrangements promoting school networking and sharing of good practice. The strategy may also set out the funding arrangements to be used. As an example, the Nordic countries have espoused an "enterprise for all students" vision that sets objectives and targets for increasing the proportions of students graduating with a practical understanding of entrepreneurship (Box 3.6).

Box 3.6. From ABC to Ph.D. – The Nordic approach to entrepreneurship education

Description of the approach

Having an integrated and holistic approach to entrepreneurship education is crucial for enhancing entrepreneurial culture and skills. Nordic countries (Finland, Sweden, Denmark and Norway) have developed such an approach which rests on three pillars:

- Long-term and cross-ministerial co-operation. Each of the four Nordic countries have developed national strategies for supporting entrepreneurship education in schools, colleges and universities: *Strategy for Education and Training in Entrepreneurship* (Denmark), *Entrepreneurship in Education and Training* (Norway), *Strategy for Entrepreneurship* (Sweden), *Guidelines for Entrepreneurship Education* (Finland). Close collaboration between employers, education providers and economic development agencies has been an essential part of the development of these strategies. In Finland, for example, 18 key stakeholders were involved in developing the strategy, such as ministries, business support providers, unions, enterprise agencies and universities.
- Developing an integrated entrepreneurship education pathway. Nordic countries have worked extensively with the suite of core programmes offered by the NGO Junior Achievement-Young Enterprise, which seek to build economic awareness in primary pupils ('our community'); financial literacy ('economics for success') and understanding of entrepreneurship ('it's my business') in lower-secondary school pupils; experimentation with starting and running a business ('company programme') in upper-secondary school students; and starting a business ('start up programme') in post-secondary school students. These have been adapted to meet the specific needs of particular Nordic countries. For example, Denmark now has a suite of four main programmes. 'Project Edison' encourages sixth and seventh grade students to develop a new product that they will showcase at a local school fair. If their idea proves successful, they go on to compete at a national fair. The aim of the project is to develop their creativity and innovation abilities. Danish eighth to tenth grade pupils can progress from this to the 'Next Level' programme, where they are asked to work on a self-set or teacher-set problem, identify a potential solution and test out its economic, social or environmental value. At older ages, students can participate in the JA-YE company and start up programmes.
- Supporting entrepreneurial teaching. There is now an increased understanding that perhaps the most effective forms of entrepreneurial teaching require teachers to act more as facilitators than lecturers (European Commission, 2008). To achieve a shift in pedagogic practices, Nordic countries have increasingly developed supportive learning materials. One such example is *Framtids Frön* (*Future Seeds*), which offers Swedish primary and secondary school teachers resources and support to develop creativity, curiosity,

Box 3.6. **From ABC to Ph.D. – The Nordic approach to entrepreneurship education** *(cont.)*

problem solving and entrepreneurial skills. Nordic countries have also found that partnering SMEs with educational institutions is critical in increasing the relevance and applicability of entrepreneurship education. Involving SMEs is more likely to ensure that the learning is practice-based and gives students the opportunity to understand the challenges faced in running and working in a small firm. Support for teacher training in entrepreneurship has also been boosted. For example, as part of its action plan, Norway expanded its funding of teacher training and university courses in entrepreneurship education and has sought to extend the engagement of education providers with the private sector.

Success Factors

One key success factor underlying the development of entrepreneurship education in Nordic countries has been the adoption of a long-term strategy, backed up by periodic action plans. While incentivising educators, firms and students to become more involved in entrepreneurship education, Nordic countries have also sought to adopt a flexible 'bottom-up' approach that tailors entrepreneurship education to meet the needs of individual countries and regions.

Alongside this, there has been a commitment to monitoring and evaluating programmes. For example Young Enterprise Denmark (2012) embarked on a longitudinal evaluation of its programmes, which showed that young secondary students on its programmes were more likely to be favourably orientated towards entrepreneurship.

Long-term cultural change has also been achieved in some cases. For example, the number of Finns who believe that their school education equips them with the skills to be an entrepreneur increased from 44% in 2009, when the national entrepreneurship education strategy was introduced, to 55% in 2012 (European Commission, 2012).

Obstacles and responses

Despite the commitment to entrepreneurship education from ABC to PhD, Nordic countries still have to negotiate a number of barriers. One issue is embedding entrepreneurship education as a cross-curricula transversal subject. There is also the perennial issue of extending business engagement and ensuring that initial and continuing teacher education supports entrepreneurial education. There is also a need for the traditional education system to better accredit the experiential learning gained from entrepreneurial education. One way of potentially achieving this is the further development of the "entrepreneurial skills pass" (*http://entrepreneurialskillspass.eu/*). This is an EU initiative that combines practical experiential learning with an on-line exam, providing students with a valuable complementary qualification to traditional academic qualifications.

Relevance for Israel

Israel has no long term national strategic or action plan to support entrepreneurship education. Whilst Israelis may feel that entrepreneurship is desirable, many of them believe that they lack the necessary skills to create and run a business. There is a need for clear incentives for teachers, employers and entrepreneurs to become stakeholders in developing student entrepreneurial competencies. The Nordic experience shows how to develop a strategy in a way that involves the relevant stakeholders, to introduce appropriate practical entrepreneurial experiences and to support teachers in entrepreneurship teaching. It also shows that it is possible to rapidly reduce the gap between entrepreneurial aspirations and skill attainments.

In Israel, a national entrepreneurship education strategy could be designed, co-ordinated and supported by a national steering committee on entrepreneurship education, which could include representatives from the relevant ministries (e.g. the Ministry of Education and the Ministry of Economy and Industry), stakeholders (e.g. the teaching profession, business support organisations, NGOs and other delivery partners) and entrepreneurs' organisations.

In parallel, the Israeli government could introduce an online web portal offering guidelines, information and teaching resources for entrepreneurship education. This portal could link to the online OECD-European Commission HEInnovate guiding framework for HEIs and Entrepreneurship360 guidance for entrepreneurship in schools and vocational education and training institutions. The former contains a detailed step-by-step approach alongside model action plans to help tertiary education institutions foster entrepreneurial mindsets and entrepreneurship. Policy can support these endeavours by offering specific awards and incentives to support the development of entrepreneurship education and work with student entrepreneurship clubs and societies across university campuses. Moreover, whilst there are examples of Israeli higher education institutions offering strong technology orientated entrepreneurship education and skills development, there is a need to broaden cross campus collaboration and involve other entrepreneurship facing disciplines (e.g. design, creative professions) as this closer collaboration is more likely to promote learning and innovation (Harrington and Douglas, 2005).

The government could also boost arrangements for initial and continuing teacher training in entrepreneurship. For example, in France prospective and qualified entrepreneurship teachers have the opportunity to participate in company internships, allowing for closer collaboration between schools and enterprises, while in Flanders (Belgium), the regional development agency has developed a website for teachers with lesson plans to develop entrepreneurial competencies (*www.competento.be*).

There is also a need to actively involve entrepreneurs in drafting entrepreneurship education guidelines and curricula and in providing education and practical training. One way of achieving this is to have an entrepreneur-in-residence in schools. This is prevalent in many universities internationally. For example, the Berkeley Center for Entrepreneurship & Innovation at New York University has an entrepreneurship-in-residence programme to support and develop the business ideas of students and staff. This could be adapted to schools and colleges, working alongside activities such as company visits, guest talks by entrepreneurs, enterprise days and weeks and case studies of role models. To support SME-school linkages, a brokerage service could be offered, similar to that organised by the Ministry of Finance and Economics of Baden-Württemberg and the chamber of commerce. This initiative partners schools with local SMEs, resulting in 95% of general education secondary schools developing links with firms.

The innovation system

Israel has a well-developed innovation system, which receives public support in various ways. The government makes significant investments in human capital infrastructure; contributes substantial funds for research; offers tax incentives to encourage multinational corporations to establish R&D activities in Israel (e.g. Intel, Hewlett Packard, Microsoft, Google, etc.); has supported the establishment of a major venture capital industry targeting high-technology start-ups; and runs a range of government programmes in support of technological innovation (Frenkel and Maital, 2012; OECD, 2012). Additional contributing factors have been the government's liberal immigration policy able to integrate thousands of Jewish immigrants into the economy and capitalise on their scientific and technical expertise as well as the military support for R&D investment which has stimulated private-sector company spin-offs in cyber-security, electronics, computers, software, communications, imaging, and process control (Frenkel and Maital, 2011).

This impression of a healthy innovation system is backed up by Israel's strong performance on most of the main indicators of the innovation system compared with other OECD countries. The number of researchers in relation to total employment is the highest among OECD countries, 17.5% compared to an OECD simple average of 8.5% (Figure 3.9). Gross domestic expenditure on R&D (GERD) amounts to 3.9% of GDP, which is the second-highest value in the OECD area only behind Korea. Business enterprises undertake 83% of total R&D spending (Figure 53), the highest value among OECD countries. Private sector firms are also active supporters of university R&D; 6.8% of higher education R&D is financed by industry, compared to 5.8% for the overall OECD area. This strong business involvement in R&D is very significant for Israel's innovation capacity, given the proximity of business R&D to commercialisation opportunities compared with government and higher education R&D spending.[6]

Figure 3.9. **R&D personnel across OECD countries, 2013**

Per thousand people employed

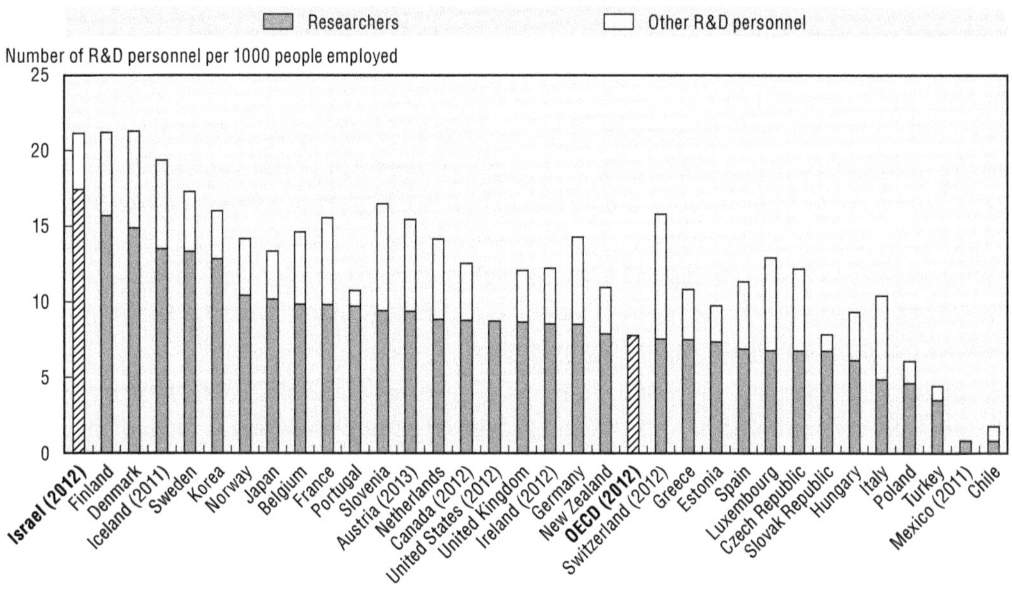

Source: OECD based on OECD (2015c), *OECD Science, Technology and Industry Scoreboard*, OECD Publishing, Paris.

StatLink http://dx.doi.org/10.1787/888933421734

The internationalisation of the Israeli R&D system is also very well developed, which can be expected to contribute to the quality of innovation through global knowledge flows. As indicated in Figure 3.10, 54% of business R&D is funded directly from abroad and 65% is undertaken by domestic companies affiliated to multinational enterprises. These are both very high values in the OECD context, and reflect the importance of foreign-backed R&D centres in ICT-related sectors in Israel.

On the other hand BERD is relatively narrowly based in terms of its sectors and origins. The share of BERD undertaken by firms in the services industry is 70% in Israel, which exceeds any other OECD country (Figure 3.11). One-half of this R&D is carried out in dedicated R&D centres, which are mostly affiliated to foreign multinational enterprises

R&D expenditure by performing sector, 2013

Percentage of gross domestic expenditures on GDP

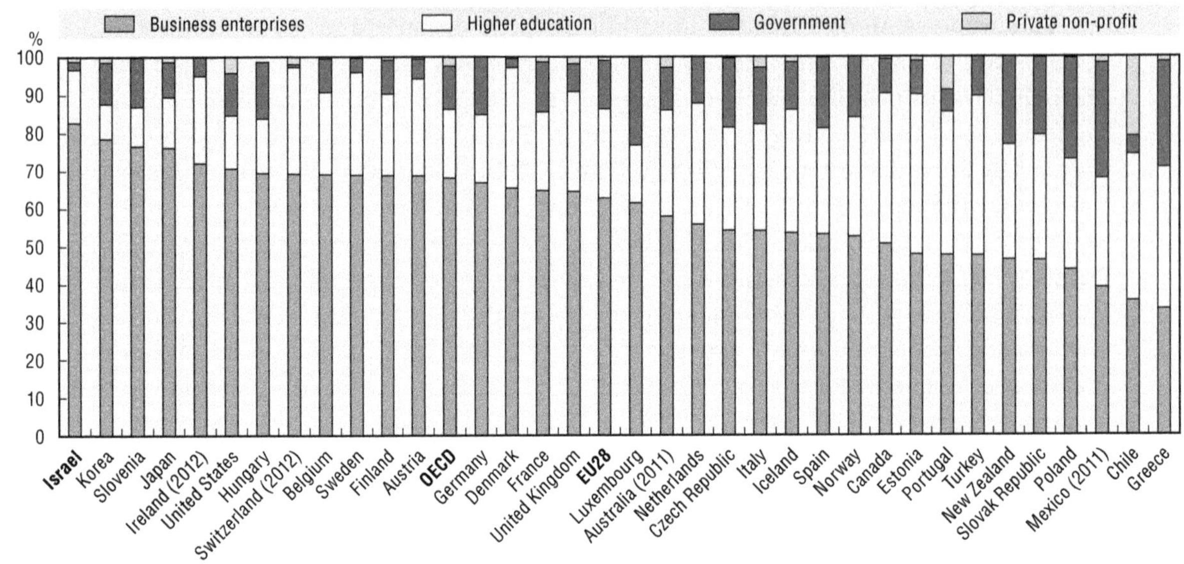

Note: This Figure appears as Figure 1.9 in this report.

Source: OECD based on OECD (2015c), *OECD Science, Technology and Industry Scoreboard*, OECD Publishing, Paris.

and mostly found in ICT. This sector alone accounts for 48% of Israel's BERD and 1.7% of Israel's GDP (OECD, 2015c). Clearly, the share of manufacturing R&D is correspondingly low (27%), which is not necessarily a concern given the high rate of services R&D and its potential to impact on manufacturing. However, Figure 3.12 shows that business R&D in manufacturing is heavily weighted towards high and medium-high R&D-intensity sectors (90%), highlighting the challenge of broadening technological innovation activities towards low technology manufacturing sectors in Israel.

Israel's innovation performance in terms of revealed technological advantage (RTA) is also strongly concentrated by sector, as measured by patents in different technology fields. This shows that Israel enjoys a world technological leadership in computer technology and has strong specialisations in other ICT-related domains such as telecommunications and basic communications (Figure 3.13). The ICT specialisation of Israel's technological innovation has declined, as ICT-related patents have fallen from 53% to 39% of the national total during the 2010s (OECD, 2013c). At the same time, the RTA has grown in medical technologies and biotechnologies, which also have multiple potential industry applications and hold the promise of fuelling further growth. Notwithstanding the emergence of these two new sectoral innovation advantages, the strong concentration of RTA raises the question of how to diversify the innovation success of Israel's ICT to other sectors.

The Israeli government provides generous support to business R&D. The volume of direct government funding of business R&D as a share of GDP is one of the largest of OECD countries (Figure 3.14), alongside which there are also generous tax breaks to R&D-active firms. However, the support is currently strongly weighted to R&D-intensive firms, particularly in ICT and biotechnologies. Non-high-technology industries conduct only 10% of industrial R&D, compared with one-quarter in other developed nations (Bank of Israel, 2014).

Indeed, as shown in Figure 3.15, only 13.5% of Israeli SMEs with innovation activity declare having received public support, far below the OECD average of 29%. Some degree of

Figure 3.10. **The internationalisation of Israel's R&D, 2011 and 2013**

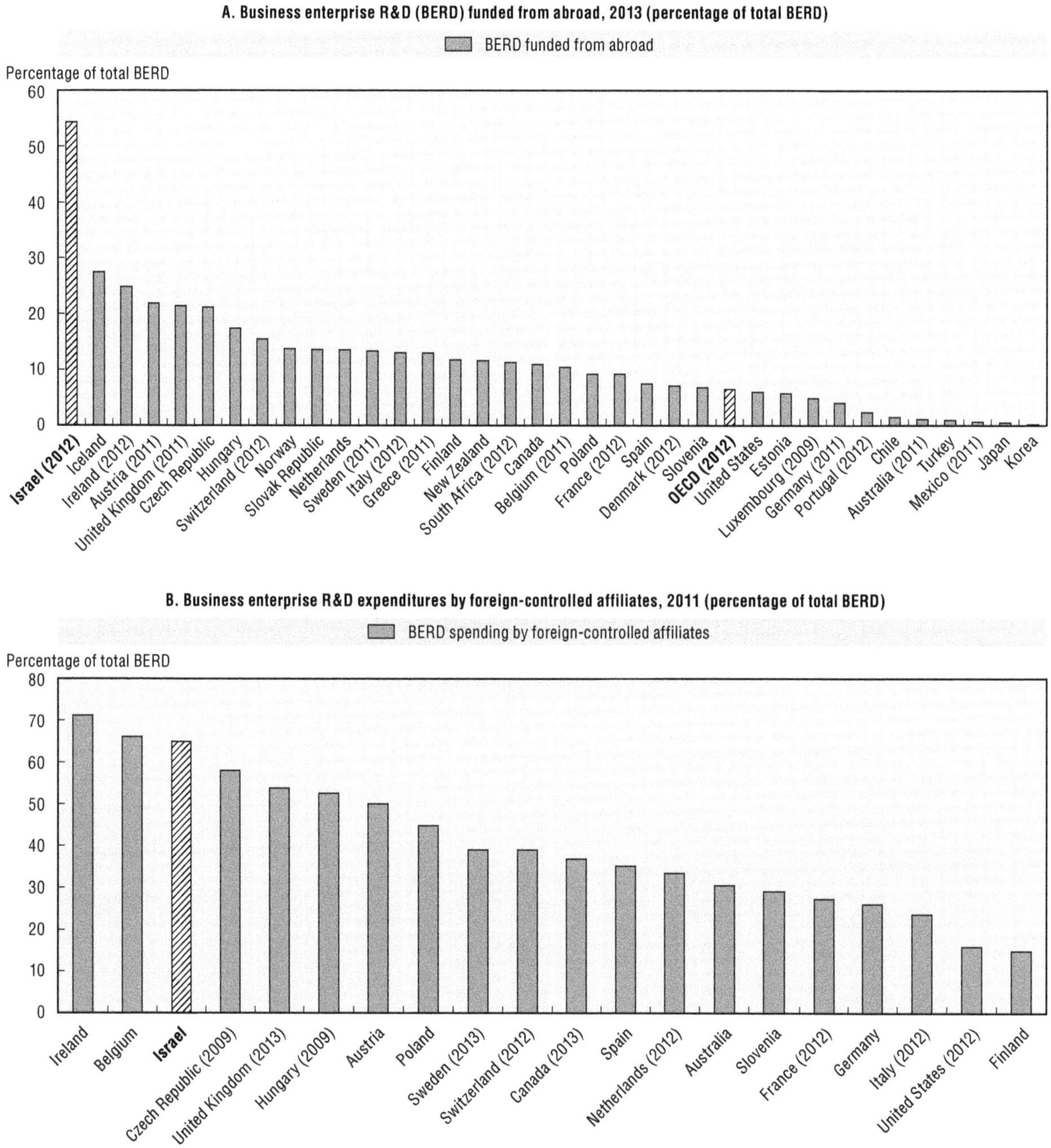

Source: OECD based on OECD (2015c), *OECD Science, Technology and Industry Scoreboard 2015*, OECD Publishing, Paris.

StatLink http://dx.doi.org/10.1787/888933421743

concentration in government support is justified to reward excellence in innovation, especially when public resources are scarce. Spreading innovation support to more small enterprises would help to narrow the wide productivity gaps that exist between sectors and business size classes, both broadening the drivers of economic growth and helping respond to high levels of inequality in Israel. This conclusion was also reached by a government committee established in 2007 to "Examine Means to Strengthen Peripheral Areas and Low Technology Industries" (i.e. the Makov Committee). This Committee recommended greater

Figure 3.11. **Share of business R&D by sector, 2013 or latest available year**

Percentage of total business enterprise R&D (BERD)

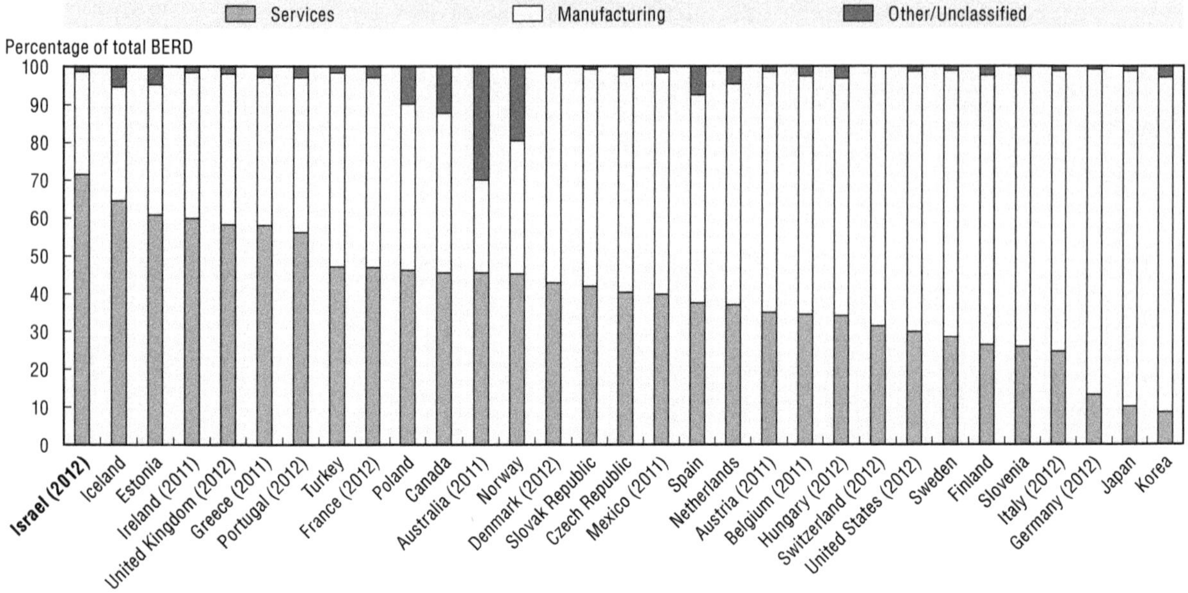

Source: OECD based on OECD (2015c), *OECD Science, Technology and Industry Scoreboard 2015*, OECD Publishing, Paris.

StatLink http://dx.doi.org/10.1787/888933421753

Figure 3.12. **Business R&D in manufacturing by R&D intensive or non-intensive sectors, 2013 or latest available year**

Percentage of total business enterprise R&D (BERD) in manufacturing

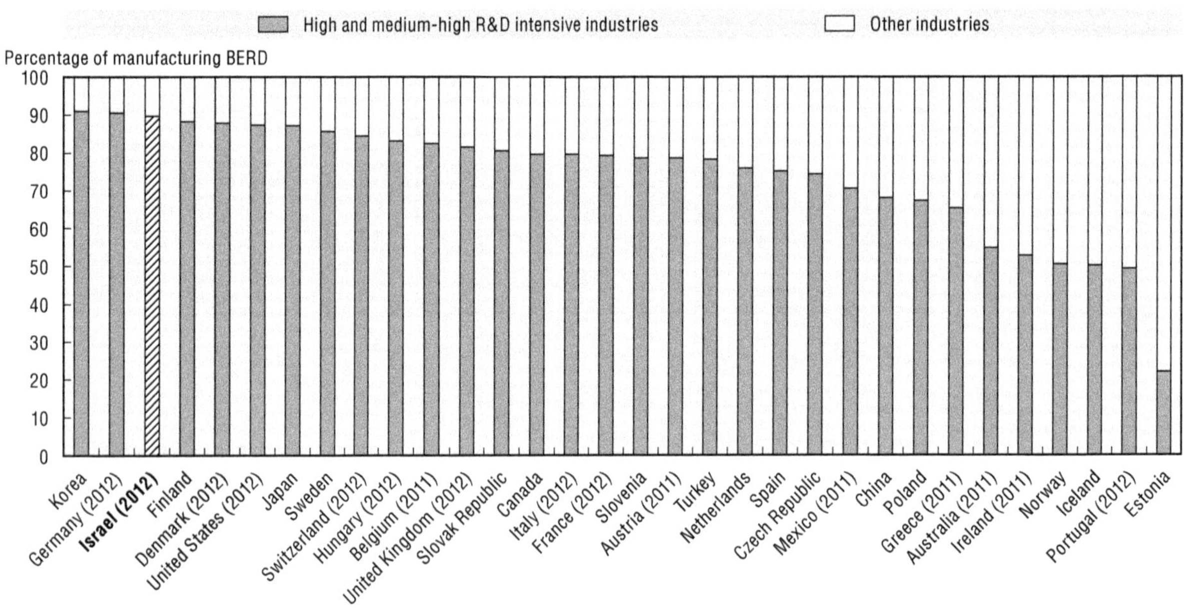

Note: High and medium-high R&D intensive manufacturing includes "chemicals and pharmaceutical products" (ISIC Rev.4 Divisions 20 and 21) and "computer, electronic and optical products, electrical equipment, machinery, motor vehicles and other transport equipment" (ISIC Rev.4 Divisions 26 to 30).

Source: OECD based on OECD (2015c), *OECD Science, Technology and Industry Scoreboard 2015*, OECD Publishing, Paris.

StatLink http://dx.doi.org/10.1787/888933421765

Figure 3.13. **The Revealed Technological Advantage of Israel, 2010-13**

Index by technology field, based on patent applications filed under the Patent Cooperation Treaty

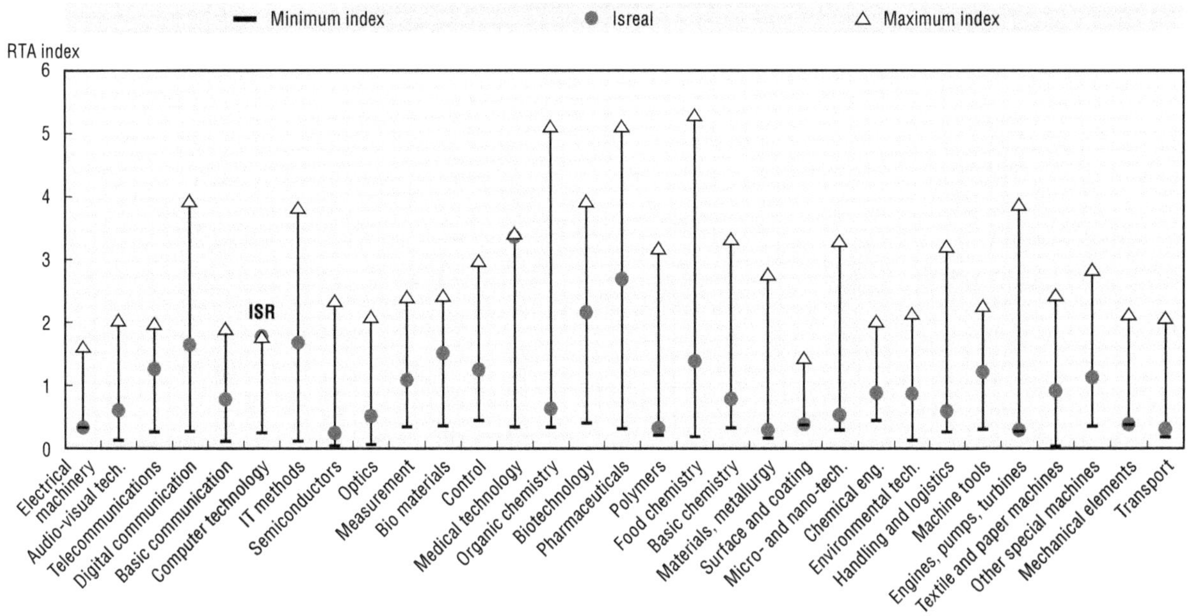

Note: The Revealed Technological Advantage (RTA) index is defined as the share of an economy's patents in a particular technology field relative to the share of total patents in that economy. The index is equal to zero when the economy has no patents in a given field; is equal to 1 when the economy's share in the sector equals its share in all fields (no specialisation); and above 1 when a positive specialisation is observed.

Source: OECD (2013c), *OECD Science, Technology and Industry Scoreboard*, OECD Publishing, Paris

StatLink http://dx.doi.org/10.1787/888933421776

Figure 3.14. **Direct government funding for business R&D, 2013**

Percentage of GDP

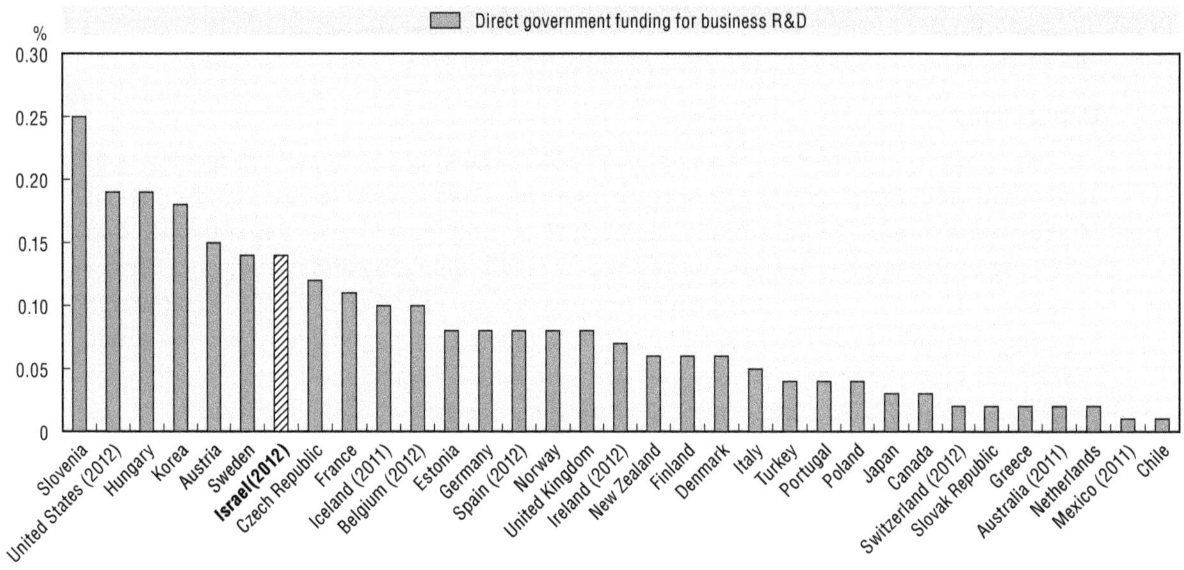

Note: Direct government funding includes grants, loans and payment for R&D contracts for procurement. Tax incentives for business enterprise R&D include allowances and credits, as well as other forms of advantageous tax treatment for business R&D expenditure.

Source: OECD based on OECD (2015c), *OECD Science, Technology and Industry Scoreboard 2015*, OECD Publishing, Paris.

StatLink http://dx.doi.org/10.1787/888933421781

Figure 3.15. **Firms receiving public support for innovation across OECD countries, by firm size, 2010-12**

Percentage of product and/or process-innovating firms

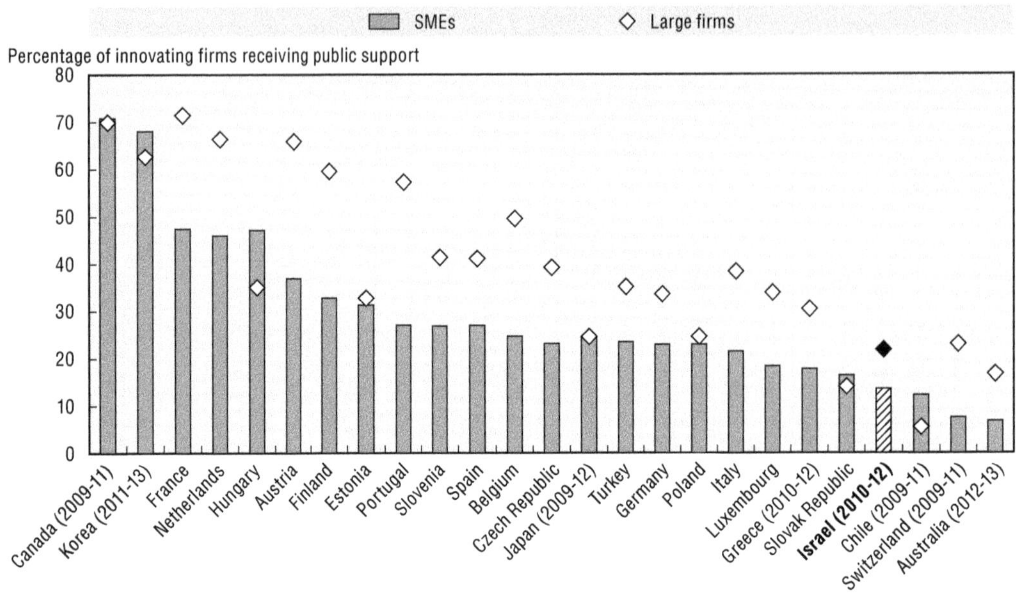

Note: International comparability may be limited due to differences in innovation survey methodologies and country-specific response patterns. Only enterprises with 10 or more employees are covered.

Source: OECD (2015c), *OECD Science, Technology and Industry Scoreboard 2015*, OECD Publishing, Paris.

StatLink http://dx.doi.org/10.1787/888933421799

investment in R&D in traditional industries to close the gap between better and poorer performing regions and industries and suggested that a combination of R&D subsidies and increased supply of engineers would lead to higher levels of R&D investment and productivity in traditional industries (Bank of Israel, 2014).

Access to finance

Debt finance

The G20/OECD High-Level Principles on SME Financing (2015) call for measures to strengthen SME access to traditional bank financing. This is very relevant in the case of Israel, where one of the important constraints on SME development is difficulties in accessing bank credit. Israeli SME owners report credit, financing and cash flow problems to present the most significant barriers to the development of their businesses (Adalya Economic Consulting, 2011). Approximately 30% report that they cannot raise the funds needed for their everyday activities and over one-half are unable to attract financing to develop or expand their operations. For more than one-half of SMEs that do succeed in raising most of the funds needed for daily operations, amounts are insufficient for development and expansion. The problems are exacerbated for new businesses, which find it nearly impossible to receive bank credit.[7]

The perceptions of SME managers are paralleled in the data on credit volumes. In relation to national GDP Israel's SME credit was 41% in 2014, which is lower than in countries such as Italy and France where business ownership is widespread, but higher than in countries such as the United States, Canada and the United Kingdom where companies tend to rely less on bank credit to finance cash-flow requirements (Figure 3.16).[8]

Figure 3.16. **Volume of outstanding (stock) business loans, Israel and selected G7 economies, 2014**

Percentage of GDP (output approach)

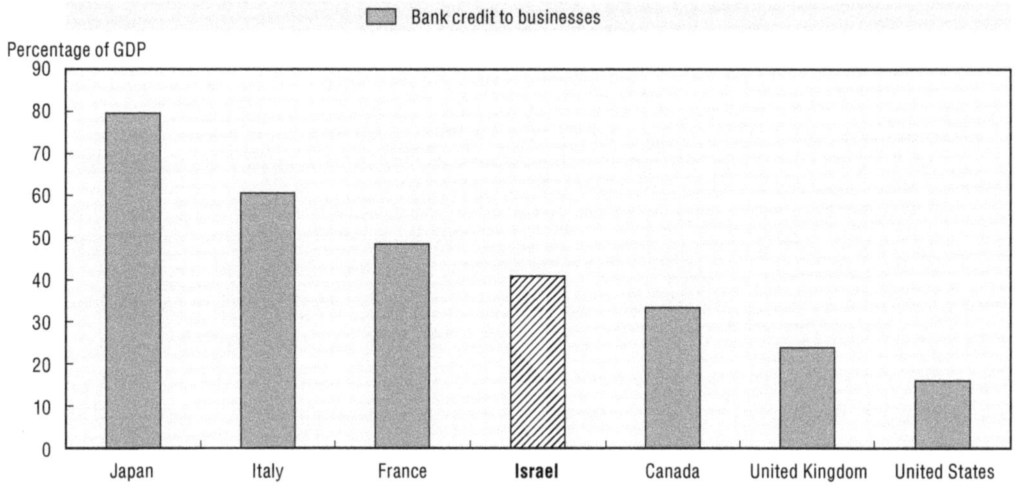

Note: The output approach (current prices) has been used for GDP data. Data on outstanding stock of bank loans in Germany are not available.

Source: OECD based on OECD Economic Outlook Database and OECD (2016), *Financing SMEs and Entrepreneurs 2016: An OECD Scoreboard, OECD Publishing*, Paris.

StatLink http://dx.doi.org/10.1787/888933421801

Furthermore, bank deposits of small firms are larger than the credit they receive, while credit for medium-sized firms is 30% greater than their deposits and credit for large firms is 65% greater than their deposits (OECD, 2014).

The terms of bank credit for SMEs are also relatively unfavourable. The interest rate spread between SMEs and large firms is quite large, standing at 1.44% in 2014 (OECD, 2016). Furthermore, although Israel's Central Bank does not collect data on loan maturity, it appears that small business credit is also often of short duration, which makes it difficult to use bank lending for long-term capital investment.

The situation has nonetheless been improving for SMEs, at least in terms of credit volumes (Table 3.3). The volume of SME loans increased by 3.4% per year in Israel during the period 2007-2014, compared to an average annual inflation rate over the same period of 2%. There has, therefore, been a real increase in SME lending. This has been associated with a rise in the proportion of SME lending out of total business lending from 41% in 2007 to 47% in 2014. The expansion in SME lending has occurred without harming the solidity of the banking sector, which has a capital adequacy ratio of 14%, two percentage points above the target set by the Bank of Israel following the implementation of the Basel II Agreement on banking laws and regulations. Furthermore, the contribution of small business lending to the total net profits of commercial banks has been growing in parallel to increased credit provision to this business segment (Bank of Israel, 2012).

The continuing difficulties in accessing finance for SMEs in Israel take place against the backdrop of a concentration of the banking system, which reduces the incentives of banks to seek out SME borrowers and to increase their choice of financial products. The two largest commercial banks (Bank Leumi and Bank Hapoalim) issue 60% of total bank credit in Israel and the five major banks together provide 95% of total bank credit in the country. Moreover, most banks are part of wider company groups where financial activities

Table 3.3. **Outstanding business loans in Israel, 2007-14**
New Israeli Sheqel (NIS) billions

	2007	2008	2009	2010	2011	2012	2013	2014
SMEs	169.3	171.2	161.6	173.8	177.7	187.0	186.7	211.9
All businesses	413.9	460.9	425.2	438.9	458.6	450.4	445.7	447.9

Note: The definition of SME lending is not related to the size of the firm which receives the credit but to the amount of bank lending. Each of the five major banks of Israel uses slightly different definitions, but small business lending is always up to between NIS 6 and 10 million, medium business lending between up to NIS 40 and 100 million, and large business lending from between above NIS 40 and 100 million.
Source: OECD (2016), *Financing SMEs and Entrepreneurs 2016: An OECD Scoreboard*, OECD Publishing, Paris.
StatLink http://dx.doi.org/10.1787/888933421872

co-exist with non-financial activities, creating opportunities for distortion in the allocation of resources and systemic risk in the case of weaknesses in other branches of the group (OECD, 2011b). Competition is held back by restrictive regulations such as on procedures to change banks, establishment of new bank and non-bank financial institutions, and sharing of credit information on customers.

As pointed out in the G20/OECD High-Level Principles on SME Financing, the absence of positive credit information is often a compounding problem, calling for improved transparency in SME finance markets. There is room for improvement in this area in Israel. The Israel Credit Data Services Law (5762-2002) rules that positive credit information on individuals can only be disclosed subject to their approval, unlike for example the United States, where positive credit information can be revealed as long as an individual does not expressly opt out. This means that only negative credit information is disseminated in Israel, which reduces the chances for SMEs with good credit history to obtain bank credit.

To address competition issues in the banking sector, the Israeli government and the Bank of Israel established in 2011 an inter-ministerial "Committee to Increase the Competitiveness of the Banking Sector", chaired by the Supervisor of the Banking Sector at the Bank of Israel and including representatives of the Ministry of Finance, Ministry of Justice, Antitrust Authority and National Economic Council. This Committee formulated a number of recommendations, some of which have already been implemented. In particular, the administrative procedures for customers to change bank have become slimmer, banking fees have been trimmed, information asymmetries have been curtailed through client reports which banks prepare for their customers showing their full assets and liabilities, and the legal framework for credit unions and online banking has been set up.

On the other hand, other recommendations are still on hold. For example, the Committee advised that institutional players such as insurance companies and pension funds be more involved in household credit and small businesses credit through closer cooperation with lending institutions; non-banking financial institutions (NBFIs) be subject to the same interest-rate ceiling as banks, on the assumption that the existing lower ceiling for NBFIs has prevented their correct pricing of credit risk; and that lending institutions deal with small businesses with turnover up to NIS 5 million as retail customers rather than as business customers, resulting in lower banking fees. Implementation of these recommendations should contribute to improving SME access to finance. In addition, the entry of additional large operators is probably needed in order to create significant competitive pressure on the main incumbents. In this respect, some efforts have been made to attract foreign banks into the Israeli market, but so far with limited success.

Equity finance

The G20/OECD High-Level Principles on SME financing also call for actions to enable SMEs to diversify their financing. Equity investment is one of the key financing instruments cited by the Principles alongside traditional debt, standing alongside asset-based finance, alternative debt, and hybrid instruments (see also OECD, 2015d). In relation to GDP, Israel has the largest venture capital market in the OECD area (Figure 1.10 reproduced below). Furthermore, unlike most other OECD countries, and notably the United States, Israel's venture capital industry is very much focused on seed, start-up and early-stage investments. By 2013, there were 70 venture capital funds in Israel, with a substantial stock of investment in the country's high-technology sector. Of these there were 8 recently-established "micro venture capital funds" managing almost USD 124 million. These are funds with less than USD 30 million, which generally invest small amounts and focus on early stage companies. Venture capital is therefore a major and dynamic component of the high-technology entrepreneurship success story of Israel.

Top ten OECD countries for venture capital investments, 2014

Percentage of GDP

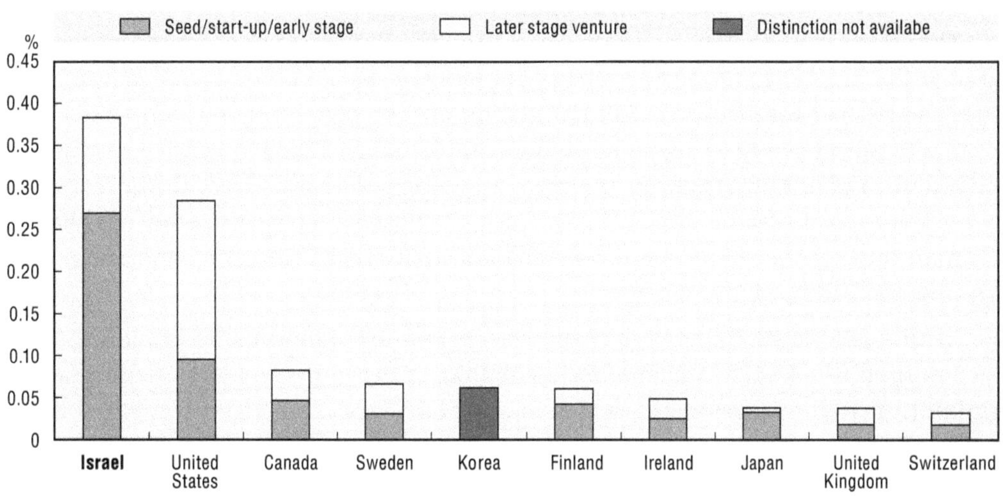

Note: This Figure appears as Figure 1.10 in this report.
Source: OECD (2015e), *Entrepreneurship at a Glance 2015*, OECD Publishing, Paris.

The development of Israel's venture capital industry dates back to the mid-1990s when lifting of government restrictions on access to foreign capital led many high-technology SMEs to issue private equity abroad. The government also intervened proactively through the establishment of Israel's first venture capital fund, YOZMA. In addition, the government offers tax incentives for venture capital investors. Foreign investors, in particular, receive tax breaks for investments in Israel-based venture capital funds or direct investments in research-intensive Israeli companies.

There are nevertheless some concerns for Israel's domestic venture capital industry, since domestic investment is a relatively small and declining share of total venture capital investments. Of the 70 venture capital funds in Israel, fifteen are branches of international funds while the remaining fifty-five are local funds which only work in Israel. A large share of venture capital investments in Israel are from non-domestic sources; two-thirds of total venture capital investments came from international funds during 2007-12, while only one-third came from domestic funds (Table 3.4). Potential regulatory barriers to the participation of domestic institutional investors in venture capital deals should be investigated in an attempt to increase the flow of funds to domestic venture capital companies.

Table 3.4. **Venture capital investments in Israel, by origins of the fund, 2007-12**

USD million and percentage values

	2007	2008	2009	2010	2011	2012
Total investment (USD million)	1 759	2 076	1 122	1 262	2 136	1 924
of which from domestic VC funds (USD million)	678	780	410	371	638	516
of which from domestic VC funds (%)	*39*	*38*	*37*	*29*	*30*	*27*

Source: Israeli Venture Capital Research Centre, (2013), *The IVC 2013 Yearbook: Israel High-Tech, Venture Capital, Startup and Private Equity Directory, www.ivc-online.com/upload/IVC2014/learnmore/pdfs/View_Sample_2013.pdf.*

StatLink http://dx.doi.org/10.1787/888933421881

Furthermore, venture capital is heavily focused on high-technology enterprises. Government could help rebalance the supply of venture capital to include high-potential firms in more traditional industries through the provision of preferential tax incentives for private investors and venture capital funds that invest in traditional sectors.

The Israeli government has also sought to stimulate smaller scale seed financing through tax incentives for business angel investment. By 2011, however, business angel investments had totalled only NIS 100 million and involved only 60 companies. This appears to reflect overly-stringent eligibility criteria for investment incentives, such as an obligation to maintain shares in the start-up companies for at least three years. The government has therefore proposed new rules for those who invest in start-ups that are less than three years old, have turnover that does not exceed NIS 1.5 million and require investments of up to NIS 3 million.[9]

In this new legal framework, fiscal incentives are generous by providing up to NIS 5 million of personal income tax deduction over the three years of the required minimum period of investment, which is therefore kept unchanged compared to the previous law. However, eligibility rules appear still somewhat rigid, for example with respect to the definition of eligible company, which can only be one in which R&D represent at least 70% of the expenses of the company, with at least 75% of these expenditures being incurred in Israel, and in which the revenues of the company do not exceed 50% of R&D expenditure.[10]

Taxation affecting small business

The Israeli government introduced a number of tax rate increases following the social protests of 2011 against high living costs and social disparities in the country. Personal income tax rates, which directly affect the self-employed and unincorporated businesses, were increased by 1% or 2% depending on the income bracket; the corporate income tax rate was raised from 25% to 26.5%; and the value-added tax (VAT) from 16% to 18%.

Despite these increases, personal income taxation levels remain favourable to business in Israel. The average personal income tax rate is low by international standards (Figure 3.17). Moreover, existing tax credits combined with a low basic tax rate (i.e. 10% on the first NIS 63 600 earned) means that average wage earners pay little or no income tax.[11] Social security contributions are also low. Israel's rate of social security contributions is 7% up to 60% of the average wage and 18.5% on earnings above the 60% threshold. Overall, this makes the country's aggregate tax wedge on employment one of the lightest in the OECD

Figure 3.17. **All-in average income tax rates and all-in tax rate less cash transfers at average wage, 2015**

One-earner married couple with two children

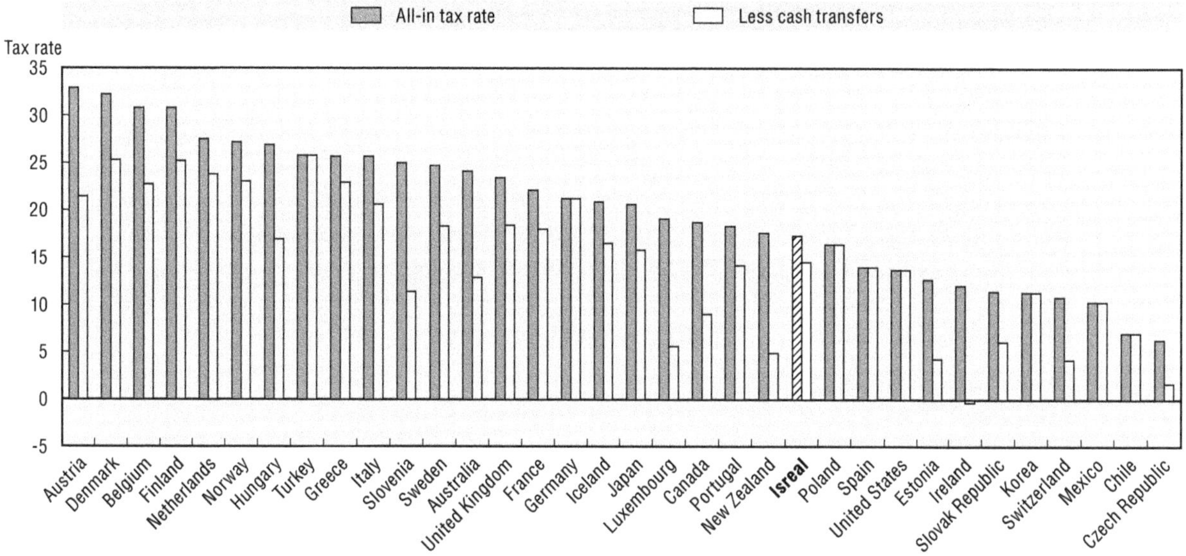

Note: The all-in tax rate is calculated as the combined central and sub-central government income tax plus employee social security contribution as a percentage of gross wage earnings. The all-in tax rate less cash transfers subtracts family benefits (in respect of dependent children) paid by general government as universal cash transfers as a percentage of gross wage earnings.
Source: OECD based on OECD *Tax Database*.

StatLink http://dx.doi.org/10.1787/888933421818

area, although mandatory contributions to private-sector pension funds increase the effective tax wedge (OECD, 2013a). In addition, Israel has run an Earned Income Tax Credit (EITC) since 2011 which helps the transition from welfare to work of low-income earners, including through self-employment. However, the Israeli EITC scheme absorbs only 0.02% of national GDP, compared with 0.4% and 0.5% of GDP in the United States and the United Kingdom (OECD, 2013a). There is therefore scope for expanding the EITC scheme in Israel, with the aim of strengthening social inclusion and reducing informality in the economy.

Formalisation can also be pursed from the demand-side of informal labour, for example through tax deductions and voucher schemes targeted to sectors where informality is widespread. Vouchers, for example, typically include a state wage subsidy whereby the employer only pays a part of the worker's salary, with the goal to cut the incentive to resort to informal labour arrangements (OECD/European Commission, 2015). An example is Denmark's Home-Job Plan, whose objective was to encourage formalisation in the sector of home-based personal services (Box 3.7).

Israel's combined corporate tax rate, at 25%, is relatively high by international standards (Figure 3.18). However, the government offers generous corporate tax breaks to foreign investors, exporters and R&D-based companies through the Law for the Encouragement of Capital Investment. For example, companies with at least 25% of taxable revenues from exports to countries at least 14 million residents are eligible for a corporate income tax rate of 16%, or 9% if they are located in a priority regional development area (i.e. the North and the South of the country). Similarly, large R&D-intensive companies are eligible for a corporate income tax rate of 8% (5% in priority areas) provided that they meet certain requirements for investment in productive equipment and employment creation. This

Box 3.7. **Denmark's Home-Job Plan**

Description of the approach

The Home-Job Plan provided tax deductions to consumers of personal and household services in the sectors of cleaning, indoor and outdoor house maintenance, gardening and babysitting. Its aim was to reduce the supply of informal labour in those sectors, but also more generally to create new jobs in construction and encourage the installation of environmental-friendly solutions in Danish households.

The programme ran as a pilot project from June 2011 to the end of 2013 with a budget of DKK 1 billion (EUR 134 million) in 2011 and DK 1.75 billion (EUR 234 million) in 2012 and 2013. It offered tax deductions of 15% over the costs incurred for buying the eligible services for each household member aged above 18 years old and up to a ceiling of DKK 15 000 (EUR 2 000) per person per year. The programme was not renewed in 2014.

The operational rules were simple. The buyer of the service had to inform the tax authority of the cost of the service and the name of the entrepreneur. The tax authority would then deduct the incurred costs from the calculation of the personal income subject to personal income tax. In more than 95% of cases the form was completed online.

The tax deduction has been widely used and its budget resources have quickly ran out each year. In 2011, for example, about 270 000 people used the tax incentive, mostly for house maintenance and repair where informal self-employment is prevalent. The average reported cost for tax deduction was DKK 9 800 (EUR 1 315), while total deductions amounted to DKK 2.7 billion (EUR 362 million). The measure was considered useful both by consumers and construction business associations. The main criticism concerned the ceiling for deductible costs (EUR 2 000), which was considered low compared with similar policies in other countries (e.g. EUR 6 600 in Sweden).

Factors for success

Budget outlays have quickly dried up every year, suggesting that this measure met a real demand from both consumers and the targeted industries. Moreover, programmes offering small tax deductions, such as Denmark's Home-Job Plan, need to be managed in a simple way to attract users and keep overheads low. Administering a voucher scheme online is generally the best way to keep costs low, although there might be a risk of excluding from the scheme the low-educated and older people. Moreover, similar interventions are better targeted at sectors where informality is known to be widespread to increase the additionality of the measure.

Obstacles and responses

With fixed-term tax incentives, such as vouchers, there is always the risk that informal arrangements kicks in again once employers and workers are no longer eligible to them. At the same time, the smaller the subsidy offered by the government (i.e. the percentage of the salary covered by the government), the higher the risk that the measure proves ineffective by either not attracting sufficient interest in the employers or by subsiding work which would have taken place in the formal sector anyway (i.e. limited additionality). Finally, if the targeted sector has a strong presence of illegal foreign workers which have no access to a government-backed voucher scheme, a similar measure may unintendedly push further down their wages by lowering the price below which employers have a convenience to resort to informal labour. The final outcome can, therefore, be the further marginalisation of illegal foreign workers.

Box 3.7. **Denmark's Home-Job Plan** *(cont.)*

It appears, therefore, important that similar measures have adequate resources to make a dent on informality. At the same time, these measures should be short-term, being second-best compared to structural reforms which reduce taxation and social security contributions more generally. Finally, in countries or sectors where there are large numbers of illegal foreign workers, this policy may bring the unintended consequence of further marginalising these workers.

Relevance for Israel

Israel has a high rate of informality, which voucher schemes such as Denmark's Home-Job Plan can help reduce, with positive effects on reduced income disparity across the society. Israel also does not have a large proportion of illegal foreign workers, which should prevent the unintended consequences of the measure mentioned above. Together with a more generous earned income tax credit, vouchers could be part of a wider business formalisation strategy in Israel.

Source: OECD/European Commission (2015), *Policy Brief on Informal Entrepreneurship*, Publications Office of the European Union, Luxembourg.

Figure 3.18. **The combined corporate income tax rate across OECD countries, 2016**

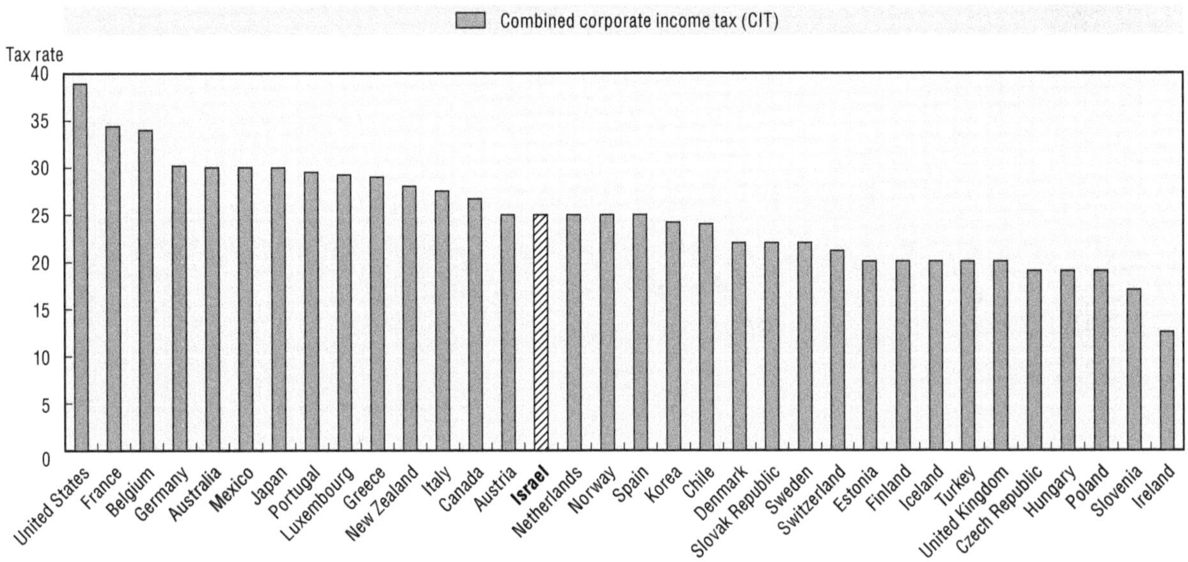

Note: The combined corporate income tax rate is given by the sum of the central government rate (adjusted, if applicable, to show the net rate where the central government provides a deduction in respect of sub-central income tax) plus the sub-central rate, for countries which have one.

Source: *OECD Tax Database.*

StatLink http://dx.doi.org/10.1787/888933421829

wide system of tax concessions helps to make Israel a business-friendly environment although there is a risk that the support may not be sufficiently effective in generating incremental activity (OECD, 2013a). In addition, the tax incentives are strongly weighted towards large enterprises and the high-technology and export-oriented businesses, leaving few resources to encourage the activity of SMEs in traditional sectors of the economy through direct government programmes such as in access to finance, training and business management consulting.

Foreign Direct Investment

Inward foreign direct investment (FDI) brings to host economies improved access to best practice technologies and international markets for the SMEs in their supply chains. In addition, FDI affiliates may generate company spinoffs, thus fostering high-impact entrepreneurship. Clearly these benefits depend both on the successful attraction of FDI ventures into the country and on the development of local supply chains by these firms.

Israel's performance in FDI attraction is relatively strong, amounting to 4% of GDP in 2015 (Figure 3.19). FDI inflows suffered a set-back following the global recession, but they are now on the path to recovering their pre-crisis levels. Overall, in the period 2005-15, FDI inflows grew at an annual average of 27% (Figure 3.20).

Figure 3.19. **FDI inflows across OECD economies, 2015**

Percentage of GDP

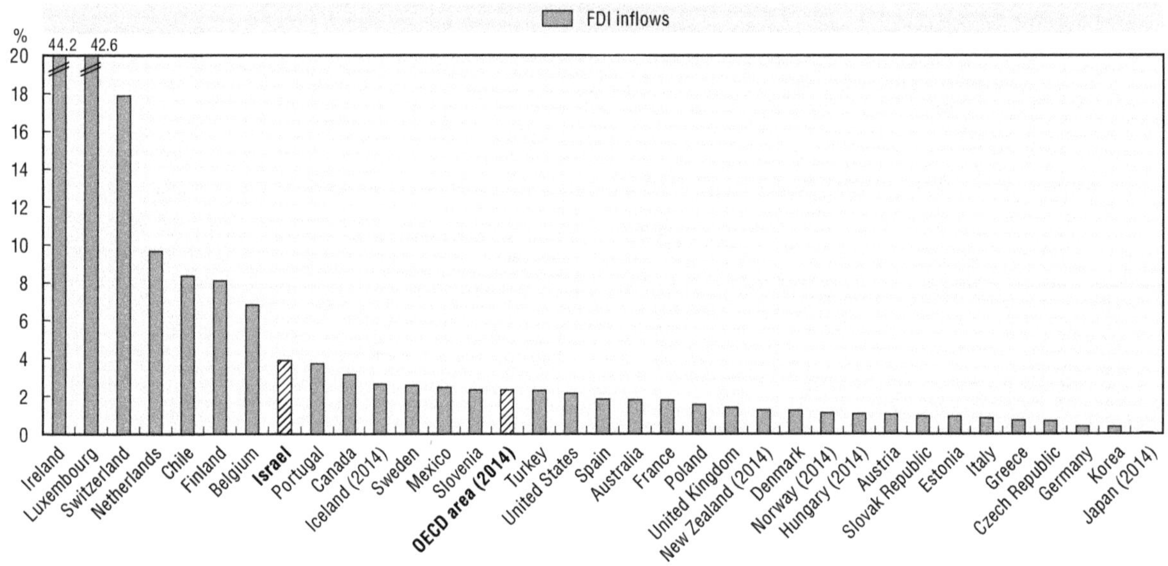

Source: OECD Globalisation Database.

StatLink http://dx.doi.org/10.1787/888933421838

Israel's strong performance in FDI attraction is the result of major assets such as a highly-educated labour force, cutting-edge R&D capabilities and favourable taxation. For example, the Law for the Encouragement of Capital Investment, which offers generous R&D incentives and employment grants, has long been targeted to foreign-owned firms. Although this law is also now open to Israeli exporter companies, it continues to be mostly used by foreign large establishments.

On the other hand, while inward FDI has a strong positive impact on Israel's high-technology economy, its potential to stimulate SME development more widely across the economy is limited by a strong sectoral bias towards ICT and, in particular, ICT R&D centres. Of the 489 foreign affiliates operating in Israel at the end of 2009, 286 were R&D centres affiliated to ICT multinationals such as Intel, Google and Microsoft. As a result, the potential trickle-down of supply contracts and technology transfer to domestic SMEs in other sectors is limited. A more diversified FDI attraction strategy coupled with increased emphasis on supply chain development could help spread the benefits of FDI more widely in the economy.

Figure 3.20. **Inward FDI flows in Israel, 2005-15**

USD billions

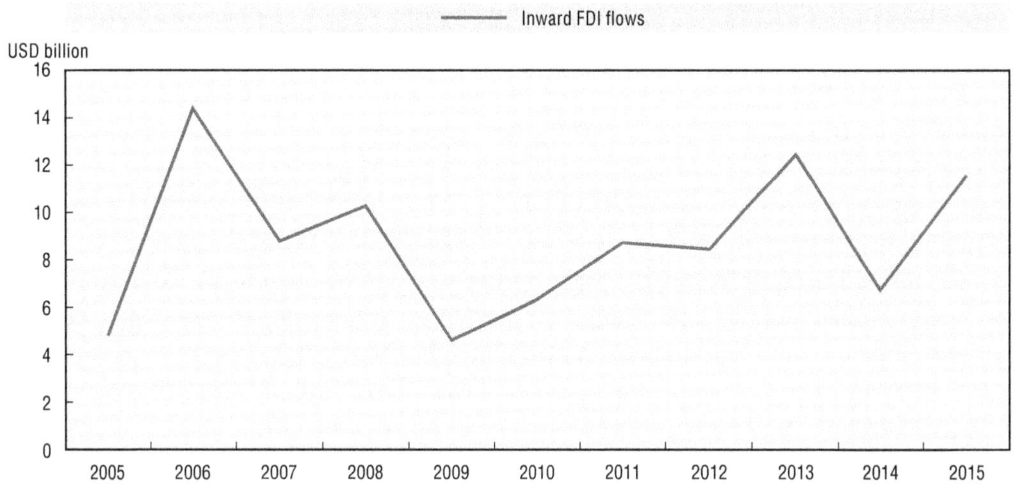

Source: OECD based on *OECD Globalisation Database.*

StatLink http://dx.doi.org/10.1787/888933421844

Moreover, most individual FDI deals in Israel are of relatively small size. For example, in 2009, only nine deals exceeded USD 100 million (Aahroni, 2009). Besides the establishment of R&D centres, these deals often involve the acquisition of domestic high-technology start-ups. Some of these promising start-ups may, however, be sold prematurely before they could have been able to generate stronger benefits for the national economy through higher wages, more knowledge spill-overs and increased managerial learning opportunities.

Conclusions and policy recommendations

Recent SME and entrepreneurship development in Israel has benefitted from strong economic growth, macroeconomic stability, a flexible labour market and relatively low taxation. Administrative burdens to business start-up are also fairly low. There are nonetheless a number of areas in which framework conditions for SMEs and entrepreneurship could be improved in Israel.

Small businesses still face difficulties in obtaining business licenses and permits. A Regulatory Impact Assessment process has recently been introduced under the responsibility of SMBA to help ensure that new legislation does not add to the overall regulatory burden on SMEs, but investment has to be made in full implementation of this process. Product market regulation is also relatively tight in Israel, leading to difficulties for new firms to enter certain markets. The Concentration Law of 2013 and recent decisions to strengthen the functions of the Anti-Trust Authority should help open up markets, but again attention will have to be paid to their full implementation.

Another challenge is to more fully exploit the potential of entrepreneurship education to strengthen the culture of entrepreneurship across the Israeli population. Whilst there are several good practice entrepreneurship education initiatives in Israel, at various levels of education, there is not yet a national entrepreneurship education strategy that could spread these initiatives more widely and offer support in terms of curriculum development and incentives, training trainers and offering pedagogical materials.

There are also a number of areas in which existing framework conditions favour high-technology entrepreneurship more than typical SMEs, contributing to a dualism between a high-income, high-productivity high-technology economy and a low-income, low-productivity traditional SME economy.

First, business R&D spending is strong in Israel, and this leads to successful patenting and research commercialisation. However, innovation policy support is mainly oriented to large companies and R&D-intensive companies, whereas greater attention to non-high-technology sectors of the economy would help spread the benefits of R&D and innovation among more people, with expected positive consequences on social inclusion.

Second, Israel enjoys one of the highest rates of workforce with tertiary education, and this helps explain, among other things, strong FDI attraction in high-technology sectors. However, the performance of upper-secondary students in the OECD PISA tests in numeracy and literacy skills is disappointing, suggesting that those who do not continue on with tertiary education may lack some basic skills to succeed in the labour market. In addition, there are weaknesses in the VET system regarding the quality of learning outcomes, training and trainer standards, and the relevance of technical education to SMEs.

Third, while the venture capital industry is actively engaged in financing start-ups and the early stages of business growth, notwithstanding some gaps in business angel finance, credit market conditions are not always the most favourable to the host of small enterprises whose sector or business model does not fit the requirements of equity financers. In particular, limited credit information and lack of competition in the banking sector are two major barriers to better access to credit for SMEs.

Fourth, Israel draws sizeable foreign direct investments. However, FDI inflows are again mostly concentrated in high-technology sectors, especially ICT. Stronger FDI inflows in non-high-technology sectors would enhance competition in the economy and bring benefits to wider segments of the society. In addition, a substantial share of inward FDI is in the form of acquisitions of innovative start-ups. There may be a case for strengthening support for the early-stage development of Israeli start-ups in order to postpone acquisitions until greater benefits have been generated for the Israeli economy in terms of wealth and managerial learning.

Given these considerations, the following recommendations are offered to improve Israel's business environment and framework conditions:

Key recommendations on business environment and framework conditions for SMEs and entrepreneurship

- Strengthen product market competition by rapid implementation of the 2013 Concentration Law and granting more powers to the Anti-Trust Authority, including the ability to apply financial sanctions to companies abusing their market power.
- Simplify the business licensing and permit system through increased monitoring by SMBA of difficulties SMEs and entrepreneurs face with permits and licenses and communication to the relevant authorities, digitalisation of the business license and permit system, and creation of a national online portal that provides comprehensive information on licensing and permit requirements across the country.
- Strengthen Regulatory Impact Assessment (RIA) of new legislation affecting SMEs and entrepreneurship by SMBA by replacing informal consultations with business associations with more rigorous RIA methodologies such as the Standard Cost Model.

Key recommendations on business environment and framework conditions for SMEs and entrepreneurship *(cont.)*

- Improve bridging between the supply of higher education graduates and their employment in SMEs by increasing SME participation in curriculum design, teaching and student placements, and providing support for upgrading productivity and management practices in SMEs to increase their demand for higher skilled workers.
- Strengthen the capacity of the Vocational Education and Training (VET) system to supply appropriately skilled workers to SMEs by increasing the share of work-based learning in SMEs (including apprenticeships, work placements and internships) as part of VET studies, experimenting with new approaches to involving employers in VET programme design and take up, experimenting with "associate degree" qualifications, developing a better labour market information system to identify industry skill needs, and promoting national training standards for VET teaching. This could all be part of a national VET strategy jointly designed by the government and industry leaders.
- Introduce a national entrepreneurship education strategy that makes entrepreneurship a mandatory and integral part of the curriculum. To support this effort, develop steering documents (e.g. curricula and syllabi) and evaluation plans, provide training and incentives to entrepreneurship teachers, and develop an online web portal offering guidelines, information and teaching resources for entrepreneurship education.
- Broaden the targeting of government expenditures on business innovation to cover more non-R&D expenditures and support greater numbers of SMEs, including in low-technology manufacturing.
- Reinforce competition in the banking sector by offering training to qualified financial or economic organisations interested in setting up credit unions and by fully implementing the recommendations of the National Committee to Increase the Competitiveness of the Banking Sector (in particular easing access to loans by very small businesses by applying regulations for retail loans rather than business loans).
- Amend regulations to enable disclosure of positive credit history information for entrepreneurs and support credit bureaus in building credit rating information through standardised computation methodologies and disclosure requirements.
- Investigate potential regulatory barriers to domestic institutional investors taking part in the venture capital market and consider tax incentives for investors making equity investments in in firms outside of high-technology sectors.
- Encourage business formalisation through both demand- and supply-side strategies, such as wider availability of the earned income tax credit and voucher schemes in sectors where informality is widespread.
- Develop an FDI attraction strategy that goes beyond high-technology sectors and supports the development of business linkages between FDI affiliates and SME suppliers.

Notes

1. After abstracting from the impact of new offshore gas fields, OECD growth rate projections for 2014 and 2015 are at 2.5% per year.
2. This trend has not been uncommon elsewhere in the OECD area; in the last twenty years, on a yearly basis, wages increased by only 1.5% in the United Kingdom, 1.0% in the United States and 0.6% in Germany, far below their respective annual GDP growth rates.
3. In 2011, Israel's civilian spending was 31% of GDP compared with an OECD average of 44% (OECD, 2013a).

4. In the Standard Cost Model (SCM), administrative burdens are calculated on the basis of the average cost of the required administrative activity (Price) multiplied by the total number of activities performed per year (Quantity). The European Commission, for example, estimates the "price" by multiplying a tariff (based on average labour cost per hour including overheads) and the time required per action, while the "quantity" is calculated as the frequency of required actions multiplied by the number of entities concerned. For further information, *http://ec.europa.eu/smart-regulation/refit/admin_burden/scm_en.htm*.
5. The OECD high-income average is a World Bank country income category which includes all OECD countries except Mexico and Turkey.
6. Data refer to 2014 and are based on the OECD Main Science and Technology Indicator Database.
7. Results based on a survey of SMEs by Adalya Economic Consulting in 2011 (Adalya Economic Consulting, 2011, p. 18).
8. Data on SME credit in relation to GDP are not strictly comparable because of the different definitions of SME loans in use in different OECD countries.
9. See "Israel to expand tax breaks to boost investment in start-ups", *www.reuters.com/article/2014/07/16/israel-taxbreaks-tech-idUSL6N0PR3DI20140716*.
10. Information retrieved from: *www.jpost.com/Business/Commentary/Your-taxes-Angel-Law-amendment-proposals-375536*.
11. The average wage in Israel is approximately NIS 110 000.

References

Aahroni, Y. (2009), *Inward FDI in Israel and Its Policy Context*, Columbia FDI Profiles, New York.

Adalya Economic Consulting (2011), *Strategic Report of Israeli Governmental Assistance to Small and Medium Businesses – Phase A*, submitted to Small and Medium Business Agency, November, Tel Aviv, Adalya Economic Consulting.

Almor, T. and S. Heilbrunn (2014), "Entrepreneurship in Israel: theory and practice", *American Journal of Entrepreneurship*, 6(2), 16-36.

Bank of Israel (2014), *Annual Report 2013*, Jerusalem.

Bank of Israel (2012), *Annual Report 2011*, Jerusalem.

Carnevale, A., P. Rose and A. Hanson (2012), *Certificates: Gateway to Gainful Employment and College Degrees*, Georgetown University Center on Education and the Workforce.

European Commission (2014), *Thematic Working Group on Entrepreneurship Education Final Report*, European Commission Directorate-General Education and Culture.

European Commission (2012), *Entrepreneurship in the EU and beyond: Flash Eurobarometer 354*, European Commission and Gallup Organization, Brussels.

European Commission (2008), *Survey of Entrepreneurship Education in Higher Education in Europe*, European Commission, Brussels.

European Commission/EACEA/Eurydice (2016), *Entrepreneurship Education at School in Europe, Eurydice Report*. Luxembourg, Publications Office of the European Union.

European Training Foundation (2014), *Mapping vocational Education and Training Governance in Israel*, Brussels.

Frenkel, A. and S. Maital (2012), *Technion Nation: Technion's Contribution to Israel and the World*, Haifa, Israel: Technion – Israel Institute of Technology.

GEM/YBI (2013), *Generation Entrepreneur? The State of Global Youth Entrepreneurship*, *www.youthbusiness.org/wp-content/uploads/2013/09/GenerationEntrepreneur.pdf*.

Harrington, K.A. and M.G. Douglas (2005), "Cross-campus entrepreneurship organising within Washington University to create an innovation environment", Paper given to the Technology Transfer Society Annual Conference, Kansas City, Missouri.

Heilbrunn, S. (2010), *Advancing entrepreneurship in an elementary school: A case study*, International Education Studies, 3(2), P174.

Innovation, Science and Economic Development Canada (ISED) (2011), "Evaluation of BizPaL Service", *www.ic.gc.ca/eic/site/ae-ve.nsf/eng/h_03356.html/*.

Israeli Venture Capital Research Centre (2013), *The IVC 2013 Yearbook: Israel High-Tech, Venture Capital, Startup and Private Equity Directory*, *www.ivc-online.com/upload/IVC2014/learnmore/pdfs/View_Sample_2013.pdf*.

JA-Worldwide (2014), *Annual Global Factbook*, Junior Achievement, United States.

Ministry of Industry Trade and Labour (MOITAL) (2012), Vocational Education and Training (VET) Background Report for Israel OECD Project: Skills Beyond School, *www.moital.gov.il/NR/rdonlyres/F14DDE94-10EC-4FEE-9311-5CBE0550DB9A/0/OECDVET29220122FinalsendtoOECD.pdf* (accessed 5th January 2015).

Musset, P., M. Kuczera and S. Field (2014), *OECD Reviews of Vocational Education and Training A Skills beyond School Review of Israel*, OECD publishing, Paris.

Natanzon, R. and R. Levi (2010), *Recommendation for the creation of models for vocational training in Israel*, Macro Institution for Political Economy, Tel Aviv.

OECD (2016), *Financing SMEs and Entrepreneurs 2016: An OECD Scoreboard*, OECD Publishing, Paris, *http://dx.doi.org/10.1787/fin_sme_ent-2016-en*.

OECD (2015a), *Education at a Glance 2015: OECD Indicators*, OECD Publishing, Paris, *http://dx.doi.org/10.1787/eag-2015-en*.

OECD (2015b), *Employment and Skills Strategies in Israel, OECD reviews on local job creation*, OECD Publishing, Paris, *http://dx.doi.org/10.1787/9789264232969-en*.

OECD (2015c), *OECD Science, Technology and Industry Scoreboard 2015*, OECD Publishing, Paris, *http://dx.doi.org/10.1787/sti_scoreboard-2015-en*.

OECD (2015d), *New Approaches to SME and Entrepreneurship Financing: Broadening the Range of Instruments*, OECD Publishing, Paris, *http://dx.doi.org/10.1787/9789264240957-en*.

OECD (2015e), *Entrepreneurship at a Glance 2015*, OECD Publishing, Paris, *http://dx.doi.org/10.1787/entrepreneur_aag-2015-en*.

OECD (2014), *Financing SMEs and Entrepreneurs 2014: An OECD Scoreboard*, OECD Publishing, Paris, *http://dx.doi.org/10.1787/fin_sme_ent-2014-en*.

OECD (2013a), *OECD Economic Surveys: Israel – December 2013*, OECD Publishing, *http://dx.doi.org/10.1787/eco_surveys-isr-2013-en*.

OECD (2013b), *PISA 2012 Assessment and Analytical Framework: Mathematics, Reading, Science, Problem Solving and Financial Literacy*, OECD Publishing, Paris *http://dx.doi.org/10.1787/9789264190511-en*.

OECD (2013c), *OECD Science, Technology and Industry Scoreboard 2013*, OECD Publishing, *http://dx.doi.org/10.1787/sti_scoreboard-2013-en*.

OECD (2011b), *OECD Economic Surveys: Israel – December 2011*, OECD Publishing, *http://dx.doi.org/10.1787/eco_surveys-isr-2011-en*.

OECD/European Commission (2015), *Policy Brief on Informal Entrepreneurship*, Entrepreneurial Activities in Europe, Luxembourg Publications Office of the European Union.

UK Commission for Employment and Skills (UKCES) (2014), *Employer Ownership of Skills Pilot Round 2 Prospectus*, London.

UK Commission for Employment and Skills (UKCES) (2013), *Employer Ownership of Skills: Building the Momentum*, London.

UK Commission for Employment and Skills (UKCES) (2011), *Employer Ownership of Skills*, London.

Varghese, N. and V. Püttmann (2011), *Trends in diversification of post-secondary education*, UNESCO, Paris.

Yair, G., K. Goldstein and N. Rotem (2013), *Country Report: Israel*, report prepared for the project "*Mapping of VET Educational Policies and Practices for Social Inclusion and Social Cohesion in the Western Balkans, Turkey and Israel*", European Training Fund, Turin.

Yemini, M. and J. Haddad (2010), *Engineer-Entrepreneur: Combining Technical Knowledge with Entrepreneurship Education: The Israeli Case Study*, International Journal of Engineering Education, 26(5), 12-20.

Chapter 4

The strategic framework and policy delivery system in Israel

This chapter examines the strategic framework and delivery arrangements for SME and entrepreneurship policies in Israel. Although many ministries and agencies have relevant policy interventions, there is no integrated, government-wide SME and entrepreneurship policy strategy. The government should craft a single strategic policy document which lays out the vision, objectives, target groups, policy measures and budgets dedicated to the support of SMEs and entrepreneurs in Israel. The SMBA is tasked with policy coordination across the government. It could be strengthened in this role by creation of an inter-ministerial committee and an inter-ministerial working group together with more adequate resources for policy coordination. The SMBA's network of MAOF business development centres is a critical part of the delivery infrastructure for SME and entrepreneurship policy in Israel. They could play a greater role in the future by delivering additional services and reaching out to more SMEs and entrepreneurs. This should be accompanied by strengthened performance monitoring and staff development in the MAOF Centres.

The strategic policy framework

Israel has gained a global reputation as a "start-up nation" (Senor and Singer, 2009) based on its success in promoting, encouraging, and supporting high-technology enterprises. This was driven by policy initiatives that began in the 1990s to attract multinational corporations to establish research and development (R&D) centres in Israel, foster the R&D activity of Israeli firms, support Israeli high-technology start-ups with R&D funds and technological incubators, stimulate the development of a venture capital industry for investment in high-technology enterprises, and promote R&D linkages between industry and academia. The well-developed policy focus on the high-technology sector continues to this day.

The Israeli government also began to develop SME and entrepreneurship policies in the early 1990s, mostly in response to the need to absorb the influx of Jewish immigrants from the former soviet areas into the workforce and take advantage of their scientific and technological skills. This included establishment of the Small and Medium Business Authority as a non-governmental entity with government funding support, which launched SME support programmes and services and advised the government on policies to support traditional SME sectors. However, for many years, the government's policy priority was concentrated on high-technology sectors, with relatively small attention to the broader issues of developing SMEs in traditional sectors.

Policy attention to SME development strengthened in the late-2000s. In 2007, the government adopted Resolution No. 2190 concerning the improvement and targeting of aid for SMEs. On the basis of this resolution, the Small and Medium Business Agency (SMBA) was created within the Ministry of Economy and Industry in 2009, replacing the non-governmental Small and Medium Business Authority. In 2011, government Resolution No. 3409 on encouraging SMEs' activities in Israel authorised the SMBA to co-ordinate all government action in the promotion of SMEs and to initiate and implement related activities. The policy agenda to be covered included:

- the supply and availability of credit to SMEs;
- collecting and disseminating information critical to the promotion of SMEs' activities;
- streamlining regulatory processes affecting the creation and operation of SMEs and reducing the regulatory and administrative burden;
- realising the productivity and innovation potential of SMEs;
- improving the capacity and capabilities of SMEs to export; and;
- increasing the participation of SMEs in government procurement.

Holding the mandate for SME and entrepreneurship development, the Ministry of Economy and Industry highlights its importance in recent work plans, listing "strengthening SMEs" as one of its core objectives, alongside a range of other policy activities relevant to the support of SMEs and entrepreneurship, including increasing competition in the economy, enhancing the skill base of the workforce, and diversifying export activity.

Specific to the objective of "strengthening SMEs", the 2016 work plan aims to remove access barriers to credit and capital; ease and reduce regulatory and bureaucratic barriers on business; assist SMEs in realising their potential in productivity, innovation, efficiency and competitiveness; and create a supportive infrastructure for the establishment of new businesses and their development.

The Ministry of Economy and Industry primarily tasks its SME and entrepreneurship policy activities to the Small and Medium Business Agency (SMBA), established in the Ministry in 2010. The Agency has the responsibilities listed in Box 4.1.

Box 4.1. **Functions of the Israeli Small and Medium Business Agency (SMBA)**

1. To initiate and implement government policies to assist SMEs;
2. To design and run SME assistance programmes;
3. To co-ordinate all the organisations involved in promoting the SME sector;
4. To establish local and regional centres dedicated to SMEs;
5. To introduce legislation pertaining to SMEs;
6. To implement guidance, public relations and educational programmes for the management of SMEs;
7. To fulfil research and surveys on the sector and establish useful databases;
8. To create additional funds and vehicles of assistance;
9. To lobby both publicly and privately to eliminate obstacles facing entrepreneurs;
10. To encourage entrepreneurial potential among specific segments of the population, such as minorities.

Source: Regulations setting up the SMBA from the Ministry of Economy and Industry website: *www.moital.gov.il/NR/exeres/54A8A7EB-8526-43E1-A8EA-210513B20FE6.htm.*

In 2011, the SMBA produced a 3-year strategic plan that focused on the following three main tasks for the Agency (Adalya Economic Consulting, 2011):

1. The operation of local development centres charged with transferring information and knowledge to SMEs (i.e. the MAOF network of business support centres).
2. The management, in collaboration with the Ministry of Finance, of the loan guarantee programme (Small and Medium Business Fund).
3. The review of legislation affecting SMEs with a view to alleviating regulatory burdens.

To improve its ability to fulfill its role, the SMBA was also to be tasked with gathering all activities under the Ministry of Economy and Industry having to do with assistance to SMEs (e.g. exporting, innovation, skills), involvement in all significant decisions regarding state guarantee funds in co-operation with the Ministry of Finance, and improving baseline data on SMEs to be able to monitor the effectiveness of SME supports in meeting their needs. The strategic plan also recommended a simplification in the range of SME and entrepreneurship programmes. However, the SMBA strategy was not a comprehensive government-wide SME policy framework, but rather an initial analysis of the most pressing issues and tasks for the Agency itself.

Entrepreneurship and SME-related policies are also within the scope of other ministries and agencies. For example, the government is implementing policies to stimulate SME and entrepreneurship development among underprivileged segments of society, including immigrants and minority populations (*i.e.* Arab, Druze and Circassian populations), which are driven by the Ministry of Immigrant Absorption and the Agency for Economic Development of the Minority Sectors (MEDA) in the Ministry of Social Equality. The SMBA co-operates with these bodies in implementing the policy support. Other examples are policies to encourage the unemployed and job-seekers to become self-employed, which are operated by the Employment Service, and policies to stimulate and strengthen SME development in the agricultural and tourism sector, which are operated by the Ministry of Tourism and the Ministry of Agriculture and Rural Development. Procurement policy is governed by the Mandatory Tenders Law under the Ministry of Finance, which includes provisions to increase the chances of SMEs being able to compete for public procurement contracts, but with no specific targets for the allocation of public tenders to SMEs. The Ministry of Finance is also involved in setting policies to improve the ability of SMEs to access financing, such as through the SMBF, the Angels' Law, and the funding of micro-credit organisations. Thus, although the support of SMEs and entrepreneurship is evident in the overall governmental agenda and consistent with policy prescriptions in major international SME policy guides such as the Small Business Act for Europe (European Commission, 2008) and the OECD Bologna Charter on SME policies (OECD, 2000), with particular strengths in policy to support high-technology sectors and businesses, Israel does not have an integrated policy document which sets out its strategic policy framework for SME and entrepreneurship development.

Going forward, the SMBA should craft a new medium-term strategic plan (e.g. for the next three or five years) to be used not only to determine its own more narrowly-defined scope of work but also to frame an overarching SME and entrepreneurship policy strategy for the government as a whole. This document should include objectives, target groups, description of policy measures, budgets and responsibilities of the various ministries and government departments and agencies in relation to the strategy.

The strategy should set out a comprehensive set of policies (e.g. access to finance, entrepreneurial, managerial and workforce skills development, innovation, access to markets, etc.) and show how they will be applied to different enterprise policy target groups. This could follow a "pipeline approach" identifying the financial and non-financial supports to be applied to entrepreneurs from different population groups and at different phases of the entrepreneurial process, and enterprises at different stages of business development, e.g. distinguishing between potential entrepreneurs, start-ups, early-stage business development, established micro and small enterprises, established medium enterprises, and high-growth potential firms.

One of the inputs to the strategy making process could be the key priorities for government intervention identified in this report. The task of the SMBA, in collaboration with other departments of the Ministry of Economy and Industry and other relevant ministries, will be to translate these and other priorities into a specific SME and entrepreneurship development strategy.

Coordination across government ministries and agencies

Although the SMBA is the main government entity responsible for support to SMEs and entrepreneurs, other branches of the Ministry of Economy and Industry and other ministries also implement policies and programmes to support SME and entrepreneurship development. Table 4.1 provides an overview of the main government institutions involved in SME and entrepreneurship policy in Israel.

Table 4.1. **Israeli ministries and agencies involved in SME and entrepreneurship policies and programmes**

Ministry/Agency	SME and entrepreneurship policy areas
Small and Medium Business Agency (SMBA) – Ministry of Economy and Industry	The Ministry of Economy and Industry has the overall mandate for SME and entrepreneurship development, which is delegated to the SMBA. The SMBA focuses on improving access to finance and know-how and reducing regulatory and administrative barriers to starting and operating a business. It administers the Small Business Loan Fund (a loan guarantee fund), together with the Ministry of Finance, and the network of local business development services (MAOF) centres.
Israel Innovation Authority (IIA)	The IIA (which replaced the Office of the Chief Scientist in January 2016) is empowered by a 2015 amendment to the 1984 Law for the Encouragement of Industrial Research and Development (R&D Law), oversees government-sponsored support of R&D in Israel. It implements the R&D Fund and supports the Technological Incubators Programme.
Foreign Trade Administration (FTA) – Ministry of Economy and Industry	The FTA is responsible for managing and directing Israel's international trade policy, including activities for the promotion of trade and export, initiating and maintaining trade agreements, and creating strategic co-operations with foreign companies. Its aim is to increase export volumes by Israeli firms and diversify exports towards new emerging markets, e.g. China and India.
Israeli Investment Center – Ministry of Economy and Industry	Its main responsibility is encouraging the development of industry and tourism in Israel. It offers taxation incentives and government grant schemes to support private investment and job creation activity in peripheral regions. Since 2014, it has adopted a special investment focus on investment projects with an expression of innovation for increased productivity and relatively high paying jobs.
Ministry of Finance	It manages policy initiatives to improve access to financing for SMEs. This includes joint management with the SMBA of the Small Business Loan Fund (a loan guarantee fund) and the Angels Law to incentivise private investments in new high-technology start-ups.
Ministry of Immigrant Absorption	The Ministry facilitates the full integration of immigrants and returning residents into society and absorption into the labour market. It Entrepreneurs Division works to incorporate new programmes into the overall policies of the Ministry to support new immigrants and returning residents in establishing and developing independent businesses in Israel. It offers a special track for establishing start-ups in the sciences and hi-tech in Israel.
Authority for Economic Development of the Minorities Sector (MEDA) – Ministry for Social Equality	Its mandate is to maximise the economic potential of minorities (Arabs, Druze and Circassian sectors) and integrate the minority business sector into the economy. It runs policy measures to increase access to financing, markets and know-how for minority-owned SMEs and nascent entrepreneurs from minority populations. It also promotes development of tourism businesses in Arab villages in partnership with the Ministry of Tourism.
Ministry for Development of the Negev and the Galilee	The mandate of the Ministry involves spreading economic development to the peripheral regions primarily through developing industrial zones and incubators to stimulate enterprise development in the Negev and Galilee, and encouraging entrepreneurs and investors to shift their economic activity to the these regions.
Ministry of Interior	This Ministry is responsible for business licensing and permits. It currently cooperates with the SMBA on interventions to reduce the complexity of the permit and licensing system at the municipal level.
Ministry of Agricultural and Rural Development	It has the mandate to support the agricultural sector by promoting agricultural development and agricultural exports. It provides financial aid to help agricultural SMEs prepare business plans and develop their activities.
Ministry of Tourism	One of its policy objectives is to stimulate start-ups and the development of SMEs in the tourism sector through the provision of grants and subsidised consultancy services.
Ministry of Defence	The Ministry manages measures to promote new ideas and technologies that can serve both military needs and future commercial applications in partnership with the OCS and the Ministry of Finance. It recently established a Business Development and SME Department as part of its International Defence Co-operation Division (SIBAT).
The Employment Service	It assists the unemployed and job-seekers to gain employment. Its activities include self-employment assistance by way of mentoring, training, and help with preparing business plans.
"Digital Israel Office" – Ministry for Social Equality	Supports the use of digital technologies across the economy including e-government for the provision of public services and e-commerce and other digital technology use in SMEs.

Source: OECD based on information submitted by the SMBA, MEDA and Israeli government website information.

Because SME and entrepreneurship policy is horizontal, transcending the scope of any one ministry or agency, managing a national SME and entrepreneurship policy agenda requires co-ordination to stave off risks of fragmentation and duplication. The coordination of SME and entrepreneurship policy is one of the functions assigned to the SMBA but needs to be strengthened. There is not a formal mechanism in place for this purpose and in practice the SMBA has only been able to achieve a limited amount of policy coordination, primarily due to the lack of sufficient authority and resources to perform the role effectively.

Because SME and entrepreneurship policy is horizontal, transcending the scope of any one ministry or agency, managing a national SME and entrepreneurship policy agenda requires co-ordination to stave off risks of fragmentation and duplication. The coordination of SME and entrepreneurship policy is one of the functions assigned to the SMBA. However, there is not a formal mechanism in place for this purpose and in practice the SMBA has only been able to achieve a limited amount of policy coordination.

One of the barriers hampering better SME and entrepreneurship policy prioritisation and achievement of greater policy synergies across government is that the SMBA is not a full-authority Agency. The authority granted to the Agency under government resolutions No. 2190 (2007) and No. 3409 (2011) is general and vague, without being specific about its granted authorities to effectively address structural problem affecting SME and entrepreneurship development. These government resolutions do not enable the positioning of the Agency as an authoritative entity within the government that is able to design long-term policy and provide efficient and effective assistance to SMEs. For example, it has not been "legislated" with the authority it needs to achieve certain parts of its mandate, particularly relating to regulatory and legislative issues affecting SMEs, co-ordination of SME support across government (e.g. ensuring receipt of information relating to SMEs from any government ministry operating support programmes, including details of the plan, device, and businesses receiving the support), setting binding uniform SME definitions for all stakeholders, and advocacy matters to ensure that the interests of SMEs are respected by all government departments and authorities and that the procedures and actions of state authorities are not having a harmful effect on SMEs. Administratively dependent on the Ministry of Economy, the SMBA lacks weight in efforts to co-ordinate all government policy actions affecting SMEs as it does not have the legitimacy needed to influence other ministries and agencies, compared to an autonomous agency.

In practice, the SMBA has found it difficult to affirm its central role in SME and entrepreneurship policy even among other departments of the Ministry of Economy and Industry, let alone with other ministries. In addition, most of the other ministries and agencies do not have an SME focal point to internally champion the SME and entrepreneurship perspective in their policies and programmes and to facilitate liaison with the SMBA, which also hinders co-ordination.

A new SME Bill, introduced in 2014 and still under discussion by the Knesset, would grant the SMBA the legal statutory standing to be the official government body responsible for SME and entrepreneurship policy and provide the relevant authorities to the SMBA to fulfil its core roles of policy co-ordination, representing the interests of SMEs within the government, reviewing regulations with an impact on SMEs, and initiating legislation relative to SMEs' interests (Box 4.2). If implemented, the SME Bill may well result in a stronger SMBA.

Policy co-ordination across government could be further enhanced through the establishment of an inter-ministerial SME and entrepreneurship policy committee. This is an approach that is common in many countries (see example in Box 4.3), but does not exist in Israel. Initially, when the SMBA was first established, it was intended to be supported by a higher-level Steering Committee consisting of the Ministry of Finance, the Ministry of Economy and Industry, and two stakeholder organisations. However, this Committee has never been activated.

The Ministry of Economy and Industry could consider reviving and broadening the mandate and membership of this higher-level steering committee to co-ordinate all public

Box 4.2. **Authorities to be granted to the SMBA under the proposed SME Bill**

- *Strategy planning*: To assist the government on planning a multi-year SME government policy in regards to SMEs and report to the government, at least once a year, on the state of the SME sector and related policies;
- *Policy co-ordination*: To consult any public entity which assists SMEs in order to co-ordinate and promote the interests of the SME sector as a whole;
- *Advocacy*: To advocate for SMEs within the public sector; for example, the SMBA will be authorised to transfer complaints and appeals made by SMEs about burdensome or discriminatory regulations to the relevant government department and to offer its assistance on alternative more SME-friendly regulations;
- *Legislative process*: To review proposed government resolutions to assess the administrative and cost impact on SMEs and to provide recommendations on legislative amendments and government resolutions affecting the life of SMEs;
- *Regulatory impact assessment*: To examine existing administrative burdens on SMEs and advise on methods to minimise them;
- *Analysis*: To create and manage a public database on the SME sector and conduct relevant research; in this regard, the SMBA is authorised to request and receive any information from public authorities needed to fulfil this duty.

Source: OECD based on the English translation of the Hebrew text of the SME Bill provided by the SMBA, 2014.

Box 4.3. **The Inter-ministerial State Council on Small and Medium Enterprises and Entrepreneurship, Spain**

Description of the approach

The State Council on Small and Medium Enterprises and Entrepreneurship is attached to the Spanish Ministry of Industry, Energy and Tourism. It is the official body for the planning and co-ordination of all the policies and measures of the various ministries and public administrations affecting SMEs and entrepreneurship, including the facilitation of their creation, growth, and competitiveness. It aims to foster dialogue and co-ordination and includes representatives of all the relevant ministries as well as representatives of SMEs.

The Council was created and is regulated by Royal Decree 962/2013, approved by the Council of Ministers on 5 December 2013. It is responsible for: informing the multiannual SME support plan; developing recommendations and proposals on priorities, mechanisms, actions and regulatory changes necessary to increase SME activity and competitiveness as well as entrepreneurship in Spain; co-ordinating the various support programmes carried out by the competent bodies and the harmonising the eligibility criteria and service standards for support to SMEs; monitoring the application of the Small Business Act for Europe in Spain to enable the evolution of policies for SME access to finance, internationalisation, public procurement, ICT adoption, and reducing administrative burdens affecting SMEs; promoting entrepreneurship in the media, educational settings and society in general; and reporting on regulatory projects and improvements.

The Council is chaired by the Ministry of Industry, with the General Secretariat of Industry and SMEs and the Directorate General of Industry and SMEs each holding vice-chair positions. Its consists of 52 members: 13 members representing ministerial departments of the General Administration of the State (e.g. Ministry of Justice, Ministry of Finance and Public Administration, Ministry of Education, Ministry of Agriculture, Ministry of Foreign

Box 4.3. The Inter-ministerial State Council on Small and Medium Enterprises and Entrepreneurship, Spain *(cont.)*

Affairs and Co-operation, Ministry of Employment and Social Security), eight representatives of State agencies (e.g. State Society for the Management of Innovation and Tourism, Centre for Development of Industrial Technology, Spanish Patent and Trademark Office, Spain Export and Investment, Official Credit Institute), one representative from each autonomous region, representatives of local governments, business and labour organisations representing SMEs, and the Council of Chambers of Commerce and Industry.

The Plenary body of the Council is composed of all members and acts as a consultative and advisory body on all matters affecting SMEs and entrepreneurship. It promotes dialogue amongst public administrations and economic and social agents in order to provide greater rationality and efficiency to SME and entrepreneurship policies and to formulate proposals for actions by the public authorities and intermediate agents to improve the growth, efficiency and productivity of SMEs. It meets at least once a year.

The Standing Committee of the Council, chaired by the Directorate General of Industry and SMEs, comprises representatives from the Ministry of Industry and the Ministry of Economy and Industry and Finance. It is responsible for co-ordinating and enforcing the work approved by the Plenary body. The Plenary body is also empowered to establish working groups to carry out the functions of the Council.

Relevance to Israel

The establishment of such an inter-ministerial council in Israel would foster a higher level of co-ordination of SME and entrepreneurship policies and measures at the national level and provide great benefit to the SMBA in carrying out is policy development and co-ordination responsibilities.

Sources for further information

Website on the State Council on Small and Medium Enterprises, Spain: *www.ipyme.org/es-ES/PoliticasMedidasPYME/ConsejoGeneralPYME/Paginas/ConsejoEstatalPYME.aspx/*.

policies and measures affecting SMEs and entrepreneurship in Israel, with representation from all the relevant ministries and agencies. The Committee could be chaired by the Minister of Economy and Industry and should meet at least twice a year to discuss SME and entrepreneurship policy priorities and objectives and agree a work plan (e.g. an annual SME and entrepreneurship policy action plan) to achieve those objectives, with functions very similar to those of the State Council on Small and Medium Enterprises and Entrepreneurship in Spain (Box 4.3). The SMBA could perform the role of secretariat functions to the Committee. One of its first tasks could be drafting a national SME and entrepreneurship strategy document. It also needs to undertake a range of research, analysis, evaluation and consultation to inform policy development and prioritisation.

The Inter-ministerial Committee should also work closely with the Knesset's Small Business Sub-Committee, which is part of the Finance Committee although, in this regard, it would also be advisable for the Knesset to set up a full SME Committee with a broader mandate than small business financing.

At a more operational level, cross-ministerial co-operation in Israel would also be strengthened by the creation of an SME and Entrepreneurship Policy Working Group, represented by SME focal points in each relevant ministry and agency. Such a working group, which could be chaired by the SMBA, could meet monthly or bi-monthly to discuss policy issues affecting the development of SMEs and entrepreneurship in the country, share information on approaches, and identify opportunities for co-operation and collaboration. The establishment of such a working group, together with an inter-ministerial committee, would go a long way in kick-starting a government-wide approach to SME and entrepreneurship policy that encompasses all the relevant departments of the Ministry of Economy and Industry as well as other ministries with programmes in support of SMEs and entrepreneurs, and enable the SMBA to more effectively and legitimately carry out its co-ordination role.

As well as strengthening the legal authority of the SMBA and establishing formal SME policy co-ordination mechanisms, it is necessary to correct the small scale of the existing financial and human resources of the SMBA compared with the tasks it needs to carry out (co-ordinating policy measures, delivering certain programmes directly and advocating for regulatory improvements). The SMBA has five divisions which cover financing (i.e. primarily the loan guarantee scheme), research and international relations, government regulations, the MAOF network of business development centres and corporate services (internal systems, ICT, etc.). However, with a staff of only 20 in 2016, comprising 6 professionals and 14 administrative assistants, the SMBA is clearly under-resourced. For example, the SMBA is asked to prepare opinions on the impact on SMEs of Knesset Bills on a weekly basis, whereas the regulation division of the SMBA is staffed with only one professional, who is therefore left with little time for proactive efforts to advocate for SME-related improvements in existing legislation, such as pushing for implementing the SME Test as part of the Regulatory Impact Assessment (RIA) regime. More staff resourcing is therefore needed to enable the SMBA to play a stronger role.

Furthermore, the SMBA does not have a secure annual programme budget but instead receives an annual allocation from the Ministry of Economy and Industry, which was approximately NIS 215 million in 2015.[1] In order to facilitate the SMBA's programme planning and reduce the uncertainty around year-to-year funding of SME support programmes, the SMBA should be allocated a multi-year budget. To take this forward, the SMBA's next three-year SME strategy can be used to determine the scale of the multi-year budget needed for the SMBA and its allocation to the specific policy pillars outlined in the SMBA strategy. The funding of the MAOF centres represents a good practice – the Ministry of Finance provided the SMBA with a three-year budget of NIS 195 million for the MAOF Centres in 2013-15. This multi-annual approach should be spread to other SMBA activities.

Dialogue with SMEs and entrepreneurs

It is good practice in SME and entrepreneurship policy that the government initiates a dialogue with representatives of SMEs and entrepreneurs to ensure that the concerns and needs of small business owners are effectively reflected in public policy making (OECD and UNIDO, 2004). Many OECD governments have therefore established SME advisory committees to allow for a structured dialogue between the government and representatives of the SME sector. The membership of these committees is generally broad, including chambers of commerce, small business associations, SME support organisations, and independent experts (see the example from Ireland in Box 4.4).

In Israel, the SMBA has formed an ad-hoc consultative advisory committee on SMEs consisting of representatives from four major business associations. Although the committee does not have an official mandate and role, the business associations have been

Box 4.4. Example of a SME Advisory Committee, Ireland

The Advisory Group for Small Business (AGSB) in Ireland, was established by the Ministry for Small Business in June 2011 as a forum to facilitate structured and regular dialogue between the government and representatives of the small business sector and to provide policy advice for onward reference to government on the key issues affecting the development and growth of the SME sector and possible solutions. The 17-member body consists mainly of entrepreneurs, nominees from the main small business and sector representative bodies, Startup Ireland, officials from the Department of Jobs, Enterprise and Innovation, the state enterprise support agencies, Enterprise Ireland, and the Credit Review Office.

The first task assigned to the Group was to carry out consultations to develop an action plan for small business, which they submitted to the Minister for Small Business in November 2011. The group has been active in promoting entrepreneur-friendly policies and procedures and has made submissions regarding the budgetary policies adopted by government in the budgetary process over the last number of years. It has also provided direct feedback on a number of proposals that had an impact on entrepreneurship.

Source: Website of the Advisory Group of Small Business, *www.djei.ie/en/What-We-Do/Supports-for-SMEs/Advisory-Group-for-Small-Business/*.

consulted on a number of occasions on issues affecting SMEs. In particular, valuable inputs have been provided on regulatory reforms with an impact on SMEs. Going forward, the SMBA could establish a more formal consultation mechanism with SMEs and entrepreneurs. This could follow the format of a series of forums with SMEs and entrepreneurs organised by the SMBA to solicit opinions and input on government regulations and policies.

The programme portfolio and mix

Israel has a well-developed policy to support the R&D activity of high-technology businesses and to provide the framework conditions in which they can thrive. At the same time, its support for non-technology based start-ups and SMEs is relatively weak, including the scale of programme support for non-R&D based innovation, new business creation in non-technology fields, promoting the growth of traditional SMEs, supporting young entrepreneurs and promoting entrepreneurship in the education system. SMBA can support a number of important programme measures in these areas, both directly and by encouraging other ministries and agencies to bend their own resources to these purposes.

Strengthening the policy focus on raising the level of innovativeness of non-technological SMEs

The SME productivity gap is most evident among SMEs in low technology manufacturing sectors, largely due to differences in capital availability, skills and innovativeness. One of the keys to addressing this productivity challenge is to promote innovation more broadly across SMEs in these sectors, with emphasis on innovation in new products, processes, marketing and organisational approaches. This will require a rebalancing of the current policy emphasis on technological innovation that is directed primarily at fostering the R&D activity of high-technology enterprises. In this regard, more SME programme support is needed to address the limited capacity of traditional SMEs to pursue innovative activity and support their efforts to develop innovation-related projects that will improve their productivity and diversification into new products and markets. To improve the innovativeness of SMEs will require attention to skills development, management capacity, business support to assist SMEs to identify opportunities to improve their businesses through innovation (e.g. diagnostic and consultancy services, and access to the financing required to implement innovation, such as for the upgrading of equipment and technology, integration of information and communications technologies and systems, training of employees, etc.). Part of this effort should involve a more coherent strategy to target the innovativeness of microenterprises, which are largely overlooked as generators of economic benefits.

Increasing programme support for new business creation, especially in non-technological fields

Apart from encouraging and supporting high-technology start-ups, government programme support for business creation has been somewhat limited. Although Israel has seen growth in the number of enterprises over the last 10 years, the economy could benefit from a higher level of entrepreneurial activity in the form of stronger and more innovative start-ups (with higher survival rates), which would have a positive impact on productivity improvements in the SME sector and create more jobs. This requires an emphasis on new start-ups that have higher levels of human capital, innovativeness and business/marketing sophistication. New entrepreneurs would benefit from enhanced know-how at the initial stages of business development through better access to entrepreneurship training, mentoring, and management development support. While including a "know-how" component, current SME programmes in Israel do not specifically emphasise policies to foster stronger start-ups as part of the business creation process. A proactive policy approach to ensure widespread access to entrepreneurship orientation and competency-building initiatives, including workshops, seminars, conference events, and mentors, across the population would help create a more informed path into the entrepreneurial pipeline.

Promoting the growth of traditional SMEs

Programme intervention has also been limited with respect to promoting the growth of the typical SME. Since productivity generally increases with firm size, increased productivity in Israel would be promoted by programmes aimed at fostering the development of microenterprises into small enterprises and small enterprises into medium enterprises, especially in the non-technological sectors where the productivity gap is the most severe.

Israel's SME policy should be more sensitive to the needs of SMEs at various stages of growth and target specific policies and programmes to remove the growth barriers and constraints. This would require adoption of a "pipeline approach" to entrepreneurship and SME policy – targeting entrepreneurship and SME development through the different phases of entrepreneurial activity and business development, i.e. potential entrepreneurs, start-ups, early-stage growth-potential micro and small enterprises, and medium-sized enterprises with the potential for integrating into global markets.

Programmes for the development of young entrepreneurs

Although Israel operates dedicated programmes for immigrants, minority populations and women, there is no special policy focus on the development of young entrepreneurs, as is common in most OECD countries. However, young people face a number of barriers in their efforts to start businesses. These include market failures in the provision of information to young entrepreneurs, lack of work experience and knowledge, difficulty in accessing financial capital, and limited business networks. Policy actions that can be developed to address these barriers include: promoting entrepreneurship skills to address the lack of knowledge and prior work and entrepreneurial experience; providing information, advice, coaching and mentoring during and after start-up; and providing financial support to compensate for the lack of initial capital and difficulty in obtaining financing (OECD/European Union, 2012).

Policy to foster integration of entrepreneurship throughout the education system

Given Israel's reputation as an entrepreneurial society, it may seem paradoxical to recommend that the SMBA adopt a policy focus on promoting an entrepreneurial culture, but this a particular policy gap in its SME policy agenda at present. One of the key policy approaches to strengthening the entrepreneurial culture is to integrate entrepreneurship throughout the educational system with the aim of promoting entrepreneurial mind sets and entrepreneurship behaviours in the population. Governments in many OECD countries now include this as a policy objective in their entrepreneurship and SME development strategies, but this not one of the stated policy priorities of the SMBA or the Ministry of Economy. Although the Israeli Ministry of Education has ad-hoc initiatives to expose students to future career opportunities and entrepreneurial pathways through linkage with the business community, the national education policy does not put a defined focus on entrepreneurial competence as outcome in curriculum guidelines (OECD/European Commission/European Training Foundation, 2014). In other countries, economy ministries often provide the policy push for integrating entrepreneurship throughout the education system and it is becoming common practice for the ministries and agencies responsible for SMEs and for education to work collaboratively to agree on a plan of action for incorporating entrepreneurship concepts across all levels of the education system, as well as across all disciplines of study.

The SMBA could play a role in promoting the more widespread introduction of entrepreneurship throughout the education system, including vocational training and university programmes on a cross-disciplinary basis, as one of the policy objectives in a new SME and entrepreneurship strategy document for Israel. This policy effort would require collaboration between the SMBA and the Ministry of Education, as well as with the Ministry of Economy unit responsible for vocational training.

Policy delivery arrangements

A number of government and public-supported are involved in delivering entrepreneurship and SME policy supports in Israel (Figure 4.1). These can be categorised by type of policy support: start-up and business development support (non-financial), financing support, access to markets, and innovation support. A number of parallel structures are in place for delivering SME policy supports – one for high-technology enterprises by the IIA (e.g. R&D funds, technological incubators), one for traditional start-ups and SMEs (e.g. MAOFs), and one for Arab Israelis (e.g. MEDA programmes, Nazareth Business Incubator Centre) and immigrant entrepreneurs (Ministry of Immigrant Absorption). However, there is no typology mapping of support programmes and target groups to identify where precise gaps may exist. Overall, it is nevertheless clear that the delivery of policy support is more developed for high-technology entrepreneurs, sectors and enterprises than for traditional start-ups and SMEs.

Figure 4.1. **Schematic of the main policy delivery structures for SME support in Israel**

Start-up and business development support

- **SMBA** – network of 35 local development centres (MAOFs) offering start-up training, counselling, subsidised consultancy and mentoring services, information and referrals
- **Ministry of Immigrant Absorption** – Entrepreneurs Division operates 6 Business Centres for New Immigrants and Returning Residents, provides entrepreneurship counsellors in regions serving these populations
- **Authority for Economic Development of the Minorities Sector (MEDA)** in the Ministry for Social Equality – business consultancy, start-up and management training, two business centres, an industrial incubator (business accelerator) targeting minority entrepreneurs
- **Nazareth Business Incubator Centre (NBIC)** – targets Israeli Arabs, since 2012; financed by Ministry of Economy and Industry to promote Arab entrepreneurship
- **Naztech** – 5-month accelerator programme (for Israeli Arabs, since 2013)

Access to markets

- **FTA** – programmes to encourage and expand exporting activity of Israeli enterprises, including SMEs (e.g. Fund for Promotion of Overseas Marketing)
- **Israel Export Institute (IEI)** – semi-government organisation(partly funded by the FTA); raises awareness of export opportunities, increases participation of Israeli companies in trade fairs; assists in locating agents/distributors in foreign markets; Centre for Small Exporters offers export training to potential/existing exporting SMEs, mentoring programmes for new exporters
- **MEDA** – *Tevel* Programme, in partnership with the IEI and the FTA to assist exporting activity of Arab SMEs
- **SME Division in Ministry of Defence** – promotes international business opportunities for SMEs in defence sector
- **Ministry of Finance** – provisions to enable SMEs to access public procurement opportunities

Financing support

- **Small and Medium Business Fund (SMBF)** – loan guarantee scheme; administered by SMBA and Ministry of Finance through co-ordinating bodies and partner banks
- **Ministry of Finance** – tax credits to investors in early-stage companies (Angels' Law); authorises funds to the Koret Foundation for micro-credit
- **Israeli Investment Center** (Ministry of Economy and Industry) – grant schemes to support private investment and job creation activity in peripheral regions
- **MEDA** – Al Bawader Private Investment Fund (2010); top up of SMBF to target Arab/minority SMEs
- **Ministry of Immigrant Absorption** – "Independent Immigrant Fund" supports self-employment activity of immigrants and returning Israelis
- **Koret Israel Economic Development Fund (KIEDF)** – NGO with partial funding from Ministry of Finance to provide microcredit and small business loans to marginalised groups
- **IIA seed capital funds** for R&D-driven enterprises
- **70 venture capital funds,** almost exclusively investing in high technology ventures

Innovation support

- **Israel Innovation Authority (IIA)** – R&D Fund - grants for innovation activities; oversees more than 30 programmes to strengthen scientific and technological innovation; promotes the development of advanced technologies in Israel and international co-operation agreements and joint ventures
- **IIA Network of 18 Technological Incubators** (public-private partnerships)
- **Hybid Fund** (2016) to promote innovative start-ups in the Arab sector (Ministry of Economy and Industry with the NBIC)
- **Technology transfer centres** in universities, facilitating linkages between academe and industry
- **Technion** – Israel Institute of Technology, Knowledge Centre for Innovation - provides training and consultancy to traditional industries on designing, planning and implementing innovation projects

Source: OECD Elaboration.

Policy delivery arrangements refer to the way public programmes are implemented. For example, business development services centres can be managed directly by the government through the recruitment of local officers in charge of the transfer of information and other services to the targeted SMEs, or alternatively the same services can be contracted out by the government to private-sector companies, which deliver them on behalf of the government.

This section focuses on the way key government agencies in SME and entrepreneurship policy in Israel reach out to their clients, namely the SMBA, the MEDA, the Israel Innovation Authority (IIA), the FTA and the Israel Export Institute (IEI), and the Ministry of Immigrant Absorption. Detailed descriptions and assessment of the SME support programmes are presented in Chapter 5.

The SMBA

The SMBA was launched in 2010, following the 2007 government resolution No. 2190, which aimed to simplify and improve the targeting of a range of existing SME support actions. The SMBA was tasked with helping deliver the SME credit guarantee fund with the Ministry of Finance, including in scaling it up and improving its efficiency, with improving the system of business development services to entrepreneurs and SMEs, and with improving policy co-ordination across government and with the private sector.

The SMBA replaced the former Israel Small and Medium Enterprises Authority, which was set up in 1993 as a not-for-profit social partnership between the government, local delivery agents and NGOs to provide business advice and assistance to prospective and existing businesses. The former agency had delivered business development services through 25 MATI business support centres located across Israel delivered by a loose group of NGOs. MATI provision continued until 2013. In 2013, MATI provided conferences, training sessions (4 127 participants), business planning (1 600), the "Initiating a Business" entrepreneurship training programme, and consulting services for entrepreneurs, including microenterprises (7 000 entrepreneurs, most of whom were micro businesses (1-4 employees) with 185 000 hours of consulting).

The government had originally opted for this approach in the belief that an NGO would be closer to the private sector and more able to understand its needs. However, in 2014 the SMBA decided to replace the MATI centre system with a new system of MAOF centres, as the result of a lack of government control and influence over the MATI centre programmes and a poor review of the impact of the MATI centres by the Auditor General, which found variable levels of quality and consistency in their support services. An SMBA survey run in 2011, for example, had found that 70% of MATI clients did not believe that they received quality support from them. The new MAOF structure aims to create national quality standards for services and assistance to entrepreneurs and SMEs, with a standardised delivery of services.

The main objectives of the MAOF centres are to increase the survival rate of businesses, improve SME productivity, accelerate SME growth, and meet the needs of minority-owned SMEs. To do so, they employ 120 staff members and have an annual budget of NIS 65 million, which is similar to the budget made available to the previous MATI system. Through this budget, the SMBA expects to serve about 12 000 entrepreneurs and SME owners each year. The range of MAOF services is also very similar to that offered under MATI, focused on government-funded training for new entrepreneurs and early diagnostic and management support services for SMEs, including referral to other relevant government services and consultants. Some co-operation exists between the SMBA, MEDA and the Ministry of Immigrant Absorption in delivering MAOF supports to marginalised groups and this is promoted through additional MAOF funding to the SMBA to serve these target groups.

The SMBA has also improved delivery of policy supports to peripheral regions by setting up MAOFs in areas of the country not previously served by the predecessor MATI network. However, the development of more support infrastructure is likely to be needed in these regions. This is particularly the case in Arab Israeli communities where SMEs and entrepreneurs lack access to adequate premises to start and operate their businesses. It will be important to support the development of industrial zones and non-technological business incubators in more peripheral regions to improve access to start-up facilities and capacity building resources.

To improve visibility and co-ordination compared to the previous MATI system, the SMBA also set up an integrated web-based information, guidance and signposting service to nascent and existing entrepreneurs (see Box 4.5).

Box 4.5. **SMBA's One-Stop Shop SME programme information service**

One of the challenges facing entrepreneurs and existing small firms is finding information that will guide them on ways to navigate government regulations, get help and assistance both from the government and outside support, and receive practical advice that will lead to business development. The SMBA website (*www.sba.economy.gov.il*) provides an integrated, comprehensive 'one-stop shop', backed up by a mobile phone app and its own Youtube channel, that provides nascent and existing entrepreneurs with the following:

- Information: regular updates of government schemes, events and notices, the opportunity to join the mailing list, and a Facebook page.
- Guidance: guides to legal issues (e.g. issues involved in incorporation, partnerships, lease agreements), marketing and sales (e.g. marketing plan), accountancy issues (e.g. compliance issues with the government). The website also offers practical business plan calculators that help entrepreneurs estimate production costs, start-up costs and cash flows).
- Signposting: offers links to MAOF local centres, links to other support providers (e.g. Israeli Chamber of Commerce) and a detailed and comprehensive search engine providing information on governmental and non-governmental finance and advice schemes.

Source: Website of the SMBA, *sba.economy.gov.il*, and information submitted by the SMBA to the OECD

The SMBA manages its two major SME and entrepreneurship support programmes, the MAOF centres and the SMBF, via intermediary organisations. This helps the SMBA deal with the scale of the operations needed on the ground but also requires an effective system of performance monitoring and control of the intermediaries so that they deliver the services appropriately. In the case of the SMBF national loan guarantee scheme, the SMBA and the Ministry of Finance have set up service-contract agreements with two independent companies to undertake the first screening of loan guarantee applications from SME applicants before sending them on to partner banks (if approved to go to the second stage). The delivery of this Israeli programme is very labour-intensive, since all guarantee decisions are made on an individual applicant basis and an extensive amount of screening and due diligence is necessary before the file is even transferred to a bank for review. The rationale for this approach is that Israeli SMEs do not have a high level of financial literary, keep inadequate accounting records, and lack the capacity to produce bankable financial proposals. Out-sourcing the management of the programme to private sector companies relieves the SMBA of having to perform these functions but it does come with high programme administrative costs. The operation of the MAOF centres is contracted out to five private sector intermediary organisations selected by the SMBA through a competitive tender process to run parts of the network under service-management agreements in five different regions of the country.

The choice of the SMBA to use intermediary organisations for the delivery of its main support programmes comes with both pros and cons. The main advantage consists in staffing economies and relief from burdensome administrative and management tasks. Clearly, if the SMBA were to manage the SMBF applications and the MAOF centres directly, it would have to hire large numbers of local officers and put in place an internal system of control and management to monitor their work on a daily basis. By contracting out, the SMBA manages to reduce staff costs and to focus on more strategic work related to SME and entrepreneurship policy. However, the outsourcing choice also has some disadvantages, such as less control on the everyday activities of the SMBF and the MAOF centres and loss of continuity if contracting companies do not perform well and need to be replaced, possibly causing a disruption in the delivery of services.

Systematic monitoring and evaluation is a very important tool for operating a system of intermediary organisations effectively. The SMBA is already engaged in an evaluation of the SMBF, which should provide useful information to help adjust the management of the programme if necessary. In parallel it should also implement a system for monitoring and evaluating the MAOF centres. An appropriate system for monitoring the allocation of funding by type of services and firm size is already in place together with monitoring of operational guidelines and quality standards. In addition, the SMBA will have to implement an assessment of the real impact of the centres on their beneficiary SMEs and entrepreneurs. This will require setting clear objectives for each of the programmes managed by the MAOF centres to evaluate whether the objectives are met, whether MAOF-supported companies do better than others, which support programmes have a stronger impact, and whether certain centres and the intermediaries that manage them do better than others.

The importance of evaluation has already been recognised by the SMBA (see Box 4.6), but there is still scope for spreading its evaluation work more widely. The same approach to impact evaluation is required for other SME policy supports, such as the SMBF, the IIA innovation policy measures, the export promotion policies, MEDA programmes, and entrepreneurial activities of the Ministry of Immigrant Absorption.

The MAOF centres also rely on a wide network of external consultants who receive referrals of SMEs and entrepreneurs from MAOF centre staff. The SMBA has created and keeps up to date a database of approximately 850 private consultants with expertise in legal, financial and business operation fields. The use of external consultants is in principle a reasonable choice as it will contribute to creating a market for private sector business support services in Israel. However, it is important that the consultants in the system are appropriately skilled and have appropriate incentives. The SMBA will need to ensure that the private consultants are able to supply high-quality services and that SME clients actually benefit from consultancy interventions. This can be achieved, for example, through client satisfaction surveys and follow-up on the quality of specific consultancy assignments. Upgrading the skills and knowledge of MAOF business advisers is also critical because their advisers make key referral decisions about what types of support are available either from

Box 4.6. **Evaluating entrepreneurship and SME policies and programmes**

The SMBA has not yet established a formal process to systematically evaluate the effectiveness and impact of all SME and entrepreneurship policies and programmes, although the SMBA strategy of 2011 made several recommendations with respect to monitoring and evaluating the effectiveness of SME support (Adalya Economic Consulting, 2011). These recommendations included:

- Consulting with international SME programme evaluation experts and organising workshops on the topic with the involvement of such experts.
- Creating an annually-updated statistical database with relevant segmentations for monitoring the status of SMEs (e.g. the distribution of businesses by turnover range, number of employees, economic sector, location, and export activity) in collaboration with the Central Bureau of Statistics.
- Creating, managing and maintaining an electronic database of entrepreneurs and businesses that receive aid from any of the relevant government organisations and agencies. This will assist in preventing duplication, monitoring the take up of assistance from different programmes, cross-checking the assistance received by any business or entrepreneur, and more effectively monitoring and evaluating the SME support system.
- Carrying out surveys and studies based on reliable information about businesses and entrepreneurs receiving assistance (including satisfaction surveys, surveys designed to test the effectiveness of certain devices, etc.).
- Identifying performance indicators for each of the individual support programmes.
- Periodically conducting a telephone survey of businesses (at least once every three years) so as to receive empirical data on trends in SME development, barriers and needs.
- Conducting satisfaction surveys (quarterly/semi-annually) among a representative sample of businesses and entrepreneurs who received services from the SMBA. Satisfaction surveys can be a useful indicator of the current level of success in delivering a proper level of service to SMEs in business development services centres, provided the surveys are carried out consistently and use the same format over time.

Moving ahead in constructing these databases would provide a framework for setting appropriate indicators of success that would enable the SMBA to draw conclusions about SME and entrepreneurship support programmes and to conduct to better inform and update policy. To date, this work has not been completed, but it is essential to the proper evaluation and management of SME and entrepreneurship support programmes.

Source: OECD based on OECD (2007), OECD Framework for the Evaluation of SME and Entrepreneurship Policies and Programmes, OECD Publishing, Paris.

the government or other support providers. This support landscape is fluid and without up-to-date support, business advisers may be ill-equipped to provide their clients with credible and accurate support.

In addition, it is important that MAOF staff members are properly trained to provide appropriate early business diagnostic analysis, are knowledgeable about existing government support programmes and services, and are fully familiar with experts and advisors in the SMBA database. MAOF staff members must therefore be properly trained and up-to-date with existing programmes and expertise available in the market for consulting services.

The Authority for Economic Development of the Minorities Sector (MEDA)

The Authority for Economic Development of the Minorities Sector (MEDA), which moved to the Ministry of Social Equality in 2015, delivers a range of policies for SME and entrepreneurship development by ethnic minority populations in the country, namely the Arabs, Druze and Circassians, which are under-represented in the entrepreneurial population. It delivers a number of programmes to SMEs and entrepreneurs as part of this mandate. It provides business advice and training to new and potential new entrepreneurs from minority populations through four business centres and an industrial incubator. In the area of access to financing, it contributes funding to the SMBF to facilitate the allocation of loan guarantees to minority-owned SMEs, co-operates with an NGO to make micro-credit available to Arab Israeli women interested in setting up a business and has launched an investment fund to provide equity finance to promising Arab-owned enterprises. Finally, it organises entrepreneurship awareness-raising events for youth in minority communities and operates the *Tevel* export programme for minority enterprises in close partnership with the Ministry of Economy and Industry's FTA and the IEI.

The Israel Innovation Authority (IIA)

The Israel Innovation Authority (IIA), housed in the Ministry of Economy and Industry, oversees all government-sponsored R&D support. The IIA replaced the Office of the Chief Scientist (OCS) in January 2016, by virtue of major amendments to the 1984 R&D Law. The IIA oversees more than 30 R&D and innovation support programmes, one of its main programmes being the "R&D Fund", which provides R&D grants to businesses at various development stages, including for high-technology start-ups and a track for businesses in traditional industries. Supported projects are funded annually, with funding confirmed if the projects meet the agreed milestones.

The IIA also oversees 18 technology incubators, which offer technical expertise, seed funding and network opportunities to high-technology start-ups. The Technological Incubators Programme has been in place for many years, initially with 24 incubators operated by the Office of the Chief Scientist. As part of a reform process that began in 2011, Israel's technology incubators are today organised as public-private partnerships, with the incubator hosts selected by the IIA through a competitive call for proposals. Successful applicant firms receive an eight-year license by the IIA that gives the winners the right to establish an incubator and submit funding applications to the IIA in support of each incubating enterprise. Of the NIS 2 million specified for each incubated enterprise, the IIA provides 85%, with the remaining 15% invested by the license holder. The license holders must make a minimal commitment of NIS 50 million for the incubator license, which provides assurances that the operator has the capability to support incubated companies further down the line. The licenses are often held by venture capital companies and technology development companies that can bring a wealth of knowledge, international exposure, capital and networks to enhance the chances of success of the incubating start-ups. This new model has attracted global interest from other countries.

The Foreign Trade Administration (FTA) and the Israel Export Institute (IEI)

The Ministry of Economy and Industry's Foreign Trade Administration (FTA) is the main agency for export promotion in Israel. It directly manages Israel's main export promotion funds, such as the "Smart Money" Programme for encouraging access by Israeli firms to overseas markets and the India-China Fund to help Israeli firms gain access to these emerging economies. The Israel Export Institute (IEI) is an important partner for some of the FTA's activities through the provision of coaching, mentoring and technical assistance to the FTA-supported firms with respect to, *inter alia*, participation in international trade fairs, identification of local agents and distributors and compliance with international industrial standards.

Ministry of Immigrant Absorption

Finally, the Ministry of Immigrant Absorption has established its own network of business centres and entrepreneurship counsellors to assist new immigrants and returning residents in starting and developing their own businesses. The Ministry of Immigrant Absorption also provides financial support for the establishment, acquisition and expansion of immigrant-owned small businesses, for example through the Self-Employed Immigrant Fund, which offers preferential start-up loans (up to NIS 125 000) to self-employed immigrants and returning residents. Some of these activities, notably those of the business information centres and counsellors, are very similar to those of the SMBA's MAOF centres, although the Ministry does co-operate with local MAOF centres to deliver subsidised consultancy and mentoring support to its immigrant clients to help in preparation of a business plan and launch of the business. Nonetheless, greater synergies should be nurtured between these two government entities on their SME and entrepreneurship support activities.

Conclusions and policy recommendations

The importance of SME and entrepreneurship policy is duly recognised in the Israeli economic policy agenda. For example, SME development is one of the main stated objectives of the Ministry of Economy and Industry, and many other government ministries and agencies have relevant actions for the support of SMEs and entrepreneurs. Furthermore, the SMBA has been created to strengthen business development services and SME access to finance and improve government regulation of SMEs and entrepreneurship.

However, the SMBA is currently lacking a full set of formal structures to formulate strategy and co-ordinate government actors around SME and entrepreneurship policy priorities. In particular, there is no comprehensive and integrated national SME and entrepreneurship policy strategy and no inter-ministerial SME and entrepreneurship policy committee or working group. In a more fully developed, adequately resourced, and legislatively reinforced authoritative role, the SMBA could address these deficiencies by ensuring that SME and entrepreneurship policy meets the market needs and government priorities, and bringing SME and entrepreneurship policy together across government.

Although the SMBA co-operates with MEDA and the Ministry of Immigrant Absorption on delivery arrangements for SME support to Arab Israeli and immigrant groups through the MAOF network, the existence of parallel support structures reinforces the need for more formal co-ordination of the system of supports by the SMBA, which has the mandate for co-ordination of all organisations involved in promoting the SME sector. An SMBA working group on SMEs and entrepreneurship could play an important role in co-ordinating the disparate structures, strengthening collaboration where appropriate to reduce fragmentation, duplication and overlaps, and identifying gaps that partnerships could best address.

The SMBA can also play a stronger role in delivering business development services to SMEs and entrepreneurs. In doing so, its management of intermediary organisations could be strengthened by increasing its monitoring and evaluation of the intermediaries and the training of their staff.

The following key recommendations are offered to strengthen the strategic planning of SME and entrepreneurship policies and improve their coordination and implementation:

Key recommendations on the strategic framework and policy delivery system

- Prepare an overarching medium-term national SME and entrepreneurship strategic policy, presented in a stand-alone document, which outlines the vision, objectives, priority pillars, target groups, and lines of action across government.
- Create an inter-ministerial SME and Entrepreneurship Policy Committee, with SMBA as its secretariat, and an inter-ministerial Working Group on SME and Entrepreneurship Policy, led by the SMBA and consisting of SME focal points from relevant ministries and agencies.
- Set up a framework of formal consultation forums with SMEs and entrepreneurs, co-ordinated by the SMBA, to solicit their opinions and input on government regulations and policies.
- Conduct an analysis of the current and future staffing and budget requirements of the SMBA and consider strengthening its resources. Strengthen the legal authority of the SMBA by making it a full-authority SME agency.
- Match the SMBA's three-year strategies with a multi-year funding commitment from the Ministry of Finance.
- Ensure that MAOF staff members are fully trained in providing diagnostic and referral services, including deep familiarisation with support programmes offered by other government departments and agencies and the competencies of consultants in the SMBA database.
- Implement a system for regular monitoring of the quality of services being delivered by each MAOF centre and their adherence to specified performance standards. Carry out evaluations of the impact of MAOF services on performance outcomes of clients using robust control group methodologies.
- Implement an evaluation system for monitoring the take-up by SMEs and entrepreneurs of policy measures across government entities, identifying performance indicators for each support device, and measuring the impact of each policy measure against these performance indicators.
- Establish a co-ordination mechanism for policy support structures, led by the SMBA, to foster communication and exchange among all entities delivering SME and entrepreneurship supports for the purpose of achieving greater collaboration and economies of scale. This could be done within the framework of a Working Group on SME and Entrepreneurship Policy.
- Undertake an assessment of the mix of the portfolio of SME and entrepreneurship programmes by programme type and enterprise target group, including contrasting expenditures and outcomes by technology and non-technology entrepreneurship. Based on the results of this assessment, increase programme support for traditional start-ups and SMEs, including programmes for non-R&D based innovation, new business creation in non-technology fields, promoting the growth of traditional SMEs, supporting young entrepreneurs and promoting entrepreneurship in the education system.

Note

1. This budget included NIS 90 million for SME training programmes, NIS 60 million for entrepreneurship training programmes, NIS 55 million for the establishment of private equity growth funds (new in 2015), and NIS 10 million for other SME support programmes.

References

Adalya Economic Consulting (2011), *Strategic Report of Israeli Governmental Assistance to Small and Medium Businesses – Phase A*, submitted to Small and Medium Business Agency, November, Tel Aviv, Adalya Economic Consulting.

European Commission (2008), *Think Small First, A Small Business Act for Europe*, Communication from the Commission to the Council, the European Parliament, the European Economic and Social Committee and the Committee of the Regions, 25 June, Brussels, European Commission.

OECD/European Commission/European Training Foundation (2014), *SME Policy Index: The Mediterranean Middle East and North Africa 2014: Implementation of the Small Business Act for Europe*, OECD Publishing, Paris, *http://dx.doi.org/10.1787/9789264218413-en*.

OECD/European Union (2012), *Policy Brief on Youth Entrepreneurship*, OECD Publishing, Paris.

OECD and UNIDO (2004), Effective Policies for Small Business: A Guide for the Policy Review Process and Strategic Plans for Micro, Small and Medium Enterprise Development, Paris: OECD.

OECD (2007), *OECD Framework for the Evaluation of SME and Entrepreneurship Policies and Programmes*, OECD Publishing, Paris.

OECD (2000), *The Bologna Charter on SME Policies*. OECD, Paris, Available online at *www.oecd.org/cfe/smes/thebolognacharteronsmepolicies.htm*.

Senor, D. and S. Singer (2009), *Start-up Nation: The Story of Israel's Economic Miracle*, Toronto, Canada, McClelland & Stewart

Small and Medium Business Agency (SMBA) (2014), "English Translation of the Hebrew text of the SME Bill", unpublished document.

Chapter 5

National programmes for SMEs and entrepreneurship in Israel

This chapter assesses programmes supported by the national government to promote the development of SMEs and entrepreneurship in Israel. It covers programmes in the areas of financing, innovation, internationalisation, entrepreneurial culture and skills, workforce skills, business advice and assistance, public procurement from SMEs and dedicated initiatives for particular social target groups. The chapter discusses many successful programmes, including SME loan guarantees, R&D grants and business advice and consultancy services. It also identifies a number of areas for potential improvement. These include extending the duration of loan guarantees, expanding support for non-technological innovation in SMEs, increasing the emphasis of export programmes on new exporters, and expanding support for workforce training in SMEs.

Access to finance programmes

The State Credit Guarantee Programme

One of the government's main programmes to improve credit flows to SMEs involves the provision of state loan guarantees. Its intervention in this area started in 2003 in order to ensure that SMEs had sufficient access to bank financing, including longer-term financing. However, the early actions were fraught with limitations, largely due to lack of co-ordination in training and technical assistance to the guarantee recipients, insufficient post-loan monitoring, and inconsistent underwriting standards and procedures (Yago and Zeldman, 2005).

During the period 2007-12, there were four government loan guarantee funds: the Small Business Fund; the Medium-Sized Business Fund (launched in 2009 in response to the economic crisis); the Exporters Fund; and the Self-Employed Immigrants Fund. In 2012, the first three of these funds merged into a single Small and Medium Businesses Fund (SMBF), managed by the SMBA and the Ministry of Finance. The Self-Employed Immigrant Fund continued operating alone through the Ministry of Immigrant Absorption. This continued separation could have costs in terms of unexploited economies of scale.

The merger of the three former funds into the SMBF was accompanied by a simplification of the application process for firms and of the reimbursement process for banks in case of default (i.e. the SMBF places a deposit in participating banks to cover guaranteed losses in case of defaults). The guarantee coverage for loans to new businesses was also increased to 85%, in order to reflect the more severe financing barriers faced by start-ups.

The first 4-year period of operation of the SMBF ran from March 2012 to March 2016. The scale of funding was boosted compared with the previous schemes, with an additional NIS 500 million allocated over the four years. This brought the fund to almost NIS 1 billion, with a target of leveraging up to NIS 4.38 billion of bank credit to SMEs. Banks were invited to tender to the Ministry of Finance and the SMBA for the provision of guaranteed loans. Banks competed on the basis of how much credit they would be willing to provide to SMEs for every NIS of government guarantee, with the range set between 5:1 and 10:1. Four banks were retained for the first round of the programme in 2012-16 – Bank Hapoalim, Bank Mizrahi, Mekantil Discount Bank, and Bank Otsar Ha-Hayal. A tender was also issued for companies to assist in the management of the programme, including the selection process for loans to be guaranteed.

A second 4-year round of the SMBF was introduced in March 2016. This aims to provide a total of NIS 6.6 billion of bank credit to SMEs, but could potentially extend to NIS 20 billion. Following the tender for the second round, one of the large banks, Bank Hapoalim, was replaced with another, Bank Leumi. Furthermore, rather than working solely with banks, as was the case in the first period, the second round involves providing state guarantees to consortia of banks and institutional investors. This works through four agreements with: Bank Leumi and Menora Mivtachim Holdings Ltd; Bank Mizrachi, Altshuler Shaham Group and Phoenix Investments and Finance Ltd; Bank Merkantil-Discount and Amitim Fund; and

Bank Otsar Ha-Hayal and the Meitav-Dash Fund. The objective of this shift to consortia including institutional investors is to increase the experience of institutional investors in financing SMEs.

Certain other changes were introduced for the 2016-20 period of the SMBF compared with its first years of operation. First, there was a reduction in the government loan comprehensive guarantee (i.e. the government guarantee for the full portfolio of SMBF loans with banks and institutional investors) from 10% to 9%, which will lead to an increase in the leverage of the SMBF from 10 to 11.1. Second, the commission (i.e. the one-time administration fee) was increased from 0.5%-1.5% in 2012-16 to 1%-2% in 2016-20, depending on the size of the business. Third, an option has been introduced to guarantee loans for export activities (for loans of up to five years). Finally, an option has been introduced to guarantee longer term loans of up to 12 years for industrial capital, including R&D. These are welcome changes. They will help increase the self-sustainability of the SMBF without jeopardising its attractiveness to banks and SMEs. In addition, they will increase the ability of the programme to support exports and longer term investment loans, since the previous round of the scheme had no specific line for export loans and had been constrained by a maximum loan guarantee period of 5 years. The operational arrangements of the SMBF are presented in Box 5.1.

Box 5.1. **The operation of the SMBF**

Firms eligible for loan guarantees

To be eligible, SMEs must have no more than 70 workers and annual turnover of no more than NIS 25 million (small business) or NIS 100 million (medium business). They must also be current with their tax obligations and not have a restricted bank account.

Types of loans guaranteed

The SMBF supports four main types of loans: i) the New Business Loan (i.e. businesses that have not started operations yet); ii) the Investment Loan (i.e. investments in plant and buildings, renovation, equipment, information technology and means of production); iii) the Working Capital Loan (i.e. cash-flow management and cash shortfalls); and iv) the Export Loan (covering loans of up to 5 years for export activities).

Guarantee coverage

The SMBF guarantees up to 70% of the loan value to existing SMEs and 85% for loans to new businesses. In addition, it will guarantee up to 60% of second and third loans to the same SME. Banks, however, are allowed to request the SMEs to deposit up to 15-25% of the loan amount as collateral, leaving the bank exposed for only the remaining 5% in case of default in these cases.

Nature of loans guaranteed

The maximum size of a guaranteed loan depends on the turnover of the firm. For existing SMEs with turnover of up to NIS 3 million and new firms which have not started operations yet, the maximum guaranteed loan amount is NIS 100 000. For businesses with turnover of up to NIS 6.25 million, the maximum guaranteed loan is NIS 500 000, while for SMEs with turnover above that threshold to NIS 100 million, the maximum loan size is set at 8% of the business turnover. The guaranteed loans carry a six month grace period, are offered at market interest rates (mostly prime plus 3%), and can extend over a period of five years (Investment Loans can extend up to 12 years).

Box 5.1. **The operation of the SMBF** *(cont.)*

Application and selection process

One of the unique aspects of Israel's guarantee programme is that the government outsources the implementation of the SMBF to two externally-contracted consulting firms, which act as co-ordinating bodies and intermediaries between the SME applicants and the banks. SMEs seeking guaranteed credit send their application to one of the consulting companies, which carry out a first assessment of the loan request based on an in-depth financial and operational analysis of the business. If the guarantee is considered warrantable, the file is transferred to one of the participating banks for approval. Final loan approval decisions are made by a Credit Committee in the bank consisting of representatives from the bank, the government and the Fund co-ordinating body. If the loan is approved, the SME can accept the loan from that bank or apply to a Credit Committee of another bank in order to obtain better terms. The whole review and approval process can take up to two months and takes six weeks on average.

Fees

The government's application fee is 1%-2% according to the size of the business, payable to the Ministry of Finance. The risk premium on approved loans ranges from 0.5-1.5% of the guaranteed loan value (i.e. annual servicing fees), depending on the size of the firm.

Source: Information submitted by the SMBA to the OECD.

From April 2012 to December 2013, 11 535 SMEs submitted loan applications to the SMBF, of which some 55% were approved and 45% were rejected.[1] This is a high rejection rate compared to many programmes in other OECD countries (OECD, 2013a), although the rejection rate decreases to 70% of applicants with larger turnover and more years in business (SMBA, 2014). The high overall rejection rate does not appear to reflect particularly high risks of default. The average default rate on SMBF-guaranteed loans is 5.2% (more precisely 4.2% for medium-sized businesses and 6.5% for small businesses). This is slightly below the average rate of 5.4% found by an analysis by the World Bank of 76 credit guarantee schemes across 46 developed and developing countries (Klapper et al., 2008).

Between April 2012 and June 2014, slightly more than 8 000 SMEs received SMBF-guaranteed loans. Table 5.1 shows the breakdown of the numbers of firms supported and their shares of the loan volume by firm size. Almost 80% of the supported firms are micro and small enterprises, although they account for only slightly more than 60% of the total loan volume. Fewer than 20% are medium enterprises (20-99 employees), but they have received nearly one-third of the total loan volume. Larger enterprises (with over 100 employees) make up a very small percentage of total clients and total loan volume. During the period, approximately one-half of the guaranteed loan volumes went to manufacturing SMEs and one-half to SMEs in other sectors, and approximately one-half went to SMEs that are less than five years old and one-half to older SMEs.

The SMBF appears to be achieving its overall objective of increasing the flow of credit to SMEs. The volume of guaranteed credit to SMEs has increased significantly, more than doubling from 2011 to 2013 (Table 5.2). In 2013, SMBF-guaranteed loans added up to NIS 2 billion, more than 1% of total bank credit to businesses in this size class (Bank of Israel, 2014). Furthermore, the tendering approach appears to have created competition between banks, which has in turn resulted in improved marketing to SMEs and appears to

Table 5.1. **SMBF-guaranteed loans, April 2012-June 2014**

Firm size (employees)	Number of firms	Percentage of firms	Loan volume (NIS thousands)	Percentage of loan volume
1-4	2 732	33.9	852 254	17.6
5-19	3 643	45.2	2 105 475	43.6
20-99	1 400	17.9	1 537 011	31.8
100+*	236	2.9	339 241	7.0
Total	8 051	100.0	4 833 981	100.0

* Even though these enterprises have more than 100 employees, their turnover might not be more than NIS 100 million, the threshold limit for obtaining the guarantee.

Source: Data provided to the OECD by the SMBA.

StatLink http://dx.doi.org/10.1787/888933421898

Table 5.2. **Approved and executed loan guarantee credit volumes, 2007-13**

	2007	2008	2009	2010	2011	2012	2013	Total
Government loan guarantees to SMEs (in NIS millions)	170	109	757	1 028	890	1 412	2 025	**6 391**

Source: OECD (2014), *Financing SMEs and Entrepreneurs 2014: An OECD Scoreboard*, OECD Publishing, Paris.

StatLink http://dx.doi.org/10.1787/888933421909

have contributed to a slight reduction in the interest rates and collateral requirements applied to SMEs. However, results from an ongoing evaluation of the impact of the programme should help throw more light on the programme effects when they become available.

There are nonetheless some potential areas for improvement of the SMBF. First, consideration should be given to how to increase loan guarantee approval rates, and hence open up credit to more SMEs. An assessment should be made of where and why the applications for guarantees are being rejected, and particularly on whether the rejections are tending to come from the two companies contracted by the Ministry of Finance to co-ordinate delivery of the programme (i.e. before consideration of applications by the banks), or by the Credit Committees of the banks themselves. If the main reason is inadequate proposals for the co-ordinators to forward to banks, then initiatives should be put into place to improve the ability of SME owners to develop bankable proposals, such as offering referrals to financial consultants in the MAOF centre database. However, if the rejections are occurring more at the second stage in the approval process, the cause could be risk aversion on the part of banks. This may call for an increase in the guarantee coverage ratios for certain types of businesses where risk is highest, although the overall coverage ratio is within the interval generally considered as appropriate for guarantee schemes (between 60% and 80%); i.e. high enough to encourage lender participation and yet low enough to limit moral hazard (OECD, 2010a).[2] Another possibility would be to increase flexibility in the scheme to facilitate a more staged approach to lending whereby the loan size increases and the interest rate decreases as the bank and the SME client develop a relationship of mutual knowledge and trust over time.

Second, consideration should be given to augmenting the share of the SMBF that is allocated to loans for new businesses given the difficulty that new entrepreneurs face in obtaining credit from senior lending institutions, as identified by SMBA surveys. This might be achieved through introduction of quotas, adjustment of coverage ratios, and training and financial literacy work with SMEs and start-ups to increase the quality of their proposals.

Finally, the fees and risk premium on guaranteed loans seem to be relatively low. This is despite the recent increase in the one-off commission to 1%-2% of the loan (depending on size of the SME). Other schemes internationally typically operate with a registration fee of about 1% plus annual fees that could range from 1% to 4% of the outstanding guaranteed loan balance, depending on the risk (OECD, 2010a). Hence, given the lack of annual fees in Israel, the total fee is towards the lower end of the range. Table 5.3 compares the fees and commissions of the SMBF with those of loan guarantee programmes in five other OECD countries. The purpose of management fees and risk premiums in guarantee programmes is to recoup some of the credit default costs and administrative expenses and ensure financial sustainability, although it is generally considered unrealistic to achieve full cost-recovery on the basis of administration and servicing fees. In Israel, there may be room to raise overall fees to higher levels, hence increasing the sustainability of the scheme and its scope to support more firms, without undue discouragement of SMEs from applying. A sophisticated approach to working out appropriate guarantee fees by individual applicant is illustrated by the credit guarantee system of Japan (see Box 5.2).

Table 5.3. **International practices in loan guarantee programme fees and commissions**

Name and country of scheme	Upfront, one-time administration fee	Annual servicing fee
Small Medium Business Fund (SMBF), Israel	Application fee of 1%-2% of loan – payable by the borrower to the Accountant General (government)	
Canada Small Business Financing Program (CSBFP)	2% of the total amount of the CSBF loan payable by the lender to the Receiver General of Canada with the loan registration. Can be financed by the borrower as part of the loan	1.25% on the end of month loan balance. Can be charged by the lender to the borrower as part of the interest rate on the loan.
Small Business Administration (SBA) 7(a) Loan Guaranty Program, United States	Lender fee is: • 0.25% for loans with a maturity of less than 12 months; • 2% of the guaranteed portion of loans of USD 150 000 or less with a maturity of more than 12 months; • 3% of guaranteed portion of loans exceeding USD 150 000 but not more than USD 700 000; • 3.5% on loans exceeding USD 700 000. • An additional 0.25% on the portion of any guaranteed loan that exceeds USD I million The lender can charge the fees back to the borrower and must submit them to the SBA; allowed to retain 25% of the upfront guaranty fee on loans of USD 150 000 or less.	Cannot exceed 0.55% of the outstanding balance of the guaranteed portion of the loan; fee is borne by the lender to the SBA and cannot be charged to the borrower.
Enterprise Finance Guarantee (EGF), United Kingdom	None to the government	2% annual premium on outstanding loan balance; paid by borrower to the Department of Business, Innovation and Skills by direct debit.
Irish SME Credit Guarantee Scheme, Ireland	None to the government	2% annual premium based on the principal balance of the guaranteed loan amount; paid by the borrower to the Department of Jobs, Enterprise and Innovation
Japan Credit Guarantee Corporation (CGC)	None to the government	Ranges from 0.5-2.2% of value of the guaranteed loan, depending on the risk assessment.

Source: Information on the Irish Credit Guarantee Scheme: *www.djei.ie/enterprise/smes/creditguarantee.htm*; on the SBA 7(a) Loan Guaranty Programme: Digler (2013); on the Canada Small Business Financing Programme: *www.ic.gc.ca/eic/site/csbfp-pfpec.nsf/eng/la03148.html#s10*; on the Enterprise Finance Guarantee: *http://british-business-bank.co.uk/understanding-enterprise-finance-guarantee/*; on the Japan CGC: CGC (2012).

Box 5.2. **Determining guarantee fees in Japan's Credit Guarantee Corporations**

In Japan, Credit Guarantee Corporations (CGCs) are public institutions, which are established pursuant to the Credit Guarantee Corporation Law and support SMEs' access to credit by serving as guarantors. Credit insurance provided by the state-owned Japan Finance Corporation serves the purposes of sharing the risks incurred by CGCs, giving rise to a system known in Japan as the credit supplementation system. There are 51 CGCs in

Box 5.2. **Determining guarantee fees in Japan's Credit Guarantee Corporations** *(cont.)*

Japan, basically one for each prefecture and, at the end of 2013, their total liabilities stood at approximately JPY 30 trillion.

What is particularly interesting about the Japanese guarantee scheme is the way that guarantee fees are established. Guarantee fees paid by applicant SMEs are determined using the Credit Risk Database (CRD). The CRD was established in March 2001 as a voluntary association mainly consisting of Japanese CGCs, with the objective of collecting and employing simple financial information (balance sheets, profits and losses, default records, etc.) to assess the financial conditions and credit worthiness of SMEs looking for loan guarantees. By using the CRD data and its risk-analysis model, it has now become faster and easier for each CGC to work out appropriate credit guarantee fees and for banks to screen loan applications. Credit guarantee fees are expressed as an annual percentage of the loan value and are used to pay credit insurance premiums, administrative expenses relating to the operation of the system, and losses when loans are defaulted.

Source: OECD based on information provided by the Japanese Delegation to the OECD, member of the Steering Group of the OECD Review of SME and Entrepreneurship Policy in Israel.

Micro-enterprise lending

The microfinance sector in Israel is active in providing small amounts of credit to individual entrepreneurs and smaller businesses. The sector is mainly driven by NGOs, but the government is active in supporting some of the microfinance institutions, principally through contributing to the funds available for business lending.

The major government contribution is to the Koret Israel Economic Development Fund (KIEDF), an initiative of the Koret Foundation of San Francisco, which is one of the largest players in the Israeli microfinance sector. It was established in 1994 as an NGO to stimulate economic development and employment opportunities in the private small business sector in Israel. One-half of its activity is funded by endowments and the other half by the government, notably by the SMBA and MEDA. In the area of entrepreneurship financing, KIEDF launched the Microenterprise Initiative in 2006 to help low-income populations, mainly women, develop income-generating activity through access to business training and financing on reasonable terms.

The KIEDF Microenterprise Initiative combines the Koret Micro Credit Fund and the SAWA Micro-Loan Fund. The Koret Micro Credit Fund operates by depositing money in Bank Hapoalim and using these deposits to guarantee bank loans to low-income entrepreneurs. The guaranteed loans can be up to USD 8 500, have a three-year term and are offered at below market interest rate. The loans support a wide variety of businesses, most of which are operated out of the home. Originally, started in Haifa, the Micro Credit Fund has now expanded across the country.

The SAWA Fund, governed by a steering committee headed by the SMBA and represented by MEDA, provides microloans direct to low-income Arab Israeli women who are interested in starting a microenterprise. From 2006-13, SAWA supported the creation and development of 4 500 microenterprises through 5 939 loans ranging from USD 500 to USD 5 500 and a total lending volume of USD 15.4 million, using the revolving solidarity-group lending model. The programme has a strong emphasis on providing training and business advice to beneficiaries alongside the credit. The microfinance services are delivered through a team of 20 female employees who travel to villages and neighbourhoods to recruit and meet with the clients. Each officer is limited to 100-120 clients so that they have the time needed to provide the "soft" support that includes guidance and advisory services. The administration costs of the SAWA programme are high, at 40% of total project costs, which reflects the scale of effort to provide the ancillary support services to the loan clients. Interest rates of 8-10% are applied to the loans and loan losses through defaults are only 2%.

KIEDF is making an important contribution to supporting microenterprise development by low-income women. Based on its successful experience in this market, there may be potential for the government to bolster the expansion of its activities to other target groups, such as marginalised youth, that are not well-served by existing financing programmes.

The government is also involved in supporting certain other specialist microfinance institutions, such as the Daroma-Tzafona Fund, which supports manufacturing enterprises in the Galilee and the Negev regions, and the Centre for Jewish-Arab Economic Development (CAEJD). However, the total lending by these institutions is relatively small. The government could seek to expand the total scale of microfinance lending either by increasing funding in order to foster the expansion of NGOs already in the market. Alternatively, it could create a government-run Microenterprise Loan Fund to offer concessional loans (with softer terms than the market – e.g. lower interest rates, longer repayment and grace periods, etc.) combined with training and business advice.

In Ireland, for example, since 2012, Microfinance Ireland (MFI), a not-for-profit lender, has been delivering the Government's Microenterprise Loan Fund. MFI provides unsecured loans of EUR 2 000 up to EUR 25 000, for terms of 3 to 5 years, to all business sectors, to businesses with fewer than 10 employees and an annual turnover of less than EUR 2 million. These loans may be used to fund the purchase of stock, equipment, machinery and business vehicles, for both start-ups and established entities.

Venture capital

The Israeli government has played a proactive long-term role in developing the national venture capital industry to its strength today. The "big push" in the early 1990s was largely propelled by the realisation that competent scientists and engineers, especially the Soviet Jewish immigrants, were able to develop innovations but were weak on entrepreneurial skills. The solution was to stimulate a private sector venture capital industry that would bring "smart capital" to the table (not only investment capital but also management advice and mentoring) and develop strong ties with foreign financial markets, especially the commercially-savvy, technology-based venture capital industry in Silicon Valley (Senor and Singer, 2011).

The initial policy action was to develop a co-investment platform in order to attract foreign venture capital companies to invest in Israeli companies. The government launched the YOZMA Fund in 1993, which had raised just over USD 200 million by 1997, approximately one-half coming from the government. The Fund was then privatised and the public sector share of the funds declined to almost zero. By 2011, it managed nearly USD 3 billion of capital and was supporting hundreds of new companies (Senor and Singer, 2011). Further information is provided in Box 5.3. In addition, the government offered tax incentives to venture capital investors. These interventions have been influential in making venture capital supply in Israel the strongest in the OECD area.

Despite this success, venture capital in Israel is too strongly focused on high-technology enterprises, leaving other sectors with few opportunities for equity finance (SMBA, 2014).

Box 5.3. **The YOZMA Venture Capital Fund, Israel**

The origins of the Israeli venture capital industry lie in a government initiative in 1993 that created the YOZMA Venture Fund. Public investment in the Fund was used to leverage foreign investment in Israeli companies, primarily from the United States. Co-investors also included financiers from Germany and Japan. This was accompanied by equity guarantees for foreign investors, programmes to link Israeli firms with foreign business angels and to encourage exits of Israeli venture firms on foreign stock exchanges.

The Israeli government invested USD 100 million at the outset to launch the Fund, which was given the objective of investing in 10 new private venture capital funds. Each fund was required to have three partners: nascent Israeli venture capitalists, a foreign venture capital firm, and an Israeli investment company or bank. The objective was to attract financing in Israeli companies at the same time as nurturing a domestic private venture capital industry by offering matched co-financing at a rate of 50-50, with the obligation to invest in start-up and early-stage companies in Israel. The ten hybrid public/private funds were established over a three-year period, each capitalised with around USD 20 million. The government retained a 40% equity stake in the funds, which the private partners had the option to buy out after five years if the fund was successful. This was a particularly attractive deal for foreign venture capital firms and provided an exit strategy for the government. The buy-out option was exercised in most cases, leading to the privatisation of the venture capital funds. In parallel, the government created an additional fund of USD 20 million through which it could invest directly in Israeli technology ventures.

The funds were mainly invested in the ICT and life science/biotechnology sectors. Initial individual investments typically ranged between USD 1 million and USD 6 million, and additional capital was reserved for follow-on investments. With the backing of prominent American, European and Israeli investors, YOZMA launched its second fund in 1995. Investment decisions regarding where and how to invest were mainly taken by the international partners.

The YOZMA initiative also developed close working relationships with several of the leading academic institutions and technology incubators in Israel. Some of the most promising companies in the YOZMA portfolio have come directly from these institutions. As part of its efforts to involve senior executives and founders of successful enterprises in its activities, YOZMA created the YOZMA III CEO Club, which became a valuable source of deal flow.

By 2000, the Israeli venture capital industry had reached the stage whereby the private sector accounted for almost all of the venture capital investments. The government phased out both the YOZMA equity programmes and the equity guarantees in the late 1990s when the success of the pump-priming efforts was evident.

Source: Baygan (2003), "Venture capital policies in Israel", *STI Working Paper* 2003/3, OECD.

To seek to extend investment to high-potential enterprises in other sectors, the government could participate in the initial capitalisation of a new venture capital fund dedicated to non-high-technology sectors, calling on private sector investors to contribute on a matching basis, much in the way Yozma originally did for the high-technology sector. This type of approach has already been tested in the government's initial capitalisation of the *Al Bawader Private Investment Fund* to stimulate private investments in Arab Israeli and other minority-owned businesses. Further, it is modelled in the development of two growth capital funds for medium-sized businesses (turnover of NIS 10-100 million) under way in 2016 by the SMBA and the Ministry of Finance that will see the government invest NIS 100 million in each fund that is expected to reach a size of NIS 300-450 million with private sector matching.[3]

Business angels

Across OECD countries, angel investors can perform an important role in bridging the seed and early-stage financing gap for high growth potential enterprises, and most of these countries operate policy measures to support angel investors, such as tax incentives, co-investment (matching) funds, encouraging the formation of business angel networks (BANs), and building the knowledge capacity of both angel investors and entrepreneurs through professional training and investment-readiness offers (OECD, 2011).

In Israel, the government has mainly intervened through tax incentives. In 2010, it passed the Angel's Law to provide tax incentives to individuals to invest in the R&D stage of Israeli companies. However, this law produced only 125 requests for investment approval and was subject to much criticism.[4] First of all, under the 2010 version of the law, investors in innovative enterprises with the Office of the Chief Scientist (OCS) label of "target companies" (the OCS was evolved into the Israel Innovation Authority (IIA) in 2015) were allowed to deduct their investment in R&D expenses (up to NIS 5 million per invested company) from their taxable income over a period of three years, but only if the company had not emerged from its start-up status.[5] Secondly, "target companies" had to prove later to tax authorities that they had been compliant with this definition for the whole duration of the benefit; had this not been the case, the investor's tax deduction could have been retroactively denied. This created much uncertainty and discouraged participation by investors in the programme.

Significant amendments to the 2010 law were therefore passed in 2015. These amendments expanded the eligible investments to include the start-up and commercialisation stage of the company, allowed investors to write off 100% of their investment for tax purposes in the first year after the investment (up to NIS 5 million) and, most importantly, clarified the entitlement to benefits at the time of the investment. The cost of the amendments to the tax authorities is estimated at NIS 50 million annually but is expected to be partially offset by other indirect taxes paid by the investee companies. On the whole, this change to the law represents a positive development which should increase the amount of informal investment available to promising high-technology start-up companies.

At the same time, the Ministry of Economy and Industry could explore complementary actions such as to encourage the development of business angel networks in peripheral regions similar to those available in the Centre of the country (e.g. the Tel Aviv Angel Group, Angel Investment Network-Israel, Israel Angel Group) and to support the development of investment-readiness programmes for new entrepreneurs.

Alternative financial instruments

The G20/OECD High-Level Principles on SME Financing stress the importance of enabling SMEs to access diverse non-traditional financing instruments and channels. In this respect, the Israeli government is examining in particular new ways to increase capital flows to SMEs whose financial needs are in the range of NIS 5-50 million. Two main options are under consideration; the securitisation of SME loan portfolios and the creation of a business development company.

Securitisation of SME loan portfolios

Securitisation refers to the sale of a loan portfolio by a lending institution to a private sector company which will finance the purchase through the issue of bonds to institutional investors (e.g. pension funds and insurance companies) and the public. This may free up resources in the lending institutions for further lending. The scale of SME loan portfolio securitisation tends to be a very small proportion of SME lending, but in Israel it is virtually absent. This has prompted the government to set up a government committee to examine ways to galvanise this market.[6] The main recommendations of the committee included setting an obligation for banks to retain 10% of the securitised portfolio to avoid the risks that only subprime loans are sold to the market, establishing a neutral taxation of securitisation transactions which will create neither incentives nor disincentives to securitisation companies and investors, and protecting the rights of borrowers whose loans are securitised. These moves are to be encouraged, although it may not be sufficient to stimulate an SME loan securitisation market, given that Israeli banks generally do not perceive a liquidity constraint with respect to their SME lending.

Business Development Company

Business Development Companies (BDCs) are publicly-traded companies that attract capital from institutional investors such as pension funds and insurance companies through the Stock Exchange to then lend or invest in SMEs. This may be an effective way of increasing debt and equity investment in medium-sized firms. Inspiration could be drawn for such a development from two experiences from the United States, described in Boxes 5.4 and 5.5.

Box 5.4. **Business Development Companies (BDCs), United States**

Description of the approach

BDCs are a form of publicly registered company in the United States that invests in the debt and equity of privately-held American small and middle market businesses, and are often eligible for government tax incentives. They were created by Congress in 1980 as an amendment to the Investment Company Act of 1940, which stipulated that the securities of private equity and venture capital firms could not be beneficially owned by more than 100 persons. This restriction had the impact of blocking their capacity to provide financing to small and growing business. The Small Business Investment Incentive Act of 1980 created a new category of closed-end investment company – the Business Development Company – that could make investments in private companies (emerging growth or expansion stage) in the form of long-term debt or equity capital without some of the restrictions of the 1940 Act, and also make significant management assistance available to them.

BDCs occupy a useful niche by helping companies grow by borrowing at low rates and making money on the spread between their borrowing rates and the rates charged to less credit-worthy SME borrowers. In this respect, BDCs are often considered as sub-prime lenders to SMEs. BDCs can offer asset-based lines of credit, working capital loans, fixed asset loans, restructuring loans, senior short- or long-term debt, subordinated debt, and mezzanine or private equity financing. Their portfolio of loans can be traded publicly without restriction or back-end fees.

The number of BDCs has grown considerably in the past ten years. There are over 40 BDCs in operation, with total assets of more than USD 40 billion and market capitalisation in excess

Box 5.4. **Business Development Companies (BDCs), United States** *(cont.)*

of USD 25 billion. Some of them are publicly traded on the stock exchange, while others are not. About one-half of the existing BDCs are managed by third party companies. However, all BDCs are subject to the provisions of the Investment Company Act, which limits how much debt they can incur (debt is not allowed to exceed equity), requires regulation by the Securities and Exchange Commission (SEC) and a code of ethics and compliance programme, and subjects them to regular examination as all mutual and closed-end funds. They are all required to file quarterly and annual reports and proxy statements with the SEC. In addition, they must comply with specific rules regarding the compensation of fund managers. BDCs must ensure that 70% of their assets are in private debt or equity investments in private or thinly-traded companies (below USD 250 million in market capitalisation). No more than 5% of the total BDC assets can be invested in any one investment and the investment size is limited to no more than 25% of any one portfolio company's total assets. BDCs must also offer managerial assistance to the SMEs in which they invest and distribute 90% of their annual taxable income to shareholders.

As long as the BDC meets certain income, diversity and distribution requirements as set out in the Investment Company Act, it pays little or no corporate taxes (if it elects to be treated as a Regulated Investment Company for tax purposes).

BDCs are particularly geared to providing funding to early-stage companies that are too small to raise public funds, do not match the investment criteria of angel investors or venture capital providers and are unattractive to banks. BDC teams select the most promising companies in their fields and provide funds in return for a debt or equity stake. They generate gains from interest payments and capital gains when acquisitions occur. The ability to selectively lend money to the right start-up companies with the potential to repay the loan or go public is paramount. With limited available financing options, the clients of BDCs are often willing to pay a high interest rate and give the BDC senior-level status on the debt as well as warrants in many cases, which add to the upside potential for the BDC investors. In return for these sometimes stringent terms, the borrowing SME can access the funds needed to increase its cash reserve; accelerate product development; invest in land, plant, and equipment to produce and bring products to market; hire staff; and purchase licenses necessary to advance R&D, etc. Thus, BDC funding can lead to company growth and innovation activity as well as job creation.

Factors of success

Investors, including institutional investors, can purchase common stock of the BDCs. This provides capital to make investments, alongside borrowings. Unlike venture capital or private equity funds, BDCs allow anyone to purchase shares in the open market; however, most of the investors and lenders in the BDCs have historically been major financial institutions. The objective is to attract investors who are interested in "investing in America's growth" on a longer-term basis and not in trading their securities on a regular basis. BDCs also often negotiate revolving lines of credit from banks at low interest rates to leverage their capacity to increase their flow of capital to target SMEs.

Investments in BDCs are attractive to investors because they have the ability to generate regular and predictable double-digit current income and moderate capital gains with lower than average risk. As of 31 October 2010, the average yield on the universe of BDCs' currently-paying dividends was over 9%. The BDCs invest principally in debt that is secured by liens on the operating assets of the borrower, including current (receivables and inventory) and fixed assets (plant, equipment and property), and is repaid by borrowers monthly or quarterly, thus entailing lower risk. BDCs lend to and invest in a diversity of

Box 5.4. **Business Development Companies (BDCs), United States** *(cont.)*

industry segments from traditional manufacturers to distributors, to ICT and energy producers, and provide to their investors the opportunity to participate in a diverse portfolio of established middle market private companies that is secured by company assets.

Obstacles and responses

The performance of BDCs depends heavily on the internal health of the economy. A rise in interest rates, for example, can have a significant impact on BDC activity. As a result, BDCs have structures to minimise their interest rate risk. Approximately 60% of their assets are in floating-rate investments – as interest rates rise, the income of the BDCs will also rise. On the other hand, the majority of their liabilities have fixed-term rates, so if interest rates rise, they are not affected.

The BDC industry also confronts regulatory and other challenges as the SEC and Congress continue to propose new and amended laws and regulations that affect them. To help present a unified voice of the BDC industry with legislators and regulators, the BDCs have therefore formed the National Association of Business Development Companies (NABDC).

Relevance for Israel

The Israeli Ministry of Economy and Industry, Ministry of Finance and Securities Authority are exploring options for attracting more investment funding from pension funds, insurance companies and other institutional investors for the purpose of investing in the SME sector, through both debt and equity instruments. The BDC approach could allow the government to achieve this objective.

Further information

Small Business Investment Incentive Act of 1980 and "BDC Primer", BDC Reporter: *http://bdcreporter.com/bdc-primer/*.

Box 5.5. **The Small Business Investment Company (SBIC) programme, United States**

Description of the approach

The Small Business Investment Company (SBIC) programme was created by the United States Congress in 1958, and is administered by the Small Business Administration (SBA) Office of Investment and Innovation. Its aim is to help small businesses raise the patient long-term capital (equity capital and long-term loan funds) they need for business modernisation and growth, which is not generally in adequate supply through banks or other private capital sources.

SBICs are privately owned and managed investment funds, licensed and regulated by the SBA to make equity and debt investments (with maturities of at least five years) in qualifying "small" businesses with a net worth of USD 18 million or less and average after-tax net income for the prior two years not exceeding USD 6 million. However, SBICs must commit to making 25% of their investments in "smaller businesses" defined as those with tangible net worth of less than USD 6 million and an average of USD 2 million in net income over the previous two years. In the past, about 90% of SBIC financing has gone to businesses with less than USD 5 million in net income.

The SBIC programme increases the overall supply of debt and equity finance capital in two ways. Firstly, licensed SBICs are able to access additional low-cost debt funds from the

Box 5.5. **The Small Business Investment Company (SBIC) programme, United States** *(cont.)*

SBA, which they can invest alongside their own capital. The borrowings come from the sale of 10-year maturity SBA-guaranteed debentures to private investors through periodic public offerings. The availability of these funds can typically increase the total capital available for investment by the SBIC by two times (but up to three times the private capital in some cases) to a maximum of USD 150 million for a single SBIC and USD 225 million for multiple SBICs under common control. This SBA leveraging provides an incentive for more individuals and/or institutions to set up investment capital funds. For example, the investor with USD 5 million might receive up to another USD 15 million through the SBA funding mechanism. In addition, many SBICs do not have to make interest payments to the SBA for the money they borrow during the first few years of operation. In lieu of regular interest, the SBA will take up to 10% of the profits as they are realised. This alleviates the burden of paying interest on the SBA guaranteed loans while the SBIC invests in long-term opportunities. Secondly, investors purchasing shares of an SBIC are eligible for tax breaks and rollovers which make it attractive for them to invest in the SBIC funds.

SBICs fill the gap for SME financing in the USD 250 000 to USD 5 million range, which is generally too small to be of interest to other private equity firms. They are also required by regulation to provide management assistance to their client companies. Most SBICs focus primarily on providing small businesses with debt or debt with equity features (60% of SBIC financing in 2013 was in the form of loans, about 24% in the form of debt with equity features, and about 16% in the form of equity). SBICs are allowed to charge interest rates to their small business clients of no more than 19% on loans and no more than 14% on debt securities. SBICs will typically focus on companies that are mature enough to make current interest payments on the investment so that, in turn, the SBIC can meet its interest obligations to the SBA. Most SBIC funds are structured as limited partnerships that surrender their license after the SBIC repays its SBA-guaranteed leverage, typically 10-15 years after being licensed. The private capital is at risk in its entirety before any taxpayer money is at risk.

The SBA uses a three-phase application and approval process to license SBICs. This can take upwards of 24 months: 45 days for review of the initial application; up to 18 months for the applicant to raise its capital base; and six months for the final licensing decision. Before it receives a license, an SBIC must prove that its management and directors are experienced individuals with a broad range of business and professional talents. In addition, it must raise between USD 5 million and USD 10 million in private capital, most of which comes from private investors, such as pension funds, insurance companies, high net-worth individuals, state development funds, or even commercial banks. The private investment company pays a USD 10 000 fee to the SBA when filing a licensing application, and an additional USD 5 000 for licensees structured as limited partnerships. When approved, the SBIC also pays a one-time up-front commitment fee of 1%, a 2% draw down fee each time it issues an SBA-guarantee debenture and a variable annual charge of around 1% of the outstanding leverage, paid semi-annually. SBICs have flexibility in determining how to operate, such as defining the investment value ranges they will serve, the preferred size of the loan or investment they choose to make, and whether to focus on certain industries or types of businesses. Once licensed, each SBIC is subject to annual financial reporting and biennial onsite compliance examinations by the SBA, and is required to meet certain statutory and regulatory restrictions regarding approved investments and operating rules.

SMEs access SBIC funding by submitting a detailed business plan, indicating their financing requirements and how the financing will be used. After due diligence performed

Box 5.5. **The Small Business Investment Company (SBIC) programme, United States** *(cont.)*

by the SBIC, the SBIC negotiates the appropriate financing structure with the SME owner(s). Because SBICs are often interested in generating capital gains, they may prefer to purchase stock in the company or advance funds through a loan with conversion privileges or rights to buy stock at a predetermined later date; however, SBICs are prohibited from taking control of the companies in which they invest. Therefore, the interests of the SBIC and their clients are compatible, both want to grow and prosper. If the SBIC financing is provided to the SME in a subordinated position, it will often allow leveraging of other financing. Industry averages show that for every SBIC dollar placed with a small business, two additional senior dollars become available from commercial banks or other sources.

The SBA also issues special provisions for the establishment of Specialized Small Business Investment Company (SSBICs), which can access additional government financial assistance for the financing of higher-risk disadvantaged small businesses or small businesses in disadvantaged areas. Furthermore, the programme can be adjusted to meet emerging needs. A recent example is the new Early-Stage SBIC programme, launched in 2012, which committed up to USD 1 billion in SBA-guaranteed leverage over a five-year period to selected early-stage investment funds using the SBA's debenture programme authorisation. The aim of this programme is to address the general shortage of venture capital for early-stage growth companies seeking financing rounds of between USD 1 million to USD 4 million, particularly those without the necessary assets or cash flow to secure traditional bank funding. If licensed as an Early-stage SBIC, the SBIC may receive SBA-guaranteed debenture leverage of up to 100% of their Regulatory Capital, to a maximum of USD 50 million for 10 years, and must invest at least 50% of their investment dollars in early-stage small businesses, defined as those that have never achieved positive cash flow from operations in any fiscal year.

Factors of success

The SBIC model is proven to support jobs and growth, filling a gap in SMEs' access to risk financing between USD 250 000 and USD 5 million and building the private equity market. Since 1958, SBICs have invested almost USD 60 billion in 107 000 "small enterprises". The businesses financed by SBICs have far outperformed national averages in terms of increases in sales, profits, assets, and new job creation and benefited from the money and management counselling made available to them by the SBICs. At the end of fiscal year 2014, there were 294 SBICs (including 30 new licensees in 2014) holding USD 22.5 billion under capital management (52.5% of which was private capital and 47.5% was SBA-guaranteed capital or commitments). In 2014, these SBICs invested USD 5.4 billion in financing in 1 085 small businesses, creating an estimated 107 912 jobs. Private investor returns are commensurate with private equity industry metrics due to the SBA leveraging. The programme is delivered at no cost to taxpayers.

The four major factors in the success of the SBIC programme are: 1) the well-defined SBA licensing process with early milestones which help potential SBIC licensees assess their likelihood of eventual funding; 2) allowing SBICs to access leverage funds from the SBA at low interest rates, which reduces fundraising burden and administrative/reporting requirements; 3) requiring the SBICs to provide expert management assistance to the client businesses, which results in improved performance of the portfolio of companies; and 4) annual regulatory audits of the SBICs by the SBA to ensure compliance with the SBIC regulation and monitor their performance against original estimates.

Box 5.5. **The Small Business Investment Company (SBIC) programme, United States** *(cont.)*

Obstacles and responses

The application process for being approved as a SBA-licensed SBIC is somewhat rigorous. Efforts have been made to streamline the licensing process, while still maintaining high due diligence and licensing standards. The SBA can now process the initial applications within two months, at which point the applicant will be advised whether the SBA has given a green light to proceed with the capital raising phase. The SBA has also reduced the approval time for SBIC requests for SBA leveraging.

In spite of the overall success of the programme, some SBICs have performed poorly. The SBA experimentation with a SBIC structure that provided for the SBA to purchase a form of senior equity security called a "participating security" in the SBIC, produced significant losses and turned out to be much more expensive than the government projected. After a thorough SBA review of the Participating Securities SBICs, the SBA decided in 2004 to discontinue their licensing and wind-down the programme. The files of poorly performing SBICs (SBICs are deemed to be poor performers when the losses incurred by a fund relative to its Regulatory Capital exceeds the maximum allowable as per the SBIC regulations) are transferred to the SBA Office of SBIC Liquidations in order to recover the leverage and minimise losses. These recoveries are critical to keeping the programme at zero cost to the taxpayer. In 2013, 5.3% of the USD 9 billion in leverage was being managed by the Liquidations Office.

Monitoring of the financial health and performance of the SBICs is critical. To improve the monitoring process, the SBA launched a new web-based system in 2013 to improve the collection of financial data and reporting, and also transparency and accountability. The SBA undertakes formal SBIC evaluations on a 12-month cycle for leveraged SBICs and on an 18-month cycle for non-leveraged SBICs. To ensure that all SBIC principals are aware of the SBIC regulations, they must complete regulatory training classes before being licensed as an SBIC.

Relevance for Israel

Israel needs more long-term non-bank financing alternatives to channel investment capital into the SME sector, such as from pension and insurance funds, and particularly directed towards SMEs in traditional, non-technological sectors. A model similar to the SBIC approach might be one to bring a systematic approach to escalating the amount of debt and equity capital available to early-stage and growth-oriented SMEs. In implementing a similar programme in Israel, the Ministry of Economy and Industry would likely need to adjust the definition of a "qualifying small business" to be more compatible with the Israeli context. Since the incentive structure for the SBICs is based on leveraging the investment fund through government-guaranteed loans to the SBIC and tax breaks for investors in the SBIC, these policy issues would have to be examined by the Ministry of Economy and Industry.

Further information

US Small Business Administration (2013), The Small Business Investment Company (SBIC) Program, Annual Report For Fiscal Year Ending September 30, 2013, Office of Investment and Innovation, (*www.sba.gov/inv/*).

SBA Office of Investment and Innovation: *www.sba.gov/content/sbic-program-overview-2*.

Small Business Investors Alliance (SBIA): *www.SBIA.org*; for SBIC Policy Guidelines, see: *www.sba.gov/content/sbicpolicy/*.

Innovation programmes

Israel Innovation Authority (IIA) programmes

The primary innovation-related government support programmes in Israel are offered by the IIA. The IIA, which replaced the Office of the Chief Scientist (OCS) and the Israeli Industry Centre for R&D (MATIMOP) in January 2016, oversees more than 30 programmes covering five main areas of activity: technology start-ups, technological infrastructure, growing companies, international R&D activity, and innovative R&D projects with technological and commercial feasibility. These programmes are supported with an annual budget of approximately NIS 1.5 billion. Estimates suggest that every NIS one million of R&D grants has led to an additional NIS 1.28 million of R&D investment by the assisted firms (Lach et al., 2008). The major interventions include the R&D Fund, the Magnet programme for university-industry R&D collaboration, and the Technological Incubators Programme. The IIA also operates a number of smaller R&D support programmes. SMEs and new start-ups can benefit from all of these programmes.

The R&D Fund

The R&D Fund supports industrial R&D by offering companies conditional grants of 50% of approved R&D expenditure for product or process development (rising to 60% of approved expenditure in the peripheral regions and to 85% for R&D projects approved from early-stage companies and entrepreneurs from Arab Israeli and Jewish Ultraorthodox populations). If a project is successful, the company must repay the grant through royalty payments. The annual budget of the R&D Fund is approximately NIS 1 billion. This is used to support approximately 1 000 industrial projects selected from approximately 2 000 applications per year. Projects are funded for one year at a time and have to report twice a year on their progress. Supported companies can apply for further funding in subsequent years to take their projects to the next stage.

Approximately 500 companies benefit from this programme per year, mainly in the fields of ICT and biotechnologies. In total, approximately 80% of the expenditure goes to SMEs. Approximately 50-60% of total funds go to companies with up to NIS 1 million in turnover (generally early-stage companies with limited revenue streams); a cumulative 70-75% of expenditures go to businesses with annual turnover of up to NIS 20 million; and the remaining 18% to larger firms. The emphasis on SME support represents a change since the 1990s, when most of the funding was allocated to large firms.

Furthermore, the Manufacturer's Association of Israel (MAI) reports that smaller firms find the R&D Fund application process quite difficult due to the time and knowledge required to apply, or the cost of hiring external consultants to assist with the application. Between 2006 and 2012, only 14% of industrial enterprises with 20-100 employees applied for R&D funding, compared to 53% of industrial enterprises with more than 100 employees (MAI, 2014). A special track of the R&D Fund has recently been established for "traditional industries (i.e. industries characterised by low investment in R&D), where consultation support is offered to companies applying for R&D funding for the first time. This type of assistance or a simplification of the application process from SMEs could also be considered for the mainstream funding.

It should be recognised that the R&D Fund is very much a programme for a selected group of R&D-intensive SMEs rather than for the larger numbers of less R&D-oriented SMEs that nonetheless have innovation potential. This target is captured in the definition of the eligible expenditures stipulated by the R&D Law (amended in 2016), which governs the activity of the IIA. This excludes the R&D Fund from investing in non-technological innovation (e.g. innovation in business, organisational and marketing models), support services or projects dealing with the management of innovation. Consequently, most of the innovation support goes to high-technology projects and businesses and largely excludes the development of innovation in traditional SMEs, except for the Traditional Industries Programme described under "smaller-scale programmes" below.

Today, there is growing recognition that business innovation goes beyond R&D and includes non-technological forms of innovation such as marketing and organisational innovations. For example, the OECD/Eurostat Oslo Manual defines innovation as "the implementation of a new or significantly improved product (good or service) or process, a new marketing method, or a new organisational method in business practices, workplace organisation or external relations" (OECD/Eurostat, 2005). In this context, there is scope for the Israeli government to support non-technological innovation more proactively. The SMBA could be a key player implementing relevant non-R&D based innovation policies. Indeed, it already manages a few small-scale initiatives through the network of MAOF centres that promote design innovation in SMEs and consulting for SME innovation.

Magnet university-business co-operation programmes

University-business co-operation primarily falls within the responsibility of the Magnet programme of the IIA, which has an annual budget allocation of NIS 200 million across all its sub-programmes. The major part of the expenditure goes to the Magnet Consortia sub-programme, which supports pre-competitive collaborative R&D projects by consortia of Israeli firms working with researchers from at least one academic or research institution for joint projects on generic technologies potentially leading to new advanced projects. Magnet provides conditional grants to firms of up to 66% of the approved costs and to academic institutions of up to 80% of their approved costs, with the remaining 20% covered by the industrial partners. The projects have a life of 3-5 years. Many of the projects are run with the Technion-Israel Institute for Technology, a public university based in Haifa (see Box 5.6).

Box 5.6. **Technion-Israel Institute for Technology, Israel**

The existence of the Technion-Israel Institute for Technology, with its strong R&D and technological programmes, Knowledge Center for Innovation, and technological incubators, is a major contributor to Israel's technological innovation performance. Technion has become a globally-significant centre of technology research and teaching with over 12 500 students and 80 graduate programmes and is a global pioneer in biotechnology, satellite research, computer science, nanotechnology, aerospace, and energy. The large number of graduates from Technion is one of the engines driving Israel's high technology economy. Technion graduates account for over 70% of the founders and managers of high-technology companies in Israel, including almost half of those listed on the NASDAQ stock market (59 of the 121). Furthermore, 74% of managers in Israel's electronic industries hold Technion degrees; 17% of Technion graduates work in (or worked in) start-ups; and a 25%, at one time, has initiated a business (Frenkel and Maital, 2012).

Source: Frenkel and Maital, 2012; American Technion Society, "Technion Global Impact", *www.ats.org/wp-content/uploads/2014/03/1.29.14Technion_Global_Impact.pdf*; American Technion Society, "Technion Business Connection", *www.ats.org/wp-content/uploads/2014/03/8.30.13Technion-Business-Connection.pdf*; *www.technion.ac.il/en/fast-facts/*.

Alongside the Magnet Consortia, there are a range of smaller programmes under the heading of Magnet. Magneton provides a grant of up to 66% of the R&D costs of an already existing relationship between a single industrial company and an academic institution. The Noffar programme provides a grant of up to 90% of the development costs to industrial companies for the transfer of academic research to an industrial application, especially in biotechnology and nanotechnology.

Overall, Magnet is an excellent example of industry-driven R&D support programmes based on fostering linkages between industry partners and academic research institutions and, although not specifically targeting SMEs, there is potential for SMEs to be involved in consortia projects.

Technological Incubator Programme

Another NIS 200 million is allocated to the Technological Incubators Programme. This was initiated by the Ministry of Economy and Industry in 1991 with the launch of 24 technology incubators. The initial impetus for the programme was to offer immigrants with scientific, engineering or technical backgrounds from Soviet countries the resources and financing they needed to develop early-stage R&D-based innovations and determine their commercial applications and market viability.

There are now 18 technological incubators in the network, spread across Israel, including 8 in peripheral regions.[7] Their goal is to support new entrepreneurs at the earliest stages of technological entrepreneurship by providing assistance in determining the technical and marketing applications of their ideas, developing a business plan, organising a team, raising capital, and preparing to enter the market with commercially-viable ventures.

The technology incubators are now all privately-owned (since 2012) but in the context of public-private partnership arrangements. Through a call for tenders, the IIA issues incubator licenses to private operator companies that, once selected, receive a license for eight years to establish and operate an incubator. The incubator operators (largely technology development companies, and venture capital funds) provide advice, mentoring by industry experts (both from within Israel and globally), and networking opportunity to the start-ups that they host. In addition, they can submit grant applications to the IIA to co-fund innovative projects in new start-up companies. Projects approved by the Incubators Committee can receive grants of between USD 500 000 and USD 800 000 (85% of this from the IIA and 15% from the incubator licensee). In exchange for investing 15% of the project funding, the licensee company can take up to 50% ownership of the incubated company, which is a great incentive for ensuring its success. Successful companies are required to repay the grant to the government (with interest) in the form of royalties of between 3% and 5% of the generated revenue. To encourage location of technological incubators in peripheral regions, the IIA offers the private sector licensees an additional USD 150 000 towards the operational costs of the incubator, and the incubated enterprises are eligible for extra financial support of USD 125 000.

The incubators are structured to accommodate 10-15 projects at a time with an incubation term for a project of about two years. Collectively, they host approximately 180 companies at any given time. In the past, as many as 40% of them have been medical device companies, 30% in ICT, 15% in clean technologies, 10% in biotechnology and pharmaceutics, and 5% in other areas such as machinery and materials.

From 1991 to the end of 2013, over 1 900 companies were admitted to the incubation programme, with 1 600 maturing and graduating from the incubators, 60% of which successfully raised venture capital. By the end of 2013, 35% of the incubator graduates were still in operation. The government investment over the 22 years totalled about USD 730 million and the amount of private investment in graduated companies exceeded USD 4 billion, i.e. for every dollar invested by the government in a tenant company, the company attracted another USD 5 from the private sector.

The Technological Incubator Programme is a success of Israeli innovation policy. Nonetheless, its incubators are primarily focused on high-technology start-ups and not on promising start-ups in non-technological sectors. The gap in provision of stimulating start-up environments for non-technology firms should be addressed by establishing a number of incubators for more traditional start-ups in the manufacturing and service sectors that are not necessarily high-technology driven, but which are nonetheless innovative in other ways. Incubation support provided to start-ups in traditional sectors can help advance their business models, improve their entrepreneurial and business management skills, and increase their growth potential. This is an area of work which could be taken up by the SMBA given adequate additional resources. The precise scale and nature of provision should be based on an assessment of the demand and the impact of the support on the economy.

Smaller-scale programmes

Another NIS 100 million is dedicated by the IIA to smaller-scale programmes. The Tnufa Programme is a pre-seed fund which assists individual inventors and nascent start-up companies in evaluating the technological and commercial potential of their innovation, preparing patent applications, building a prototype, preparing a business plan, etc. It provides grants of up to 85% of approved expenses up to a maximum of USD 65 000 per project. The Upgrade Programme covers 75% of the cost of up to 250 hours of consultancy to perform a diagnostic of the R&D possibilities for companies. The Mumad Programme encourages the transfer of technology from the defence sector through support to start-ups spinning out of large defence companies. Finally, the Traditional Industries Programme is a line of the R&D Fund created in 2005 to back continuous technological improvement projects in firms in typically low-technology sectors, such as textiles, plastics, auto parts, etc. It offers grants of up to 50% of R&D costs (e.g. for designing and introducing new products or production processes). In parallel, it can provide professional advice and parallel grants for activities such as foreign marketing, training and acquiring intellectual property.

The Traditional Industry Programme and the Upgrade Programme are particularly relevant to SMEs in non-high-technology sectors that could benefit from a diagnostic assessment of their innovation potential and assistance with implementing continuous improvement projects. Such additional support is needed because smaller and traditional businesses are often less equipped to manage the process of innovation. This often has to do with a lack of knowledge and skills of owners and senior managers to identify opportunities to improve the performance of their businesses (e.g. productivity, expansion, diversification) through innovation in products, processes and services. Classical, non-technology SMEs need a proactive nurturing approach to stimulate them to follow an innovation path and undertake R&D projects. Efforts of the Kibbutz Industries Association provide a good example of a successful initiative to build the capacity of traditional SMEs to engage in innovation activities and to meet the requirements for R&D support from the IIA (Box 5.7). A similar programme, working through a SME consortia approach and facilitated by the MAOF

Box 5.7. The Kibbutz Industries Association – building capacity to manage the innovation process

The Kibbutz Industries Association (KIA) represents about 250 industrial companies, ranging from 20 to 2 000 employees, which operate on Israel's kibbutzim[8] and collective moshavim, mostly in peripheral areas. Kibbutz industry focuses predominantly on traditional manufacturing (e.g. agri-food, plastics, metal and machinery, rubber goods, chemicals for agriculture, textiles and leather, etc.). A decade ago the KIA resolved to encourage more proactively R&D activities among its members when it found that only 5 of its members were recipients of government-funded R&D grants. KIA's member companies were first encouraged to identify their product improvement needs and then to apply to the Upgrade Programme offered by the Office of the Chief Scientist in the Ministry of Economy and Industry, where they could receive a subsidy of 75% to cover the costs of 250 hours of consulting time to perform a diagnostic of their R&D possibilities. Many of the KIA members that completed the Upgrade Programme continued by applying for the R&D Fund for funding to implement their R&D projects. Finally, the KIA provided networking opportunities for its members to share challenges and solutions related to their own innovation processes. Thanks to these efforts, approximately one-half of the KIA members are today engaged in innovation activity, mostly R&D-based.

The Kibbutz Industries Association (KIA) is also active in backing technology-based start-ups via a Fund aimed at start-ups which have gone through one of the Technological Incubators but are finding it difficult to become financially self-sustainable. The KIA Fund provides NIS 2-3 million to each start-up, with a target to support five per year. Finally, in 2014 the KIA launched another new Fund to encourage the development and use of advanced technology in kibbutz companies, including in agriculture. This new fund will support the creation of partnerships and the integration of businesses with innovative advanced technology that can be tailored to particular kibbutz businesses.

Source: OECD based on information provided by Kibbutz Industries Association (KIA) during the OECD study mission.

centres in partnership with industry and sector associations, could play an important role in helping SMEs develop an innovation mind-set and identify projects that could be supported by the IIA R&D programmes.

Start-up accelerators

Israel also has a growing number of start-up accelerators, totalling more than 200 in 2016, mostly focused on technology innovations. They are located in various parts of the country, but tend to be more prevalent in and around Tel Aviv, due to the high concentration of start-ups and venture capital funds, and areas with more concentrated innovation eco-systems. These accelerators target both start-ups at the idea stage and start-ups that have passed the proof-of-concept stage and can demonstrate a working prototype. They aim to fast-track entrepreneurs from idea to viable business plan or to fast-track their "market ready" product development. The assistance is generally provided over a period of three to six months depending on the accelerator. During their time on the programme, the participating entrepreneurial teams have access to co-working spaces, some seed-capital, business consulting, coaching and mentoring, opportunities to meet with potential investors, and linkages to markets. Some of the accelerators are initiated or funded by local authorities (e.g. the Create Tel Aviv accelerator is partially funded by the Tel Aviv Municipality and housed at a city-funded start-up work space), while others are driven by the private sector (e.g. the Microsoft Ventures Accelerator in Tel Aviv, the Citi accelerator for fintech start-ups, the IBM Alpha Zone accelerator, and the Sushi Venture Partners "Startupbootcamp" in Haifa) and higher education institutions (e.g. StartHub at the Academic College of Tel Aviv-Yaffo, Q-start accelerator at Al-Qasemi College in Baqa al-Gharbiyye, and Zell Entrepreneurship Programme at the Interdisciplinary Center Herzliya). These developments are relatively recent but expanding rapidly, and building excitement and momentum around new innovative start-ups in a variety of locations.

The Israel Investment Centre

The Israel Investment Centre operates under the aegis of the national Law for the Encouragement of Capital Investment with the aim of increasing economic activity in peripheral regions by supporting capital investment (mainly plants and machinery) in the establishment or expansion of enterprises, creating jobs, and promoting innovation and productivity in these regions. The Investment Centre is an important player in the Israeli policy landscape, but its grants (up to 20-24% of the total investment cost) and tax incentives (reduced corporate tax of up to 12.5% depending on the priority of the peripheral region) for investing in the peripheral regions are primarily targeted at large companies rather than SMEs. In 2014, it invested NIS 1.33 billion in large companies (more than 100 employees), NIS 184.3 million in medium-sized companies (20-99 employees), and NIS 28.5 million in small companies (5-19 employees). Nonetheless, the Investment Centre has tried to reach out to SMEs more proactively in its programmes aimed at the integration of socially disadvantaged groups (Jewish Ultraorthodox, minorities, disabled people and single parents) in the workforce through the offer of generous wage subsidies in the range of 20%-27.5% of the total wage costs. It could also consider adjusting its selection criteria for investment projects in the peripheral regions to increase the emphasis on entrepreneurial and innovative projects and projects carried out by SMEs. In fact, in 2014, a particular emphasis was placed on support for investment projects demonstrating productivity-enhancing innovation and creation of higher-paying jobs. In the future, increasing emphasis should be placed on innovation as an eligibility criterion for this investment support.

Green innovation programmes

Israel has a long tradition in innovation related to natural resources, primarily water and solar energy, owing to the arid nature of large swathes of its land. A number of policy interventions can support SME innovation in this area. The Investment Centre, in collaboration with the Ministry of Environmental Protection, provides grants of 20% of the costs of investment projects directed towards cutting greenhouse gas emissions and improving energy efficiency. SMEs are eligible but not explicitly targeted. It also offers grants of between NIS 250 000 and NIS 750 000 (depending on the size of the company) to encourage manufacturers to connect to the natural gas grid as a source of energy diversification. The IIA earmarks some of its incentives to environmental-related R&D. It has also recently launched two technology centres devoted to water management and renewable energies in the Negev region. These centres bolster long-term collaborative research between industry and research organisations and have five-year budgets of NIS 35 million (the water management centre) and NIS 57 million (the renewable energy centre). Finally, the SMBA, in collaboration with the Ministry of Environmental Protection, carries out energy surveys of small enterprises consuming high energy inputs with the objective of identifying energy inefficiencies in the production process and proposing alternative solutions to lower costs and emissions.

Non-technological innovation programmes

Innovation policy in OECD countries increasingly stresses the importance of non-technological forms of innovation, such as marketing, design, organisational and managerial changes, alongside more traditional R&D-based policies. While Israel is a leader in R&D support for science-based sectors such as ICT, biotechnologies and nanotechnologies, it lags in its support for non-technological innovation, which holds the potential to embrace a wider group of firms and sectors. Non-technological innovation programmes are particularly relevant for diversifying traditional SMEs and increasing their productivity. Rather than focusing on supporting R&D projects to find path-breaking, new-to-market innovations, the emphasis of this type of programme is in supporting the typical SME to adopt new-to-firm technologies and managerial practices in areas such as marketing, e-commerce and workforce development, as well as to orient these SMEs to the concept of innovation management.

One of the two key actors in support for non-technological innovation in Israel is the Technion Knowledge Centre for Innovation. It offers training and consultancy to encourage managerial innovation in traditional industries through three main programmes: Moving Up, Moving Up-North and the Managing Innovation Forum. The first supports innovation in traditional larger SMEs through the establishment of groups of 7-10 managers who participate in a six-month programme that includes lectures on innovation, meetings to share experiences, and assistance from business mentors to plan and implement the innovation projects that they design for their companies. The second programme offers similar assistance targeted to smaller traditional SMEs in the north of the country. The third programme targets managers from both high-technology and non-high-technology SMEs who come together on a monthly basis to hear industry experts on the topic of innovation. In the forum, managers are exposed to models of innovation that have already been implemented in other Israeli companies and advised on how to orchestrate innovative processes in their own organisations.

The other key actor pursuing non-technological innovation is the SMBA. It has recently launched a tender process for the establishment of a social impact business accelerator aimed at encouraging innovation in traditional SMEs to be operated by a private-sector company with experience in business management support. The accelerator is expected to cater for promising companies with less than 20 employees, to last for five years, accommodate 10-20 enterprises per year, and be based on the principle of co-funding by the private-sector organisation winning the tender. The extension of business accelerator support in the country from its current focus on high-technology start-ups to support for existing SMEs with growth potential is in line with business accelerator practices in other OECD countries and responds to evidence that fast-growing firms can be found in any sector of the economy, including low-technology ones, with stronger proportional incidence in the services industry (OECD, 2013b). Further investment in business accelerators for existing non-R&D based SMEs with growth potential would help to improve SME productivity and growth in Israel more generally.

The SMBA also runs a small-scale programme (with an annual budget of NIS 2 million) to promote the use of industrial design in SMEs by providing consultancy and grants for new design and packaging (up to NIS 200 000 per firm and up to 60% of development costs). The SMBA also provides advice on innovation management to SMEs through its network of MAOF centres. It could strengthen its work in this respect by hiring specialised innovation agents, as done in Denmark, who should in principle be better able to provide innovation-oriented support than existing MAOF local officers who are not specifically recruited or trained for their innovation expertise but rather for their management consultancy capability more generally. Box 5.8 offers the example of the Innovation Agents programme in Denmark, which provides specialised innovation diagnostics and referrals to SMEs.

Box 5.8. **Innovation Agents, Denmark**

Description of the approach

The Innovation Agent programme was launched in 2007 as a pilot project in selected regions of Denmark and expanded to the whole country in 2010. Its aim is to strengthen innovation in SMEs through linkages with research organisations. In particular, a total of thirty trained Innovation Agents carry out a free innovation diagnostic analysis (the "innovation check") of Danish SMEs and provide support towards the implementation of the proposed actions.

The basic approach of the Innovation Agent scheme is as follows:

- SMEs are identified and contacted by the Innovation Agents, although SMEs can also request assistance from the programme directly or be referred to it by other business advisory services.
- An Innovation Agent carries out an in-depth innovation diagnostic analysis of the small business based on a standard methodology and field visits with managers and relevant workers.
- The Innovation Agent then submits a short report to the participant SME which summarises the main innovation-related challenges and opportunities and proposes possible solutions, including a list of relevant research organisations, external experts and public innovation support schemes which can contribute to the future innovation endeavours of the company.
- The Innovation Agent can further support the implementation of the suggested actions by directly establishing contacts with relevant knowledge institutions or experts or by helping SMEs to apply for public support schemes.
- Finally, the Innovation Agent carries out an assessment of the innovation diagnostic analysis to which participating SMEs are required to provide feedbacks.

Companies recruited in the scheme should fit with at least two of the following three criteria: 1) have at least 10 employees; 2) be at least two years old and have positive financial accounts; 3) have expressed an interest for knowledge-based support and show some innovation potential.

The Innovation Agent scheme is a joint project involving nine independent Danish research and technology organisations, with the Danish Technological Institute acting as the leader organisation. Funding comes from the Danish Council of Technology and Innovation.

Factors for success

The programme addresses many of the barriers to innovation experienced by SMEs, such as lack of knowledge about the innovation process, lack of capacity to undertake innovation, and limited awareness of external innovation services. Evaluations suggest that it has been successful in boosting innovation activities in Danish SMEs. Since 2010, more than 2 300 innovation checks have been carried out; more than 60%of participating SMEs have subsequently launched technological and non-technological innovation

Box 5.8. **Innovation Agents, Denmark** *(cont.)*

projects; almost 60% have established relationships with private or public innovation actors such as cluster organisations, private consultants, and universities; and as many as 85% state that they would recommend the scheme to other small enterprises.

A further key success factor has been the professional profile of the Innovation Agents, who are selected based on their ability to combine understanding of technology with knowledge of the small business *modus operandi*. This ensures that innovation checks and recommendations focus on delivering business value to SMEs in the form of improved competitiveness and increased sales/exports. Also, the formal association of the "Innovation Agents" programme with the highly respected GTS "Advanced Technology Group" (a network of nine independent Danish research and technology organisations) contributes to the programme's credibility and attractiveness.

Obstacles and responses

A critical factor for the success of such a programme is the active participation of top-level managers in the innovation checks and their commitment to implementation of the recommended actions. This is why the Innovation Agent programme has a strong focus on ensuring that top-level management is sufficiently involved and supportive of the process, for instance by formally requiring the participation of SME managers throughout the whole process of the programme.

Relevance to Israel

A similar programme in Israel could promote innovation activities among non-R&D based SMEs as long as the innovation agents explore both the technological and non-technological innovation potential of participating SMEs. Moreover, the existence of MAOF centres already provides a platform from which innovation agents would be able to operate throughout the country.

Further information

Further information available at:

- Innovation Agents, *www.innovationstjek.dk/innovationstjekket.aspx*.
- GTS – Advanced Technology Group, *http://en.gts-net.dk*.
- Danish Ministry for Higher Education and Science, *http://ufm.dk/en/research-and-innovation/cooperation-between-research-and-innovation/collaboration-between-research-and-industry/innovation-agents/innovation-agent*.

Source: OECD based on information provided by the Danish Delegation to the OECD, member of the Steering Group of the OECD Review of SME and Entrepreneurship Policy in Israel.

Alongside these initiatives, it would be appropriate to expand support for collaborative innovation in small non-high-technology firms, since these rarely have the resources to invest in long-term uncertain innovation projects on their own. The Innovation Networks programme from Denmark offers a good example of a network-based approach to innovation in SMEs (see Box 5.9).

Another concern in Israel is that the domestic market is not benefiting enough from the high-technology development that is occurring in Israel. Israel's high-technology enterprises focus almost exclusively on international markets and interactions with multinational corporations. Innovation support is not being used to promote productivity increases that could arise across a range of domestic sectors through the integration of

Box 5.9. **Innovation Networks, Denmark**

Description of the approach

Innovation networks are defined by the Danish legislation as "a framework for cooperation, knowledge sharing and knowledge development between companies, knowledge institutions and other relevant players within a sector or a professional or technological area". The programme was established in 2008, and there are currently 22 government-funded innovation networks covering fields such as medical technologies, energy, ICT, robotics, food processing, offshore oil, and the services industry.

A key feature of the innovation networks is that they provide both technological and non-technological innovation support to companies, i.e. they address managerial and organisational issues as well as product and process development. Furthermore, some of the networks are focused on sectors that are largely based on non-technological innovation. For example, one of the networks is entitled "Service Cluster Denmark". It has 1 100 members and provides member companies with access to the latest knowledge in the field of innovation in services.

The approach to establishing the networks is as follows:

- An open competition for funding is launched by the government;
- National partnerships are formed and submit applications for government funding. The partnerships consist of research organisations, knowledge institutions and key actors such as leading companies, industry organisations, trade unions and regional or national authorities;
- The winners of the competition are selected by the Danish Ministry of Higher Education and Science. Partnerships are chosen to be innovation networks only if there is considerable growth potential within the selected focus area. Moreover, there must be a significant target group of companies, and Danish knowledge institutions need to have substantial expertise in the area concerned;
- The selected partnerships establish the secretariats of the innovation networks and launch their activities.

The main responsibilities of the networks are to implement knowledge dissemination activities, kick-start joint development projects and provide innovation services to SMEs, for example by helping them with applications for funding and support from other public innovation programmes.

The 22 existing innovation networks receive government co-financing (up to a maximum 50% of the total budget) for the period 2014-2018, while the rest of the funding comes from private companies, regional funds, etc. Companies also have to finance their own participation in the activities of the innovation networks and, in some cases, are expected to pay a membership fee. Public funding is therefore mainly used to cover the management costs of the networks.

Factors for success

In 2013, approximately 6 000 companies participated in activities organised by the innovation networks; two-thirds of them were SMEs. The 22 networks contributed to the introduction of innovations in 780 companies, a large majority of which (563) were small companies with less than 50 employees. The positive contribution of the innovation networks is also supported by an evaluation of cluster policy in Denmark, which showed how the probability to introduce innovations by "network companies" is four times higher than in similar firms which do not participate in networks (DASTI, 2011).

Box 5.9. **Innovation Networks, Denmark** *(cont.)*

A key success factor has been the ability of the innovation networks to connect actors in highly specialised areas across different regions and clusters of Denmark. This makes it possible to exploit innovation and growth potential in areas where there is no critical mass of knowledge at the regional level. Moreover, the innovation networks have helped create a one-stop-shop for access to commercially-relevant knowledge in very specific focus areas, thus improving the functioning of the national innovation system.

Obstacles and responses

One of the main challenges has been increasing the internationalisation of participant companies and, in particular, establishing strategic collaborations between the Danish members of the networks and relevant companies or research institutions abroad. To do this, a separate organisation has been established to support the innovation networks with their internationalisation efforts, namely Cluster Excellence Denmark.

Relevance to Israel

In Israel there is a need to increase innovation support for the typical non-high-technology SME, in particular with regard to non-technological innovation. The innovation networks in Denmark support a broad range of SME innovation activities with networks focused on a range of specific technologies, industries or cross-cutting innovation themes such as service innovation. This broad and yet structured approach to innovation support ensures that Danish SMEs have access to technological as well as non-technological innovation.

Further information

Further information available at:

- Danish Ministry for Higher Education and Science, *http://ufm.dk/en/research-and-innovation/cooperation-between-research-and-innovation/collaboration-between-research-and-industry/innovation-networks-denmark*.
- Cluster Excellence Denmark, *www.clusterexcellencedenmark.dk/da-DK/UK/About-the-support-function.aspx*.
- DASTI (2011), *The Impact of Cluster Policy in Denmark*, Copenhagen, *http://ufm.dk/en/publications/2011/the-impact-of-cluster-policy-in-denmark*.

Source: OECD based on information provided by the Danish Delegation to the OECD, member of the Steering Group of the OECD Review of SME and Entrepreneurship Policy in Israel.

new technologies and ICTs developed by these high technology enterprises within the country, for example, in the commercial and retail sectors. Greater emphasis on promoting the integration of these innovations in traditional enterprises would help address the productivity gap in the SME sector. For example, exchange forums could be organised to share knowledge on the high-technology developments coming out of Israel and their application in traditional SMEs. Consultants could be engaged to work with traditional SMEs in sector clusters to examine how these relevant new technologies could improve their production, operational and managerial processes.

SME internationalisation programmes

The Israeli government has developed a number of programmes that aim to address the barriers that SMEs tend to face in accessing international markets and supply chains in Israel and other OECD countries, including lack of staff skills, lack of knowledge of foreign market opportunities and foreign laws and regulations, and lack of working capital to finance export development activity (OECD, 2008, Adalya Economic Consulting, 2011). The Foreign Trade Administration (FTA) is the main government body responsible, complemented by the Israel Export Institute (IEI) and some export finance initiatives.

Foreign Trade Administration

The FTA, in the Ministry of Economy and Industry, runs programmes to develop linkages with foreign buyers, promote the participation of Israeli companies in international trade fairs, and foster international opportunities for Israel companies through trade agreements with other countries. It currently has a particular focus on the diversification of export products (to increase non high-technology exports) and of export markets (to increase sales outside of the tradition partners of the United States and the European Union). It assists approximately 1 500 companies a year, 90% of which are SMEs as defined by an annual turnover of less than NIS 100 million.

The FTA programme most relevant to SMEs is the "Smart Money" Programme, an initiative launched in 2014 to foster export growth of Israeli companies in international markets, with preference for entering China, India and Japan. This programme provides financial assistance and subsidised professional consultancy services to support companies in implementing their targeted marketing programmes, up to 50% of eligible costs, such as for market research, promotional materials, marketing activities in the target country(ies), and legal services. Funding is granted in collaboration with the Israel Export Institute (IEI), which provides coaching and mentoring support to the assisted SMEs.

On the other hand, one of the deficiencies of the "Smart Money" Programme is that travel costs of SMEs to attend international trade fairs, explore international markets or meet international buyers are not considered eligible for grant support. In many OECD countries, a common practice is for governments to offer a cost-sharing grant to SMEs to cover some of the travel expenses incurred for these purposes. This serves as an incentive for SMEs that may otherwise forgo the opportunity to explore and develop export markets. The FTA could consider amending its list of eligible expenses to include travel costs, which are a barrier especially to new and small exporters.

Two other significant FTA programmes for SMEs are the India-China Fund and the International Projects and Tenders Fund. The India–China Fund (budget of NIS 100 million) seeks to foster growth in Chinese and Indian markets by offering funding support of up to NIS 2.5 million over three years to help qualifying Israeli companies (with at least NIS 15 million in turnover) develop new marketing activities. Eligible costs include staff salaries, local consultancies, office space and the adaptation of products to the local market. If the company succeeds in the new market, it must pay back 100% of the funding support granted for marketing activities. From September 2011 to mid-June 2014, 63 of the 160 submitted applications had been approved, mainly from sectors such as medical devices, agriculture, software, telecommunications, water and energy. The International Projects and Tenders Fund provides grants of up to half of the costs related to preparing tender applications by Israeli companies in international projects. Grants cover eligible costs associated with conducting the project feasibility study and preparing the tendering documents and become repayable if the project succeeds (i.e. the grant converts to a loan).

Israeli Export Institute (IEI)

The IEI is an important partner of the FTA in providing assistance to export-oriented clients and collaborating in the organisation of international exhibitions for Israeli companies. Its activities include intelligence on foreign markets, market research, marketing counselling, courses and training on international marketing, assistance with meeting international standards and identifying local agents and distributors, and advice on trade agreements and logistics. In addition, the IEI Small Exporters Assistance Centre offers training, consulting and guidance for first-time and small exporters.

On the other hand, although the IEI offers export training, it tends to be in the form of one-off courses and seminars. A more comprehensive approach would consist in the development of activities along the different stages of export promotion, from awareness-raising events among groups of companies potentially interested in exporting, to export-readiness courses to instruct new and occasional exporters on how to export for the first time or expand export volumes, and advanced bespoke training for more experienced exporters. Consultancy and mentoring are common types of support for high-growth potential SMEs across a range of OECD countries such as Canada, the United Kingdom and Denmark (OECD, 2013b). Enterprise Ireland, the main government SME and entrepreneurship support agency, illustrates a good practice in addressing the export development needs of SMEs through a range of activities tailored to the different stages of export activity (see Box 5.10).

Box 5.10. **SME Exporting Assistance: the case of Enterprise Ireland Programmes**

Description of the approach

Enterprise Ireland runs a number of programmes to assist SMEs in developing export and internationalisation activity. To be eligible, SMEs should have 10-249 employees, be operating in the manufacturing and internationally traded services sectors, and have an established trading record. Funding awards are determined by the need for financial support for the project, potential employment and sales growth, previous funding provided to the company, and the company's regional location.

The support offered spans the stages of regular Export Awareness seminars for potential exporters, Exploring Export workshops for pre-exporters, building the export skills and capacity of new and currently exporting SMEs, and supporting new and existing exporters to undertake market research on new export markets. Overall, there is a suite of programme support available with specific activities aimed at particular types of exporters and potential exporters. Some of the main programmes are discussed below.

Get Export Ready Programme

In 2011, Enterprise Ireland established a Potential Exporters Division and launched the "Get Export Ready" programme aimed at pre-export and early-stage exporting companies. The programme provides practical measures for new and early exporters focusing on export readiness, the importance of research, developing a value proposition and the skills of export selling. It offers workshops, seminars and training; mentoring support; access to market information; online access to "how to" guides, links to relevant information, and self-assessment tools and templates; access to a Get Ready to Export helpdesk; access to advice from successful exporting companies; and help with preparing an export plan, as well as access to a range of Enterprise Ireland financial supports. To promote the programme

Box 5.10. **SME Exporting Assistance: the case of Enterprise Ireland Programmes** *(cont.)*

and encourage SMEs to explore an export path to growth, Enterprise Ireland also regularly conducts export awareness seminars in locations around the country.

First Flight Programme

First Flight helps first-time exporters and currently exporting SMEs manage the risk of entering new markets. The programme offers a systematic market-readiness assessment to help SMEs research, prepare and develop an export strategy. This programme is specifically targeted to high-growth potential start-ups that want to learn about the key factors that will contribute to the success of exporting activity and build their export development skills and capacity. Participating enterprises attend a full-day introductory workshop and are then matched to an experienced business mentor who will assist them in undertaking an export readiness assessment and the development of a First Flight Action Plan (i.e. export strategy). The workshops are offered at no charge, and Enterprise Ireland covers 100% of the mentor cost.

Market Access Grant

The Market Access Grant provides up to 50% of EUR 150 000 of eligible costs met by an SME to undertake an intensive six-month market research project to examine a new export market or the potential for introducing a new product or service into an existing export market. Eligible costs include salary costs of an employee placed in the market for up to six months, in-market consultancy fees and rent, and marketing costs up to the time of market launch.

Relevance for Israel

Israel does not have a cohesive array of programme support to proactively identify SMEs with export potential or with the potential to expand their existing export activity and provide them with the appropriate assistance. Based on the more systematic and programmatic approach of Enterprise Ireland, this could be achieved by delivering export awareness sessions on a regular basis to interest potential exporters, offering opportunities for SMEs to identify their export potential and develop their export-readiness, investing in the development of exporting skills and human resources within SMEs, followed by the grant support to develop their export plans and strategy, including the necessary market research, and to defray some of the costs for travel to international fairs and exploratory visits to targeted countries. Such an approach would enable Israel to better build a pipeline of new SME exporters.

For further information:

- Get Export Ready: *www.enterprise-ireland.com/en/Export-Assistance/Get-Export-Ready/.*
- First Flight Programme: *www.enterprise-ireland.com/en/Export-Assistance/Building-Export/First-Flight-Initiative.shortcut.html.*
- Market Access Grant: *www.enterprise-ireland.com/en/funding-supports/Company/Esetablish-SME-Funding/Market-Access-Grant.html.*

Export financing

Governments often offer loan guarantees to banks to stimulate lending to SMEs for foreign trade activities, given the high risks involved. Before 2012, Israel operated a loan guarantee fund specifically dedicated to exporting firms but, together with other two funds, this was merged into the SMBF as part of a strengthening of Israel's loan guarantee activity in general. The SMBF no longer explicitly specifies that the guarantee can be used to cover export development activity, although it might qualify under the Working Capital Loan provisions. The issue of inadequate export financing for Israeli firms was fully explored by Horowitz-Reshef (2014) who recommended that the government implement a state guarantee programme for exporting activity. In lieu of another guarantee programme, the Ministry of Finance and the SMBA should designate "export financing" as one of the loan categories to be covered under the existing SMBF so that it is very clear to SMEs and programme managers that this is one of the intentions of the programme and so that take up for this purpose can be monitored.

Another policy tool that is important for the support of SME exporting is insurance to cover the risk of export transactions, especially with respect to payment defaults by foreign customers. In Israel, this is available through both public and private providers. The government is involved through the Israel Foreign Trade Risks Insurance Corporation (ASHRA). This is a government-owned company, backed by a state guarantee, which insures medium- and long-term export credit transactions (one to ten years) and investments abroad. The involvement of AHSRA helps to minimise political and commercial risks and increases the credibility of the exporter in dealing with its foreign customers. In addition to offering export insurance, ASHRA supplies exporters with professional information on the credit-worthiness of foreign customers and assists them with obtaining financing for transactions through the transfer of insurance policies to banks or by issuing guarantees directly to the banks. Private sector providers include the Israel Credit Insurance Company. However, there is no available data on the extent to which these providers meet the needs of new and small exporters.

SME workforce skills development programmes

Work-based learning is critical for developing initial occupational skills and deepening workforce skills, knowledge and abilities. However, while large firms tend to make use of a range of internally-organised training activities for their employees such as job rotation, learning and quality circles, self-learning and learning at work stations, the use of these approaches is generally much lower in SMEs, as is the frequency of apprenticeship placements in SMEs (OECD, 2013c).

In OECD countries, governments have typically sought to encourage workforce training in SMEs by offering financial subsidies to help cover the costs of training (e.g. in the form of grants or tax subsidies), offering publicly-funded advisory services aimed at identifying training needs and developing training plans and referring SMEs to appropriate training providers, and promoting national training standards that recognise the continuing professional development undertaken by employees. However, Israel offers little support for workforce skills development within SMEs. Examples of countries with important workforce skills development programmes of this kind include Korea, France and Ireland. This is an important potential area for expanded government support in Israel.

As a first step, developing a more formal framework for recognising workplace learning, with a common and unified set of qualifications has obvious advantages in upskilling the SME workforce because workers learn more and at a quicker speed if their training is workplace based. The workplace is the best place to gain exposure to soft skills development (e.g. dealing with customers) and working in peer groups and with mentors (Lerman, 2014). The benefits for SME employers are also clear. Workplace training allows employers to directly observe the capabilities and potential of workers, thereby easing recruitment decisions. It further eases information asymmetries because recognised qualifications can provide a high level of assurance about the skill levels.

A second step would involve providing advisory services to help SMEs understand the benefits of workforce training for their businesses and recognise their training needs. There is increasing policy emphasis internationally on peer learning for SME managers, often as part of broader SME development interventions. Box 5.11 provides the example of a local approach to workforce development in the United States which mixes financial assistance for apprenticeships in SMEs with the use of business advisors to help SMEs identify their training needs and adapt the provision of apprenticeship training by local colleges to SME needs.

Box 5.11. **Apprenticeship Carolina**

South Carolina has seen a dramatic increase in the involvement of its SMEs in apprenticeship programmes, with an increase of 652% in numbers of firms involved and a 600% increase in apprentice numbers between 2007 and 2014. By 2014 the 16 technical colleges in South Carolina have worked with more than 10 000 apprentices. The entry point for ApprenticeshipCarolina is often the offer of an annual USD 1 000 tax credit (for up to four years) for each registered apprentice taken on by the firm. In addition, an outreach programme has been critical to the success of the approach. This has sought to actively engage with the business community through a state-focused website (*www.apprenticeshipcarolina.com*) and the use of trained staff with a business background to connect with employers. The business advisors actively work with firms to help them diagnose their workforce development needs and help define ways that they can upskill their workforce. At the same time they work with teachers and lecturers in the technical colleges to help develop the content of traditional apprenticeship programmes (4 years) or for programmes that may only require a one year apprenticeship taking into the account of needs of local employers. Overall, ApprenticeshipCarolina shows that a small tax incentive and a proactive approach to engaging with firms can help increase the level of training in SMEs.

Source: Website of the South Carolina Technical College System: *www.apprenticeshipcarolina.com*.

The MAOF centres could trial a peer-learning programme for SMEs in Israel, in combination with a new financial subsidy programme, with a particular focus on favouring exchange of information on improving managerial practices in SMEs in low and medium technology industries. This would involve it in setting up private-led "communities of practice" in groups of SMEs for mutual learning and development. This could be self-standing or attached to other interventions.

A third step would be to support networking and clustering arrangements to allow SMEs to collaboratively work with suppliers, customers, training providers and the public sector in developing and implementing appropriate training provision. One example of this is the CME Manitoba consortia programme in Canada, which brings networks of 10-12 non-competing companies together to achieve improvements in business performance. Key to the process is SME learning circles, which involve participants in mentoring peers from other SMEs in the learning circle through presentations, discussions and site visits. CME Manitoba further supports these activities by training the mentors and acting as a broker between different learning circles to encourage the sharing of best practice.

Business diagnosis, advice and consultancy programmes

The main government business advice and consultancy support for SMEs in Israel is provided by the SMBA's local MAOF centre network, although certain other government programmes include advice and consultancy for specific types of SMEs, for example exporters or firms hosted in technological incubators.

The first stage of the MAOF centre advice and consultancy support involves an in-house diagnostic analysis of client SMEs to identify their business development needs. Subsequently, firms are matched with an appropriate consultant in the SMBA database of approximately 850 external consultants across the country who can offer support on subjects ranging from starting a business through to exporting and environmental regulatory compliance. Firms can claim up to 60% of the consultancy costs. The amount of consultancy support that can be offered varies with the type of firm. Nascent entrepreneurs receive up to 10 hours of assistance, micro firms (1-4 employees) receive up to 20 hours, small firms (11-50 employees) receive up to 100 hours, and medium-sized firms are eligible for up to 150 hours of consultancy support. The MAOF centres also provide signposting of SMEs to other government programmes that are relevant to their situation as identified by the business diagnosis and the request of clients.

The business advice and consultancy services available from the MAOF centres is nonetheless still fairly limited in scale and scope, despite recent growth in budget. The MAOF centre operational budget was NIS 200 million in 2015. This is substantially below the annual budget of NIS 354 million for capital investment in manufacturing for example (Bank of Israel, 2013). From July 2014-June 2015, the 35 MAOF centres nationwide provided business advice and support services to 25 000 businesses, including 11 500 self-employed entrepreneurs, 9 600 very small businesses, 1 900 small businesses, and 2 000 medium-sized businesses. A scaling up of the MAOF support should be considered, which could be based on an evaluation of the impact of the support provided on key objectives such as SME productivity, exporting and growth.

In addition, there is a need for greater diversity in the MAOF programmes. In particular, two additional advice and consultancy activities would be useful additions to the MAOF programme portfolio given appropriate budget provision. These are initiatives that are commonly provided in other OECD countries but not currently offered in a substantial way in Israel and that would sit best in the MAOF centre framework.

First, the MAOF centres could introduce coaching and consultancy services that are dedicated to growth-orientated businesses. This type of programme is increasingly offered in other OECD countries, based on evidence that high growth potential businesses – which are found in all sectors – are more likely than firms in general to create jobs and foster productivity growth (Storey and Greene, 2010; OECD, 2010). For example, five Danish "growth houses" were set up in 2007, one for each of the Danish regions. The aim of these growth houses is to target growth potential firms, regardless of age, sector, and ownership structure. Another example of the increased orientation in targeting support to growth businesses is given in Box 5.12.

Second, the MAOF centres do not have an explicit objective or intervention for providing management advice for business restructuring situations, for example when a business is facing difficulties as a result of changing technologies, markets and competition or sudden shocks and needs to make quick changes to turn around. The Early Warning programme in Denmark is a good example of how the MAOF centres could help

Box 5.12. The Single Business Service and Entrepreneurs' Infrastructure Programme, Australia

In 2014, the Australian government embarked on an AUD 484 million programme to target public support towards growth-oriented businesses. This is part of its wider AUD 1.4 billion programme to improve Australian business competitiveness. Support is in two forms: a Single Business Service which is a universal service available to all Australian businesses; and an Entrepreneurs' Infrastructure Programme (EIP) designed to offer tailored and targeted services to growth-orientated businesses.

Description of the approach

Australian SMEs and entrepreneurs can access the Single Business Service through web-chat, by telephone or via an on-line form. The aim is to make information simple and easy for SMEs and entrepreneurs to use. Services offered include easy to access information on business relevant topics (e.g. start-up, finance, counselling for small businesses in difficulties, IT, licencing and regulation), signposting to other sources of support (e.g. training support through the Industry Skills Fund, a grant and loan finder, sources of financial counselling support) and a referral service that seeks to signpost eligible firms to the EIP.

The EIP focuses on three integrated streams:

- Business management. This is available for established firms (three years old) that have a willingness to engage with change and have growth potential. Those that are successful are able to benefit from business growth evaluations from a network of more than 100 advisers from senior private sector management roles. These evaluations are conducted at the firm's premises and result in a detailed report and recommendations for future improvements. Businesses can use these reports to aid applying for Business Growth grants (up to AUD 20 000 of matched funding) and access to dedicated workshops and learning events.
- Research connections. Eligible SMEs (those that can demonstrate a need for research support from a research institution and can match government funding) can receive a brokerage services designed to foster links with research institutions. This can lead to up to AUD 50 000 of financial assistance to bring in outside research capabilities to the SME.
- Commercialising ideas. New and existing businesses with a novel product or service that can be commercialised can apply for support designed to increase the visibility of their innovation, provide critical networking capabilities and facilitate the use of experienced and independent advisers. Such services may include coaching to develop presentation skills, facilitated and qualified introductions, linkages to markets and investors and the availability of matched funding of up to AUD 250 000.

Obstacles and responses

As with any new system of business support, there are obvious challenges in making growth-oriented SMEs aware of the Single Business Service and EIP. It is likely, at least initially, that these new pathways will have limited up-take. Another challenge is that the triaging system is dependent on the experience and training of the business advisers. UK experience of the Business Link service showed that poor quality of business advisers contributed to negative perceptions of the service and its ultimate closure (Sear and Agar, 1996).

Relevance to Israel

The EIP is an example of an intervention that targets growth-potential SMEs with a tailored package of coaching and consultancy services, matched finance and leveraging-in of outside business support. This type of intervention would support much needed growth

Box 5.12. **The Single Business Service and Entrepreneurs' Infrastructure Programme, Australia** *(cont.)*

and productivity increase in SMEs outside of high-technology sectors where such support is difficult to access in Israel. The EIP approach is particularly valuable because it focuses on providing an integrated pathway for growth-potential businesses, one that recognises that SMEs often require a mix of financial and business assistance services if it is to work.

Further information

Australian Department of Industry (2014a, b).

companies facing economic hardships to turn around and renew with growth or to close down in a managed way that minimises social and economic costs for business and its customers and other stakeholders (Box 5.13).

Box 5.13. **The Early Warning programme, Denmark**

Description of the approach

Early Warning is a national programme providing free, impartial and confidential counselling to Danish SMEs facing the risk of bankruptcy. Since 2007, the Early Warning programme has helped over 4 000 Danish SMEs to deal with severe economic challenges and helped keep alive about two thirds of these companies.

The purpose of Early Warning is: i) to help viable companies survive a severe slump and renew with growth; ii) to reduce economic losses for society, creditors and entrepreneurs by helping non-viable companies to close down quickly; iii) to promote an entrepreneurial culture and help recognise failure as a natural part of entrepreneurial endeavours; iv) to give bankrupt entrepreneurs a second chance by helping them to avoid unmanageable debt and loss of self-esteem so that they may start a new company within a foreseeable future.

The Early Warning organisation comprises 10 specially trained consultants collaborating with 15-20 insolvency lawyers and a group of approximately 100 voluntary advisers consisting of current and former directors of large corporations, owners of smaller companies, board members and chairpersons as well as a few professionals (accountants, lawyers, financial advisers, psychologists, coaches etc.).

The overall approach of Early Warning is as follows:

1. The Early Warning organisation receives a request for help from a company owner facing a severe economic crisis.
2. A consultant undertakes an initial screening of the company and provides an assessment of the economic situation and the future prospects of the company.
3. If the company can be saved, one of the voluntary advisers will be assigned to the company to support a turn-around of the company.
4. In case the future prospects are unclear or negative, Early Warning will organise a meeting with an insolvency lawyer to determine if the company can be fully or partially reconstructed, or if the company shall be closed/declared bankrupt.
5. A voluntary adviser can be assigned to assist a bankrupt entrepreneur with economic and personal advice following a declaration of bankruptcy.

Box 5.13. **The Early Warning programme, Denmark** *(cont.)*

Factors for success

The experience with the Early Warning programme in Denmark is extremely positive. Two impact evaluation studies comparing participants in the Early Warning programme with a control group show that Early Warning companies that survive are capable of maintaining or increasing their turnover, employment and export. Moreover, the Early Warning companies that are declared bankrupt do so with less debt to the public sector such as unpaid income tax and VAT than the corresponding control group. Both evaluations find that the economic benefits of the Early Warning programme outweigh its economic costs (social considerations are not part of the evaluation studies).

The key success factor for the Early Warning programme is the group of voluntary advisers that bring with them the experience and skills needed to turn around companies going through a moment of difficulty. Furthermore, there is a strong focus in the Early Warning organisation on facilitating exchange of experiences and the joint development and testing of methodologies to assist in the best possible way the viable and non-viable companies in the programme

Obstacles and responses

One of the main challenges facing the Early Warning programme is that company owners facing difficulties often resolve to come only when problems have become almost unmanageable. As a result, many of the companies that could have been saved end up being closed down. Early Warning is currently exploring different approaches to getting in contact with companies at an early stage when their crisis is still relatively manageable. These efforts are expected to increase the future success rate of the Early Warning programme in Denmark.

Relevance to Israel

The MAOF centres do not currently advise on business restructuring for SMEs which are faced with economic hardships. However, this service could practically be provided by the same staff members responsible for the early diagnostic analysis of the strengths and weaknesses of client firms. In this case, however, before signposting to existing public programmes, firms which approach the MAOF centres with already-identified problems should be helped to find a path to long-term economic recovery, if necessary with the help of government-supported external consultants. Once back on their feet, these firms could then be signposted like any other firm to standard SME support programmes to help them renew with growth. This type of programme could also help reduce "fear of failure" in the Israeli population by showing that business failure is socially accepted and that bankrupt entrepreneurs are entitled to a second chance in their professional life.

Further information

Further information available at:

- Early Warning programme, *http://startvaekst.dk/earlywarning.dk/earlywarning_experiences_from_denmark*.

Source: OECD based on information provided by the Danish Delegation to the OECD, member of the Steering Group of the OECD Review of SME and Entrepreneurship Policy in Israel.

Alongside this more diverse programme offer, the MAOF centres should seek to better link their managerial support with the financial assistance available from other public programmes. In particular, the MAOF centres currently do not systematically link into the national loan guarantee scheme. Offering management support alongside finance would be beneficial, as shown for example by the evaluation of New Zealand Growth Services Range

Programme where a combination of financial and business advice support led to higher sales growth in the targeted companies (Morris and Stevens, 2010). In addition, those SMEs that do not receive loan guarantee assistance from the SMBF could be automatically re-directed towards the business consulting and signposting services offered by MAOF for alternative support.

SME public procurement programmes

Government support for the access of SMEs to public procurement contracts has the potential to increase public sector supplier diversity, enhance competition and generate economic development benefits, including encouraging large firm led supply chain firms to work with their smaller suppliers. Public procurement programmes generally aim to help SMEs overcome specific barriers that they often face in accessing and winning public procurement contracts, namely obtaining information about tender opportunities, developing skills to write tender bids, meeting eligibility criteria if public tenders specify requirements in terms of business size or experience, meeting proportionally higher fixed-costs in relation to the preparation of tender bids, and in some cases meeting the quantity and quality requirements of the tendered contract.

The OECD estimates the scale of government procurement in Israel at 15% of GDP, compared with an OECD average of 12% (OECD, 2013d). Central government purchasing is led by the Accountant General, but there are more than 300 procurement units in government departments at the national and local level, around 160 000 suppliers and 700 000 procurement activities conducted each year in Israel (Bezalel, 2013a). SMEs in Israel have free access to information on public tenders either from newspapers or online websites, while the existence of provisions for the cutting of bids into smaller lots reinforce the chances of SMEs winning public contracts (Bezalel, 2013b). However, Israeli SMEs suffer from most of the other barriers motivating SME public procurement programmes in other countries. These include requirements in the Mandatory Tender law (5752-1992) that often stipulate that the tenderer must be of a certain minimum size or have particular experience in an industry.

One approach to increasing public procurement from SMEs is the use of set-asides, i.e. policies that earmark a certain volume of public procurement contracts to SMEs. Israel does not operate set asides for small businesses or new businesses. This is in contrast to various other OECD countries (e.g. the United States, the Netherlands, Mexico and Slovenia) where there are clear targets for the involvement of SMEs in public tenders. In the USA, for example, the Small Business Administration has set-asides that reserve 23% of direct contracts and 40% of subcontracts to SMEs whilst in Mexico there is a set aside of 50% of the volume of low-value contracts (OECD, 2013d). In Europe, such set-aside quotas are not permitted by competition regulation but some governments have set explicit targets. Set-asides or targets for the value or volume of contracts from SMEs or new and young firms could be introduced as an important part of the public procurement policy framework in Israel.

Another potential policy tool that is currently lacking in Israel is a well-developed system of e-procurement. This would facilitate the access of SMEs to procurement opportunities by reducing the bureaucracy and fixed costs associated with the public tendering process. The case of Korea (Box 5.14) illustrates how the complexity of the tendering process can be reduced to support SMEs. International evidence also suggests that small enterprises are more likely to apply for and win small-sized contracts (PwC et al., 2014), and these are often tendered by local municipalities. Thus, there is scope for the

Box 5.14. **The Korean On-line Procurement System (KONEPS)**

The KONEPS is an integrated e-commerce marketplace that has given Korean SMEs increased access to public procurement. All public tender notices are published on KONEPS, which uses an integrated system of e-bidding, e-ordering, e-contracting and e-payment. It is used by 45 000 government agencies and 244 000 registered businesses. In 2012, 66% of all Korea's public procurement budget of USD 100 billion went through KONEPS. The advantages of the system to Korean SMEs is that it allows information to be swiftly accessed, eases searching of tender opportunities and reduces administrative transaction costs. To support awareness of KONEPS, the government runs nationwide training sessions, has a web-based call centre and markets the service to both government departments and SMEs. This has led to an estimated USD 6.6 billion in transaction cost savings to the private sector. Because the system offers end-to-end functionality and an online market place where sellers and buyers can come together, the number of SMEs involved in KONEPS doubled over the last decade and the SME share of the online market place for government goods increased from around one-quarter in 2006 to three-quarters by 2010.

Source: Seo, K. (2013).

national government to set the example by launching an e-procurement system which can subsequently be integrated by local authorities posting their own tenders.

Additional components of an effective system to promote public procurement from SMEs may include training and support to government procurement officers in how to ensure that their procurement processes are open to SMEs and on-line guidance for SMEs in the form of a step-by-step guide for contracting with the government.

Support for social target groups[9]

The main Israeli programme in support of entrepreneurship by disadvantaged and under-represented groups is the Initiating a Business programme, which is managed by the SMBA and delivered through the MAOF centres. The programme was inherited from the MATI system, which saw the participation of 7 000 individuals from groups such as the unemployed, seniors (older than 45 years old), Ultraorthodox Jews, the disabled and new immigrants in 2013. Activities in the programme include 56 hours of theoretical and practical training in how to set up a new business followed by up to 20 hours of external consultancy support to help make the business sustainable. Although not formally evaluated, SMBA survey evidence suggests that 30% of participants have gone on to open a business after they have completed the course. In addition, the SMBA works with the Joint Distribution Committee of Israel to deliver workshops for Ultraorthodox Jews and disabled people in order to prepare them for entry into the "Initiating a Business" programme.

Other Israeli ministries also offer small-scale targeted support. The Ministry of Immigrant Absorption offers new immigrant entrepreneurs training and access to a loan of up to NIS 125 000 to start a business. The IIA has launched a dedicated scheme for Ultraorthodox Jews looking to develop a high-technology business that offers up to 200 hours of subsidised mentoring together with an underwritten loan of up to NIS 2 million. There are also examples of relevant programmes from non-governmental actors. These include for example the "We Dream" programme of *StarTau*, the entrepreneurship centre at Tel Aviv University, which delivers training and provides network opportunities for women techno-entrepreneurs, or the Sunbeam programme for young entrepreneurs (see Box 5.15).

Box 5.15. **The Sunbeam programme, Israel**

Supported by the Safra Foundation, the Sunbeam programme offers young people (20-35 years old) support to set up a business or develop a young business (under one year old). The programme provides training support to help them with their business plan; consultancy support to develop their business; and workshops and seminars to improve their business network. In addition, Sunbeam has 400 voluntary mentors who provide advice and assistance to young entrepreneurs and guidance and support on accessing financial loans from organisations such as the KIEDF micro loan fund. Young entrepreneurs are able to access cheap loans of up to 90 000 NIS, repayable over a five year period. Data collected by Sunbeam suggests that it has supported the development of more than 1 000 new businesses in Israel which has led to the creation of 3 000 new jobs, largely in Israel's peripheral regions.

Source: www.edmondjsafra.org/general-philanthropy/keren-shemesh-israel; www.ksh.org.il, http://en.ksh.org.il/entrepeneurs/become-a-keren-shemesh-entrepeneur/.

Although these are good examples of inclusive entrepreneurship programmes, there are still challenges in increasing the scale and uptake of the services. For example, specialised support for Ultraorthodox Jews is still in its infancy. This is likely to require an increased emphasis in the future given both the challenge of increasing the labour market participation of this group in appropriate ways, including entrepreneurship, and the increasing weight of Ultraorthodox Jews as a proportion of the Israeli population. Another pressure stems from ageing of the Israeli society, which is likely to make senior entrepreneurship more relevant in the future given that older people have a stronger tendency than other population groups to participate in the labour market through running their own businesses. Many OECD countries have already launched programmes which equip seniors with the skills and knowledge to launch second careers in entrepreneurship that could provide models for Israel (see OECD/European Commission, 2012; OECD/European Union, 2016). For instance, in Belgium the non-profit organisation NEOS runs a Start50+ programme with financial support from the Flemish regional government that offers free coaching to seniors interested in launching their own business.

More could also be done in Israel to strengthen the sustainability of businesses started by people from disadvantaged and under-represented groups in entrepreneurship by integrating business advice with financial support (OECD/European Union, 2015). Business advice and assistance alone, in fact, are unlikely to be sufficient to solve undercapitalisation problems commonly affecting businesses run by entrepreneurs from deprived social groups, who are often financially constrained. Under-capitalised businesses are more likely to fail. This has made the combination of soft loans and grants with training and advice a common approach to supporting entrepreneurship for social target groups (Botti and Corsi, 2011). In addition, the sustainability of supported businesses can be increased by continuing support provision after the immediate start-up event. Box 5.16 gives the example of an integrated approach to backing youth entrepreneurship in France. In the case of Israel, a financing component could be integrated into the Initiating a Business programme.

Box 5.16. **Créajeunes, France**

Description of the approach

In response to youth unemployment in France, Adie (the *Association pour le droit à l'initiative Economique [Association for the right to economic initiative]*) set up CréaJeunes to meet the entrepreneurial aspirations of young people from poorer backgrounds. The initiative is designed to help young (18 to 32 year old) disadvantaged people in France to set up a sustainable business.

CréaJeunes recognises that unemployed and disadvantaged young people often have ideas and commitment but lack experience, business skills and finance to be able to set up their own businesses. To support these ambitions, an integral part of the programme is six weeks of group training (for groups of 5-10 young people) that consists of: a personal development module designed to develop personal skills (e.g. public speaking, confidence building, time management, IT skills); a business start-up module (e.g. market research, selling); and three other modules that focus on the legal, accountancy and finance issues involved in business start-up and development. Subsequently, participants are offered the support of a volunteer coach who is available to meet with them (usually once a week) for two to four months to discuss their business ideas and to deal with issues that may arise over the start-up period. CréaJeunes participants are also offered the potential to access financial support through a EUR 1 000 bonus, the micro-loans available from Adie and financial support from other funders. This post start-up support can last for up to 18 months.

Some 58% of participants are under 26 years old and 46% are women. Many are also in receipt of unemployment benefits or other social security payments. The programme has expanded since 2007 to over 20 French cities. Survey evidence collected by Adie shows that CréaJeunes has helped more than 5 000 young people, with a third going onto create a new business, a third finding employment and the rest either in training or continuing with their business project.

Factors for success

One of the key success factors of CréaJeunes is that it provides an integrated package of support combining business advice, training, life skills coaching and support in accessing start up finance. Another important feature is that CréaJeunes support is available over up to 18 months after business set-up. This longer-term support is designed to tackle the problem of early failures from under-resourced start-ups. The design of CréaJeunes benefits from the Adie NGO's previous experience of operating a suite of similar programmes to support micro businesses (0-9 employees) in rural communities and deprived urban areas and among unemployed adults. Cost efficiency is also achieved by providing a proportion of financing as quasi-equity loans ("loans of honour") and reimbursable advances alongside straight start-up grants.

Obstacles and responses

One of the challenges addressed by the CréaJeunes programme is that it seeks to provide business advice and assistance to young people from "hard-to-reach" populations where experiences of multiple disadvantage are common. It may be very difficult for disadvantaged young people to access relevant other sources of support. CréaJeunes seeks to support young people with business advice and assistance but this may not be enough without access to other social services support.

Box 5.16. **Créajeunes, France** *(cont.)*

Relevance to Israel

There is a need to support entrepreneurial aspirations amongst entrepreneurs from socially disadvantaged groups in Israel to increase labour market participation and deal with demographic challenges. CréaJeunes shows that an offer of business and life-skills training and microfinance can support disadvantaged young people to successfully enter the labour market by starting businesses. CréaJeunes is also notable because it offers support over a longer time period. While such support can be costly, there is evidence that such interventions can increase the chances of disadvantaged entrepreneurs such as the unemployed being able to create wealth and jobs in their own community (Caliendo and Kritikos, 2010).

Source: www.adie.org/sites/default/files/links/Dossier_presse_campagne_jeunes_2013.pdf, Buron (2011), Crépon et al. (2014).

Conclusions and policy recommendations

Israel has many examples of successful national support programmes for SMEs and entrepreneurship. However, there is also significant variation across the SME and entrepreneurship programme areas in the extent to which programmes exist that would be relevant to meeting SME and entrepreneurship development needs and there are some significant programme gaps to fill.

There are particular strengths in existing programme interventions for entrepreneurial financing, innovation, and internationalisation, although there are nevertheless some potential areas for improvement even in these intervention areas.

In financing support, the loan guarantee programme, the SMBF, has been revamped with expanded resources and streamlined management, the government is active in supporting microfinance institutions and it also played the decisive role in triggering the creation of Israel's venture capital industry. The interventions could nevertheless be strengthened in certain ways to reach more entrepreneurs and fill gaps in the types of financing offered, including increasing the numbers of businesses reached by the loan guarantee scheme (including start-ups), expanding the coverage of microfinance initiatives to other needy parts of the population alongside women, expanding venture capital and business angel activity to sectors outside of high technology and R&D-based activity, promoting appropriate finance sector innovations (e.g. loan securitisation, crowdfunding and special vehicles to attract institutional investors into SME financing), and providing related training and business development services to clients supported or rejected by public finance initiatives.

Innovation support is a widely recognised success story of Israel thanks to its comprehensive support of business R&D across the different stages of the business lifecycle. The IIA in particular offers several high-quality programmes, which include a range of grants to R&D and R&D collaboration and a technology incubator programme. However, to some extent, Israel has been victim of its own success in R&D support and has neglected the potential of non-technological innovation for productivity gains in traditional SMEs. This could be addressed by supporting innovation grants, external knowledge inputs and collaborative innovation, and incubator and accelerator services for non-technological SMEs and start-ups and by increasing the focus of the investment centre subsidies on entrepreneurship and innovation.

In the area of support for internationalisation, the FTA and IEI run exporting programmes that are open to SMEs, including funding for export development, coaching and mentoring and export training. On the other hand, it is not always easy for first-time exporters and small exporters to access this support.

While, overall, programme support is relatively strong in the areas of financing, innovation and internationalisation, there are some bigger gaps in programme provision in the areas of workforce skills development, advice and consultancy, public procurement and support for needy social target groups.

One of the most important gaps is in the area of workforce skills development. The main issues concern the lack of a uniform qualification framework for recognising workplace-based learning, limited advice to SMEs on their training needs, and limited financial subsidies for SMEs for training purposes.

In the area of business advice and consultancy, the new MAOF centre network provides important support to SME management through its company diagnostics and its specialised consultants. The budget for these activities is nonetheless low compared with other areas of programme intervention and it remains a modest programme following its revamp, with a very restricted number of SMEs that can be reached compared with the vast SME population. In addition, there are certain relevant types of advice and consultancy that are not provided by the MAOF centres, such as peer learning, and dedicated support for high-growth companies, or support for business restructuring. There is also scope for increasing the integration between MAOF services and financial support programmes, which would provide a way of reinforcing the funding and take up of MAOF services as well as better supporting SMEs. Finally, the MAOF approach is essentially one that focuses on counselling services rather than direct consultancy intervention, and there is a need in the long run to consider whether a shift towards consulting services targeted at business development and growth could provide better benefits to the taxpayer.

There is also potential for increased action to promote SME procurement. Unlike many other OECD countries, Israel does not make significant use of SME set-asides or targets in terms of the value of purchases that should come from SMEs, and there is not a well-developed e-procurement system. Furthermore, there is not yet a programme of training for public procurement officials in making their systems and approaches SME-friendly.

Support for needy social target groups is relatively small in scale. It is also relatively focused on combatting social exclusion by helping potential entrepreneurs to start businesses rather than helping entrepreneurs to sustain or grow their business. In particular, there are opportunities to upscale support to people from disadvantaged and under-represented groups in entrepreneurship, by expanding existing programmes and replicating them for other groups, and by creating pathways by which they can better access mainstream financial support and advice.

Based on the analysis brought forward in this chapter, the following policy recommendations are offered to strengthen the existing offer of SME and entrepreneurship support programmes:

Key recommendations on national SME and entrepreneurship support programmes

Finance programmes

- Increase the share of the SMBF resources allocated to loans for new businesses through introduction of quotas, adjustment of coverage ratios for new businesses and training and financial literacy work with start-ups to increase the quality of their proposals.
- Introduce greater flexibility in the SMBF to facilitate a more staged approach to lending whereby the loan size increases and the interest rate decreases as the bank and the SME client develop a relationship of mutual knowledge and trust.
- Reinforce the provision of microfinance and associated soft support such as training and business advice by fostering the expansion of NGOs currently active in this market and/or creating a government micro-enterprise loan fund combined with training and business advice.
- Provide additional incentives for venture capital funds and private equity firms to invest in non-high-technology growth-oriented enterprises or, alternatively, supply the initial capitalisation for a new seed/venture fund for this purpose based on the principle of matching public and private sector funding. The two private equity funds that will start operations in 2016 are good models for a broader intervention.
- Encourage business angel investment through the development of regional business angel networks, support of investment-readiness programmes for new entrepreneurs who could benefit from angel investment, and launching a state matching fund to stimulate angel investment in non-R&D based start-ups and early-stage SMEs.
- Support the diversification of finance sources and instruments for SMEs and entrepreneurship, including through setting up alternative finance mechanisms such as Business Development Companies and legal and support frameworks for SME loan securitisation by which institutional actors such as pension funds and insurance companies can invest in SMEs. Design incentives so that institutional investments are channelled to SMEs in traditional industries as well as high-technology enterprises.
- Boost MAOF centre activities for strengthening the financial literacy skills of SME owners, such as offering referrals to financial consultants in the MAOF centre database, focusing on their ability to prepare bankable proposals and understand credit access practices.

Innovation programmes

- Facilitate the transfer of technology developed by Israeli high-technology companies and R&D centres to domestic SMEs to improve their productivity. This could be achieved by the creation of intermediate technology institutes that make technical expertise and facilities available to SMEs that do not have the resources to develop in-house R&D, creating exchange forums to share knowledge on the high-technology developments coming out of Israel and their application in traditional SMEs, or engaging consultants to work with traditional SMEs in sector clusters to examine how these relevant new technologies could improve their production, operational and managerial processes.
- Create a fast-track lane in the IIA R&D Fund to simplify the application process for SMEs with smaller R&D projects.
- Establish closer co-operation between the IIA and the SMBA so that the MAOF centres, which are managed by the SMBA, can become local entry-points for SMEs interested in using the R&D incentives of the IIA. This could include MAOF support to SME consortia to develop an innovation mind set and identify projects that could be supported by the IIA R&D Fund.

Key recommendations on national SME and entrepreneurship support programmes *(cont.)*

- Encourage the Israel Investment Centre to increase the share of its budget for capital investment in SME-led projects by reducing eligibility requirements as to export and turnover thresholds for its subsidies.
- Establish incubators and accelerators for more traditional start-ups and existing SMEs in the manufacturing and service sectors that are not necessarily R&D-driven, but which are nonetheless innovative in other ways.
- Provide more funding and technical assistance (awareness raising, mentoring, counselling, etc.) for non-technological innovation (e.g. design, marketing, organisational approaches, and innovation management) in SMEs.
- Strengthen the MAOF centre advice on innovation management to SMEs by hiring specialised innovation agents.
- Expand support for collaborative innovation in small non R&D-based firms by supporting networks of SMEs for innovation activity.
- Continue support for the greening of the economy by encouraging more SMEs to join the natural gas grid and re-launching the Investment Centre's greenhouse gas reduction programmes.

Internationalisation programmes

- Design a more comprehensive approach to export training and advice for SMEs including awareness-raising events among SMEs potentially interested in exporting, export-readiness courses to instruct new and occasional exporters on how to export for the first time or expand export volumes, and advanced tailored advice for more experienced exporters.
- Adjust eligibility criteria for export programmes to facilitate participation by new and small firms with exports worth less than NIS 1 million (approximately USD 250 000) and make travel costs eligible for new and young firms to attend international trade fairs, explore international markets or meet international buyers.
- Launch a new dedicated programme for SME export promotion combining financial support with advice on exporting, export logistics management and adoption of digital infrastructures conducive to e-commerce.
- Keep the MAOF centres up-to-date about the various export promotion tools that the government provides through the FTA and the IEI and ensure that MAOF centres hire experts in exporting among their consultants and mentors.
- Introduce a more formal approach to backing the creation, operation and expansion of export consortia in Israel in order to spread the benefits of government funding among larger numbers of exporting firms and to foster the transfer of export-related knowledge among consortia members.
- Designate "export financing" as a specific loan category under the SMBF to ensure that firms can use state-backed loan guarantees when applying for bank loans to finance their export activity.

Key recommendations on national SME and entrepreneurship support programmes *(cont.)*

Workforce skills development programmes

- Set up a publicly-funded advice and brokerage service to increase the awareness of SME managers about the advantages of workforce training, develop training plans for SMEs, and refer SMEs to appropriate training providers, potentially as part of MAOF centre activities.
- Pilot a financial incentive scheme (such as a voucher, grant or tax subsidy) to assist SMEs in engaging professional training providers for workplace-based training.
- Expand the support offered by MAOF centres to include organisation of in-company workforce training packages for SMEs.
- Promote national training standards that recognise the continuing professional development undertaken by employees.
- Support networking and clustering arrangements to allow SMEs to work collaboratively with suppliers, customers, training providers and the public sector in developing and implementing appropriate training provision.
- Pilot an approach to peer learning in SME management development by setting up private-led "communities of practice" brokered and supported by MAOF centres, based on the idea of SME learning circles through which SME managers can advise and mentor peers.

Business diagnosis, advice and consultancy programmes

- Scale up the budget and activities of the MAOF centres for business diagnosis, advice and consultancy services with a particular emphasis on providing more support to SMEs with strong growth potential and expanding the range of services offered to cover significant niche areas that do not get adequate attention.
- Introduce dedicated and tailored coaching and consultancy services for growth-orientated businesses in MAOF centre activities.
- Introduce a management advice and support programme to help companies requiring business restructuring either to turn around or to close down in a way that reduces social and economic costs for the entrepreneurs and their customers.
- Consider strengthening the specialisation of MAOF staff by creating two tracks, one for manufacturing and one for services firms, reflecting the different development challenges of these two types of SMEs.
- Better link the managerial support of the MAOF centres with the financial assistance available from other public programmes. As part of this, ensure that those SMEs that do not receive loan guarantee assistance from the SMBF are automatically re-directed towards alternative support from the business consulting and signposting services offered by MAOF centres.

Public procurement programmes

- Develop online guidelines for SMEs in the form of a step-by-step guide for contracting with the government.
- Implement a national e-procurement system in order to simplify administrative procedures for businesses to reduce the comparative disadvantage of SMEs in accessing procurement opportunities.

Key recommendations on national SME and entrepreneurship support programmes *(cont.)*

- Collect data on the number and volume of public procurement contracts awarded to SMEs to ascertain whether SMEs have fair access to public procurement, making use of set-aside quotas or targets for the value of contracts from SMEs if they are found to experience discrimination.
- Provide training and support to government procurement officers in how to ensure that their procurement processes are open to SMEs.

Programmes to support entrepreneurship in specific social target groups

- Launch additional specialised support programmes for self-employment and entrepreneurship for people from disadvantaged and under-represented social groups in entrepreneurship, including youth, women, Arab Israelis, and Ultraorthodox Jews.
- Develop more comprehensive interventions for these groups, which integrate training and business advice with financial assistance and offer some follow-on support after the immediate start-up event.

Notes

1. Data provided by the SMBA. 95% of the applicants were small businesses with less than 20 employees.
2. The median coverage rate among 76 schemes studied by the World Bank was 80% (Klapper et al., 2008).
3. "Cognito Capital and Peninsula Chosen to Establish Growth Capital Funds for Investment in Small and Medium-Sized Businesses: Total Investment NIS 1 billion", Press Release, 1/4/2016, Ministry of Economy and Industry.
4. "Bennett: New angels law is world's most daring", GLOBES, 16 July 2014. Online at: *http://globes.co.il/en/article-bennett-new-angels-law-is-worlds-most-daring-1000955499*.
5. Target companies are Israeli private companies in which 75% of the investment amount must be used for R&D expenses, the R&D expenses must in each year covered by the investment comprise 70% of the overall expenses of the company, at least 75% of the R&D expenses must be expended in Israel, and the company's revenue cannot exceed 50% of the amount of its R&D expenses in the year of the investment and in the following tax year (Ministry of Finance, 2012).
6. The Committee included the Bank of Israel, the Israel Securities Authorities, the Ministry of Finance, the Ministry of Justice and the Israel Tax Authority.
7. Data on Israeli incubators Israeli incubators are from *www.science.co.il/Technology-Incubators.asp/*.
8. Kibbutz is a Hebrew word for "group" and refers to a voluntary democratic community in Israel where people live and work together on a non-competitive basis, founded on the principles of communal ownership of property, social justice, and equality. In 2010, there were 270 kibbutzim in Israel, their factories and farms accounting for 9% of Israel's industrial output.
9. Programmes for the Israeli Arab minority are discussed at length in the specifically dedicated chapter of this report.

References

Adalya Economic Consulting (2011), *Strategic Report of Israeli Governmental Assistance to Small and Medium Businesses – Phase A*, submitted to Small and Medium Business Agency, November, Tel Aviv, Adalya Economic Consulting.

American Technion Society (undated), *Technion Global Impact*, Haifa, *www.ats.org/wp-content/uploads/2014/03/1.29.14Technion_Global_Impact.pdf*.

American Technion Society, *Technion Business Connection*, Haifa, *www.ats.org/wp-content/uploads/2014/03/8.30.13Technion-Business-Connection.pdf*.

Australian Department of Industry (2014a), *Entrepreneurs' Infrastructure Programme Business Management Elements Transitional Programme Guidelines*, Canberra.

Australian Department of Industry (2014b), *Establishment of the Entrepreneurs' Infrastructure Programme Discussion Paper*, Canberra.

Bank of Israel (2014), *Annual Report 2013*, Jerusalem, Bank of Israel.

Bank of Israel (2013), *Structural Issues in Israel's Economy,* Bank of Israel, Jerusalem.

Baygan, G. (2003), "Venture capital policies in Israel", *STI Working Paper* 2003/3, OECD Publishing, Paris.

Bezalel, J. (2013a), *Israeli Government Procurement*, Ministry of Industry, Trade and Labour, Jerusalem.

Bezalel, J. (2013b), *Israel Government Procurement Administration*, Accountant General – Ministry of Finance, Jerusalem.

Botti, F. and M. Corsi (2011), *Measuring the Social Performance of Microfinance in Europe*, *Working Papers CEB*, 11.

Buron, G. (2011), *Young people and Adie: a secure path towards autonomy*, EMN Newsletter, No. 9.

Caliendo, M. and A. Kritikos (2010), "Start-ups by the unemployed: characteristics, survival and direct employment effects", *Small Business Economics*, 35.1, 71-92.

CGC (Credit Guarantee Corporation) (2012), *Credit Guarantee System in Japan 2012*, Tokyo, Credit Guarantee Corporation.

Crépon, B., E. Duflo, E. Huillery, W. Parienté and J. Seban (2014), *Les effets du dispositif d'accompagnement à la création d'entreprise CréaJeunes : résultats d'une expérience contrôlée*, J-PAL, Paris.

DASTI (Danish Agency for Science, Technology and Innovation) (2011), *The Impacts of Cluster Policy in Denmark – An impact study on behaviour and economical effects of Innovation Network Denmark*. Ministry of Science, Technology and Innovation, Copenhagen, *http://ufm.dk/en/publications/2011/the-impact-of-cluster-policy-in-denmark*.

Digler, R.J. (2013), *Small Business Administration 7(a) Loan Guaranty Program*, CRS Report to Congress, 1 May, Washington, DC, Congressional Research Service.

Frenkel, A. and S. Maital (2012), *Technion Nation: Technion's Contribution to Israel and the World*, Haifa, Israel: Technion – Israel Institute of Technology.

Horowitz-Reshef, R. (2014), *Financing Israel's export economy*, Fellows Programme, No. 82, February, Jerusalem, Milken Institute Fellows Programme.

Klapper, L., T. Beck and J.C. Mendoza (2008), *The Typology of Partial Credit Guarantee Funds Around the World*, World Bank Policy Research Working Paper Number 4771, November, Washington, DC, World Bank.

Lach, S., S. Parizat and D. Wasserteil (2008), *The Impact of Government Support to Industrial R&D on the Israeli Economy*, Tel Aviv, Applied Economics Ltd.

Lerman, R.I. (2014), *Expanding Apprenticeship Training in Canada: Perspectives from International Experience, Taking Action for Canada: Jobs and Skills for the 21st Century*, Canadian Council of Chief Executives, Ottawa.

MAI (Manufacturers' Association of Israel) (2014), *Policy Recommendations for Increasing Productivity in Small and Medium-sized Enterprises in Israel*, Tel Aviv, Manufacturers' Association of Israel.

Ministry of Finance (2012), *Opportunity Israel: Enhanced Legislation, R&D Incentives, Grants and Support Programs*, International Affairs Department, Fall, Jerusalem: Ministry of Finance.

Morris, M. and P. Stevens (2010), "Evaluation of a New Zealand business support programme using firm performance micro-data", *Small Enterprise Research*, 17(1), 30-42.

OECD (2014), *Financing SMEs and Entrepreneurs 2014: An OECD Scoreboard*, OECD Publishing, Paris.

OECD (2013a), Thematic Focus: Credit Guarantee Schemes, ch. 3, 41-68, in *Financing SMEs and Entrepreneurs 2013: An OECD Scoreboard*, OECD Publishing, Paris, *http://dx.doi.org/10.1787/fin_sme_ent-2013-en*.

OECD (2013b), *An International Benchmarking Analysis of Public Programmes for High-growth Firms*, OECD LEED Programme, Paris.

OECD (2013c), *Skills Development and Training in SMEs*, OECD Publishing, Paris, *http://dx.doi.org/10.1787/9789264169425-en*.

OECD (2013d), *Public Procurement Review of the Mexican Institute of Social Security*, OECD Publishing, Paris, *http://dx.doi.org/10.1787/9789264197480-en*.

OECD (2011), *Financing High-Growth Firms: The Role of Angel Investors*, OECD Publishing, Paris, *http://dx.doi.org/10.1787/9789264118782-en*.

OECD (2010), *High-Growth Enterprises: What Governments can do to Make a Difference*, OECD, Paris, *http://dx.doi.org/10.1787/9789264048782-en*.

OECD (2008), *Removing Barriers to SMEs' Access to Global Markets*, OECD Publishing, Paris.

OECD/European Commission (2012), *Policy Brief on Senior Entrepreneurship*, OECD Publishing, Paris.

OECD/European Union (2016), *Inclusive Business Creation: Good Practice Compendium*, OECD Publishing, Paris, *http://dx.doi.org/10.1787/9789264251496-en*.

OECD/European Union (2015), *Policy Brief on Sustaining Self-Employment*, OECD Publishing, Paris.

OECD and Eurostat (2005), Oslo Manual – Guidelines for Collecting and Interpreting Innovation Data, Paris, OECD.

PwC, ICF, GHK, and Ecorys (2014), *SMEs' Access to Public Procurement Markets and Aggregation of Demand in the EU*, Brussels, European Commission. *http://ec.europa.eu/internal_market/publicprocurement/docs/modernising_rules/smes-access-and-aggregation-of-demand_en.pdf*.

Sear, L. and J. Agar (1996), "Business Links and Personal Business Advisers: Selling Services Irrespective of Client's Needs?", *Paper presented at the 19th ISBA Conference*, Birmingham

Senor, D. and S. Singer (2011), *Start-up Nation: The story of Israel's economic miracle*, Random House LLC.

Seo, K. (2013), "Design, Implementation & Roll-out of e-Procurement", presentation to the OECD Public Procurement Workshop, *www.oecd.org/gov/ethics/Public-procurement-workshop-Kuwait-Korea-2-June-2013.pdf*

SMBA (Small and Medium Business Agency) (2014), *Financing SMEs and Entrepreneurs: An OECD Scoreboard Israel*, Jerusalem, Israel Ministry of Economy and Industry.

Storey, D.J. and F.J. Greene (2010), *Small business and entrepreneurship*, Financial Times Prentice Hall.

US Small Business Administration (2013), *The Small Business Investment Company (SBIC) Program, Annual Report For Fiscal Year Ending September 30, 2013*, Office of Investment and Innovation, (*www.sba.gov/inv/*).

Yago, G. and B. Zeldman (2005), *Building Israel's Small Business and Micro-enterprise Sector: Israel Entrepreneurial Finance Initiative*, Santa Monica, CA, Milken Institute.

OECD Studies on SMEs and Entrepreneurship
SME and Entrepreneurship Policy in Israel 2016

Chapter 6

The local dimension to SME and entrepreneurship policy in Israel

This chapter considers the extent to which SME and entrepreneurship policy actions are adapted to differing local conditions in Israel and the role of regional policy and local government authorities in SME and entrepreneurship development. The national government's regional policy offers capital investment incentives to encourage mobile industrial investment to locate in the under-developed northern and southern regions of the country, but could do more to support entrepreneurship and innovation and to build local supply chains and clusters. Local government authorities in Israel have an influence on SME and entrepreneurship development through supporting the availability of appropriate sites and premises, simplifying local business regulations and supporting SME access to local public procurement. However, most are very small, and lack budgets and professional capacities for SME and entrepreneurship development. Government can support the local level through capacity-building activities in these areas and by encouraging inter-municipality co-operation.

The statistical data for Israel are supplied by and under the responsibility of the relevant Israeli authorities. The use of such data by the OECD is without prejudice to the status of the Golan Heights, East Jerusalem and Israeli settlements in the West Bank under the terms of international law.
This document and any map included herein are without prejudice to the status of or sovereignty over any territory, to the delimitation of international frontiers and boundaries and to the name of any territory, city or area.

The role of local government

Local government responsibilities

Although Israel is often divided into six districts for statistical and planning purposes, which can also be combined into three major regions, there is no elected administrative structure at the district or regional level and there is no policy coordination at this level. Furthermore, neither regional development agencies nor regional development strategies exist. The only relevant level of sub-national government for SME and entrepreneurship policy in Israel is therefore the local government authorities.

Israel has 232 local authorities, which are mostly small. The local authorities are classed into three kinds: cities (urban municipalities with populations greater than 20 000), municipalities (covering settlements with populations of between 2 000 and 20 000), and regional councils (coordinating sets of settlements with population of less than 2 000 each). Of the 232 local authorities, 170 have less than 25 000 inhabitants and a further 34 have less than 50 000 inhabitants. Only 28 local authorities have populations of 50 000 or more, of which 6 have populations of more than 200 000. The two largest local authorities are Jerusalem with a population of 815 000 and Tel Aviv-Yafo with a population of 415 000.

Economic development is not a general statutory duty of the local authorities. However, they do have an influence on SME and entrepreneurship development through their roles in business licensing, land use planning and property development and their ability to make discretionary funding of SME and entrepreneurship actions from their own budgets.

Business licensing

Business licensing largely falls within the remit of local authorities, although some permits are awarded by other types of authorities (for example fire authorities), which cover different geographical areas. There is a wide range of permits which are necessary for businesses, and there are plans to streamline the system by reducing the numbers and combining permits at national level. Meanwhile, some local authorities have tried to streamline business licensing (e.g. Jerusalem), at least in as much as this is related to actions determined by the local authority itself, through the development of one-stop shops and better coordinated provision of information.

Planning permission

Local authorities have responsibility for the award of planning permission for business property development either individually or in combination with neighbouring authorities. Although a 2008 government decision called for the establishment of local planning committees for every municipality with more than 15 000 inhabitants, this policy is still not fully implemented and so local planning decisions are often made by combined planning committees covering several municipalities, particularly for smaller settlements. The fact that planning powers often rest with very small local authorities can have certain adverse consequences for the development of sites and premises for SMEs and entrepreneurs. Sometimes local authorities take an excessively long time to reach planning decisions, reflecting low capacities to handle files (BIMKOM, 2012; Hamdan and Jabareen, 2006; Charney, 2013). The fragmentation of power across small authorities can also encourage competition among local authorities to approve industrial zones, given that zones generate revenues for local authorities from the business taxes paid. As a result many competing and under-occupied small sites are often approved, while larger industrial sites are not put forward. Furthermore, local authority planning decisions must be in line with the national spatial plan (TAMA 35) while the majority of land (93%) is publicly owned and managed by the Israeli Land Authority. The way in which land has been zoned at national level and released for use by the Israeli Land Authority has often not been well integrated with local economic development needs, such that appropriate business sites and premises are lacking in some localities.

Industrial site provision

Local authorities in Israel can play an important role as investors and developers of commercial property. The extent to which they are able to develop industrial and business property is nonetheless dependent on their professional and financial resources. Central government grants compensate to some extent for lower direct tax revenues per capita in poorer local authorities since grant allocations are weighted by the level of socio-economic development and the degree of peripherality of the local authorities. Despite this, local authority revenue per capita is greater on average for authorities with higher socio-economic rankings. The larger local authorities can also pull together a greater critical mass of funding given their larger population sizes. It is therefore the largest local authorities that are most active in property development. Indeed, the three largest local authorities (Jerusalem, Tel Aviv-Yafo, and Haifa) all have their own municipally-owned development companies (Jerusalem Development Agency, Tel Aviv-Yafo Economic Development Authority, and Haifa Economic Corporation respectively), dealing mainly with property development. On the other hand, smaller local authorities often do little commercial property development, leading to shortages of appropriate sites and premises.

Local economic development programmes

Some of the larger local authorities have been involved in small-scale actions to support SMEs and entrepreneurship. For example, some participate in the sponsorship of business incubators and accelerators in their localities and some have participated in the past in the funding of the business support activities of the MATI business centres, which preceded the new MAOF business centre network. Israeli local authorities in general, however, are not very active in using their own discretionary funds to promote local economic development actions, such as in access to finance, workforce training, consultancy and mentoring or bending procurement to SME development needs. Limited budgets stand in the way of more active involvement for most local authorities.

Potential capacity-building support

Even where local authorities do not have substantial dedicated budgets for SME and entrepreneurship development they can still have a positive impact, by simplifying regulations and procurement processes, co-operating in the planning of industrial zones or simply in providing information to SMEs and entrepreneurs on the local availability and specifications of premises, public procurement, and regulations. The central government could assist by supporting the development of stronger capacities among local authorities in these areas, including by preparing appropriate guidelines for local authorities and supporting the sharing of information among them on good practices. For example, in terms of the planning process, the government could produce clearer planning guidance notes that take into account the needs of SME development, and provide capacity building training for local authorities involved in the planning process, helping them to make strategic decisions and to cooperate with neighbouring authorities. Similarly, to support industrial site provision, the central government could provide capacity building training at the local level on how to bring forward development as well as provide some funding from central sources to allow the smallest local authorities to work effectively on industrial sites.

Co-ordination among local authorities

Policy co-ordination across levels of government can be problematic when regional and local governments operate SME and entrepreneurship interventions that are not fully coherent with national interventions. In Israel, this is not a major problem since local authorities are generally not engaged in SME and entrepreneurship development programmes, beyond business licensing and property development, and there is no regional level of government. More formal coordination with national policy is possible for the largest local authorities. For example the Jerusalem Development Agency has an advisory council including representatives of the state (various ministries) as well as the city, meaning that any strategies produced (for example the Regional Innovation Strategy – see Kaufman et al., 2007) are coordinated with national priorities.

On the other hand, one of the future opportunities in Israel is to facilitate greater co-operation among local authorities in SME and entrepreneurship development. For example there are relatively few cases of shared industrial zones, perhaps due to the difficulty of coming to agreement over the use of revenues. Shared zones could be encouraged further in the future. There are also some examples of co-operation among associations of local authorities promoted by the Centre for Mayors and Regional Development of the American Jewish Joint Distribution Committee (JDC) Institute for Leadership and Governance, which offers a model for other potential inter-local authority co-operation efforts. One of the most important areas of co-operation supported by JDC is the development of regional clusters in Eastern Galilee, Western Galilee, Eastern Negev, Western Negev, and Beit HaKerem Valley. In each case the relevant local authorities co-operate in the preparation of regional cluster development strategies. A cluster organisation is set up in each case (with powers similar to a municipal company) which can receive government funding, participate in competitive bids, and hire employees. The cluster organisations also co-ordinate joint actions funded by the member local authorities. The most developed cluster is the Western Galilee Cluster, which was formed in 2009 and coordinates 10 local authorities. There are four main pillars supporting the cluster: the intra-authority pillar (the cluster acts as an executing arm for municipal projects); the governmental pillar (an interlocutor for governmental initiatives looking for a local implementation framework, and for local initiatives seeking partnership with government offices); the civilian pillar (a regional anchor point for civil society organisations); and the economic pillar (acting as a lever for economic development initiatives and networking between them). As a result, a joint regional employment and training centre and a business incubator have been put in place, as well as new collaboration mechanisms and a regional strategic plan. The clusters have attracted financing from the Ministry of the Interior and the Ministry of Finance, which value the economies of scale and improved contacts with local government. As a result, the programme has a budget of more than NIS 15 million.

Another example of inter-local authority co-operation for SME and entrepreneurship development is the "Negev Circles" initiative, which aims to strengthen regional collaboration for the local exploitation of procurement opportunities from the transfer of Israel Defence Forces (IDF) bases to the Negev. The programme includes representatives not only of local authorities but also government offices, security forces, social organisations and businesses. They work together to develop initiatives to offer local entrepreneurs access to business opportunities provided by industrial parks and by IDF training camps.

There is significant scope to expand these types of co-operation among local authorities. National government could contribute with some funding and capacity building support. It could also support the establishment of formal structures for such collaborations. An example of this type of approach is the inter-municipal economic development company. An example of the operation of such a company in Belgium is shown in Box 6.1.

Box 6.1. **Inter-municipal cooperation company Leiedal, South West Flanders**

Description of the approach

This model shows the way in which an inter-municipal company can operate, giving services related to planning as well as support to entrepreneurship. Whilst such cooperation is voluntary, this could prove a template for such cooperation in Israel.

The Leiedal inter-municipal company for regional development groups together local authorities in the region on a voluntary basis for the common provision of planning and economic development services. The company was established in 1960 and supplies services to 13 municipalities in South West Flanders. These are centred on the town of Kortrijk (75 000 inhabitants) and all have populations of less than 50 000 people.

The company was initially established to supply services such as local spatial structure and zoning plans but has expanded, now employing more than 50 people and operating in three general fields: entrepreneurship and economic development; space and environment; and people and society. Within the field of entrepreneurship, a major part of its work relates to the planning and development of sites for businesses, particularly SMEs. For this it has capabilities in research, planning, and implementation which do not exist in the individual municipalities. Leiedal also organises provision of advice and other support to entrepreneurs and seeks to provide premises adapted for innovative businesses as part of its strategy.

Factors for success

The major reason for the success of this company as an inter-communal project is that it adds expertise and services to a region which could not afford them as individual municipalities. For this to be effective there needs to be a common understanding of the problems of the area, and the area itself needs to be a cohesive economic unit.

Obstacles and responses

The fact that the company has slowly been given more responsibilities as it has proved its capabilities has been a useful way of developing on the basis of mutual trust, which is clearly an obstacle to the rapid establishment of such a company.

The way in which the company has been set up means that there is no direct private sector representation and that the Board consists purely of representatives of the municipalities.

Box 6.1. **Inter-municipal cooperation company Leiedal, South West Flanders** *(cont.)*

This limits its ability to provide a regional vision for development. The representation of all municipalities additionally limits the ability of the company to develop larger strategic projects which do not benefit every one of them. Since this is a small region dominated by a single urban settlement, this has not caused problems. However the composition of the Board and the avoidance of "cake splitting" can be an issue. Partly as a result of this, other studies show that leadership is a key factor in effective inter-municipal cooperation (CoE et al., 2010).

Relevance for Israel

Although legal instruments are in place for cooperation between municipalities in Israel there have been only limited collaborations in the field of economic development. Many economic development services could be provided on an inter-municipal basis using structures such as the inter-municipal company, such as provision of information on public procurement and business regulation, planning and development of shared industrial zones, development of regional cluster strategies, and offering of basic SME development support such as access to loans and business development advice.

Sources for further information

- CoE, UNDP, and LGI (2010), Intermunicipal Cooperation Toolkit, Council of Europe (CoE), the United Nations Development Programme (UNDP) and the Local Government Initiative (LGI) of the Open Society.
- Leiedal (2014), Beleidsplan 2014-2019 [Policy Plan, in Flemish].
- Pisman, A., P. Vervoort and I. Loris (2013), Inter-communal cooperation and spatial planning in Flanders.

Tailoring policies to local conditions

Local variations in SME and entrepreneurship activities and conditions

Figure 6.1 shows the evolution of the number of enterprises and of the rate of enterprise births per head at district level in Israel. The Central, Haifa, Jerusalem and Tel Aviv districts can be seen as the broad core, whereas the Northern and Southern districts represent the broad periphery. The Figure shows that there are significant differences in performance in generating SMEs and entrepreneurship. The northern and southern periphery and Jerusalem are trailing the average on both enterprise numbers and enterprise birth rates. Furthermore, relative gaps are not changing over time. This would tend to suggest the need for a stronger policy for enterprise development in the periphery and Jerusalem if these areas are to develop as entrepreneurial economies.

The existence of important local differences in the rate of business creation is confirmed by the Global Entrepreneurship Monitor (GEM) survey. For example, the 3.0% of the adult population involved in total early-stage activity (TEA) in the Negev region in the south of Israel is much lower than the average of 5.0% nationally (Menipaz et al., 2011). Similarly 33% of entrepreneurs with young businesses are in Haifa and the North and 31% in the Centre, compared to only 18% in the Southern Region (Menipaz et al., 2013).

There are also significant local differences in earnings from self-employment, as shown in Figure 6.2. Across the main population groups, earnings from self-employment were higher in Tel Aviv and the Centre than in Haifa, Jerusalem, the North and the South.

Figure 6.1. **Number of enterprises per capita and enterprise births per capita in Israeli districts, 2005-11**

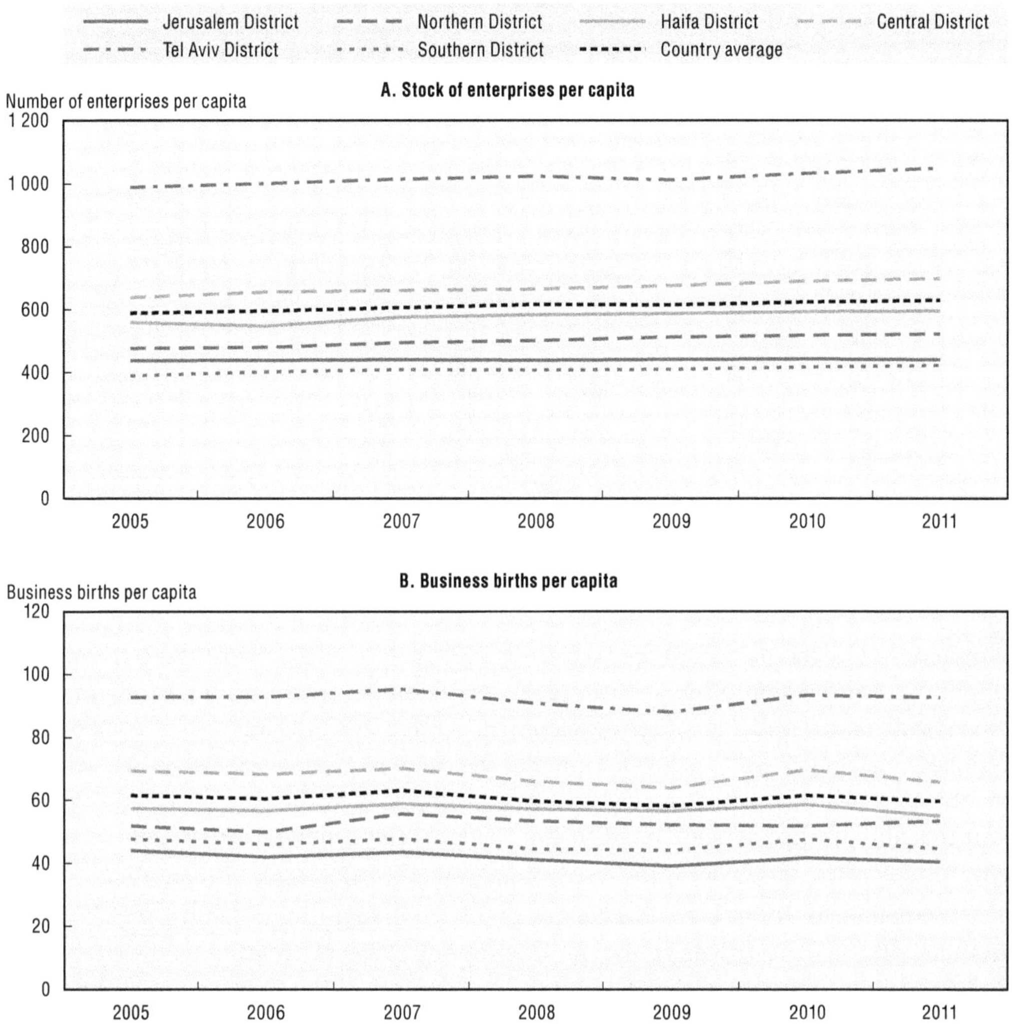

Note: these figures relate to the location of business registrations and may therefore probably be biased towards Tel Aviv and the Centre since this is where the majority of lawyers and registration agents are located.
Source: Central Bureau of Statistics.

StatLink http://dx.doi.org/10.1787/888933421913

The local differences overlap to a significant extent with the distribution of the Arab Israeli population, which is relatively concentrated in districts with low earnings from self-employment, particularly in the northern district. This suggests that there can be synergies between addressing the regional entrepreneurship gap and increasing the integration of Arab Israeli populations in the economy. It highlights the potential benefits of additional entrepreneurship training, advice, consultancy and access to finance support in peripheral and Arab-dominated localities.

Building local clusters and supply chains

The majority of SME and entrepreneurship policies and programmes in Israel are delivered by national government ministries and agencies in a standardised or "spatially-blind" way across the country. Certain policy measures weight their spending towards the

Figure 6.2. **Self-employed earnings per capita by main ethnicity of the local authority district, 2011**

New Israeli Sheqel (NIS)

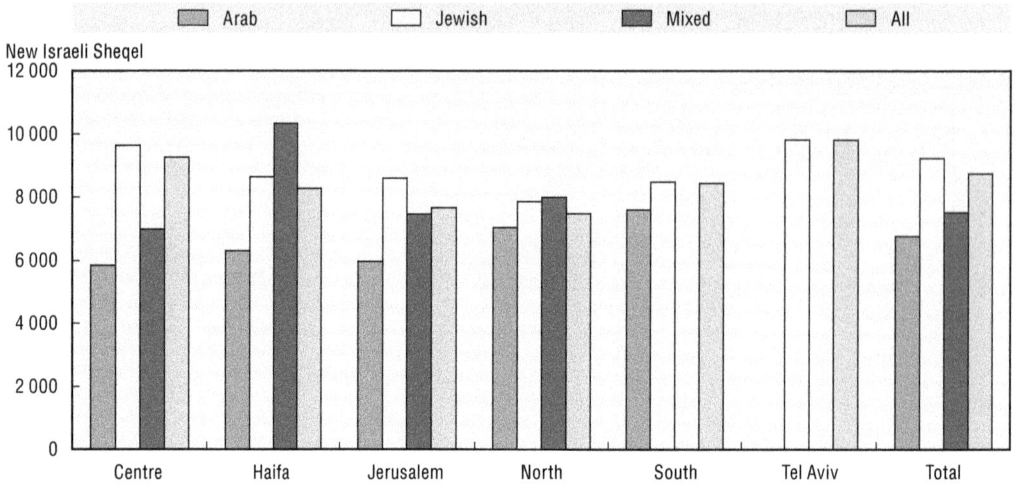

Note: "Mixed" are majority Jewish municipalities where there is a non-Jewish population of at least 25%.
Source: Central Bureau of Statistics.

StatLink http://dx.doi.org/10.1787/888933421926

periphery, but in general the design and overall availability of the measures is no different according to the region (Kipnis, 2010, 2013). For example, there is a weighting of SMBA expenditure on the MAOF business development centres that favours centres located in the periphery enabling them to carry out more of the same services available elsewhere in the country. Similarly the high technology incubators supported by the IIA are located across the country (and are not concentrated in the Central region where innovation activity is concentrated), but the services which they deliver are the same across the country.

The main exceptions are the activities of the Israel Investment Centre, which targets financial and tax incentives to mobile investment projects locating in the peripheral regions and the activities of the Ministry of Development of the Negev and Galilee, which provides business and transport infrastructure and undertakes investment promotion in order to promote economic development in these peripheral regions (Salman et al., 2005). In addition, the Ministry operates a few direct actions to support SMEs as part of this strategy, including Tourism Incubators (in the Galilee) and a programme ("A Classroom in a Factory") to assist immigrants from Ethiopia in integrating within local SMEs.

One of the features of this generally "spatially-blind" approach is that partnership among ministries and agencies in designing relevant actions is often underdeveloped in Israel with respect to adapting policies to distinct local needs and opportunities. In the area of innovation policy, for example, the IIA operates a technology incubator programme with incubators spread across the whole country. However, these have been funded as individual initiatives and their technology focus has not been specifically linked to the strengths and potentials of particular locations, such as the presence of relevant university research or local cluster specialisations. Greater co-operation between the IIA and other ministries could help to link the technology incubators with strategies for regional development. The Centre for Expertise Programme (OSKE) in Finland illustrates a way in which place-based regional policy can be integrated with national innovation policy in a way that could more deliberately promote the development of regional clusters in Israel (Box 6.2).

Box 6.2. **The Centres of Expertise Programme (OSKE), Finland 1994-2013**

Description of the approach

The Centre of Expertise Programme's objective was to create new innovations, products, services, enterprises and jobs based on national excellence. It supported the specialisation of regions and division of duties between them in order to create internationally competitive centres of expertise. At the same time, the Centre of Expertise Programme aimed to enhance the attractiveness of regional innovation environments, in order to draw international companies, investments and top experts to Finland. The programme formed part of the national innovation strategy, but combined this with local and regional development.

In pursuit of these goals, the programme worked on the principle that there should be one Centre of Expertise in each region, based on regional strengths, and that these should collectively support a set of Competence Clusters of national importance. The regional centres were set up based on local circumstances and institutions and several centres supported each cluster.

In the final period, the programme consisted of 21 regional Centres of Expertise which supported 13 national Competence Clusters. From a regional point of view, a centre of expertise could contain several fields of expertise belonging to different clusters. The objectives and measures of Centres of Expertise were defined in accordance with the needs and opportunities of businesses, both in the region and the entire cluster, and of other actors in the innovation system. The Centre of Expertise acted as a network of regional operators implementing the national Centre of Expertise Programme in their region together with other members of the cluster, with activities based on a regional structure comprising businesses, universities, institutes of higher education, research institutes and technology centres.

Centres of Expertise were initially selected through a competitive process with applications being judged centrally against a menu of competence clusters which had also been determined by a process of applications. Although there was naturally a bias towards high technology, some were in other areas such as tourism and culture.

Factors for success

This was a long term approach (starting in 1994), providing a framework for a national approach to innovation support but at the same time accommodating regional specialisation.

A wide range of stakeholders were involved at all levels and the programme worked on the basis of partnership. This allowed the definition of clusters and participation by Centres of Expertise to be largely consensual and for the programme to become a forum for coordination between the "triple helix" of research, government, and the private sector.

The approach of defining Centres and Clusters by a process of competitive applications allowed structures and ways of working to be built from the bottom up even within a nationally-defined framework and objectives.

Obstacles and responses

There are some inherent contradictions between national innovation policy (meaning that there should be a concentration on national priorities and competences and those actions should take place where there is the biggest concentration of expertise) and regional policy (ensuring equitable development of different regions of the country). These contradictions remain, even though the OSKE system did give to some degree a forum where issues could

Box 6.2. **The Centres of Expertise Programme (OSKE), Finland 1994-2013** *(cont.)*

be discussed. The system has been more successful at supporting innovation than supporting lagging regions, particularly because some of the regions do not have strong expertise on a national level. As a result there has been some suggestion that instruments for regional development and for innovation should be more clearly divided.

The emphasis on regional centres to some degree caused the programme to become inward looking, even though effective innovation requires internationalisation. In the latest phase, each cluster had a single coordinator who was specifically responsible for creating shared aims within the cluster, but also for cooperation outside it, including with other countries. Clusters were chosen with internationalisation potential as one of the criteria.

As with all such programmes, there has been a need for renewal, to avoid institutional structures becoming self-justifying and unimaginative in their approach. The programme was terminated in 2013 on the basis that self-sustaining clusters and expertise had been developed and that this could form the basis of actions based around the EU's smart specialisation strategy.

Relevance for Israel

Israel's approach to supporting innovation through the Office of the Chief Scientist (now the IIA) has been centralised and has had a limited local and regional component, meaning that innovation activities tend to be concentrated in the core districts ("Silicon Wadi"). Although technology incubators have been spread throughout the country, they have not had any sectoral specialisation and have been relatively poorly connected to the regional innovation system, even connections with universities happening through proximity rather than design (Shefer et al., 2002).

The Finnish experience shows that even more remote areas can participate in a programme of national clusters and that through this regional development and national innovation objectives can be combined. An approach of this nature, perhaps based around the existing technology incubators, could act as a stimulus for local development in Israel's peripheral regions. This would additionally form part of development of regional policy from a traditional "core-periphery" model to a more place-based system.

Sources for further information

- Ministry of Employment and the Economy of Finland (2009), Evaluation of the Finnish National Innovation System – Full Report, Helsinki.
- Ministry of Employment and the Economy of Finland (2010), chapter 4.2, "The OSKE programme in international perspective", in Osaamiskeskusohjelman (2007-13) väliarviointi, Helsinki.
- The Research and Innovation Council of Finland (2010), Research and Innovation Policy Guidelines for 2011-2015, The Research and Innovation Council of Finland, Helsinki.

Websites

- *http://erawatch.jrc.ec.europa.eu/erawatch/opencms/information/country_pages/fi/supportmeasure/support_mig_0033.*
- *www.ccdr-lvt.pt/files/aa3f8753ce509dca676a94c436cfd9a4.pdf.*
- *www.hyvinvointiklusteri.fi/en/.*
- *www.tekel.fi/in_english/science_parks_in_action/programmes_and_networks/oske/.*

Another feature of this "spatially-blind" approach is that, apart from the inter-municipality collaborations discussed above, there is no policy aimed at developing locally-specific clusters or local supply chains, despite the existence of some potential for developing regional clusters in Israel. For example, an OECD study concluded that there is a significant opportunity to establish a clean-tech sub-cluster in the Negev region specialised in research, demonstration and testing, linked into the broader Israel clean-tech cluster. A number of actions could be undertaken to build up existing nascent activity in the sub-cluster: the promotion of collaborative innovation projects, the creation of a clean-tech technology validation centre, a green strategy at the regional (Negev) level, the creation of a regional cluster management organisation, and the transformation of Eilat into a focal point as Israel's model green city (Potter et al., 2012). However, there has not yet been a specific strategy to promote this cluster at the Negev level.

Similarly, in respect of FDI attraction, there is currently a lack of localised FDI-SME linkage programmes in Israel that could create local SME supply chains and capabilities in the regions. Ireland is a good example of an OECD country that uses inward investment to develop local supply chains. Enterprise Ireland and IDA Ireland currently operate a global sourcing initiatives which aims to strengthen the connections between Irish-owned firms and the foreign-owned bare of companies in Ireland. It involves meeting with multinationals operating in Ireland to discuss their procurement practices and identifying domestic SMEs with relevant products and services that can compete with overseas supplies with the aim of identifying import substitution opportunities. Actions to develop local strategies for developing supply chains (including training and investment in selected companies with the greatest potential to be part of the supply chain) could be introduced in Israel through cooperation between the Israel Investment Centre, the Industrial Cooperation Authority, the SMBA and interested municipalities.

Increased efforts to build local FDI-SME supply chains and local clusters would be supported by a shift in both the enterprise policy and the regional policy approaches in Israel. In the case of enterprise policy, more emphasis could be placed on identifying and overcoming locally-specific barriers to SME and entrepreneurship development and building local clusters and linkages. In the case of regional policy, a greater emphasis on promotion of entrepreneurship and innovation could be included in order to support bottom-up development. Thus whereas Israel can currently be characterised as operating a "traditional" regional policy approach based on compensating for the disadvantages of location via investment subsidies for mobile businesses, modern approaches to regional policy increasingly stress the use of a range of soft support and financial support to develop peripheral regions based on exploiting their unique assets and overcoming local barriers to entrepreneurship and innovation in areas such as firm capabilities, specialisations and business linkages of universities and research institutions, skills, and business networks (Reut Institute et al., 2010; McCann and Rodriguez-Pose, 2011). The differences between the two approaches are summarised in Table 6.1.

Some of the collaborations among local authorities in the development of regional clusters represent the first steps along this type of approach. These types of approaches need to be extended to become an integral part of regional and enterprise policy in Israel, with the collaboration not just of the local authorities but also relevant ministries and agencies, such as the Ministry of Development of the Negev and the Galilee, the IIA and the SMBA, as well as local authorities and business, research and education stakeholders. The

Table 6.1. **Traditional and modern approaches to regional policy**

	Traditional Regional Policy	Modern Regional Policy
Objectives	Compensating temporarily for location disadvantages of lagging regions	Tapping into underutilised entrepreneurship and innovation potential in all regions
Unit of Intervention	Administrative units	Functional economic areas
Strategies	Sectoral approach	Integrated development projects
Financial tools	Subsidies and state aids	Mix of hard capital (infrastructure) and "soft" capital (business support, credit availability, networking systems)
Actors	Central government	Multi-level governance involving different tiers or levels of local, regional and national government working in partnership and alongside the private and civil society sectors
Policy prioritisation	Sectoral logic and capital investment	Place-based approach Smart Specialisation principles – focus on innovation and SMEs
Incentive Tools	Absorption and expenditure criteria	Outcome oriented policies

Source: OECD based on OECD 2009.

locally-specific measures to be promoted in this way could include support for the emergence of local entrepreneurial ecosystems, clusters and supply chains.

In a more comprehensive manner, the European Union has developed an approach to developing regional "smart specialisation strategies" to encourage economic development based around specific regional assets. Box 6.3 explains the approach, which offers a model of how the process could be started in Israel involving a range of partners in regional strategy development including relevant ministries, the SMBA, local authorities and stakeholders from the business, research and education sectors.

Box 6.3. **The EU Smart Specialisation Strategies**

Description of the approach

National/Regional Research and Innovation Strategies for Smart Specialisation – known as Regional Innovation Strategies (RIS3) or Smart Specialisation Strategies (S3) – seek to provide a strategic approach to economic development and are based on targeted support for research and innovation activities. The strategies aim to promote integrated, transformative and place-based approaches to economic development. The agenda is focused upon making innovation a priority for all regions, focusing investment and creating synergies, improving the innovation process and enhancing governance and stakeholder involvement. Specifically, the Smart Specialisation approach aims to:

- establish a process for developing a vision;
- identify specialisation, competitive advantage and potential for excellence in activities appropriate to the local context, building upon national/regional strengths;
- set strategic priorities for future development policy and investments dovetailing with key national/regional priorities, challenges and needs for knowledge-based development;
- develop policies to maximise the potential for knowledge-based development in different kinds of local contexts – including strong or weak, and high-technology or low-tech;
- support technological as well as practice-based innovation and aim to stimulate private sector investment;
- engage and involve stakeholders to encourage innovation and experimentation; and,
- build upon sound research and analysis from a strong evidence-base, incorporating rigorous monitoring and evaluation systems.

Box 6.3. **The EU Smart Specialisation Strategies** *(cont.)*

Smart Specialisation is the basis for the investments to support research, innovation and entrepreneurship through the European Union (EU) Cohesion Policy and its Structural and Investment Funds. The EU's Cohesion Policy aims to promote balanced and harmonious development across the territory of the EU.

Factors for success

While it is too early formally to assess the effectiveness of Smart Specialisation Strategies, the OECD undertook a recent enquiry into progress to date (OECD, 2013). The report identified a number of key issues that are likely to support success.

A consistent approach to assessment and diagnosis of potential is important in order to generate systematic understanding and to enable international comparisons. This also enables priorities to be chosen in a clear and systematic manner. The EU's strategy of encouraging peer reviews of strategies has been helpful in this respect.

The process and objectives of S3 enables a focus on particular local strengths and consideration of areas beyond generic areas for development (e.g. ICT, life science, biotechnology, health, materials, nanotechnology, logistics, transport, mobility, energy/ green energy, green/clean technologies). Peer reviews have assisted in challenging regions which have not made detailed analyses.

The adoption of the process as part of EU Structural and Investment Funds programmes ensures that there are adequate resources to make it possible to implement the strategies and realise the stated objectives with the agreed policy mix. The EU approach to co-financing has ensured effective ex ante evaluation in this respect, and will additionally enforce comprehensive monitoring and evaluation system to enable learning from experience.

Obstacles and responses

Given the early stage of development of S3 across Europe, the ways in which actors at the national, regional and local levels have responded to obstacles is currently being identified. Early analysis from the European Policies Research Centre (Strathclyde University, UK) (EPRC, 2012) has drawn a number of key conclusions:

- S3 is proving useful in promoting innovation policy in different types of regions rather than just those with high-technology and/or R&D assets;
- considerable uncertainty remains about how the approach will be implemented, some advanced regions have the necessary elements but see little value-added formalising this in a S3 strategy document while others lack the most basic capacity and elements for innovation policy rendering such an approach unrealistic;
- leadership is a critical issue in delivering on the S3 strategies when developed;
- S3 can have most impact where it can enhance regional innovation capacities and support existing efforts;
- while promoted as a strategy for all kinds of regions, putting together the S3 strategy for some regions will entail much time, effort and resources while generating limited benefits;
- S3's most positive effect may be through building capacity especially in regions with little experience of developing strategy and policy for innovation.

Relevance for Israel

Moving to a more place-based approach to regional and enterprise development will require coordination of a number of different stakeholders. To start this process it will be important to have clear written objectives and a strategy. The S3 approach shows a way of

Box 6.3. **The EU Smart Specialisation Strategies** *(cont.)*

doing this that could be implemented at regional level (districts or groups of districts) in the Israeli context.

Further information

- European Commission (2010), Regional Policy contributing to smart growth in Europe 2020. SEC (2010) 1183.
- European Commission (2012), Guide to Research and Innovation Strategies for Smart Specialisation (RIS 3).
- EPRC (2012), "Smart Specialisation" and Cohesion Policy – A Strategy for All Regions? European Policies Research Centre, Strathclyde University, Glasgow.

Conclusions and policy recommendations

There is no regional level of government and no regional development agencies in Israel. The relevant subnational level of government is rather the local authorities, the majority of which have relatively small populations. It is rare for Israeli local authorities to operate their own local economic development programmes. They nevertheless have some important impacts on SMEs and entrepreneurship through their powers and responsibilities in the areas of business licensing, planning permission for commercial property and industrial site provision. There are a number of constraints for SMEs and entrepreneurs in these areas of local authority responsibility, which in large part reflect limited local authority budgets and professional capacities. Central government could make a significant difference by offering capacity-building support to help improve local authority practices in these areas.

There are also opportunities to facilitate greater co-operation among Israeli local authorities in SME and entrepreneurship development, for example in developing shared industrial zones, in providing shared information on local procurement and regulations or developing joint cluster development initiatives or supply chains. There are some examples of such inter-municipal collaboration, but there is scope to do more, for example by encouraging the creation of inter-municipal co-operation companies for SME and entrepreneurship support services.

Israel is also characterised by significant local variation in SME densities and start-up rates, with the north, south and Jerusalem lagging behind the centre regions on several measures. This suggests the need for stronger SME and entrepreneurship support in the peripheral regions. Most existing national government SME and entrepreneurship programmes are "spatially blind" in the sense of offering standard and common support throughout the country. At the same time, the main existing regional policy subsidy instrument operated by the Israel Investment Centre puts relatively little emphasis on the promotion of entrepreneurship and innovation. Both the national enterprise and regional policy approaches would benefit from an increased emphasis on identifying and overcoming locally-specific barriers to the development of SMEs and entrepreneurship, with particular emphasis on developing local supply chains and regional clusters. This type of more place-based approach to SME and entrepreneurship development can be encouraged by establishing local strategies and actions with the co-operation of a range of relevant government ministries and agencies together with private sector and other stakeholders. This type of process can most easily be started up through voluntary collaboration of municipalities at a local level, but this will require targeted support. Furthermore, SMBA should participate in discussions regarding regional development to ensure that SME and entrepreneurship development policy instruments are appropriately applied.

With these considerations in mind, the following specific recommendations are suggested:

Key recommendations on the local dimension of SME and entrepreneurship policy

- Provide capacity-building support to local government authorities on local actions for streamlining local business licensing procedures and assisting entrepreneurs through the process of obtaining licenses, making the local planning system more effective and opening up local public procurement to SMEs. This could take the form of professional training, preparation of guidelines and disseminating information on the practices of the best performing local authorities as examples for others to follow.
- Encourage participation of local authorities in national efforts to open up public procurement to SMEs, including simplification of procurement procedures for SMEs, training for officials in good practice procurement methods and participation in a national e-procurement system or SME set-aside system if introduced.
- Offer funding and brokerage for co-operation projects amongst groups of smaller local authorities for joint SME actions. These can include joint projects for property development, business licensing simplification, local public procurement from SMEs, and local cluster and supply chain development.
- Expand support for SME and entrepreneurship development in the regional development programme for the southern periphery and develop a relevant set of SME support actions for development in the northern periphery.

References

BIMKOM (2012), *Outline Planning for Arab Localities in Israel*, Bimkom – Planners for Planning Rights, Jerusalem.

CoE, UNDP and LGI (2010), Inter-municipal Cooperation Toolkit, Council of Europe (CoE), the United Nations Development Programme (UNDP) and the Local Government Initiative (LGI) of the Open Society.

EPRC (2012), *Smart Specialisation' and Cohesion Policy – A Strategy for All Regions?* European Policies Research Centre, Strathclyde University, Glasgow.

European Commission (2012), *Guide to Research and Innovation Strategies for Smart Specialisation* (RIS3), European Commission, Brussels.

European Commission (2010), *Regional Policy contributing to smart growth in Europe 2020*, SEC (2010) 1183, European Commission, Brussels.

Hamdan, H. and Y. Jabareen (2006), "A Proposal for Suitable Representation of the Arab Minority in Israel's National Planning System', *Adalah's Newsletter*, Volume 23, March 2006.

HMRC (2008), Study of the impact of the Enterprise Investment Scheme (EIS) and Venture Capital Trusts (VCTs) on company performance, HM Revenue and Customs Research Report 44, HM Revenue and Customs, London *http://webarchive.nationalarchives.gov.uk/20140207061336/www.hmrc.gov.uk/research/report44.pdf*.

Kaufman, D., A. Malchi, N. Solomon and D. Bendel (2007), *Regional Innovation Strategy to Promote Growth in Jerusalem*, November 2007 J-RIS project.

Kipnis, B. (2013), *Greater Tel Aviv as a Global City – A Vehicle for Reviving the National Periphery*.

Kipnis, B.A. (2010), "Polarization, Spread and Upgrading of Urban Functions: From a Dominating 'First City' to a 'Network of Cities' Structure".

Leiedal (2014), *Beleidsplan 2014-2019* [Policy Plan, in Flemish], Intercommunale Leiedal, Kortrijk.

McCann, P. and A. Rodriguez-Pose (2011), *Why and When Development Policy Should be Place-Based*, Ch. 10, pp. 203-214, in *OECD Regional Outlook 2011: Building Resilient Regions for Stronger Economies*, OECD Publications, Paris, *http://dx.doi.org/10.1787/9789264120983-en*.

Menipaz, E., Y. Avrahami and M. Lerner (2013), *National Report for Israel by the Global Entrepreneurship Monitor 2013*, Ira Center for Business Technology and Society, Ben Gurion University.

Menipaz, E., Y. Avrahami and M. Lerner (2011), *GEM 2010 Israel National Entrepreneurship Report*, Ben Gurion University of the Nagev, Beer Sheva, *www.gemconsortium.org/docs/2290/gem-israel-2010-report*.

Ministry of Employment and the Economy of Finland (2010), "The OSKE Programme in International Perspective", ch. 4.2 in *Osaamiskeskusohjelman (2007-13) väliarviointi*, Ministry of Employment and the Economy of Finland, Helsinki.

Ministry of Employment and the Economy of Finland (2009), *Evaluation of the Finnish National Innovation System* – Full Report.

OECD (2009), *Regions Matter: Economic Recovery, Innovation and Sustainable Growth*, OECD Publishing, Paris, *http://dx.doi.org/10.1787/9789264076525-en*.

Pisman, A., P. Vervoort and I. Loris (2013), *Inter-communal cooperation and spatial planning in Flanders*, presented at the conference "Cities as Seedbeds of Innovation".

Potter, J., P. Cooke, K. Chapple, D. Rehfeld, G. Theyel, D. Kaufmann, M. Malul and M. Rosenboim, (2012), *Clean-Tech Clustering as an Engine for Local Development: The Negev Region, Israel*, OECD Local Economic and Employment Development (LEED) Working Papers, 2012/11, OECD Publishing, *http://dx.doi.org/10.1787/5k98p4wm6kmv-en*.

Reut Institute, JDC Institute for Leadership and Governance, Jewish Agency for Israel (2010), Israel 15 Vision, Leapfrogging the Periphery.

Salman, N. and R. Folkman (2005), *Development of the Negev and Galilee – For Jews Only? A Proposal for Equal Development for Jews and Arabs in the Negev and Galilee*, Policy Paper, Jerusalem, July 2005, Or Watch Project, Sikkuy Association.

Shefer, D. and A. Frenkel (2002), *An Evaluation of the Israeli Technological Incubator Program and Its Projects*, Technion – Israel Institute of Technology, Haifa.

The Research and Innovation Council of Finland (2010), *Research and Innovation Policy Guidelines for 2011-15*, The Research and Innovation Council of Finland, Helsinki.

Chapter 7

Entrepreneurship and SME development in the Arab Israeli population

Arab Israelis account for approximately 20% of the country's population but their incomes and labour market participation are much lower than the national average. Stronger SME and entrepreneurship development in the Arab Israeli community could promote national growth and help address inequality. Although the overall business start-up rate for Arab Israelis appears to be similar to the population as a whole, it is less likely to be opportunity-driven and start-up rates for Arab Israeli women are low. Existing Arab-owned SMEs are relatively small and heavily concentrated in low productivity sectors. The barriers that need to be addressed include reliance on constrained local market demand, limited workforce and management skills, poor access to finance, and difficulties finding appropriate business premises. The government has taken important steps forward with the creation of a dedicated Authority for Economic Development of the Minorities Sector (MEDA) and the introduction of a new 5-year economic development plan for the Arab sector to be implemented across all government ministries and agencies. However, a larger-scale effort is needed, with greater emphasis on the use of public procurement, improving business management and supporting access to finance for Arab Israeli SMEs and entrepreneurs. Enhanced resources are also needed for policy co-ordination and outreach by MEDA.

Socio-economic conditions of Arab Israelis

Statistics in Israel divide the population between Jews (75.0%), Arabs (20.7%), and Others (4.3%). The Arab Israeli population can be further subdivided between Moslems (17.5% of the total population), Arab Christians (1.6%) and Druze (1.6%) (CBS, 2014a). In Israel, the term "minority" is not used to apply to sub-groups of the Jewish population or to refer to immigrants (29% of Jews were born abroad in 2009). Arab Israelis are therefore the largest minority population group targeted by government policy.

The incomes of most Arab Israelis are very low. Approximately 50% fall below the national poverty threshold. This compares to an average poverty rate of approximately 20% in Israel and an average of 11% across OECD countries (OECD, 2009). One of the main causes is a low rate of engagement in the labour force. Less than one-half of Arab Israeli adults are in the labour force (46.0% in 2014), compared to two-thirds of the Jewish population (CBS, 2014b). Greater rates of Arab Israeli self-employment and expanded employment in Arab-owned SMEs would help respond to this problem.

To a significant extent, the Arab Israeli and Jewish Israeli communities are spatially distinct. The great majority of Arab Israelis live in well-defined, ethnically-homogeneous and densely-populated villages and towns. Nine out of ten of these settlements have fewer than 25 000 inhabitants. The largest, Nazareth, has fewer than 70 000 inhabitants. Most Arab Israeli settlements are in the Northern district and to a lesser extent in the adjoining Haifa district. Fewer than 20% of Arab Israelis reside elsewhere, mostly in Jerusalem, Haifa and in parts of the Greater Tel Aviv metropolitan area (Goldblatt and Omer 2014). This spatial pattern implies the need for some special policies for Arab-owned businesses, designed for and delivered in the places where the Arab Israeli population is concentrated.

The distribution of the Arab Israeli population interacts with the core-periphery nature of Israel's economy. Most Arab Israelis live far from Tel Aviv, the centre and economic core of the country, and a limited road network and poor public transportation serving Arab Israeli towns and villages impede travel to the centre or Jewish areas for employment. There are also limited cross-flows of finance and sales and supply linkages between the Arab and Jewish Israeli business sectors.

These issues need to be taken into account in the design of policy to support Arab Israeli SMEs and entrepreneurship. In addition, policy should recognise the increasing education rates and desire for labour market participation among Arab Israeli women, who suffer the highest rate of unemployment of any social group in Israel.

Arab Israeli early-stage entrepreneurship

According to the Global Entrepreneurship Monitor (GEM), the rate of early-stage entrepreneurial activity in the Arab Israeli community appears to be similar to the average for the Israeli population (Table 7.1). In 2009 and 2010, it appears to have exceeded the national level, while in 2012 and 2013 it appears to have fallen behind. Both Arab Israeli

Table 7.1. **Rate of total early-stage entrepreneurial activity in Israel and its Arab population, 2009-13**

	2009	2010	2012	2013
National	6.1	5	6.5	10
Male		7	7.7	13.7
Female		4.4	5.1	6.6
Arab	7.2	6.5	6.1	8.5
Male	9.4	6.5	4.4	13.2
Female	4.9	6.5	7.9	4

Note: Total early-stage entrepreneurial activity (TEA) is defined by GEM as the percentage of the adult population (18-64 years old) who are either nascent entrepreneurs (actively involved in setting up a new business less than 3 months old) or who are currently an owner-manager of a business less than 42 months old.
Source: Global Entrepreneurship Monitor (GEM).

StatLink http://dx.doi.org/10.1787/888933421949

women and Arab Israeli men are involved in early-stage entrepreneurship activities, but the female Arab Israeli entrepreneurship rate appears to have been substantially below that of Arab Israeli men in 2013.

Indicators on the motivations for entrepreneurship and the technology-orientation of entrepreneurs suggest that the nature of the businesses created by Arab Israeli entrepreneurs may be less likely to deliver high incomes and growth than those of Israeli entrepreneurs more generally (Menipaz et al., 2013). First, in 2013 only 66.4% of Arab Israeli male entrepreneurs reported that their projects were opportunity-driven, compared with 83.8% of Jewish Israeli male entrepreneurs (excluding recent immigrants). Even more strikingly, only 27.5% of Arab Israeli female entrepreneurs were opportunity-driven, compared to 93.7% of Jewish Israeli female entrepreneurs. Second, only 8.3% of Arab Israeli male early-stage entrepreneurs were involved in medium or high technology ventures, compared to 14.0% of all Israeli male early-stage entrepreneurs. This nonetheless represents a substantial step forward from earlier years, when technology-based ventures were 'almost entirely absent from the Arab Israeli sector' (GEM 1999). By contrast, no surveyed Arab Israeli women entrepreneurs were in a technology-driven segment in 2013.

Perceptions of entrepreneurship in the Arab community are similar to those in the Jewish population (Table 7.2). However, the Arab Israeli population perceive significantly fewer good business opportunities, even though they have a higher intention of starting a business within 3 years.

Table 7.2. **Perceptions of entrepreneurship in Israel's Arab and Jewish populations, 2013**

Percentage of the adult population

	Men		Women	
	Arab	Jewish	Arab	Jewish
Perceive good opportunities to establish a business	36.7	55.3	34.5	46.3
Perceive to have entrepreneurial skills	48.1	49.2	24.1	27.1
Intend to establish a business within 3 years	38.8	33.8	33.8	17.2
Perceive entrepreneurship as a respectable career path	69.4	59.8	69.9	55.3
Think successful entrepreneurs receive status and prestige	73	86.1	69.7	80.1
Know entrepreneurs who have formed a business over the last 2 years	46.2	54	27.4	32.2

Source: GEM (2013).

StatLink http://dx.doi.org/10.1787/888933421952

Characteristics of Arab-owned SMEs

There were an estimated 20 000 Arab-owned employer businesses (i.e. with at least one employee in addition to the owner) in Israel in 2014. This represented 10.3% of employer businesses; a low density when compared to the Arab community's 20% population share. The majority (77.5%) of Arab employer businesses were located in the Northern district, where they accounted for 32.3% of all businesses. A significant minority (16.5%) were in the Central district. The remaining 6% were in the South. In addition, there were approximately 28 800 self-employed Arab Israelis, 21 000 male and 7 800 female in 2013 (CBS, 2013). This again is a relatively low rate. The self-employed (without employees) represented 5.6% of employed Arab men and 4.1% of employed Arab women. This compares to figures of 9.6% and 6.5% respectively for the Jewish population.

Arab-owned SMEs tend to be smaller than other Israeli SMEs, and there is a relative shortage of Arab-owned businesses among medium-sized and larger firms in Israel. As shown in Table 1.2, reproduced below, the share of Arab-owned businesses in all Israeli businesses is inversely related to firm size. Whereas Arab-owned enterprises accounted for 11.5% of Israeli enterprises with 1-5 employees in 2014, they represented only 3.1% of enterprises with 50 or more employees.

Distribution of Arab- and Jewish-owned employer businesses by enterprise size, 2014

	Arab-owned		Jewish-owned		Total	
Firm size (by no. employees)	No. (thousands)	Per cent	No. (thousands)	Per cent	No. (thousands)	Arab share (per cent)
1-5	15.5	77.2	118.6	68.1	134.1	11.5
6-19	3.7	18.6	38.7	22.2	42.4	8.8
20-49	0.6	3.2	10.7	6.1	11.3	5.6
50+	0.2	1.0	6.2	3.6	6.4	3.1
Total	20.0	100.0	174.2	100.0	194.2	10.3

Note: This Table appears as Table 1.2 in this report. Data are drawn from the Ministry of Economy and Industry register of businesses, which includes businesses with at least one employee. Arab-owned businesses are defined as those in which 50% or more of owners and employees are Arab or Druze. Discrepancies are due to rounding.
Source: MEDA.

The distribution of employment in SMEs follows a similar pattern (Table 7.3). More than 66% of employment in Arab-owned employer businesses was in firms with fewer than 20 employees in 2014, compared with only 28% for Jewish-owned businesses. By contrast, only 17% of employment in Arab-owned employer businesses was in firms with 50 or more employees, compared to nearly 60% in Jewish-owned employer businesses. The total employment share of Arab-owned employer businesses was only 4.3%. This is less than one-half of the Arab shares in the number of employer enterprises, and less than one-quarter of the Arab Israeli population share.

The density of Arab-owned employer businesses is 118 per 10 000 population. This is significantly lower than the national average of 641. In addition, Arab-owned businesses are concentrated in low value-added sectors with high competition and low barriers to entry. As shown in Table 7.4, Arab-owned SMEs are over-represented in construction, commerce, transportation and low-tech and mid- to low-tech manufacturing. This is likely to play a part in keeping them small. By contrast, there is significant under-engagement in

Table 7.3. **Distribution of employment in Arab- and Jewish-owned employer businesses by enterprise size, 2014**

Firm size band (by no. employees)	Arab-owned			Jewish-owned			Arab share (%)
	No. employees (thousands)	Per cent employees	Average number of employees	No. employees (thousands)	Per cent employees	Average number of employees	
1-5	32.26	32.9	2.3	295.3	12.5	2.5	10.7
6-19	35.94	33.4	9.7	369	15.6	9.5	8.9
20-49	18.08	16.8	30.1	315	13.3	29.4	5.4
50+	18.29	17	91.5	1387.1	58.9	223.7	3.1
Total	107.6	100	5.4	2366.8	100	13.6	4.3

Note: The Arab share is the share of employees in Arab-owned businesses as share of total number of business employees in Israel (%). Arab-owned businesses are defined as those in which 50% or more of owners and employees are Arab or Druze. Discrepancies are due to rounding.
Source: MEDA.

StatLink http://dx.doi.org/10.1787/888933421960

Table 7.4. **The distribution of Arab- and Jewish-owned employer businesses by industry sector**

Industry sector	Arab owned		Jewish owned		Share of Arab businesses (%)
	No. businesses (thousands)	Per cent	No. businesses (thousands)	Per cent	
All sectors	19.97	100	174.2	100	10.3
Manufacturing	2.5	12.3	15.8	9.1	13.7
Hi tech	0.04	1.6	1.2	8.8	3.2
Hi-medium tech	0.07	2.8	2.4	14.6	2.8
Mid-low tech	1.16	46.4	3.6	25.1	24.4
Low tech/Traditional	1.23	49.2	8.5	51.6	12.6
Construction	5.5	27.4	22.8	13.1	19.3
Financial and business services	1.8	9.2	54.4	31.2	3.3
Commerce	6.3	31.6	37.4	21.5	14.4
Agriculture	0.8	3.8	7	4	9.9
Transport, storage, and communications	1.7	8.4	8.4	4.8	16.7
Land transportation	1.66	97.6	6.1	72.6	21.4
Services for transportation	0.04	2.3	1.2	14.3	3.2
Communications	0.006	0.1	0.1	1.2	5.7
Other	0	0	1	11.9	0
Hospitality industry and food services	0.8	4.1	9.4	5.4	7.8
Hotels and hospitality industry	0.03	4.4	0.8	8.5	3.6
Restaurants and food services	0.77	95.6	8.6	91.5	8.2
Health, education, and community services	0.7	3.3	19.1	10.9	3.5

Note: Arab-owned businesses are defined as those in which 50% or more of owners and employees are Arab or Druze.
Source: MEDA.

StatLink http://dx.doi.org/10.1787/888933421973

health and education services and financial and business services. According to information from the Authority for Economic Development of the Minorities Sector (MEDA), only 1.4% of Arab-owned employer businesses were in the fast-growing ICT sector in 2014, compared to 7.8% of Jewish-owned employer businesses.

The Israeli Export Institute also reports that Arab-owned businesses generate a strikingly low share of exports. In 2011, exports from Arab-owned businesses totalled only USD 33 million, equivalent to approximately 0.1% of total Israeli exports.

There is no nationwide information on differences in characteristics of established Arab-owned enterprises by gender, but an academic study of small enterprises owned by

Arab women in Northern Israel showed that all were micro or small: 70% had no employees and 2% had 5-8 employees. Some 65% of the businesses were located outside the home, and a high proportion (71%) was registered. Most of the businesses were shops (62%) or personal services businesses (27%), although 9% were in production (Heilbrunn and Abu Asmah 2011).

Constraints on Arab Israeli SME and entrepreneurship development

Surveys of Arab SME owners by MEDA, academic studies and information from Arab SME stakeholders indicate that there are important constraints to Arab Israeli SME and entrepreneurship development. These take the form of limited market demand and intense competition in sectors in which the majority of Arab-owned businesses operate, low skill levels in Arab-owned SME workforces and difficulties recruiting skilled workers, management skills and practices that are not in tune with the needs of growth, productivity upgrading and diversification, difficulties accessing external finance, and shortages of efficient industrial and commercial premises in Arab local authority districts. These constraints are examined below.

Local market demand

Arab-owned SMEs in Israel find it difficult to grow to medium and large size or increase their profits and wages because they are concentrated in retailing and other sectors characterised by intense competition and low profit margins and because they tend to rely on local markets where incomes and income growth are low. Additional issues concern competition from unregistered firms in the informal sector, which have lower costs, and from retailers in the West Bank, which can offer consumer products and vehicle fuel at much lower prices than in Israel because of low applied tariffs on imports to the West Bank (UNCTAD, 2014). There are some signs of Arab Israeli entrepreneurs starting up in high-technology sectors with higher value-added and greater expansion opportunities, and this should be encouraged. However, for the majority of existing businesses, actions are needed to find new markets.

There are two major immediate opportunities that could be promoted with appropriate policies – tapping into public procurement contracts and tapping into contracting from large corporate firms. As well as bringing new markets, this type of initiative could help Arab-owned SMEs to increase their investment and upgrade their operating practices. Current Israeli policies to open up central and local government procurement to SMEs do not include any dedicated actions for Arab-owned firms. However, a potentially very effective intervention for Arab-owned SMEs could consist of raising the awareness of public buyers of the existence of viable bidders in the Arab Israeli business community, increasing the awareness of the Arab Israeli business community on how to access the procurement market, and providing matchmaking between the potential buyers and suppliers. Bidding consortia could also be promoted among Arab-owned SMEs to enable them to bid for larger orders and share their experience in bidding. As well as promoting this type of action with public procurement offices, this type of initiative has also proven effective in other countries in increasing purchasing by large firms from minority-owned small businesses. Box 7.1 discusses the example of a programme in the UK, which was initially funded by the public sector but now operates with membership fees. Box 7.2 gives a second example that operates across Europe.

An even greater stimulus could be provided by creating set-asides for public procurement from Arab-owned SMEs, as is the case in the USA. This would essentially set compulsory

Box 7.1. Minority Supplier Development, United Kingdom

Description of the approach

Minority businesses typically find it difficult to break out of the restricted level and composition of demand in their local market, primarily as a result of relatively low incomes in the local community. Support in tapping into the market opportunities embodied in national public and private procurement can help them break out of this local market trap. At the same time it can help public and corporate purchasers meet their objectives in terms of expanding and increasing competition in their supplier base and meeting their public and corporate social responsibility objectives.

In the United Kingdom, an action-research project called Supplier Development East Midlands (SDEM) was started by local academic experts, who also monitored the outcome (Ram et al., 2007). Legislation in the United Kingdom does not allow minority business set-asides in public procurement, as in the United States. The project therefore relied instead on creating awareness amongst public procurement departments and large corporates in the East Midlands region of the opportunities of purchasing from ethnic minority businesses. The initiative quickly established itself, sponsoring exchanges of contracts that in terms of value were in excess of five times the cost of the initiative.

Having demonstrated its success, the initiative evolved into a private not-for-profit company operating nationally called Minority Supplier Development UK Ltd (MSDUK). MSDUK is now a network of some 60 public and corporate purchasing organisations and 3 000 ethnic minority business suppliers. It organises a range of events to enable the buyers and suppliers to interact, including Meet the Buyers Days, Supplier Diversity Days, Business to Business networking and an annual conference. MSDUK is linked to partner networks in other countries, such as the US Minority Supplier Development Council, thereby offering its members access to some global corporate procurement opportunities. It also offers supplier certification, which enables corporates to be sure that they are indeed buying from ethnic minority businesses.

MSDUK is funded by corporate membership fees and cost recovery from minority business and corporate business participation in services such as conferences and courses.

Factors for success

As intermediary organisations, the SDEM and its successor MSD UK relied initially on goodwill (with a view to eventual commercial return) on both purchasing and supplier business sides. MSDUK now operates on a cost recovery basis, meaning that clients have become persuaded of the effectiveness of the intervention and the commercial value of supply chain diversity.

Obstacles and responses

Given the innovative nature of the activity, public funding was necessary at the outset. The social climate had moved in favour of promoting minority enterprises, and policy analysts had reached a view of the need for public action to overcome the structural barriers they face. Nevertheless, an enlightened and experimental approach on the part of public officials was a prerequisite for such expenditure to be made, resting on a conviction that the intervention was essentially a demonstration project that could raise awareness of potential commercial benefits. The burden of project funding was indeed shifted in time to the private sector actors who acknowledged the benefit to them from the intervention.

Box 7.1. **Minority Supplier Development, United Kingdom** *(cont.)*

Relevance for Israel

A ceiling on the expansion of the Arab Israeli business sector seems to be set partly by the demand limitations of its current clientele. With public sector trigger funding, this type of initiative could facilitate the access of Arab-owned businesses to public and large firm procurement markets as a way of breaking out of their local markets.

Sources of further information

Organisational websites: *www.msduk.org.uk.*

Shah, M. (2014), Supplier Diversity in the UK, *Minority Business Entrepreneur*, July-August 2014.

Ram, M., N. Theodorakopoulos and I. Worthington (2007), *Policy transfer in practice: Implementing supplier diversity in the UK*, Public Administration, 85, 799-803.

Box 7.2. **Supplier Diversity Europe**

The Supplier Diversity Europe programme was established in 2003 on the initiative of the Migration Policy Group, a not-for-profit think tank based in Brussels. It was initially funded by a range of public bodies including national governments, private foundations, and corporate sponsors. It now operates in the UK and France on the basis of membership fees.

The programme builds the capacity of large member organisations to operate supply chains that offer a 'level playing field' that is open to minority suppliers. Recently it has developed an 'Accessible Supply Chain' benchmark, which is an accreditation system for corporates aimed at supporting and measuring their progress on supplier diversity. This provides a set of practical indicators for measuring diversity outcomes and assists corporates to set up time lines for their objectives in this connection.

In the case of Israel, such a supplier development initiative could emphasise opening up market opportunities for Arab-owned SMEs from Jewish-owned businesses. The fact that some Arab-owned businesses already have subcontracting links with Jewish-owned firms and the fact that a corporate initiative has been successfully established for boosting the employment of Arabs in Israeli hi-technology firms suggests that some parts of the Jewish-business sector may be willing to participate in such a scheme. It could also target foreign-owned large businesses operating in Israel and corporates operating in other countries, particularly neighbouring Arab countries.

Source: Migration Policy Group's website: *www.migpolgroup.com/.*

targets for the proportion of contracts or contract values allocated to Arab-owned enterprises. This could be measured purely directly or in addition include subcontracts awarded by lead firms winning public procurement contracts.

At the same time, success in participating in public and corporate procurement processes is likely to require upgrading of the output of Arab-owned SMEs regarding quality, design, timeliness and flexibility. Not all Arab-owned companies have found it easy to do this (Drori and Lerner, 2002). Consultancy support and finance for investment could be offered to help Arab-owned SMEs to meet required standards for public and corporate procurement.

Workforce skills

The vast majority of the workforces of Arab-owned SMEs in Israel are drawn from the Arab Israeli population. However, the Arab Israeli population is characterised by relatively low rates of educational attainment. This has adverse effects on the quality of the workforces that Arab-owned SMEs can recruit. Only 20% of Arab Israeli adults have had tertiary education compared to 45% of the total Israeli population. Similarly, only 36% of Arab Israeli students have received a high school diploma meeting the admissions standard for university compared with 50% of Jewish students (OECD, 2011). On average, Arab Israelis have 11 years of education, compared with 14 years among the Jewish Israeli population; and 25% of Arab Israelis have between 0-8 years of study, compared to 4.6% of Jewish Israelis. With respect to higher education, Arab Israeli students concentrate on certain subjects (for example, they constitute 42% of pharmaceuticals and 36% of all nursing students) and are underrepresented in others (only 6% of engineering students and 3% of business and industrial administration students are Arab) (IATA, 2013).

On the other hand, there have been notable recent improvements in educational attainment among Arab Israeli women, which holds out promise for increasing the scale and quality of Arab Israeli women's entrepreneurship if actions are taken to address other barriers faced by this population group. The share of Arab Israeli women with no education has dropped from 13.6% in 1990 to 7.5% in 2010, whereas the share of high school graduates increased from 18.4% to 27.7%. The number of Arab Israeli women with 16 or more years of education jumped from 1.8% to 10.3%, with the majority of them gaining academic degrees (Shihadeh and Moadi, 2011). Indeed, the proportion of adults in the labour market with tertiary education is now higher among Arab Israeli women than Arab Israeli men.

Arab-owned SMEs also suffer from low labour market participation in the Arab Israeli workforce. Only 64% of Arab Israeli men and 28% of Arab Israeli women are in employment (CBS, 2014b, Table 12.10). This limits the ability of a significant proportion of the Arab Israeli workforce to gain work experience and learn skills on the job. The government has established a network of Employment Orientation Centres targeted at the Arab Israeli population which offer training, placement, vocational guidance, soft skills coaching and retraining services. It is hoped that this will increase both labour force participation and skill levels in the Arab Israeli workforce (OECD, 2015). In this respect, there could be a particular emphasis on increasing the labour market engagement of the Arab Israeli female labour force. The reasons for low labour force participation by Arab Israeli women are not only cultural but are also the result of their economic situation, for example regarding costs of childcare (Schlosser, 2011). Policy could target Arab Israeli females with 12 years of education for extra training for employment and to support them into entrepreneurship.

As shown in Figure 7.1, the education rate and the labour force participation rate are closely linked. Increasing the education levels of the Arab Israeli population could therefore increase human capital both through the direct education outcomes and through opening up the opportunity for increased work experience and learning of skills on the job.

Alongside lack of Arabic language skills among non-Arab Israelis (Habib et al., 2010), one of the reasons that Arab-owned SMEs are largely dependent on Arab Israeli workforces is the limited geographic mobility of the Arab and Jewish workforces. Arab-owned enterprises tend to be located in Arab settlements where there is limited Jewish residence or Jewish in-commuting. On the other hand, there is significant migration and commuting

Figure 7.1. **Labour force participation rates by sex and years of education, Arab Israelis and Jewish Israelis, 2013**

Ratio of the labour force to the working age population

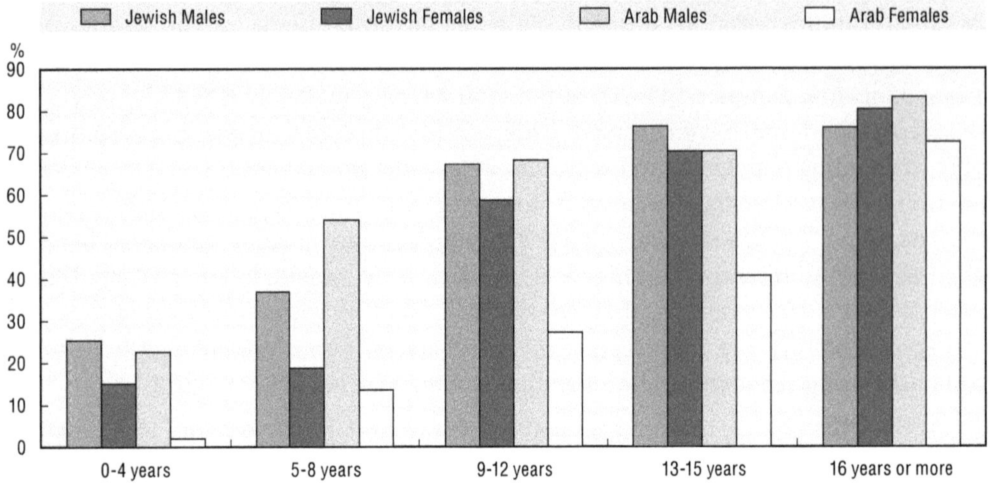

Source: Central Bureau of Statistics (2013), *Statistical Abstract of Israel 2013*, Jerusalem.

StatLink http://dx.doi.org/10.1787/888933421930

of Arab Israelis to Jewish areas, reflecting better job opportunities in Jewish-dominated areas. Thus, according to MEDA information, one-in-five Arab Israelis resided outside of Arab-dominated areas and one-quarter of Arab Israeli employees were employed in Jewish-owned businesses in 2014. Ironically, efforts to increase mobility could have a negative effect on the development of Arab-owned SMEs if they lead to increased out-migration or out-commuting of relatively skilled Arab Israeli workers. Work by the OECD comparing local labour markets in Israel illustrates this problem. Areas with high levels of skills demand and supply were typically the larger cities (Haifa, Tel Aviv) and in the centre of the country, while areas with low levels of skills demand and supply were in more peripheral and less densely populated areas – where the Arab population is concentrated (OECD, 2015).

Attention should therefore be paid to developing workforce skills in Arab localities. Measures that can be applied on the supply side include subsidies for training in Arab-owned SMEs and joint training activities for networks of SMEs in Arab settlements. This will need to be accompanied by measures to promote the demand for higher workforce skills by Arab-owned SMEs through promoting new SME management strategies.

Management skills and practices

The management skills and practices of Arab-owned SMEs are affected by the tendency for the general education levels of Arab Israelis to be lower than the Israeli average. This may affect the approach of Arab Israeli business owners and managers to operating and developing their businesses and call for post-formal education management skills and development support. In addition, Arab-owned SMEs are frequently family businesses, in which the extended family provides managers, workers, social connections and other support (Drori and Lerner, 2002). There is often a gap between traditional family business management approaches and the practices necessary to grow and diversify a business and expand into national and international supply chains and markets.

However, lack of management skills and sub-optimal management practices are not always recognised by Arab Israeli SME managers as a constraint on the development of their businesses. Therefore many who could potentially benefit do not come forward for the training or consultancy programmes that are available. Reaching out to some Arab Israeli SME owners and managers could nonetheless quickly have a knock-on effect across the wider Arab Israeli business community. Bloom et al. (2013), for example, report on a programme in India which provided free consulting (for 5 months, from an international firm) on modern management practices to a randomly chosen set of large-sized, low-productivity textile firms and compared their performance to control firms. The programme yielded very positive results in terms of increased levels of productivity at enterprise level. Moreover, while many SME managers did not immediately recognise the potential for them to benefit, the new management techniques introduced to participants in the programme quickly diffused throughout the sector as other enterprise owners and managers heard of the successes in the firms that had benefitted from the programme and copied their new methods.

By contrast, Arab Israeli women entrepreneurs and microbusiness owners frequently do acknowledge that they have problems with management skills and competences. A study by Heilbrunn and Abu Asbah (2011) found that a high proportion of women microbusiness owners in northern Israel cited lack of management experience and absence of counselling opportunities as constraints: out of 372 respondents, 348 cited lack of management experience as a problem and 350 cited absence of counselling. This was a higher number than for financial issues (226) or bureaucracy (282). However, many women micro entrepreneurs are likely to require a specific management skills and development programme that is more tailored to their personal experiences and how they would like support to be delivered than the support available to SME managers in general. One of the most promising policy approaches that could be tried in this area is to organise peer support for women's enterprise development. Box 7.5 describes a programme example in Ireland that could provide inspiration for a programme for Arab women entrepreneurs in Israel.

The SMBA's consultancy and training programmes delivered through the MAOF business development services centre network is accessible to Arab-owned businesses. The most notable access point is the MAOF centre established in Nazareth, an Arab dominated city. In principle, the MAOF concept of offering support based on demand is sufficiently flexible that it should be possible to ensure that the support offered is appropriate to Arab-owned businesses, given than each centre is free to tailor its services to meet the needs of its local business community (whether Jewish or Arab or both). The success of the Nazareth centre in delivering services that meet the needs of the local Arab-owned business base should be evaluated after it has been in operation for some time (it was established in 2014) in order to learn lessons for other MAOF centres that also deal with Arab-owned businesses. In addition, it may be appropriate for SMBA and MEDA to produce guidelines for involving Arab-owned businesses in MAOF support programmes, for example in the language and communication channels for promotion, or in the employment of Arabic-speaking staff.

Having recognised some of the management weaknesses of Arab-owned SMEs, it should also be recognised that there is also a small and growing pool of highly-skilled young Arab Israeli entrepreneurs who have graduated from prestigious Israeli technology institutes. There are also a handful of older, highly-educated Arab Israeli businessmen who have returned to Israel to establish technology businesses after following professional careers in Europe or the USA. The further growth of these skilled groups should be encouraged. Furthermore, some of these people could be encouraged to act as a voluntary or paid resource for advice and mentoring of other Arab-owned businesses.

Box 7.5. Going for Growth, Ireland

Description of the approach

Going for Growth is a networking and mentoring organisation for women business owners in Ireland who have run their businesses for at least 2 years and are ambitious for them to grow. It involves an annual two-day forum and a series of small round table sessions that explore a series of relevant questions related to growth. These events foster networking among ambitious business women and offer practical peer-to-peer learning from more experienced "Lead Entrepreneur" business women in a confidential, community spirit. The programme is designed to offer role models, build self-confidence and provide access to appropriate networking opportunities for women entrepreneurs interested in developing their businesses to attain scale. Some 450 businesswomen have participated in networking at annual forums and round tables over eight cycles since its establishment.

Factors for success

Public funding was important for launching the initiative. It was initially supported and funded by the European Social Fund (ESF), the government Department of Justice and Equality, and Enterprise Ireland, the national enterprise development agency. Enterprise Ireland continues its support and more recently KPMG has become a sponsor. The organisation now also raises funds directly through membership fees paid by participants who have successfully completed a cycle and who wish to become members of the Going for Growth Community. The Lead Entrepreneurs give their time on a voluntary basis, which helps to keep the cost of the initiative manageable.

Progress of participants is closely monitored. After the completion of each cycle that progress is reported in terms of aggregated increases in revenues, additional employment created and numbers of first time exporters. These are impressive and serve to attract high calibre candidates for the following cycle.

Another key to the success of the initiative has been the calibre of those involved. The programme was founded by a former consultant who had used her expertise on questions of entrepreneurship and small business growth to form an advisory service to government and enterprise support bodies. Her experience equipped her to understand the difficulties typically faced by women in business, which enabled her to specify precise objectives for the organisation and to design activities to fulfil the need. Her advisory work with policy makers also helped her to persuade nationally successful entrepreneurs to participate in the initiative from the outset. At the same time, participation by new businesswomen is through a competitive process, which aims to ensure that the participants can benefit from each other's involvement, and lead entrepreneurs are carefully selected businesswomen who have successfully led their companies through all the difficulties of start-up and expansion.

Obstacles and responses

In order to be successful, such a programme needs to attract women entrepreneurs who are ambitious to grow their businesses as well as successful women Lead Entrepreneurs. In Ireland, this was achieved by recruiting experienced, nationally renowned businesswomen to the programme, conferring value on participation so that many more apply each year than there are places available, and obtaining international recognition for the programme. Going for Growth, for example, was awarded the European Enterprise Promotion Award 2015, Investing in Entrepreneurial Skills. Positive testimonials from former participants and well-prepared informational videos of the event add another layer of endorsement that encourages other successful and ambitious businesswomen to apply in the annual recruitment drive.

Box 7.5. **Going for Growth, Ireland** *(cont.)*

Relevance for Israel

There is potential for the emergence of a new cohort of more ambitious and educated women entrepreneurs in the Arab Israeli community. However, Arab Israeli women entrepreneurs often identify lack of family support, absence of counselling, lack of management experience and lack of networking opportunities as constraints to the development of their businesses. A dedicated entrepreneurs' network for Arab Israeli women fostering peer learning and interaction with role models could complement the organised business support services supplied by the SMBA and MEDA. If some successful Jewish businesswomen could be persuaded to participate that could also provide a bridge to the wider national business community.

Whereas Arab Israeli women entrepreneurs could get support from the existing Association of Businesswomen in Israel (JASMINE), which includes both Arab and Jewish members (*www.hasmine.org.il*), a dedicated programme for Arab Israeli women entrepreneurs is likely to be able to recruit more Arab Israeli members, respond better to their particular concerns and give support in more appropriate locations and settings.

A pilot Going for Growth cycle was implemented in Finland in 2014, and the Going for Growth organisation is keen to see similar organisations set up in other countries and link up with them. There is therefore an opportunity for a quick start in Israel through a link with Going for Growth and provision of appropriate public trigger and operating funding.

Sources of further information

Organisational website: *www.goingforgrowth.com.*

Finally, it is valid and necessary to promote the diversification, innovation and productivity upgrading of Arab-owned SMEs not just through management skills and consultancy support, but also through an expanded range and scale of subsidy programmes for upgrading Arab-owned businesses. This could include financial support for capital investment, technology development projects, marketing projects, and International Standards Conformity programmes. Businesses with potential for upgrading and modernisation of their products, processes, organisation approaches and marketing methods should be targeted. This could include businesses in traditional manufacturing sectors and tourism. It could also focus on high-potential Arab-owned businesses including ICT-intensive business services in medicine and pharmaceuticals and other fields where expertise is available from newly emerging cadres of Arab professionals, and producers of Arabic web content and internet-based consumer products, such as computer games, personal apps, and business IT services.

Access to finance

Lack of access to finance is an important constraint to the ability of Arab-owned SMEs and entrepreneurs to invest in the fixed capital often required to increase their productivity and to obtain the working capital needed for growth or entry into supply chains. Arab Israeli entrepreneurs are often obliged to start up with relatively limited internal financial resources drawn from wealth and assets acquired from their regular income. Existing Arab-owned SMEs may struggle to expand on the basis of internally-generated revenues, since many operate in low margin lines of business. At the same time, they have limited access to external bank and non-bank credit and other financial products such as equity.

The most important issue is lack of access to credit. This is reported as a major constraint by more than one-half of Arab-owned employer businesses. The volume of bank credit to SMEs in Israel is low in general. However, the difficulties for Arab-owned SMEs are even greater. The issue is partly one of treatment of collateral. First, in Israel, a given amount of collateral releases a larger amount of credit for larger than smaller firms (Ministry of Economy/SMBA, 2014). This disproportionately penalises Arab-owned SMEs because of their smaller size distribution. Second, Israeli banks generally only accept non-movable assets as collateral. This affects Arab-owned SMEs disproportionately since they rarely hold a proper deed of ownership for their property at the land registry office[1], which reflects weaknesses in the Israeli system of property registration and the limited access of Arab-owned businesses to formal leases on state-owned land. Limited access to credit for Arab-owned SMEs also partly stems from limited competition among the retail banks. As a result, innovative products for SME finance that could address the problems faced by Arab-owned businesses are not common and existing product offers by banks are not well communicated, for example in the area of export finance. Finally, there are very few formal non-bank credit institutions in the Arab Israeli sector to compensate.

The government has promoted a number of responses to the problem of lack of access to credit for Arab Israeli SMEs and entrepreneurs, but these efforts are not yet sufficient given the scale of the problem. One of the most important interventions is the allocation by the MEDA of NIS 18 million additional funding to the State Loan Guarantee Fund in 2012, earmarked for guaranteeing bank loans to Arab-owned businesses. This is an important intervention that makes no demand on the public finances beyond the initial funding injection (Yashiv and Kasir (Kaliner), 2014). According to SMBA data, approximately 10% of loan volumes went to minority-owned SMEs, which is in line with the share of minority-owned firms in the total business population (mostly Arab-owned). However, more detailed information on the characteristics, performance and payments record of Arab Israeli beneficiaries is needed for a rigorous assessment of the impact of the scheme in the Arab sector and whether the approach should be expanded or adjusted.

At the same time, MEDA has promoted non-bank finance for Arab Israeli SMEs and entrepreneurs at a modest scale through support for the SAWA Microfinance Fund (part of Koret Israel Economic Development Funds, KIEDF). SAWA microfinance loans target women from Arab Israeli minorities. The loans do not carry interest but they do include commission fees. The Fund employs a team responsible for finding female entrepreneurs interested in receiving support, provides consulting services, follows them up until the loan is approved, and stays available to the entrepreneurs for further advice, guidance and support. The Fund's steering committee is headed by the SMBA and the MEDA is one of the members. During the period 2006-13, SAWA delivered 4 260 business microloans of between USD 1 000 and USD 7 000, with a total value of USD 8.16 million. Funding initially came through Kiva, a global crowd funding platform aiming to expand access to financial services to excluded populations. The MEDA contributed NIS 11 million in 2011 to expand these loans, representing around 40% of SAWA's total funds. This type of intervention by the MEDA could be repeated and expanded to support for other microfinance initiatives, credit unions and cooperative banks that exist in the Arab sector. However, evaluation evidence will need to be collected on the impact of the MEDA's participations in these schemes in terms of additional new business creations and business expansions to justify the support in the long run. Furthermore, a clear "graduation" facility needs to be introduced, whereby entrepreneurs with growth ambitions for their enterprises can be accompanied from microcredit support into mainstream business development support services.

In parallel to strengthening loan guarantee and microfinance support, any future reforms to increase banking competition in Israel should include special measures designed to encourage the retail banks to reach out to the Arab Israeli business sector. For example, banks could be encouraged to increase their range of credit products in ways useful to the Arab Israeli community, become less restrictive in their collateral requirements, and link up with microcredit schemes.

The MEDA has also moved forcefully in supporting the supply of equity capital to high-potential Arab-owned businesses through its establishment of Al Bawader, a venture capital investment fund for Arab-owned start-ups favouring firms with regional export potential. This has been the MEDA's flagship finance sector intervention involving a commitment of NIS 50 million of public funds. Alongside this, Al Bawader has leveraged more than NIS 120 million of funds from the private sector, mainly from Pitango, the major venture capital fund in Israel. The entry of private Jewish investors into the scheme is solid evidence of market confidence in the potential for high-growth businesses to emerge from the Arab Israeli population, including in high-technology industries. There are also interesting synergies with the construction of new incubators. This is enabling a few promising Arab-owned start-ups to be given premises, introductions to support services and access in some cases to venture capital investment. Although only seven enterprises have been funded to date, disbursement of the fund is going to plan and it is expected to support up to 30 enterprises in total, in both seed funding and subsequent stages.

There may be further potential to support the supply of finance to Arab Israeli SMEs and entrepreneurs. Informal investor financing is already significant in the Arab Israeli population. Menipaz (2011) indicates that 4.8% of Arab Israeli females and 4.2% of Arab Israeli males had invested their own money in the last three years in an entrepreneur who set up a new business, which compares with only 1.3% of non-immigrant Jewish Israeli females and 2.3% of non-immigrant Jewish Israeli males. However, 53% invested in a close family member, compared with 32% of non-immigrant Jewish investors, while only 5.3% invested in strangers with a good business idea, compared to 9% of non-immigrant Jewish Israeli investors. Policy may be able to build on the greater propensity of Arab Israelis to invest in the businesses of other people by creating and supporting informal investor networks, including angel investor networks, in the Arab Israeli population and encouraging them to invest more frequently in the businesses of others not in the close family.

The MEDA's prioritisation of venture capital and financing for high-technology business appears to be an appropriate approach given the importance of shifting perceptions that the Arab Israeli business sector is not capable of modernisation. It has been associated with the emergence of a number of high-technology ICT Arab-owned businesses that demonstrate the potential in the Arab Israeli business community. Given changed perceptions, improvements in management practices in other medium-tech businesses could trigger a responsive supply of finance from conventional sources. At the same time, however, further support for debt finance to traditional Arab-owned SMEs should now be considered. This could include special provision for the Arab Israeli business sector in banking competition reforms such as temporary quotas or targets for Arab Israeli business clients. In addition, it should include further targeted measures for loan guarantees and microfinance for Arab-owned businesses.

Lack of industrial and commercial premises

Business development beyond backyard workshops, shops, and small-scale office-based services depends on the availability of land for industrial and commercial use. However, most Arab Israelis live in a densely-built and densely-populated environment of towns and villages surrounded by and separated from each other by state-owned land. In these settings, it has been very difficult for small, and virtually impossible for medium-sized, businesses to create or obtain modern premises.

The development of dedicated "industrial zones" is needed, which in Israel is a term used to designate a particular land use and can involve quite small areas of land, of only a few hundred square metres. However, at present only 3.5% of all industrial zones in Israel are within or adjacent to Arab local authority areas. This has impacts on the financial income of Arab local authorities; only 23% of their revenues are from taxes on business property compared to 34% of Jewish municipal revenues (CBS Municipalities dataset).

A number of structural issues will have to be addressed in order to increase the number, surface area and standard of industrial zones in Arab local authority areas, or in nearby locations accessible to Arab-owned businesses. First, assembly of land for redevelopment can be difficult within existing Arab settlements. Little land is available for redevelopment, given the density of construction. Moreover, much of the land is dispersed across different land owners who have an effective right of veto over a development. More sites for business development need to be made available.

Second, access to land for industrial zone development in or near Arab settlements is often contingent on land use zoning changes, which could then allow planning permission to be given. However, the zoning process is not rapid and flexible. Moreover, there is often a lack of detailed plans at the municipal level, particularly in minority municipalities. The Ministry of Interior is working with local authorities to rectify this, but it is taking a considerable period of time. The planning system at local level therefore needs to be reinforced.

Third, access to land for industrial development is often constrained by the difficulty of obtaining leases. Land cannot easily be purchased on the market: only 7% of the territory of Israel is privately owned (some of it by Arabs; Sandberg 2010); 12% is owned by the Jewish National Fund to promote Jewish settlements and economic activity; and 81% is owned by the state. Access to land is therefore largely on time-bound leases purchased from the state. Entrepreneurs and property development companies wishing to obtain rights to the use of state-owned land for the construction of a factory, workshop or office can apply to the Ministry of Economy and Industry, although the Ministry does not have to respond and is entitled to reject any request. If it supports the application, the Ministry forwards the request to the Israel Lands Administration. Arab Israeli business people report that proposals for industrial land development have often received negative responses and/or suffered extreme delay. Due consideration of the economic and social development needs of the Arab Israeli population is therefore need in state land leasing.

Fourth, both Arab-owned businesses and Arab local authorities lack finance for the purchase of leases and the development of industrial sites, premises and associated infrastructure (both utilities on the zone and connection to national and local transport networks). There is a vicious cycle involved. Arab-owned businesses are often operating in inappropriate and constrained premises; this makes it more likely that they remain small and inefficient; which limits the internal and external financing of the businesses themselves and the business tax revenues of Arab local authorities needed to develop better sites and premises. Both public financing for zone development and better local authority competences in attracting and facilitating private development are required.

In an attempt to improve site and premises availability for Arab-owned businesses, the MEDA has made significant recent direct investments in the development of industrial zones in or adjacent to Arab-dominated local authority areas. Table 7.2 sets out allocated budgets and status of the work in 2014. Out of the total funding of NIS 201.5 million, NIS 20 million was dedicated to buying private land in three localities. In the others, the zones were to be built on publicly-owned land, which was transferred without payment. The rest of the allocated funds are for the construction of infrastructure – electricity, communication, roads, water and sewage, public grounds, lighting and sidewalks. Five of the zones were fully in operation by October 2014, with one more in partial occupation.

Table 7.5. **Central government support for the development of industrial zones in Arab communities 2010-16**

Community	Net size (ha.)	Budget (million NIS)		Status of work in 2014
		Govt. Decision 4193	Govt. Decision 1539	
Cana	19.1	9	0	Completing development of infrastructure
Nazareth	11.5	9	14	Development of infrastructure
Sakhnin	5	9	9	Development of infrastructure
Rabat	22	5	8	Completing development of infrastructure
Yarka	35	7	0	Upgrading of the existing industrial area (zone processed and populated)
Jadida	2.5	10.5	0	Detailed design for new industrial zone
Araba	2	9	1.5	Completed and populated
Kafr Qasem	50	3	4	Expansion of existing zone completed and populated
Taiba	28	12	0	Upgrading of infrastructure on existing zone completed (zone processed and populated)
Baqa	6	19.5	0	Upgrading of infrastructure and expansion of existing zone completed (zone processed and populated)
Ar'ara	3.5	17	0	Development being finalised; 50% populated
Umm al-Fahm	12.5	10	8	Development being finalised
Maghar	n.s.	0	4	Not stated
Shefar'am	n.s.	0	13	Not stated
Tamra	n.s	0	5.5	Not stated
Dalyat Hacarmel-Isfiya	n.s.	0	4	Not stated
Tira	n.s.	0	2.5	Not stated
Qalansawe	n.s.	0	8	Not stated
TOTAL		120	81.5	

Note: The budget allocation from Government Decision 4193 covers the period 2012-16. The budget allocation from Government Decision 1539 covers the period 2010-14.
Source: Information submitted by the Minorities Economic Development Authority (MEDA) to the OECD.

StatLink http://dx.doi.org/10.1787/888933421986

A number of further actions can be taken to further accelerate and expand provision of appropriate sites and premises for Arab Israeli SMEs and entrepreneurs, alongside further direct MEDA investments. It is important, first of all, to allow for more Arab industrial zones and related infrastructure within the land use and planning system. National government support could also be offered to develop the professional capacities of Arab municipalities in the development and promotion of industrial zones and for developing local public-private financing agreements. To this end, the existing municipalities support programme of the MEDA should continue to be supported and scaled up as necessary. The smallest municipalities need to be encouraged to cooperate in groups in order to find the critical mass necessary for economic development impact.

Finally, policy could encourage the location of Arab-owned SMEs on existing or new industrial zones in accessible Jewish local authority areas. A downside of such an approach is that Arab-owned businesses transferring to new sites may lose some of their customers, suppliers and human resources as a result of the transfer. However, this should be limited for short-distance moves to locations with good transport and public transport links to the source location. Furthermore, relocations may deprive Arab municipalities of business tax revenues, since revenues from relocated Arab-owned businesses will be paid to the new host local authority. MEDA has brokered an arrangement in Dalit el Carmel to support Arab-dominated local authorities to negotiate a share in the tax revenues raised from Arab-owned businesses on zones in Jewish-dominated local authorities proportional to the share of active Arab-owned businesses. This approach could be expanded to other municipalities and linked to a shared investment by the Arab and Jewish authorities in the new, expanded or improved industrial zones in the Jewish-dominated areas. So that such agreements are not negotiated on a purely case-by-case basis, national guiding principles on revenue sharing could be set up. Government Resolution 2365 of December 2014 called for the formation of an inter-ministerial team whose role would be to consolidate and recommend guiding principles and policy devices for the promotion of income-sharing, and this should be pursued and implemented.

The spearheading and co-ordinating role of the MEDA

The first official Government of Israel report into the disadvantaged socio-economic status of Arab Israelis was published in 2003 (Or Commission, 2003). The Government accepted its conclusions but several years passed before policies were adopted (Trajtenberg Commission, 2012). The first step was the creation in 2007 of the MEDA, which was initially in the Office of the Prime Minister and is now housed in the Ministry for Social Equality. Its mandate is to maximise the economic potential of the Arab, Druze and Circassian minority populations and integrate them into the economy.

Since 2010, the government has enacted a number of decisions designed to improve the economic situation of Arab Israelis. Some of the government measures and resources are aimed generally at employment, education, infrastructure and transportation for minority populations. Others are more closely targeted at Arab Israeli business development. The major decisions aimed most strongly at Arab Israeli business development are listed below:

- Decision 1539 of March 2010 provided support for the economic development of 13 Arab communities with a population of approximately 350 000 for the period 2010-14, with a budget allocation of NIS 778.5 million. The MEDA had responsibility for general oversight of the programme and for direct management of NIS 250 million.
- Decision 4193 of January 2012 provided resources for measures to increase employment, education, infrastructure and regulatory enforcement for minorities. The MEDA had direct responsibility for managing the budget of NIS 730 million for 2012-15.
- Decision 4432 of March 2012 expanded Decision 4193 to cover an additional 58 Arab towns. The MEDA had direct responsibility for managing the budget of NIS 250 million for 2012-15.
- Decision 922 of January 2016 takes over from the previous Decisions by creating a new resource allocation mechanism for the Arab sector, ensuring that Arab citizens will be budgeted by each ministry in line with their 20% share in society or with preferential

resources. It has been estimated that the new mechanism will lead to allocations of approximately NIS 10-15 billion for the development of Arab communities during 2016-20. The resources will be allocated in various fields such as education, transportation, welfare services, employment and housing guided by a new 5-year economic development plan for the Arab sector.

The MEDA has had a key role in support to date, either in initiating or delivering programmes directly (with corresponding budgetary allocations), or in monitoring and co-ordinating programmes led by other government ministries. Approximately two-thirds of the allocated resources for 2010-15 were under the direct management or oversight of the MEDA. Together with the MEDA, the SMBA has also been a key implementation agency for access to financing and business development programmes for Arab Israeli SMEs and entrepreneurs.

The annual operational budgets for the MEDA have been NIS 16 million (2011), NIS 14 million (2012), NIS 18.9 million (2013) and NIS 21.1 million (2014). This includes funding that the MEDA can award to other government ministries for projects to support minority populations in areas of employment promotion, business development, local economic development, higher education and education, where there is no direct budget allocation to the line ministry for this purpose.

More information is provided in Table 7.6 on the nature of public programme support for Arab Israeli business development and the role of the MEDA and implementation partners in the period 2010-2015.

The MEDA will also have a key role in administering the new 5-year plan for the Arab sector. The new plan will expand support for Arab Israeli SMEs and entrepreneurs, both for domestic development and for exporting. The Ministry of Finance will also allocate NIS 200 million to the Economy Ministry for continuing the operation of One Stop Employment Centres until the end of 2020. In addition, 42.5% of all funds allocated to new industrial developments will be designated to Arab localities and to regional industrial areas in which at least one of the localities is Arab.

The MEDA is also active with the SMBA in developing incubators and accelerators for Arab-owned start-ups and SMEs, particularly those with a high-technology focus. They have recently collaborated, together with the 8200 Alumni Association, in the establishment of a non-profit Hybrid start-up accelerator for start-ups in the Arab Sector launched by the Nazareth Business Incubator Centre. This has two locations, in Nazareth and Tel Aviv, and can take Arab-owned start-ups from other parts of Israel. The first intake was May 2016 of 10 selected start-ups in a variety of fields. Over 5 months, they will receive assistance in networking, mentoring, validating their early products, and becoming market-ready functional companies. This initiative demonstrates a strong policy commitment to include the Arab population in the Israeli high-technology sector.

An important function of the MEDA is to co-ordinate policy intervention for the economic and social development of minority populations across the different ministries and agencies of government. This is important for providing an impulse for strengthening activities for the minority population across government and for prioritising actions and identifying policy gaps. In the past it has been difficult for the MEDA to obtain information from other ministries and agencies to judge the extent to which ministries and agencies were undertaking specific or additional actions for minorities. However, the MEDA's co-ordination capacity has been strengthened by Decision 922 of 2016 and the creation of

Table 7.6. **Main government programmes for Arab Israeli business development and the role of MEDA and implementation partners**

Programme	Public budget (NIS)	MEDA activities	Implementation partner(s)	Government Decision or originator
Industrial zones	231.5 million (2012-16)	Development or improvements of industrial zones in 12 towns and planning for new industrial zones	Ministry of Economy and Industry	4193 and 1539
Transportation	• 30 million (2010-14) • 80 million per annum from 2010 with no deadline • 0.5 million (2010-14)	• Development of public transport infrastructure • Public transport subsidies • Campaign to encourage use of public transport	Ministry of Transport	1539
Municipality infrastructure support	9.5 million (2010-14)	Integrating local government into administration of existing industrial zones	Ministry of Economy and Industry	1539
Employment Centres	75 million (2012-16)	Setting up 6 centres	Ministry of Economy and Industry	4193 and 1539
El Bawader investment fund	80 million from public funds (2010-17)	Leveraging private capital	MEDA, El Bawader Fund and Pitango Venture Capital	MEDA
State Loan Guarantee Fund (SLGF) expansion	18 million allocated for minorities in 2012	MEDA assisted in making the fund accessible and raising awareness	SMBA and Ministry of Finance Accountant General	Ministry of Finance
Tevel/export promotion	3 million (2013)	Assistance in locating potential export companies, guidance, initial training	Israeli Export Institute, SMBA and Overseas Market Promotion fund	Israeli Export Institute
Microfinance	10 million	Participating in steering committee, raising awareness	MEDA, SMBA and Koret Israel Fund	MEDA and SMBA
Business development support services	4.4 million (2012)	Business plan guidance, management training etc.	SMBA	1539
Business centres (incubators)	2.16 million	Support for 2 centres for Arab entrepreneurs	SMBA	1539 and 4193
Business accelerators	To be allocated at a later date	Support for accelerators for Arab entrepreneurs	SMBA, Cisco and PresenTense	4193
Tourism business in Arab villages	25 million (2010-14)	Investment in infrastructure, and grants and subsidised access to business consulting services	Ministry of Tourism	1539

Source: Information submitted by the Minorities Economic Development Authority (MEDA) to the OECD and *www.diplomacy.co.il/current-events/1439-pm-netanyahu-holds-special-cabinet-%20discussion-on-economic-development-in-the-minorities-sector*.

the new 5-year economic development plan for the Arab sector. A steering committee has been established for the new plan headed by the Director of the MEDA and composed of the Director Generals of all relevant ministries as well as representatives of the Arab Local Authorities Forum. The Committee will meet every six months to monitor the plan's progress. Each ministry will designate a senior public official who will be in charge of the implementation of the plan within the ministry. This may enable the MEDA to have a more authoritative and continual grasp of the scale and nature of the reforms being undertaken on the initiative of ministries as well as more clarity about the budgets allocated.

The MEDA nonetheless operates with a small staff and operating budget relative to the initiatives it has to develop directly and the work required for coordination of minority economic development initiatives across ministries and agencies. It had only 13 senior professional staff in 2014 both to deliver initiatives directly and co-ordinate other ministries. Its new role is likely to require an increase in its staffing and resources.

A specific inefficiency with respect to policy co-ordination in Israel results from the fact that responsibility for municipality development in the Druze sector does not lie with the MEDA, although the MEDA has responsibility for other actions to support the economic development of the Druze and is responsible for municipality development for Arab Israelis. Bringing responsibility for the Druze municipality development into the remit of MEDA would be in line with a recommendation of the State Comptroller's Office from 2013, which recommended that all minority economic development related activity should be under the MEDA's responsibility.[2]

Better monitoring and evaluation data are also required to support the prioritisation and design of actions for Arab Israeli SMEs and entrepreneurs. GEM has carried out surveys of the entrepreneurial population in Israel in 1999, 2007, 2009, 2010, 2012 and 2013. In most of these, the Arab sub-sample consists of around 400 observations. While this appears adequate to capture the main entrepreneurship indicators reliably for Arab Israelis it does not permit any detailed analysis. The sample could potentially be boosted for the Arab Israeli population or special surveys undertaken. Another data source is the comprehensive register of Arab employers compiled by the Central Bureau of Statistics and its periodic surveys of these businesses to complement the quarterly industrial survey of the Ministry of Economy and Industry. This provides basic information on Arab-owned business demography and structure. The register could be further exploited for periodic in-depth surveys of Arab-owned business activities and constraints by the Central Bureau of Statistics or independent analysts, and potentially used as a sample frame to obtain beneficiary and control group information for evaluations of Arab Israeli business development programmes.

The most important data improvement needed for guiding policy for Arab Israeli SME and entrepreneurship development is the introduction of impact evaluations of projects and programmes. This will help determine what has worked best and justify and prioritise new funding. The limited general data on Arab Israeli SME and entrepreneur activities and barriers is a problem, but does not prevent evaluation at a project level that can undertake their own surveys of beneficiaries or comparisons of treatment and control group effects, even without linkages to national monitoring or business register data.

The MEDA should also have a greater role in increasing the awareness of Arab Israeli entrepreneurs about the government support programmes open to them. An important action it could take in this area is to create and manage a single, integrated information portal on business development services and supports for Arab Israeli SMEs and entrepreneurs. This would include all relevant national programmes. In addition, Arab-dominated local authorities could be encouraged to help diffuse the information and add information on their own support. Such a knowledge portal would also assist policy makers and providers to identify gaps in provision.

In seeking to address the issue of outreach of public programmes to Arab Israeli entrepreneurs, the MEDA should pay particular attention to the gender dimension of support for the Arab Israeli minority. There appear to be some substantial gender gaps in rates of participation by women and men entrepreneurs across the whole range of SME interventions in the Arab sector – provision of finance, entrepreneurship support, business services and other interventions – with frequently low rates of participation by Arab Israeli women. The introduction of gender-based targets for participation in public programmes for Arab Israeli SMEs and entrepreneurship could help reduce the scale of this problem. In addition, there are relatively few gender-targeted measures for the Arab Israeli SME and entrepreneurship development. There are many good models for women entrepreneurship support internationally that could be tested for Arab women entrepreneurs in Israel, such as women entrepreneur networks and coaching and mentoring by and for women entrepreneurs (OECD/European Union, 2015; OECD/European Union, 2016).

There are lessons to be learned from the USA's Minorities Business Development Agency and Small Business Administration in putting together an enlarged agenda for the MEDA and ensuring coherence with other agencies delivering relevant support, notably the SMBA (see Box 7.3). Specifically, the experience of the USA illustrates the need to have close

Box 7.3. Institutional arrangements and responsibilities for minority economic development in the USA

Unusually among OECD countries, the USA, like Israel, has two government agencies engaged in support for minority businesses: a general small business support agency (the Small Business Administration) and an agency for ethnic minority businesses (the Minorities Business Development Agency).

The Small Business Administration

The US Small Business Administration (SBA) was founded in 1953 as an autonomous agency of government. The head of the organisation has a seat in Cabinet. The SBA's function is to "aid, counsel, assist and protect the interests of small business concerns".

The SBA provides assistance to SMEs in four ways:

- Access to finance. The SBA provides loans and loan guarantees for small firms. It had a total loan portfolio in 2013 of USD 107 billion and in that year made new loans amounting to USD 30 billion to 47,000 enterprises.
- Entrepreneurial skills and business consultancy. The SBA delivers education, information, technical assistance and training in over 1,800 locations throughout the United States and US territories. Within this activity, the 8(a) Business Development Program assists eligible socially and economically disadvantaged individuals to grow their businesses over a period of up to 9 years.
- Public contracting. The SBA facilitates SMEs' access to federal contracts and monitors the Federal government's implementation of its statutory obligation to set aside 23% of all prime contract dollars to SMEs. Within that total, various socially and economically disadvantaged populations have special allocations, such as (ethnic) minority-owned, women-owned and locationally disadvantaged businesses.
- Advocacy. The SBA reviews Congressional legislation, testifies on behalf of small business, assesses the impact of the regulatory burden on SMEs, maintains an SME database, and conducts research on American small businesses and the small business environment.

The Minorities Business Development Agency (MBDA)

The MBDA was founded in 1969. It is a bureau of the Department (ministry) of Commerce and is much smaller than the SBA, with an annual budget of USD 30 million. It is the only federal agency dedicated to advancing the establishment and growth of minority-owned firms. To be eligible for its support, minority-owned businesses must have attained a certain size in terms of turnover. The current threshold is annual revenue of USD 1 million. MBDA assists eligible businesses by providing a range of business services and links to capital, contracts and market opportunities through online and personal referrals. It operates a national network of more than 40 MBDA Business Centers.

Box 7.3. **Institutional arrangements and responsibilities for minority economic development in the USA** *(cont.)*

The MBDA recognises two types of minority businesses. The main group is businesses that are at least 51% minority-owned, operated and controlled. The second group is "minority-controlled" enterprises. In this category, at least 30% of the economic equity of the firm is minority-owned and minority managers or owners control the day-to-day operations of the firm and retain a majority (not less than 51%) of the firm's voting equity.

Factors for success

Between them, the two public agencies offer a comprehensive set of measures for minority business support in the USA. The SBA provides comprehensive support for all SMEs, within a "mainstreaming" philosophy for minority businesses, i.e. minority businesses can benefit from all SBA support services but are not specially singled out. At the same time, the SBA operates special online information portals and publications in minority languages (especially Spanish) to help raise awareness of minority businesses about what is on offer. Furthermore, minority businesses are included in the SBA's 8(a) Business Development Program for disadvantaged SMEs.

The MDBA provides complementary specialist support for minority businesses once they reach a certain size (USD 1m turnover). This aims to help them overcome particular obstacles that might otherwise block their expansion and integration into national and international markets. The MBDA fosters business links for minority businesses and in particular encourages access to procurement markets that might otherwise be difficult for minority businesses to break into.

Thus there is some overlap but also a clear division of responsibility between the two public agencies. This is one way of addressing the perennially difficult balance between 'mainstreaming' and group-specific targeting. The proper functioning of the system depends on good communications and cross-agency links and referral systems. From the perspective of minority businesses, the arrangement offers a clear growth pathway, giving an incentive for ambitious minority ventures to grow on standard start-up lines and thereafter to become eligible for MBDA programmes to help overcome group-specific barriers.

Obstacles and responses

Abuses occurred in the minority business support system in the US when federal contracts under SBA support program 8(a) were awarded to non-minority businesses. In those cases inter-agency communication was flawed and the contract awarding entity had not checked bidding firms' real eligibility, making the process open to fraud. The remedy was to improve cross referencing and create a robust register of minority businesses open to public scrutiny.

Both the SBA and the MBDA make use of a non-government organisation, the National Minorities Supplier Development Council (NMSDC), to issue certification of minority status to businesses to give them eligibility for those public programmes and statutory set-asides that are specifically for minority businesses. The main criterion for certification is that individual business owners must be at least 25% Asian, Black, Hispanic or Native American; their personal status is established via a combination of screenings, interviews and site visits. The SBA and MBDA both refer applicants to their programmes to the NMSDC for certification.

The effectiveness of SBA lending programmes has been criticised both for the relatively small scale of SBA intervention compared to the number of small businesses in the country and for its drain on the US public finances. Its operations have not been self-financing because they have incurred a high level of bad debts. However, the counter-financing

Box 7.3. **Institutional arrangements and responsibilities for minority economic development in the USA** *(cont.)*

because they have incurred a high level of bad debts. However, the counter-argument has been made that its lending losses were a valid response to helping SMEs weather the recessionary conditions of the late 2000s. In addition, evaluation evidence has shown that the minority SME set asides in public procurement have been effective in overcoming the structural disadvantages of minority businesses (Chatterji et al., 2013).

Relevance for Israel

As in the USA, Israel has two main public agencies for the support of minority businesses, one mainstream agency, SMBA, and one specialist agency, MEDA. There may be lessons from the USA concerning the combined scope and mix of the policies and programmes operated and the details of policy intervention. Multiple actions are operated across the areas of access to finance, entrepreneurial skills and business consultancy, procurement and advocacy. The SMBA and the MEDA operate a similar range of programmes. Examination of evaluation evidence on what works in these approaches in the USA could provide inspiration for the further development of similar programmes in Israel, although this would require local testing and evaluation to account for differences in the Israeli and USA circumstances, including in terms of the smaller size bands of the targeted enterprises in Israel.

There may also be lessons for how the two Israeli agencies combine. In the USA, there is a clear division of roles. The US SBA provides mainstream support for business establishment and development that is open to minority enterprises, and uses special outreach channels to raise the awareness of minority businesses about these services. The US MBDA aims to support established minority businesses with at least sales of at least USD 1 million p.a. to diversify outside their own community. Few Arab-owned firms in Israel would meet this eligibility criterion and the MEDA in Israel therefore aims to support start-ups and micro-businesses as well as larger firms. Partly as a result, there is a greater overlap in the responsibilities and target groups of the mainstream and specialist agencies in Israel. However, in both cases there are strong and effective working relationships among the specialist and mainstream agencies.

Sources of further information

Agency websites and government portals: *www.mbda.gov/*; *www.sba.gov/*; *www.nmsdc.org/*; *http://business.usa.gov/*; *www.setasidealert.com/index.htm*.

Chatterji, A.K., K.Y. Chay and R.W. Fairlie (2013).

collaboration between the agency responsible for general SME support and the agency responsible for business development among minorities. In addition, it underlines the importance of having separate programmes for start-ups and for support to market access for established minority enterprises with proven competitiveness and efficiency, particularly through the route of public procurement.

Overall, the MEDA also needs a specific and integrated strategy to strengthen the Arab Israeli business sector. This strategy should extend the current policy package in three main ways:

1. Demand needs to be assured by way of increased market access. Public and private corporate buying agents need to be reoriented in their purchasing behaviour to favour inclusion of minority businesses.

2. Arab-owned enterprises need to improve the efficiency of their business operations. Current efforts in this direction are generally weak throughout Israel and there is scope here for the MEDA to lead the field by undertaking and evaluating an experimental intervention drawing on the design of projects in other countries.
3. To enable Arab-owned businesses to consolidate management improvements and expand their operations their access to finance needs to be improved. Current funding initiatives are laudable but limited in scope, being focussed on high-technology, potentially high-growth start-ups, and not systematically linked to upgrading of existing employer businesses, which need to increase their productivity and competitiveness beyond the Arab market.

The different facets of this intervention strategy are interrelated and mutually reinforcing. Measures addressing each of them therefore need to be introduced simultaneously.

Conclusions and policy recommendations

In its short period of existence, the Israeli government has launched an impressive range of projects and programmes for Arab Israeli SME and entrepreneurship development, funded from a variety of different sources and spearheaded and co-ordinated by the MEDA. None of the current interventions shows signs of failure in implementation or lack of relevance. However, the scale of need considerably exceeds the resources currently available and a further step up of support for Arab Israeli SMEs and entrepreneurship is required, even given the new 5-year funding package foreseen in the economic development plan for the Arab sector 2016-20.

A key recommendation is therefore that the level of funding should be increased for the MEDA and for programmes aimed at Arab Israeli SMEs and entrepreneurship run by other government bodies. This scale up of resources should be on the basis of detailed evaluation of the existing projects and programmes and the creation of an overall strategic programme which can guide the MEDA interventions and underpin its coordination with other Ministries and programmes.

A reinforced programme for support of Arab Israeli SMEs and entrepreneurs needs to address a number of issues. Policy needs to focus on helping Arab Israeli SMEs and entrepreneurs to break out of local markets, strengthening SME workforce skills, building SME management skills and competences, providing subsidies for investment and innovation, improving access to finance and increasing access to suitable premises. Overall, the key requirement for strengthening the Arab Israeli business sector is to achieve diversification of new and existing businesses towards higher value-added and higher growth potential sectors and markets.

This can be led by the MEDA working with national government ministries and agencies. However, the role of the MEDA should be strengthened to enable it to better co-ordinate and prioritise policy across and to undertake greater outreach to the Arab Israeli SME and entrepreneur community.

Specific recommendations offered for future policy development are as follows:

Key recommendations on SMEs and entrepreneurship in the Arab Israeli population

Open up public procurement to Arab Israeli businesses

- Introduce public procurement measures dedicated to Arab-owned SMEs and start-ups, through setting a quota or target for the share of contracts or volume of business for Arab-owned enterprises, supporting the development of bidding consortia among Arab-owned enterprises and requiring prime contractors to offer a proportion of subcontracts to Arab-owned businesses.

Build workforce and management skills

- Introduce incentives for Arab-owned SMEs to undertake in-company workforce training and offer in-company workforce training programmes for networks of Arab-owned SMEs.
- Expand dedicated management development programmes for Arab Israeli SMEs and entrepreneurs offering advice, consultancy and mentoring on business innovation, upgrading of equipment and technology, expanding markets and participating in local and international supply chains.
- Ensure that university business incubator programmes across the country give support to Arab Israeli students and staff in proportion to their numbers and needs by setting target quotas for Arab Israeli participants and/or creating a specific university incubation programme for Arab Israeli entrepreneurs.

Introduce a dedicated financial incentive programme for investment and innovation

- Launch a time-limited, "challenge fund" type programme of subsidies for capital investment, R&D, product and marketing development and meeting international quality standards in Arab-owned SMEs, both in traditional manufacturing and tourism sectors and emerging knowledge-intensive business services.

Improve access to finance

- Include special provisions such as quotas for Arab businesses within financial competition reforms.
- Provide financial and technical support to existing microfinance institutions, credit unions and cooperative banks serving the Arab Israeli business community to help them expand their operations.
- Develop a graduation facility for the MEDA microcredit programmes whereby entrepreneurs with growth ambitions for their enterprises can be accompanied into mainstream business development support services.
- Promote the development of business angel networks targeting investments in Arab-owned enterprises.
- Explore the potential for equity and loan crowdfunding based within – but open to expansion beyond – the Arab Israeli community.

Provide industrial sites and premises

- Continue central government investment in the creation of industrial zones in and around Arab-dominated local authority areas at such a scale as to ensure that there is an adequate supply of local premises for Arab-owned businesses.
- Make regulations and land use planning decisions more favourable to the establishment of industrial zones and business premises in and around Arab-dominated local authority areas in particular by streamlining the decision-making of planning authorities, establishing

Key recommendations on SMEs and entrepreneurship in the Arab Israeli population *(cont.)*

planning authorities for individual Arab-dominated areas where possible, and providing planning policy guidance notes supportive of SME development.

- Produce and disseminate guiding principles on sharing of business tax revenues between Jewish- and Arab-dominated municipalities in the case of joint industrial zones and broker partnerships among local authorities for joint industrial zone development.
- Provide training and guidance to professionals in Arab-dominated local authorities to increase their ability to finance, develop, manage and market industrial zones.

Improve policy co-ordination and outreach

- Transfer responsibility for economic development support of Druze municipalities to the MEDA.
- Organise periodic in-depth surveys of Arab Israeli business development trends and issues and introduce more systematic monitoring and evaluation of policy activities implemented for minority businesses. Establish a unit within the MEDA for research and evaluation to assist in particular in scaling up successful experimental projects, making the case for increased funding for the MEDA and securing the greatest impacts from this funding.
- Create and manage through the MEDA a single, integrated information portal on business support for Arab Israeli SMEs and entrepreneurs.
- Apply gender targets consistently for participation in public programmes for Arab Israeli SMEs and entrepreneurship, establishing rolling targets that they are feasible at the outset and increase over time as expectations and awareness are raised.
- Strengthen gender-targeted measures for Arab Israeli women entrepreneurs, e.g. creation of women's cooperatives and sponsorship of women's business organisations, networks and mentoring (including by senior Jewish businesswomen).
- Increase funding for the MEDA in order to enable it to co-ordinate policy across government and develop the necessary statistical and evaluation base as well as to scale up its direct interventions for Arab Israeli SMEs and entrepreneurs that have the greatest net benefits.

Notes

1. Shaul Katznelson, the Export Institute's head of the Economics Department. Interview at *www.haaretz.com/news/features/2.475/israeli-arab-exports-in-a-country-near-you-1.452142*.
2. State Comptroller's Office, Report No. 63?'- 111-113 published 5/2013.

References

Bloom, N., B. Eifert, A. Mahajan, D. McKenzie and J. Roberts (2013), "Does Management Matter? Evidence from India", *The Quarterly Journal of Economics*.

CBS (2014a), *Israel in Figures 2014*, Central Bureau of Statistics, Jerusalem.

CBS (2014b), *Statistical Abstract of Israel*, Central Bureau of Statistics, Jerusalem.

CBS (2013), *Statistical Abstract of Israel*, Central Bureau of Statistics, Jerusalem.

Chatterji, A.K., K.Y. Chay and R.W. Fairlie (2013), "The Impact of City Contracting Set-Asides on Black Self-Employment and Employment", University of California at Santa Cruz, Department of Economics, *Working Paper Series*, February, at *www.escholarship.org/uc/item/479755b2*.

Drori, I. and M. Lerner (2002), "The Dynamics of Limited Breaking Out: The Case of the Arab Manufacturing Businesses in Israel", *Entrepreneurship and Regional Development: An International Journal*, 14.2, 135-154.

GEM (1999), *Global Entrepreneurship Monitor 1999 Israel Executive Report*, Tel Aviv University Faculty of Management, *www.gemconsortium.org/country-profile/73*.

Goldblatt, R. and I. Omer (2014), "The Association between Land-Use Distribution and Residential Patterns: the Case of Mixed Arab-Jewish Cities in Israel", *Journal of Urban and Regional Analysis*, Vol. VI, 1, p. 15-34.

Habib, J., J. King, A. Shoham, A. Wolde-Tsadick and K. Lasky (2010), "Labour Market and Socio-Economic Outcomes of the Arab-Israeli Population", *OECD Social, Employment and Migration Working Papers* No. 102, OECD Publishing, *http://dx.doi.org/10.1787/5kmjnrcfsskc-en*.

Heilbrunn, S. and K.M. Abu-Asbah (2011), "Disadvantaged and Embedded: Arab Women Entrepreneurs in Israel", *International Journal of Business and Social Science*, Vol. 2 No. 11 Special Issue, June.

IATA (Inter Agency Task Force on Israeli Arab issues) (2013), *Arab Citizen Employment in Israel Critical Concern and Great Potential*, by Avivit Hai, July 2013, at *http://iataskforce.org/resources/view/1052*.

Menipaz, E., Y. Avrahami and M. Lerner (2013), *National Report for Israel by the Global Entrepreneurship Monitor 2013*, Ira Center for Business Technology and Society, Ben Gurion University.

Menipaz, E., Y. Avrahami and M. Lerner (2011), *GEM 2010 Israel National Entrepreneurship Report*, Ben Gurion University, Beer Sheva, *www.gemconsortium.org/country-profile/73*.

Ministry of Economy/SMBA (2014), *An Analysis of the Obstacles Faced by SME's in Access to Finance and Suggested Solutions*, Note for the OECD Mission.

Minorities Economic Development Authority (MEDA) (2014), Note supplied to the OECD secretariat, unpublished.

OECD (2015), *Employment and Skills Strategies in Israel*, OECD Publishing, Paris, *http://dx.doi.org/10.1787/9789264232969-en*.

OECD (2011), *Higher Education in Regional and City Development*, The Galilee, Israel, OECD, Paris, *http://dx.doi.org/10.1787/9789264088986-en*.

OECD (2009), *OECD Economic Surveys: Israel 2009*, Volume 2009/21 – January 2010, Supplement No. 3, OECD Publishing, Paris, *http://dx.doi.org/10.1787/eco_surveys-isr-2009-en*.

OECD/European Union (2016), *Inclusive Business Creation: Good Practice Compendium*, OECD Publishing, Paris, *http://dx.doi.org/10.1787/9789264251496-en*.

OECD/European Union (2015) *The Missing Entrepreneurs 2015: Policies for Self-Employment and Entrepreneurship*, OECD Publishing, Paris, *http://dx.doi.org/10.1787/9789264226418-en*.

Or Commission (2003), *Israeli Arabs: The Official Summation of the Or Commission Report*, 2 September 2003, Jewish Virtual Library at *www.jewishvirtuallibrary.org/jsource/Society_&_Culture/OrCommissionReport.html*.

Ram, M., N. Theodorakopoulos and I. Worthington (2007), *Policy transfer in practice: implementing supplier diversity in the UK*, Public Administration, 85, 799-803.

Shah, M. (2014), Supplier Diversity in the UK, *Minority Business Entrepreneur*, July-August 2014.

Shihadeh, M. and F. Moadi (2011), *The Education Budget and Participation of Arab Women in the Labor Market in Israel: an Analysis of Gender and Ethnicity*, The Galilee Society with Rikaz, Mada al Carmel and I'lam.

Trajtenberg Commission (2012), Creating a More Just Israeli Society, Israel Prime Minister's Office, Jerusalem. English version at *www.bjpa.org/Publications/details.cfm?PublicationID=13862*.

UNCTAD (2014), *Palestinian Fiscal Revenue Leakage to Israel under the Paris Protocol on Economic Relations*, United Nations Conference on Trade and Development, Geneva, *http://unctad.org/en/Publications Library/gdsapp2013d1_en.pdf*.

Yashiv, E. and N. Kasir (Kaliner) (2014), *The Labor Market of Israeli Arabs. Key Features and Policy Solutions*. Tel Aviv University, January.

Chapter 8

Medium-sized enterprises in Israel

This chapter provides an assessment of the performance of medium-sized enterprises[1] in Israel with respect to number of firms and employment, labour productivity and innovation. It identifies a significant productivity gap affecting traditional medium-sized enterprises in traditional manufacturing. It then examines Israel's policy framework in six main areas relevant to improving growth, productivity and innovation in medium-sized enterprises: workforce skills development, improving management skills and practices, access to finance, supply chain development, public procurement and innovation. A particular focus is on developing programmes to support medium-sized enterprises in traditional manufacturing sectors.

The relevance of MSEs

Israel's economy benefits from high levels of business R&D and a very strong high-technology sector. However, at the same time it experiences relatively low levels of productivity and innovation among its medium-sized enterprises (MSEs), especially in traditional sectors. While productivity has increased in export-intensive high-technology industries such as medical equipment, optical equipment and metrology equipment, electronics and chemicals it has stood still or even decreased in traditional industries. Gaps in labour productivity compared to the OECD average in 2013 ranged from 50% to Israel's disadvantage in the clothing sector and 30% to Israel's disadvantage in the construction sector (Bank of Israel, 2014).

One of the key problems identified in this report and elsewhere (Ben-Nahum and Erez, 2012) is that Israel's high-technology and traditional sectors operate as dual economies, with little bridge between them, an issue which is particularly relevant for MSEs. While MSEs in high-technology sectors receive considerable support including R&D funding and schemes for technology transfer, policy intervention for the much larger numbers of MSEs in traditional industries is limited. However, successful MSEs are key to boosting economic growth and are often part of the population of high-growth firms. They have established track records, comprise a stable part of the economy, and have in place organisational systems that can be built on in order for growth to take place. They can also be seen as being 'anchor firms', as cluster enablers, as a magnet for supply and service firms, as orchestrators of networks, and as generators of spillovers (Feldman, 2003; FRIDA, 2013). Appropriate policies and programmes for this segment of the enterprise population could therefore have important benefits.

The SMBA has a key role to play in supporting high-growth MSEs, whether in high-technology or traditional sectors. Interventions should be designed to foster and provide support for greater levels of innovation among high-growth MSEs through collaboration with a variety of kinds of organisations, to support exporting into international supply chains and increasing access to investment finance.

The targeted MSEs are considered here as those with between 20 and 99 employees, to correspond to the definition used by the SMBA. On this definition, MSEs made up 6.5% of the total number of employer enterprises and accounted for one-fifth of total private sector wage jobs in Israel in 2012 (Table 8.1). Most of these MSEs were in the lower end of the size

Table 8.1. **Employer enterprises and employee jobs by business size class, 2012**

Absolute numbers and percentage values

	Micro (1-4 employees)	Small (5-19 employees)	Medium (20-99 employees)	Large (100+ employees)	Total
Number of employer enterprises	172 792	54 227	16 105	3 582	246 706
Per cent	70.0	22.0	6.5	1.5	100.0
Number of employees	283 893	482 494	641 373	1 851 747	3 259 507
Per cent	8.7	14.8	19.7	56.8	100.0

Source: OECD based on data supplied by SMBA.

StatLink http://dx.doi.org/10.1787/888933422011

band; 4.9% had between 20 and 49 employees (smaller MSEs) and accounted for more than half of wage jobs in this business segment (11.4%), while only 1.6% of total enterprises had between 50 and 100 employees (8.6% of total business sector jobs).

Ministries and agencies in various OECD countries have focused policies and programmes on MSEs, following their own definitions, reflecting recognition that the barriers faced by these enterprises differ in many ways from those of other enterprises. By way of comparison, the Confederation of British Industry (CBI, 2014) found that firms with a turnover in the range of GBP 10-100 million face particular challenges, which are partly the result of a policy gap. They are too large to benefit from policies tailored to small businesses but too small to win the attention that firms in the London Stock Exchange command. Moreover, there is a lack of demand for policies from this target group. In Finland, the government has observed that MSEs (50-249 employees) grow faster than all other size bands other than small firms and has designed targeted support in the form of business accelerators.

Productivity and innovation performance

Labour productivity

Figure 8.1 shows labour productivity by enterprise size in Israel and other OECD countries for the total business economy. It indicates that the value added per employee of large and medium firms in Israel is relatively low in Israel compared with other OECD averages, but that the gap in Israel between MSE productivity (on the OECD measure of 20-29 and 50-99 employees) and large firm productivity is small compared with most other OECD countries. This would tend to suggest that poor productivity performance is not just an issue for MSEs in Israel, but rather a feature of Israel that extends to larger firm sizes. However, these statistics are dominated by productivity performance in the service sector and disguise an important MSE-specific productivity issue in Israeli manufacturing.

Figure 8.1. **Labour productivity by enterprise size, total economy**

Value added per person employed, thousands of USD, current PPPs, 2013 or latest available year

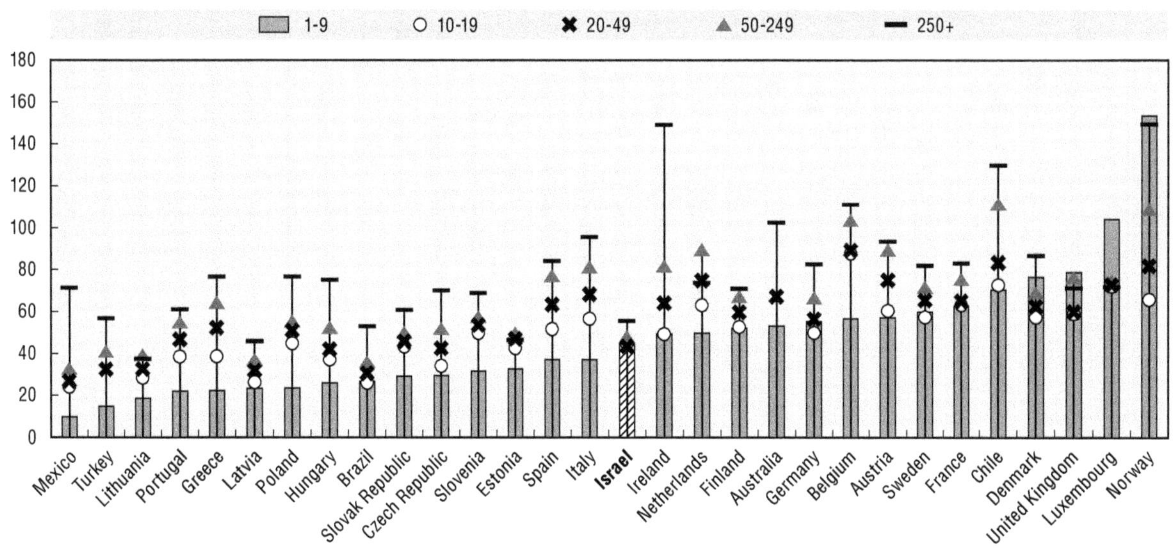

Note: data for Mexico refer to 2014, data for Ireland refer to 2011, data for Israel refer to 2012. For the United States, labour productivity is constructed as value added per employee.

Source: OECD (2016), *Entrepreneurship at a Glance 2016*, based on OECD Structural and Demographic Business Statistics (database).

StatLink http://dx.doi.org/10.1787/888933421997

Figure 8.2 breaks down the statistics between services and manufacturing and focuses on the differences between MSE productivity and large firm productivity. It shows that while MSE productivity is higher than that of large firms in Israeli service industries, the gap between MSE productivity and large firm productivity is larger in Israel than in many other countries. This suggests that productivity upgrading for manufacturing MSEs should be the particular target of policy for this group of firms in Israel.

Figure 8.2. **Labour productivity by enterprise size, manufacturing and services**

Value added per person employed, index 250+ = 100, 2013 or latest available year

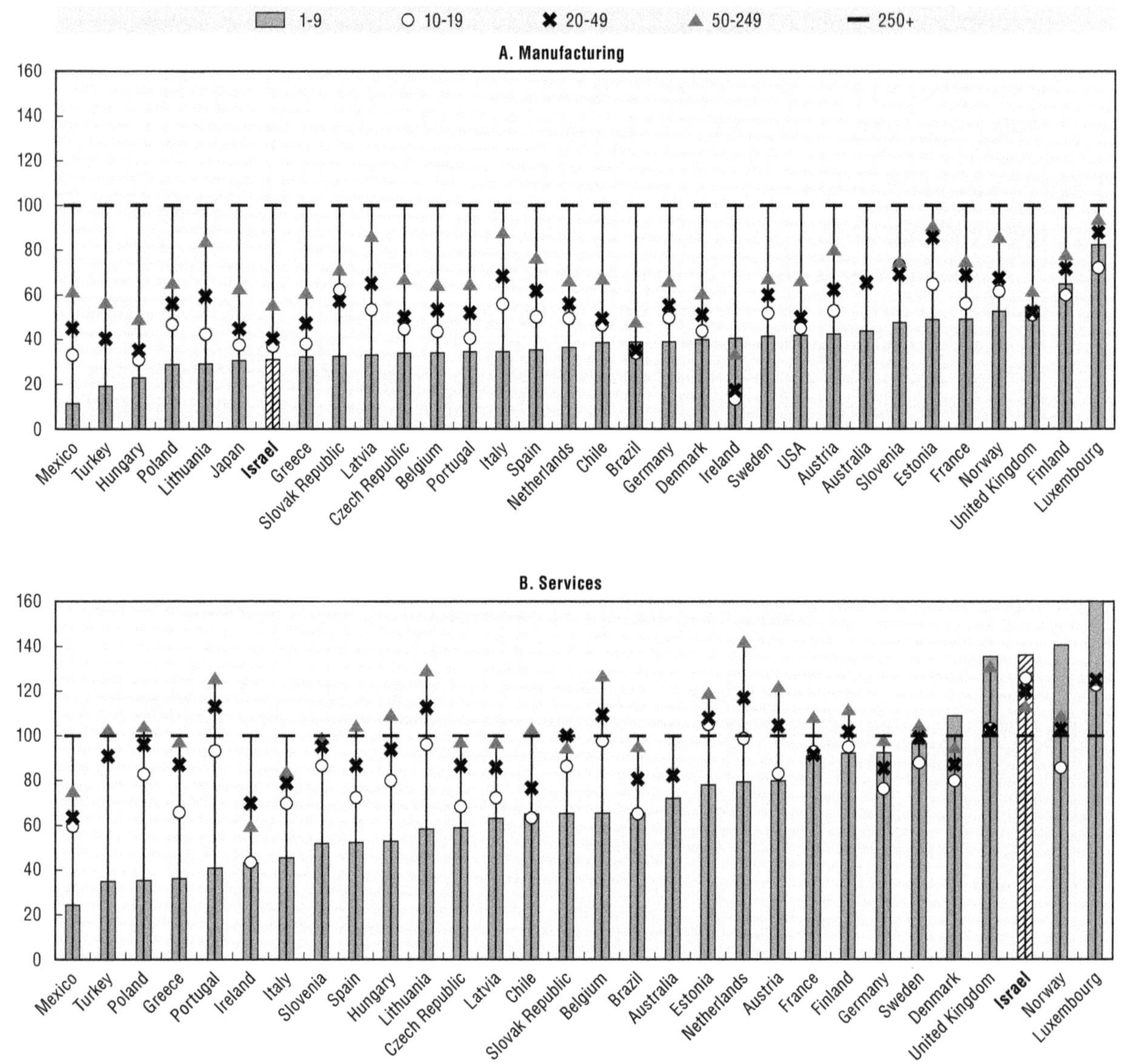

Note: For manufacturing, data for the United States on labour productivity is constructed as value added per employee. For manufacturing and services, data for Mexico refer to 2014, data for Ireland refer to 2011, and data for Israel refer to 2012. The size-class classification for Mexico is based on establishments.

Source: OECD (2016), *Entrepreneurship at a Glance 2016*, based on OECD Structural and Demographic Business Statistics (database).

StatLink http://dx.doi.org/10.1787/888933422002

Innovation

One of the reasons for the productivity lag in manufacturing MSEs is limited innovation activity. Table 26 shows that the share of MSEs in R&D activity is low in manufacturing compared with the total business economy. MSEs accounted for only 9.2% of total manufacturing R&D compared with an MSE share of 22.5% across all business activity in the period 2010-2012.

Table 8.2. **R&D expenditure by business size class and industry, 2010-12**

NIS million and percentage values

	5-9 employees	10-19 employees	20-49 employees	50-99 employees	100+ employees	All
Total manufacturing, NIS million	..	89	324	549	8,546	9 508
(% contribution)	..	0.9	3.4	5.8	89.9	100
ICT, NIS million	86	716	2 113	1 780	7 141	11 835
(% contribution)	0.7	6.1	17.9	15	60.3	100
R&D centres*	239	950	1 855	950	8 462	12 455
(% contribution)	1.9	7.6	14.9	7.6	67.9	100
Total business sector	324	1 756	4 341	3 297	24 256	33 976
(% contribution)	1	5.2	12.8	9.7	71.4	100

Note: This category overlaps with what in the CSI are defined as "professional, scientific & technical activities"
Source: OECD based on data supplied by the Israeli CBS.

StatLink http://dx.doi.org/10.1787/888933422022

Table 8.3 indicates that the small share of manufacturing R&D accounted for by MSEs is more the consequence of the majority of MSEs being in low and medium-low technology industries that undertake little R&D in general than a tendency of MSEs to undertake less R&D than other firms in these industries. The weak R&D performance of manufacturing MSEs is particularly a feature of smaller MSEs (20-49 employees). This is true across all segments of technology intensity, although the gap is especially pronounced in medium-low technology sectors such as plastic and metalworking.

Table 8.3. **Manufacturing R&D expenditure by size class and technology intensity, 2010-12**

NIS million and percentage values

	10-19 employees	20-49 employees	50-99 employees	100+ employees	Total
Total manufacturing	89	324.2	549	8 545.8	9 508.3
(% contribution)	0.9	3.4	5.8	89.9	100
Manufacturing by technological intensity:					
High technology	40.6	228.1	410.5	6 597.7	7 276.9
(% contribution)	0.6	3.1	5.6	90.7	100
Medium-high technology	9.2	62.9	63.2	1 454	1 589.3
(% contribution)	0.6	4	4	91.5	100
Medium-low technology	9.2	20.5	60.8	316.5	407
(% contribution)	2.3	5	14.9	77.8	100
Low technology	30.4	11.6	14.4	155.8	212.2
(% contribution)	14.3	5.5	6.8	73.4	100

Source: OECD based on data supplied by the Israeli CBS.

StatLink http://dx.doi.org/10.1787/888933422032

The Community Innovation Survey provides information that covers different types of innovation in manufacturing. As shown in Table 8.4, there is a substantial gap in overall innovation activity between smaller (20-49 employees) and larger MSEs (50-99 employees) and large companies with more than 100 employees. The gap between manufacturing

Table 8.4. **Technological innovation in manufacturing by type and business size class, 2010-12**

Percentage of enterprises

	Innovation activity	Technological innovation	New to market technological innovation	Product innovation	Process innovation	Process and product innovation
10-19 employees	20.5	18.5	11.4	11.7	15.2	8.4
20-49 employees	33.1	30.2	12.6	20	20.2	10.1
50-99 employees	54.3	48.4	26.4	37.4	34.2	23.3
100+ employees	68.1	63.8	47.3	54.5	45.1	35.8
Total	37	32.9	19	24.1	23.7	14.9

Source: OECD based on data supplied by the Israeli CBS.

StatLink http://dx.doi.org/10.1787/888933422040

MSEs and large manufacturing firms is particularly large in the areas of new to market technological innovation and product innovation, as well as combined process and product innovation in the case of smaller manufacturing MSEs.

MSEs are a more homogenous group in non-technological innovation, although the gap in innovation performance with larger companies is also wide with respect to organisational and marketing innovation (Table 8.5).

Table 8.5. **Non-technological innovation in manufacturing by type and business size class, 2010-12**

Percentage of enterprises

	10-19 employees	20-49 employees	50-99 employees	100+ employees	Total
Organisational innovation	29.1	32	33.9	56.4	35.4
Market innovation	22.4	31.7	36.7	48.1	36.1

Source: OECD based on data supplied by the Israeli CBS.

StatLink http://dx.doi.org/10.1787/888933422050

Policy levers for MSE development

Six main policy levers are typically used to improve the productivity, innovation and growth performance of MSEs: workforce skills development, improving management skills and practices, strengthening access to finance, supply chain development, targeted public procurement and innovation support. This section assesses current policy arrangements in Israel for each potential policy lever as they affect MSEs and potential areas for improvement.

Workforce skills development

Israel's vocational education and training (VET) system is not working well for MSEs, which are more dependent on it than larger firms given their more limited levels of internal training activity. There are relatively small numbers of participants in engineering and technical training, limited sector-specific training and the mix of courses does not have a good match to key skill needs. At present no analysis has been carried out on a national scale on the training needs of MSEs to guide VET provision, in spite of the recognition of a serious shortage of skilled professionals like welders, metalworkers and electricians. In particular, Israel is yet to develop a holistic vision with regard to skills provision for growing firms spanning all parts of the education and learning system up to graduate level and continuing professional development. Such a vision is important for supply chain improvement and requires inputs from employers and industry associations. Such a training needs assessment should be used to develop more vocational-technical, skills and lifelong learning opportunities for MSE employees. This means not just a focus on technical skills but includes those developed in business schools, the humanities and social sciences (OECD, 2011).

The approach to upgrading VET provision should involve regionally-delivered programmes that include collaboration between local VET colleges and universities to tailor training to meet the needs of MSEs in the region. An example of an innovative way of taking this kind of approach forward is Coventry University in the United Kingdom. Coventry University was formerly a polytechnic specialising in engineering. It has brought into the university a college of further education, now named Coventry University College, in order to provide a more comprehensive skill set and training to local industry, including engineering and accountancy. The College draws on the excellence in teaching and learning and the extensive experience of Coventry University. It operates independently from the University, as a separate organisation, in its own building and with its own staff; all based on the Coventry University campus. All of the courses have been designed around the standards for professional body accreditation, which means that students are prepared and have the opportunity to secure an additional award from a professional body alongside normal studies. The College also runs stand-alone professional qualifications which provide an individual with industry-specific skills. This model could be adapted by Israel's universities in order to leverage their particular research and teaching resources by creating in-house programmes that meet the needs both of MSEs and students from technical through to degree-level qualifications.

In addition, the MAOF centres are providing some relevant training support to MSEs in the form of specialist workshops and short courses where there is a demand for them from companies. This function could be encouraged further with more diagnostic analysis of MSE training needs by the MAOF centres accompanied by a targeted offer of subsidised courses and longer courses.

Improving management skills and practices

Support initiatives for improving management skills and practices are limited in Israel. However, there are examples of good practice. For example, Technion University runs a number of programmes targeted at high-level skills. Key features are that they cater for top management, have the effect of creating networks, and have a practical mentoring element. In particular, the following programmes are noteworthy:

- The Managing Innovation Forum delivers courses for management in larger firms in both high-technology and traditional industries. It holds a series of monthly lectures and meetings presented to top management, research and development leaders, and CEOs.
- The Moving Up programme is targeted specifically at senior executives in traditional industries. It is an outcome of collaboration between Technion University and the Ministry of Economy and Industry. The format consists of six workshops, one a month, lectures, case studies, guest lectures and mentor meetings. In the workshops, participants listen to lectures that focus on the theme of managing innovation in the organisation. Major subjects include innovation strategy, the journey of the idea, change management and leadership, teamwork, innovation in a global world, innovation marketing strategy and strategic human resources. The programme provides participants with a variety of tools focused on encouraging and implementing innovation processes in their organisations. Participants are guided by business mentors in project definition, planning and implementation.

- Moving up North is an adaption of Moving Up to SMEs in traditional industries in Israel's northern periphery. The goal is to encourage collaboration and innovative initiatives among the participating companies through a series of practical workshops on managing organisational innovation processes.

This type of programme could also be operated in a selection of other universities in the country and MSEs could be encouraged to participate in them and join the networks. In addition, a universal scheme could be rolled out to upgrade management skills and practices in high growth potential firms in Israel, for example by the SMBA. An example of such an approach is the Management 4 Growth programme run by Ireland's SME and entrepreneurship agency (see Box 8.1). Another example is the Growth Accelerator in the Netherlands (Box 8.2).

Another important avenue to provide management development support involves management consultancy programmes. The main initiative for delivering such support to MSEs in Israel is the MAOF business development centres. According to an SMBA survey, MSEs are often aware of this support but have a low level of satisfaction with it. This appears

Box 8.1. **Management 4 Growth Programme, Ireland**

Description of the approach

During recent years Enterprise Ireland operated Management 4 Growth, a subsidised programme for management and leadership development in manufacturing or internationally-traded services business with 10+ plus employees (including large firms).

The programme had three elements:

1. Executive education learning modules specifically geared towards companies ready to make a more significant footprint in international markets. The content focused on management competence, practical tools and techniques and case studies and includes inputs from industry keynote speakers.
2. Appointment of a business advisor/coach working directly with each participating management team to apply the tools and techniques to their own business challenges.
3. Peer networks established to support participants from multi sector backgrounds. These peer networks focused on individual participant challenges and encouraged peer-to-peer learning during the programme with the ultimate aim of building networks that would be sustainable into the future.

The government subsidised 50% of the fee that the company paid to participate in the programme. The total amount depended on the number of people in the management team being trained. For a company with the CEO and one manager, the total programme cost would be approximately EUR 20 000 and the subsidised fee payable by company would be approximately EUR 10 000. For a CEO plus two managers, the costs of the programme would be approximately EUR 24 000 and the subsidised fee approximately EUR 12 000.

Enterprise Ireland updates its leadership and management development programmes to meet client demand. Its current offer includes "Excel at Growth" short programmes (involving a virtual classroom, a one-day face-to-face implementation workshop, and a follow-up two-hour in-company management team advisory sessions), Innovation 4 Growth (involving a business adviser coach to support the development of a company's Innovation initiative), Leadership 4 Growth (involving coaching and mentoring of senior management teams by international executive education organizations) and Platform 4 Growth (combining cleaning and face-to-face delivery for management teams in SMEs seeking to scale up).

Box 8.1. **Management 4 Growth Programme, Ireland** *(cont.)*

Factors of success

One of the factors behind the success of this type of intervention is the integration of educational modules with business advisory and coaching sessions. This ensures that learning is embedded in-company and therefore more than just the participant is benefitting from the programme experience. This has subsequent positive learning implications for other employees within the participating company and has led to the development of in-company learning cultures.

In addition the creation of multi-sector peer learning networks considers management practices and leadership challenges that are common to all industries. This means that participants can understand that many of the challenges that they face are not unique to their specific industry and helps them together to identify solutions to key difficulties that they face.

Obstacles and responses

It can be difficult to customise module elements considering the diverse audience in the room. The core educational team there seeks to deliver content that is directly relevant to the audience by designing 'just-in-time' material along with the support provided by business advisors and coaches. However, no matter how well planned, some of the material will inevitably be irrelevant to some participants during specific modules. Constant feedback and communication with the participants is the only way in which this issue can be minimised.

Relevance to Israel

A programme of this kind can help management in Israeli MSEs to understand and respond to issues their companies are facing in upgrading productivity, innovation, competitiveness and exporting. It can also help build networks among firms for management development and commercial collaborations. It also has the potential to build bridges between the dual economies of the traditional and high-technology sectors at senior levels in Israel companies.

Further information

- Enterprise Ireland's Website: *www.enterprise-ireland.com/en/Management/Leadership-and-Management-Development/*.
- OECD (2013) An International Benchmarking Analysis of Public Programmes for High-Growth Firms: *www.oecd.org/industry/high-growthreport.htm*.

Box 8.2. **The Growth Accelerator, the Netherlands**

Description of the approach

The rationale for the Netherlands Growth Accelerator programme, introduced in 2008, was that the country was lagging behind other countries in the number of fast-growing companies and their rate of growth. The objectives of the Growth Accelerator Programme are to support and facilitate the growth of two hundred MSEs from a turnover of approximately two million Euros to a turnover of twenty million Euros in a period of five years; and to ensure that each company has a Strategic Picture, a Growth Strategy and Growth Path, including milestones and a Personal Development Plan. The programme is run by the High Growth Stars Consortium: a joint-venture between PwC, AKD Advocaten & Notarissen, de Baak, Philips Innovation Services and the platform for growth businesses Port4Growth. The first companies entered the programme in 2009. The total budget for the first five years was EUR 5 million (2009-2014).

Box 8.2. **The Growth Accelerator, the Netherlands** *(cont.)*

The average firm is aged 5 to 10 years at the beginning of the programme and has 15 employees, with an average EUR 3.6 million turnover in a fast-growth industry such as IT, services, high-technology and healthcare. It has a highly ambitious managing director who owns the company and is approximately 40 years old. By 2013, over 130 firms had joined the programme, with 25% in a high-technology sector (such as IT, telecoms, sensors), 25% in creative industries (fashion, digital printing), 15% in industrial design, 6% in agrifood and 5% in chemicals 5%, There were also several firms from other sectors such as recruiting, accounting and real estate.

The programme has four phases over five years. 1. Planning (year 1) including a working strategic picture and from this a growth strategy and pathway (Growth Path) and a personal development plan. The programme puts great emphasis on personal development of the participating company's Director-Manager. 2. Realisation (years 2 and 3). The organisation and its surroundings are prepared for growth. 3. Growth Start (year 4). This begins with an assessment to identify any potential gaps that would inhibit growth. 4 Executing the Growth Plan and Personal Development Plan established in year 1. In addition each Director/manager will construct a new Strategic Picture and Growth Strategy/Path for the next five years.

Factors for success

A particular strength of the programme is its professional programme management, which focuses on continuous programme improvement, and its high-expertise impartial support service providers. It is also important that it delivers wide-ranging support across different aspects of MSE business development. The programme was evaluated in 2011, which showed that participants achieved an increase in turnover of 22 percentage points, an increase in number of employees of 8 percentage points, an increase in turnover in foreign countries of 55 percentage points and an increase in investment in innovation and product development of 45 percentage points compared with a control group.

Obstacles and responses

Two main weaknesses were identified in the programme. First is that there has been quite low take up of the programme by potential beneficiaries. This could reflect the fact that the programme lasts for 5 years, which is a relatively long period of time and could be a deterrent to companies. It could also reflect eligibility criteria and a lack of awareness by MSEs about the programme. The second is that the programme needs to be connected to other available programmes that are active in supporting entrepreneurs so as to enhance better value for money.

Relevance for Israel

This national programme is designed to support high-growth MSEs, with a particular focus on established firms with the potential to grow. Targets addressed in the Netherlands Growth Accelerator include developing an enterprise culture, a greater sense of ambition and greater confidence in the ability to design growth strategies among managers as well as building networks and relationships. These are areas where MSEs in Israel also need support. The main parts of the model should be easily transferred to Israel since the programme's approach and content is well described in manuals and workbooks. Specific subparts and work formats can be adapted to fit local learning cultures.

Further information

- Programma Groseiversneller's website: *www.groeiversneller.nl/*.
- Website: *www.akd.nl/en/about-akd/news/growth-accelerator-study*.
- OECD (2013) An International Benchmarking Analysis of Public Programmes for High-Growth Firms: *www.oecd.org/industry/high-growthreport.htm*.

to reflect the greater demands of MSEs for specialised consulting as compared with smaller firms, and suggests the need for introduction of a special track for MSEs, potentially focusing specifically on high-growth potential SMEs, in MAOF consulting services.

Access to finance

The scale and terms of investment loans available to MSEs, particularly those in traditional sectors, suffer from a number of weaknesses present in the Israeli financial system related to a general under supply of credit, limited competition between banks, lack of long-term loans and long-term loan guarantees. Some 94% of MSEs (20-99 employees) use short-term bank credit lines (including credit cards), the largest proportion in the SME sector. On the other hand, only 30% access bank loans and only 7% of MSEs obtain bank loans through state guarantee funds, compared to 18% of firms with 6-10 employees and 9% with 11-20 employees. Furthermore, bank loans are generally limited to two year durations. This suggests that MSEs are overly focused on short-term financial fixes rather than longer-term investment finance models. One of the approaches available to address this problem is to expand the terms of loan guarantees that can be offered to MSEs under the SMBF, which are generally limited to 5-year maximum terms, although in 2016 an option was introduced to guarantee longer term loans for industrial capital.

MSEs also need working capital to finance the short-term costs of periods of growth and the opening up of export markets. Factoring can be a useful source of such working capital. It involves converting credit transactions (usually invoices) into cash by selling commercial debt. The threshold to enter the factoring market is an annual turnover of NIS 5 million, thus making it particularly appropriate for MSEs. Factoring is still relatively new but it is growing. In 2001, the company CLAL Factoring Ltd entered the market, followed by other companies. The total market had grown to NIS 6-7 billion by 2014, with some 500-600 companies using the service, mostly SMEs. Intervention to build the use of this form of credit could focus in particular on financial education initiatives for MSEs, to increase awareness of this financing option.

Venture capital and private equity is particularly appropriate for financing the growth of MSEs, but is limited for smaller investment amounts outside of high-technology sectors, despite the large volume of early-stage venture capital in Israel overall and the recent announcement of the establishment of two new growth capital funds for MSEs (turnover of NIS 10-100 million) to be operated by the SMBA and the Ministry of Finance. Tax incentives have existed in law since 2011 for business angels and offer substantial tax breaks. However, like venture capital, there is a lack of angel investment for MSEs in non-technological sectors. The UK's Enterprise Investment Scheme is an example of an initiative designed to increase the flow of equity finance to MSEs as a way of stimulating innovation (see Box 8.3).

Finally, there is significant untapped potential in Israel to stimulate the flow of equity and debt finance to MSEs through the development of crowdfunding. Crowdfunding is important for MSEs because of the shortage of smart investment. An advantage of crowdfunding is that platforms reach a wide variety of knowledgeable investors who are able to identify the kinds of viable opportunities offered by MSEs rather than by SMEs in general. However, further regulatory change will be necessary to make equity and debt crowdfunding more accessible to non-high-technology MSEs in Israel.

As indicated in the OECD/G20 High-Level Principles on SME Financing, it is important to design regulation that supports a range of financing instruments for SMEs, while

Box 8.3. **The Enterprise Investment Scheme (EIS), United Kingdom**

Description of the approach

EIS is designed to help smaller higher-risk trading companies to raise finance by offering a range of tax reliefs to investors who purchase new full-risk ordinary shares in qualifying companies (HM Revenue and Customs 2013). The tax relief is intended to offset some of the risk for investors by offering tax relief proportional to the cost of shares they purchase through the scheme. If they make a loss when their EIS shares are sold, they can claim loss relief. The EIS offers both income tax and capital gains tax reliefs to investors.

The scheme is targeted at SMEs: the Gross Assets of the company – or of the whole group if it is the parent of a group – cannot exceed GBP 15 million immediately before any share issue and GBP 16 million immediately after that issue. The company must have fewer than 250 full-time employees (or their equivalents) at the time the shares are issued (500 for a knowledge-intensive company). Other rules include that:

- Companies are not allowed to raise more than GBP 5 million of state aid risk finance including EIS in any 12-month period, or a total of GBP 12 million (GBP 20 million for a knowledge-intensive company).
- Income Tax relief is available for investors at 30% of the cost of the shares, to be set against the individual's Income Tax liability for the tax year in which the investment was made on a maximum annual investment of GBP 1 million.
- Capital Gains Tax can be deferred if reinvested in EIS shares within a certain amount of time. Any profit on the sale of shares will be exempt from Capital Gains Tax if Income Tax relief is given and the shares are held for a qualifying period.
- Losses from the disposal of shares can be offset against Income Tax (instead of Capital Gains Tax) if Income Tax relief has been given and not withdrawn.
- Investors can also invest through an EIS Fund, which will invest on their behalf in a number of qualifying companies.
- The SME must be an unquoted company at the time the shares are issued. That means it cannot be listed on the London Stock Exchange or any other recognised stock exchange. It can subsequently become a quoted company without the investors losing relief, but only if no arrangements for it to become quoted were in existence when the shares were issued.
- For the EIS rules the Alternative Investment Market (AIM) and the PLUS Markets (with the exception of PLUS-listed) are not considered to be recognised exchanges, so a company listed on those markets can raise money under the EIS if it satisfies all the other conditions. The PLUS-listed market is regarded as a recognised stock exchange and shares listed on that market at the time of issue do not qualify for EIS.
- HMRC offers 'Advance Assurance', a free service, to companies that intend to raise money under EIS.

Factors of success

The scheme was evaluated in 2008 (Cowling et al., 2008). The evaluation indicated that across all companies EIS led to increased fixed asset formation, sales, employment and productivity and reduced gearing. This results from the increased investments in the participant firms. Underlying this increased investment is the award of tax relief to investors in SMEs under less restrictive conditions than general legislation (e.g. with no requirement for a lead investor) and with lower reporting requirements for SMEs seeking to raise funds in this way compared with public listing. According to the British Business Bank (2015) it underpins the majority of business angel finance in the UK and therefore plays

Box 8.3. **The Enterprise Investment Scheme (EIS), United Kingdom** *(cont.)*

a pivotal role in supporting a vibrant early-stage equity culture. In 2012-13, GBP 1 016 million was invested in almost 2 400 businesses.

Obstacles and responses

While results indicate that EIS investments have a positive effect on capacity building (fixed asset formation, sales growth etc.) in recipient companies, these effects are relatively small. However, the scheme appears to be associated with differentials in impact depending on the size, age and sector of the recipient company. Adjustments could therefore be made to focus the scheme on the types of companies for which the impacts are greatest. A recent assessment of the availability of finance to SMEs by the British Business Bank (2015) identified that despite the increasing use of equity finance, there are several weaknesses in the finance market: the persistence of the equity gap, especially at the venture stage; a lack of institutional investment; lack of awareness of finance options on the part of small businesses; and insufficient data for more detailed analysis of market trends.

Relevance to Israel

EIS is relevant as a way of increasing the flow of equity investment to Israeli MSEs that have not been publicly listed. This approach might be possible for Israel because it increases the flow of finance to companies and could also contribute to the building of a strong and visible set of complementary investment mechanisms targeted at MSEs. In order for Israel to start up an EIS approach it would need to identify target groups of investors and types of investee MSEs. Key to the scheme would be agreement by the SMBA and Ministry of Finance on the best fit within existing arrangements as to where the scheme and availability of advice to both firms and investors would be supported.

Further information

- Website of the programme: *www.gov.uk/government/publications/the-enterprise-investment-scheme-introduction.*
- Cowling, M., P. Bates, N. Jagger and G. Murray (2008), *Study of the Impact of Enterprise Investment Scheme (EIS) and Venture Capital Trusts (VCT) on Company Performance*, HM Revenues & Customs Research Report 44. *https://ore.exeter.ac.uk/repository/bitstream/handle/10036/67875/hmrc44.pdf?sequence=1*
- British Business Bank (2015), *Small Business Finance Market 2015-2106*, *http://british-business-bank.co.uk/wp-content/uploads/2016/02/British-Business-Bank-Small-Business-Finance-Markets-Report-2015-16.pdf*

ensuring financial stability and investor protection. In Israel, the balance of regulation concerning crowdfunding is more strongly towards investor protection than supporting the development of a new financing instrument for MSEs. There are examples of crowdfunding companies in Israel, e.g. OurCrowd, as outlined in Box 8.4. However, the existing crowdfunding legislation requires companies wishing to access crowdfunding to obtain approval from the IIA. This is normally only given for R&D-based companies. In addition, only equity-based crowdfunding is permitted; crowdfunding loans are not permitted by the legislation (Shenhav & Co, 2013).

There are also important regulatory requirements placed on crowdfunding organisations and platforms and on MSEs seeking to raise funds in terms of the information that has to be provided to investors and the types of investors that are allowed to make investments.

Box 8.4. **The "OurCrowd" crowdfunding platform, Israel**

OurCrowd is an equity-based crowdfunding platform, built exclusively for a select group of accredited investors to provide venture capital funding for Israeli venture capital start-ups. Membership in the community is vetted and offered only to people who meet the stringent accreditation criteria. Accredited investors who are accepted into the community can make minimum investments of USD 10 000 per deal. The initial focus of OurCrowd will be the dynamic early stage funding market in Israel and only companies that have passed a rigorous due diligence process will be added to the platform.

Source: OurCrowd website, *www.ourcrowd.com/*.

In Israel, any offer of shares to more than 35 offerees is considered an offer to the public and requires a prospectus to be issued. This is a burden on the MSE and the crowdfunding organisation. Exceptions are private placements under the 1968 Securities Law, which allows a company to offer securities to an unlimited number of accredited investors and can offer securities to foreign investors. Pure business crowdfunding (i.e. an offer to a large number of non-accredited investors) is not yet available. In several OECD countries, such as the USA, crowdfunding investments by retail (non-accredited) investors are now allowed without requiring issue of a prospectus. Accompanying restrictions on the total amount of investments that can be made or on the proportion of personal wealth that can be invested by individuals help to keep this in line with the need for appropriate investor protection. Furthermore, in Israel, there is also no official guideline to distinguish between an offer and publication. Hence each offer has to be reviewed and evaluated. While these regulations may originally have been conceived with investor protection interests in mind, they are far more restrictive than the leading countries in the development of crowdfunding, and do not take up the option of using thresholds for investment values by individual retail investors below which restrictions are more limited to obtain a different trade-off between developing a new financing instrument and ensuring investor protection.

New crowdfunding laws were introduced at the end of 2015 by the Israel Securities Authority, in recognition of the promise of new trends in financing to respond to the obstacles faced by small start-ups when approaching banks, institutional investors and venture capital funds. The new law is an amendment to the Securities Law and the Joint Investment Trust Law (The Law for the Encouragement of Investment in High-Technology Companies). The new law provides an exemption for small companies (not just in the field of high-technology) from the need to issue a prospectus when crowdfunding and raising small amounts of financing from various investors. These amended regulations aim to make it easier for firms to raise capital by selling shares to the public (see Box 8.5). However, Barnea & Co (2016) point out that the applicable regulations that will determine the parameters of the exemption have yet to be published so that how lenient the Securities Authority will be is yet to be made clear. Whether Shenhav & Co's (2014) verdict on the proposed legislation (that it would be still too restrictive) proves to be correct remains to be seen.

Israel could draw on recent international models of new crowdfunding regulation. The United States has been the forerunner by passing a law in 2012 governing equity-based crowdfunding (Box 8.6). Canada is following suit through a proposed new set of rules that will make it easier for SMEs to raise capital up to CDN 1.5 million through approved and regulated equity crowdfunding portals without issuing a prospectus. In order to protect

Box 8.5. **Main principles of new crowdfunding regulation in Israel**

- At the beginning of 2016 it was expected that investments of up to NIS 10 000 (i.e. approximately USD 2 500) per investor for each investment, and NIS 20 000 per investor in the aggregate per annum (i.e. approximately USD 5 000) will be exempt.
- In addition, the relevant company will be limited in the aggregate amount it can raise through crowdfunding per annum, and the expectation is that the cap will be several million NIS.
- In the interest of protecting the public, the regulations will require that at least one accredited investor participates in the crowdfunding and that such crowdfunding is executed through an internet portal regulated by the Securities Authority.
- Following laws already adopted in the United States and England, the new law also provides for the establishment of high-technology funds. These funds are to be traded on a new index on the Tel Aviv Stock Exchange (TASE).
- Public and institutional investors can now invest in funds, which in turn invest in a wide variety of Israeli high-technology companies; reducing investors' exposure when compared to investing in lone ventures. This new model provides an alternative for high risk high-technology companies seeking financing and/or looking to be traded on TASE.
- The Securities Authority is seeking legislative approval regarding new regulations to provide additional concessions to high-technology companies. Such concessions include the right to submit annual reports and prospectuses in English (as supposed to Hebrew) and to prepare financial reports according to the principals of US GAAP (rather than IFRS).
- These proposed changes will save Israeli high-technology companies significant expenditures when registering on TASE, and allow them to attract investments from US investors, without having to turn to the NASDAQ.

Source: Barnea & Co (2016).

Box 8.6. **The Crowdfund Act under the JOBS Act, USA**

The Jumpstart Our Business Startups Act (JOBS Act) was passed by the US Congress and signed into law in April 2012. The JOBS Act removed a Securities and Exchange Commission (SEC) regulation preventing small businesses from solicitation of investors to obtain capital, thereby enabling them to solicit securities-based funding from the general public through the Internet, social media or elsewhere – known as "business crowdfunding".

Securities-based crowdfunding allows investors to receive a financial return through the purchase of equity, debt, or revenue-based securities. The JOBS Act expands these investment opportunities to non-accredited investors, who have been historically excluded from this process. This dramatic institutionalisation of crowdfunding as a form of start-up financing has been alluded to as an important step towards the "democratisation of access to investment".

Key points of the Crowdfund Act include:

- A company will be able to crowdfund up to USD 1 million over a 12-month period without the requirement to register the shares for public trading with the SEC. The fewer rigorous compliance requirements for start-ups mean lower costs, although the company must still file some basic information with the SEC.

Box 8.6. **The Crowdfund Act under the JOBS Act, USA** *(cont.)*

- Companies that seek to crowdfund a securities-based round must have background checks undertaken on all principals with 10% or greater ownership in the company and provide full and adequate disclosures with a business plan and a full description of their ownership and capital structure. Companies seeking to raise up to USD 100 000 must provide tax returns and a financial statement, while those raising up to USD 500 000 must provide financial statements reviewed by an independent public accountant. If the amount is over USD 500 000, the company must provide audited financial statements.
- Crowdfunding portals must, alongside the legally-required background checks, do a full review of the company, disclosures, and the raise in order to approve a company prior to fundraising.
- Intermediaries seeking to help companies raise capital through crowdfunding are required to register with the SEC, make sure investors are advised of the risks, and take measures to avoid fraud. The Crowdfund Intermediary Regulatory Association has formed as a self-regulating organisation representing the crowdfunding industry.
- Individuals with annual income or net worth of less than USD 100 000 may invest up to USD 2 000 or 5% of their annual income or net worth, whichever is greater, over a 12-month period. Individuals with annual income or a net worth of USD 100 000 or more may invest up to 10% of their annual income or net worth, capped at USD 100 000 maximum aggregate amount, over a 12 month period. Investors can fund one company or several companies as long as they remain within these annual limits.
- An investor must wait a minimum of 12 months before selling her/his securities unless the sale is to a family member, the issuing company, or an accredited investor, in addition to other restrictions normally placed on the transfer of securities.
- A crowdfunding round does not prevent a company from raising capital through other legal channels.
- Companies crowdfunding are also exempt from the 500 shareholder cap pursuant to rules and regulations of the SEC and can increase that number to 2 000 before being required to register with the SEC. This allows companies to grow with greater flexibility before choosing to go public or selling out to a larger company.

Source: www.crowdfunder.com/blog/crowdfunding-law/.

investors, equity investments by individuals would be limited to no more than CDN 2 500. In the United Kingdom, crowdfunding is regulated by the Financial Conduct Authority (FCA), which in 2014 introduced new rules which allow for equity and peer-to-peer lending crowdfunding. The principles include a cap on investment of 10% of "net investible assets" for inexperienced investors, which does not apply to sophisticated investors (based on self-declaration). Platforms need to be authorised by the FCA, to which they have to report, and are only allowed to approach investors who have signed the required declarations and passed an examination. They must also clearly communicate investment risks and, in the case of peer-to-peer lending, must maintain adequate capital buffers (Shenhav & Co, 2014).

Supply chain development

A supply chain is a set of organisations directly linked by one or more upstream and downstream flows of products, services, finances, or information from a source to a customer. Participation by traditional manufacturing MSEs in supply chains can play an important role in supporting their competitiveness, innovation, and growth, for example by providing new markets, supporting collaborative innovation, and improving their responsiveness to changing market conditions and customer needs. In Israel, stronger supply chains could also help bridge the gap between traditional and high-technology sectors and promote growth and technology development in traditional manufacturing. Furthermore, it could play a role in developing innovative clusters in new sectors for Israel such as water, energy, health and biotechnology, in which there are nascent R&D and start-up activities but not full cluster ecosystems.

Some actions have been undertaken in Israel to support supply chain development, but primarily in the private sector. For example, Intel, the US electronics multinational, has a wide circle of suppliers in Israel. It also creates opportunities for service companies, provides science and engineering education, and undertakes R&D in the Computational Intelligence Institute that it founded in 2011. At the beginning of 2012, Intel signed a memorandum with the Ministry of Education to help with the Ministry's flagship strategic programmes to advance science and technology education. However, Israel lost out to Ireland in the race to set up the new Intel fabrication plant. Since then, in 2014, the Israeli government agreed to give Intel a NIS 1.5 billion grant towards the USD 6 billion it will invest in its next generation fabrication plant in Kiryat Gat. The plant will employ an additional 1 000 people and possibly contribute to new buyer-supplier relationships in the local economy. The example of Intel suggests that multinational enterprises can be harnessed as a driver for productivity growth and innovation in MSEs.

Business associations also undertake many activities to support supply chain development. In many cases, their membership encompasses enterprises of different sizes and different activities across an industry's supply chain, which makes them well placed to identify the main challenges for different sectors and to suggest specific policies for better MSE integration in supply chains. Supply chain management has also become the focus of support in colleges and universities. For example, the Galilee International Management Centre organises study programmes on supply chain management and procurement. It provides training on such topics as the role of outsourcing in the supply chain system, supply chain and quality control management, monitoring and evaluation in the international and global arena and negotiation and communication skills.

The SMBA could develop a programme in collaboration with multinational anchor firms and universities and colleges, guided by information and contacts from business associations that would seek to build supply chain linkages with manufacturing MSEs through a range of brokering activities combined with training, consultancy and financing for potential MSE suppliers. Specific actions that could be taken by the SMBA to support existing initiatives include paying consultants to provide a diagnostic service to MSEs to help them identify strengths, weaknesses, opportunities and threats in the supply chains within which they operate. The service could also help MSEs develop an explicit supply chain business strategy. The SMBA could also provide a portal for existing/potential subcontractors to broker new business opportunities in the supply chain giving better visibility of the routes available to gain access to them. It should do this in conjunction with business associations as well as colleges and universities.

Targeted public procurement

Public procurement represents a viable growth mechanism for MSEs, given both the scale of public procurement, which accounts for between 9% and 25% of GDP in OECD countries, and the potential for scalability that MSEs normally have in place in comparison with smaller enterprises. A number of OECD countries have established rules public procurement rules that are intended to act as a driver for SME innovation and growth. For example, in 2005 the UK's Department of Environment, Food, and Rural Affairs set up the Sustainable Procurement Task Force, followed by the Local Government Sustainable Procurement Strategy, to increase the access of SMEs to public procurement. Similarly procurement laws in Finland have been designed to facilitate SME participation by establishing two key principles: all contracts should be subject to an open bid and all bidders should be treated impartially.

In Israel, information on tendering has been centralised at national level and made available on-line to all businesses through recent reforms and the country is in the process of setting up an e-procurement portal to increase access to procurement. In principle the new processes should make it more feasible for MSEs to win contracts. However, in practice this seldom happens. Thus an SMBA survey in 2013 found that 70% of MSEs had not attempted to participate in public tenders in the past year. The explanation was that this resulted from a lack of knowledge on how to apply and the complexity of the process. Preparing for submitting a tender requires management attention, skill and time commitment. Professional advisors are available for large firms and institutional tenderers, and many use a professional team, but such practices are not available to MSEs. What is needed is a subsidised unified, advanced and focused training system for MSEs, with local support where possible and online more generally (Adalya Economic Consulting, 2011). Defence spending could also be more actively utilised to encourage innovation in MSEs.

Innovation support

OECD (2014) concluded that Israel is one of the top performers in developing pro-innovation policies and generating innovations, especially in the ICT fields. There is a challenge, however, in supporting innovation in MSEs in traditional manufacturing. Only 4% of government support for R&D in 2004 was directed to traditional sectors (OECD 2011b). Public support for academic R&D is low and funds need to be funnelled towards research linked with long-term priorities – water, energy and health – sectors where there are opportunities for MSEs. Moreover, traditional Israeli industries spend about one third of the R&D budget of comparable firms in the US and one-half of the budget of comparable European firms. As such, support for innovation in traditional Israeli industries potentially has a high yield.

MSEs are eligible for a range of IIA R&D support programmes (Box 8.7). Furthermore, the IIA has recently created a special track of the R&D Law dedicated to subsidising R&D in Traditional Industries (industries characterised by relatively low investment in R&D). This track offers separate evaluation and discussion for projects. Private consultation is also offered to firms applying to the track for the first time. The IIA also supports several R&D centres and technological incubators. However, the support is still strongly focused on R&D funding, whereas broader support for innovation is needed for many traditional manufacturing MSEs.

One approach that can stimulate innovation in MSEs without being solely focused on R&D is to develop partnerships between MSEs, college-based researchers, and college graduates to work together on project development in MSEs. An example of such an approach in the UK is provided in Box 8.8. This could provide a good model for a new type of MSE innovation programme in Israel.

Box 8.7. **A selection of Israeli R&D programmes catering to MSEs**

MAGNET: This supports pre-competitive R&D within a consortium that includes a number of commercial companies together with research personnel from at least one academic or research institution. The R&D focuses on new generic technologies that will lead to new generation advanced products. The industrial partners can receive a grant of 66% of approved R&D costs and the academic partner can receive 80% of approved R&D costs. A foreign company may be included in the consortium if it can bring a unique contribution to the relationship.

Mini-MAGNET: This provides further support to an already existing relationship between industry and an academic institution. The grant in this case amounts to 66% of the approved R&D costs.

NOFAR: This supports applied academic research that has aroused business interest but is not yet directed to a specific product. The objective is to advance the research to a point where it is ready for a cooperative venture with a commercial partner. A minimum requirement of this programme is for a company or incubator to invest 10% of the development costs complementing the 90% grant given by the government.

Technology Dissemination Through Users Groups: This is designed for the dissemination and adaptation of new generic technologies that were developed in Israel or abroad and are useful to any group of industries organised as a user group.

Source: Website of the IIA.

Box 8.8. **Knowledge Transfer Partnerships (KTP), United Kingdom**

Description of the approach

The KTP scheme supports UK businesses wanting to improve their competitiveness, productivity and performance by accessing the knowledge and expertise available within UK universities and colleges. It is run by Innovate UK, formerly the Technology Strategy Board. A KTP is a relationship formed between a company and a university or college of further education (the 'Knowledge Base' partner) aimed at facilitating the transfer of knowledge, technology and skills to a company partner that formerly had no access to them. Companies and organisations from a broad range of industrial and commercial sectors are eligible to participate. The scheme includes a wide range of technical and professional skills that are important for innovation and improvements in the whole of a sector's supply chain.

The more specific aims of KTPs are to: facilitate the transfer of knowledge through projects undertaken by high-caliber, recently-qualified people under joint supervision from a company and an academic institution; provide company-based training for recently-qualified people to enhance their business and specialist skills; stimulate and enhance business-relevant training and research undertaken by the academic institutions; increase the interaction between businesses and academic institutions, and awareness of the contribution academia can make to business development and growth.

Each partnership employs one or more recently-qualified people (known as an Associate) to work in a company on a project of strategic importance to the business, whilst also being supervised by the Knowledge Base Partner. Projects vary in length between 6 and 36 months. The Associates are either postgraduate researchers – university graduates – or individuals qualified to at least NVQ Level 4 or equivalent.

Box 8.8. **Knowledge Transfer Partnerships (KTP), United Kingdom** *(cont.)*

Factors for success

The success factors lie in the benefits for each partner. The scheme offers benefits to the research associates, companies, and the universities and colleges. A recent evaluation of the programme by Regeneris Consulting Ltd showed that the benefits to Associates include higher salaries, a professional management qualification and, for three-quarters of them, employment in the host company. The company benefits from an increase in the overall value of the business (over half), an increase in sales (nearly two thirds), increased profits, and new jobs created.

KTPs provide academic institutions with the potential to apply knowledge and expertise to important business problems; develop business-relevant teaching and research materials; identify new research themes and undergraduate and postgraduate projects; publish high-quality research papers; gain a relevant and improved understanding of business requirements and operations; lead rewarding collaborations with innovative businesses; assist strategic change in businesses, and supervise and act as mentors for postgraduates working on company-based projects. Failure rates are low.

Obstacles and responses

The level of commitment from each participating business is high, which means that companies need to be aware of what is expected of them. Furthermore, overall satisfaction levels among beneficiaries of the programme could be higher, especially among supported businesses. Some KTP activities are seen to offer less value than others, timescales for recruiting the right Associate are seen to be long, and the KTP portal is not well regarded or designed. Mandatory training provided to the associate is inflexible and does not always add value to the project being undertaken. Finally, arrangements for promoting the KTP scheme are unclear and there are uncertainties and overlaps in the roles of the KTP Advisor and KTP offices in generating partnerships and proposals.

The policy responses that could be taken to help address these problems include better targeting of partnerships to identify where the biggest impacts and returns can be made and reducing the complexity and bureaucracy associated with the timescale for the recruitment of the Associate. The programme could also make better use of existing skills and capacity as well increase the number of companies and universities and colleges involved.

Sources of further information

- InnovateUK, *www.gov.uk/government/organisations/innovate-uk*.

Conclusions and policy recommendations

A key policy challenge for Israel is to overcome important weaknesses in productivity and innovation in MSEs in traditional manufacturing sectors. Israel has not yet developed a specific strategy for this group of firms, but it is a priority. When developing an overall strategic document for SME and entrepreneurship policy in Israel, the SMBA should pay particular attention to this group of firms. A multi-pronged approach will be needed that combines actions for workforce skills development, improving management skills and practices, access to finance, supply chain development, targeted public procurement and innovation. New programmes in these areas focused on traditional manufacturing MSEs will help both to increase national productivity and inclusion and help bridge the gap between the dual economies of traditional and high-technology sectors. Formalised cooperation between government ministries and agencies, universities and colleges and representatives of MSEs will be critical to designing effective policies.

The following key recommendations are offered for future policy development in this area:

Key recommendations on medium-sized enterprises

- Develop a specific MSE component in the new national strategy document proposed in this report for SME and entrepreneurship policy.
- Undertake a national training needs analysis for MSEs in collaboration with the Ministry of Education, the Ministry of Economy and Industry, universities, colleges, unions and MSE employers and adapt VET programmes and MAOF centre short courses in line with the findings.
- Introduce additional management development programmes for MSEs in selected universities based on good practices developed by Technion University, including a management and leadership programme for existing high-potential MSEs.
- Introduce a dedicated consultancy track for MSEs in MAOF centres with more specialised consultants and more intensive diagnosis, consultancy and mentoring.
- Extend the maximum term of SMBF loan guarantees to repayment periods of 10-15 years and ensure that MSEs have the same access to these guarantees as smaller enterprises, introduce tax incentives for angel investments in non-R&D based MSEs, and make further improvements to the regulatory environment for crowdfunding.
- Introduce a national supply chain development programme for MSEs involving brokering relationships among potential supply chain partners, developing marketing and marketing platforms, targeted training and mentoring, and support for introduction of supply chain management software and management procedures.
- Open up defence procurement to MSEs in traditional industries and set up an information portal where details of how to apply are placed and other support offered to potential bidders in co-operation between the Ministry of Defence and the Ministry of Economy and Industry.
- Introduce a programme to stimulate non-R&D based innovation in traditional manufacturing MSEs involving knowledge transfer partnerships between MSEs, college-based researchers, and college graduates.

Note

1. Medium-sized enterprises are defined in this chapter according to the definition followed by the Israeli Small and Medium Business Agency (SMBA), i.e. "companies with between 20 and 99 employees".

References

Adalya Economic Consulting l.T.D (2011), *Strategic Report of Israeli Governmental Assistance to Small and Medium Businesses – Phase A, http://adalya.co.il/en/adalya-economic-consulting.*

Bank of Israel (2014), *Annual Report for 2013*, Jerusalem *www.boi.org.il/en/NewsAndPublications/PressReleases/Pages/26-03-2014-Research.aspx.*

Barnea & Co (2016), *Finally, Crowd Funding Comes to Israel, www.barlaw.co.il/client-updates/finally-crowdfunding-comes-to-israel/.*

Ben-Nahum, Y. and M. Erez (2012), *Accelerating Innovation in Israeli Industry*, Ivey Business Journal, March/April 2012, *http://iveybusinessjournal.com/publication/accelerating-innovation-in-israeli-industry/*.

British Business Bank (2015), *Small Business Finance Market 2015-2106, http://british-business-bank.co.uk/wp-content/uploads/2016/02/British-Business-Bank-Small-Business-Finance-Markets-Report-2015-16.pdf*.

Confederation of British Industry (CBI) (2014), *Stuck in the Middle: Addressing the Tax Burden for Medium-Sized Businesses, www.cbi.org.uk/media/2791233/stuck_in_the_middle.pdf*, accessed 19 August 2014.

Cowling M., P. Bates, N. Jagger and G. Murray (2008), *Study of the Impact of Enterprise Investment Scheme (EIS) and Venture Capital Trusts (VCT) on Company Performance*, HM Revenues & Customs Research Report 44. *https://ore.exeter.ac.uk/repository/bitstream/handle/10036/67875/hmrc44.pdf?sequence=1*

Feldman, M.P. (2003), "The Locational Dynamics of the US Biotech Industry: Knowledge Externalities and the Anchor Hypothesis", *Industry and Innovation*, 10(3), 311-328.

FRIDA (2013), *Fostering Regional Innovation and Development through Anchors and Networks*, Final Report Summary: *A Cross Regional Comparison in an Evolving International Context, http://cordis.europa.eu/result/rcn/54992_en.html*.

OECD (2016), *Entrepreneurship at a Glance 2016* (forthcoming), OECD Publishing, Paris.

OECD (2016), *Financing SMEs and Entrepreneurs 2016: An OECD Scoreboard*, OECD Publishing, Paris, *http://dx.doi.org/10.1787/fin_sme_ent-2016-en*.

OECD (2013), *An International Benchmarking Analysis of Public Programmes for High-Growth Firms*, OECD LEED Programme, Paris, *www.oecd.org/industry/high-growthreport.htm*.

OECD (2011), *Higher Education in Regional and City Development: The Galilee, Israel*, OECD, Paris, *http://dx.doi.org/10.1787/9789264088986-en*.

Shenhav & Co (2013), *Crowd funding – legal and other issues, www.iati.co.il/resources-category/3/presentations*.

Shenhav & Co (2014), *Crowdfunding – Current Status and Proposed Changes www.shenhavlaw.com/wp-content/uploads/2014/06/Crowd-Funding-Presentation.pdf*.

ORGANISATION FOR ECONOMIC CO-OPERATION AND DEVELOPMENT

The OECD is a unique forum where governments work together to address the economic, social and environmental challenges of globalisation. The OECD is also at the forefront of efforts to understand and to help governments respond to new developments and concerns, such as corporate governance, the information economy and the challenges of an ageing population. The Organisation provides a setting where governments can compare policy experiences, seek answers to common problems, identify good practice and work to co-ordinate domestic and international policies.

The OECD member countries are: Australia, Austria, Belgium, Canada, Chile, the Czech Republic, Denmark, Estonia, Finland, France, Germany, Greece, Hungary, Iceland, Ireland, Israel, Italy, Japan, Korea, Latvia, Luxembourg, Mexico, the Netherlands, New Zealand, Norway, Poland, Portugal, the Slovak Republic, Slovenia, Spain, Sweden, Switzerland, Turkey, the United Kingdom and the United States. The European Union takes part in the work of the OECD.

OECD Publishing disseminates widely the results of the Organisation's statistics gathering and research on economic, social and environmental issues, as well as the conventions, guidelines and standards agreed by its members.

OECD PUBLISHING, 2, rue André-Pascal, 75775 PARIS CEDEX 16
(85 2016 03 1 P) ISBN 978-92-64-26230-0 – 2016

www.ingramcontent.com/pod-product-compliance
Ingram Content Group UK Ltd.
Pitfield, Milton Keynes, MK11 3LW, UK
UKHW051459290926
15471UKWH00008B/1301

9 789264 262300